DATE DUE

S

ASSESSMENT CENTERS IN HUMAN RESOURCE MANAGEMENT

Strategies for Prediction, Diagnosis, and Development

George C. Thornton III
Colorado State University

Deborah E. Rupp
University of Illinois

LEA LAWRENCE ERLBAUM ASSOCIATES, PUBLISHERS
2006   Mahwah, New Jersey   London

Lawrence Erlbaum Associates, Inc., Publishers
10 Industrial Avenue
Mahwah, New Jersey 07430
www.erlbaum.com

Cover design by Kathryn Houghtaling Lacey

Library of Congress Cataloging-in-Publication Data

Thornton, George C., 1940–
  Assessment centers in human resource management : strategies for prediction, diagnosis,
and development / George C. Thornton III, Deborah E. Rupp.
      p.   cm.
  Includes bibliographical references and index.
  ISBN 0-8058-5124-0 (cloth : alk. paper)
  ISBN 0-8058-5125-9 (pbk. : alk. paper)
  1. Assessment centers (Personnel management procedure).   I. Rupp, Deborah, E., 1975–
II. Title.

HF5549.5.A78T485   2006
658.3′125—dc22   2005051239
                                                                      CIP

Books published by Lawrence Erlbaum Associates are printed on acid-free paper,
and their bindings are chosen for strength and durability.

Printed in the United States of America
10 9 8 7 6 5 4 3 2 1

To students who have inspired me
throughout my career
GCT

To the members of the DACLab, a constant source
of intellectual stimulation and inspiration
DER

To assessees past, present, and future whose lives
have been affected by assessment centers
GCT and DER

Contents

Series Foreword

Jeanette N. Cleveland
The Pennsylvania State University

Edwin A. Fleishman
George Mason University

Series Editors

There is a compelling need for innovative approaches to the solution of many pressing problems involving human relationships in today's society. Such approaches are more likely to be successful when they are based on sound research and applications. This *Series in Applied Psychology* offers publications that emphasize state-of-the-art research and its application to important issues of human behavior in a variety of social settings. The objective is to bridge both academic and applied interests.

Early psychometricians such as Galton, Binet, and Cattell developed tests, which required some level of manipulation, dexterity, mechanical comprehension or visual/perceptual ability. With the onset of World War I, more cognitive group paper-and-pencil tests became dominant. In conjunction with German and British military officer selection, one objective was to assess "leadership" at a more Gestalt level using more complex job simulations as well as interviews, paper-and-pencil tests of human ability. These programs were precursors to our own U.S. Office of Strategic Services program during World War II which used multiple raters to evaluate intelligence agent candidates using multiple assessments, including traditional paper-and-pencil tests, group discussions, stress interviews, and situational exercises. By the late 1950s at AT&T, the Management Progress Study was underway including the incredibly informative assessment and longitudinal validity studies of leader identification. The assessment center movement came out of these early developments.

We are pleased to welcome the book, *Assessment Centers in Human Resource Management: Strategies for Prediction, Diagnosis, and Development* by George C. Thornton III and Deborah E. Rupp into the *Series in Applied Psy-*

chology. Dr. Thornton is internationally known for both his scholarly work and professional expertise in assessment centers. Dr. Rupp is also well known for her work on assessment centers and perceptions of organizational justice and fairness. Together, these two authors apply their areas of expertise to interpret the state of current research and practice of assessment centers in an increasingly changing, global, and complex workplace.

There has been significant research on the use of assessment centers as selection and assessment tools. Thornton and Rupp explore the change in goals of assessment centers from selection and identification of management potential to the use of assessment centers in actual skill acquisition or development. The authors describe how the basic elements of assessment centers have remained constant, including candidate evaluation by multiple trained assessors. Importantly, the authors identify how modifications to assessment centers have allowed them to be adapted effectively to address the changing nature and demographics of work.

Furthermore, the book updates the interpretation of theory, research, and practice on this approach drawing from several disciplines, including psychology, management, and labor and industrial relations. Case examples of actual assessment centers are presented early on in the book. The influence of technology, use in international contexts, and web-based assessment are a few of the new issues addressed. The discussion incorporates recent changes in the integration and interpretation of multiple sources of validity evidence related to prediction, diagnosis, and development in the global workplace and workforce.

The book is a timely and innovative discussion about a technique and process of selection, diagnosis, and development of managerial leadership that has deep historical roots in industrial and organizational psychology, testing, and human resource management. The book is intended for students and academics that are interested in learning more about assessment center developments and want an up-to-date treatment of this topic. The book will be useful to those conducting research on evolving assessment center practices. A target audience includes consultants and human resource managers who are interested in developing and implementing assessment center practices.

Preface

The theme permeating this book on assessment centers is continuity and change. We describe what has remained the same and what has changed in the 50-year history of the assessment center method. The basic elements of the assessment center method have remained the same: observation and judgments by multiple trained assessors about overt behaviors relevant to dimensions of performance displayed in simulation exercises. Continuity is also seen in the traditional assessment centers carried out in many public safety agencies (e.g., police and fire jurisdictions) in the United States.

Change has been evident in each of the elements of the assessment center method. Assessment center developers have experimented with modifications in reaction to changes regarding:

- the nature of work
- the globalization of business
- the structure of organizations
- workforce diversity
- human resource management systems
- theoretical and empirical advances in the research literature
- technological innovations in assessment

We evaluate the pros and cons of many of these modifications.

One major focus regarding change, deals with changing goals surrounding the purpose of assessment center programs and the ways in which assessment centers and their component parts have been used. Although some have observed there is a decreased incidence of traditional assessment centers for promotional purposes in private industry, there is an increased use of assessment centers for developmental purposes. This evolution has led to the need for a clearer differentiation in the definitions of the purposes of assessment centers and in specifications for how assessment centers are designed and operated for those different purposes.

In this book, we clearly differentiate between assessment centers used for prediction, diagnosis, and development. Historically, the most predominant applications involved prediction for selection of external applicants and promotion of internal candidates. Later, many organizations used the method for the diagnosis of strengths and developmental needs on performance dimensions in order to determine training needs. More recently, we have seen the emergence of truly developmental assessment centers that are designed to foster actual skill acquisition both in the course of the program itself and immediately following the program. We devote an entire chapter to this new form of assessment center. In it, we explore such issues as the identification and use of "developable" dimensions, the incorporation of rich, developmental feedback, and how developmental assessment centers might be structured from start to finish.

In comparison with Thornton (1992), this book includes expansion of several topics: assessment centers and human resource management, court cases involving assessment centers, innovations in assessment center operations, cross-cultural considerations including workforce diversity, and assessor training. In each area, theory and research relevant to assessment center operations are explored.

Our chapter on validity has been significantly expanded. In it, we discuss the validity of assessment centers using the modern definition of validity expounded in the *Standards for Educational and Psychological Tests* (American Educational Research Association, American Psychological Association, National Council of Measurement in Education, 1999). This definition calls for the interpretation of a variety of evidence relevant to the intended interpretation of assessment information. For the first time, we integrate several strands of evidence related to the use of assessment centers for prediction, diagnosis, and development. This presentation is markedly different from the former discussion of validity in terms of the outdated categories of "content, criterion, and construct validity." To give a sneak preview of our "bottom line," we conclude that assessment centers do have validity to accomplish the purposes of prediction, diagnosis, and development.

We have written this book with the same intended audiences and with the same style as Thornton (1992). The target audiences include students who are learning about assessment centers, practitioners including human resource managers and consultants who may be considering the implementation of assessment centers, and academicians who are researching the method and wish to understand current issues.

We have strived to provide a clear interpretation of theory, research, and practice for the nonacademic audiences. We have drawn on diverse sources from subdisciplines of psychology such as industrial/organizational, social, personality, developmental, and cognitive psychology, as well as other disciplines such as psychometrics, management, organizational behavior, human resource management, and labor and industrial relations. Theory and research in these areas have informed the practice of assessment centers and helped explain the effectiveness of the method for various purposes. We attempt to interpret this literature as it applied to assessment center operations.

After our discussions of the pros and cons related to several controversial topics, we provide our conclusions. Although it is not fashionable in some academic circles to appear to be an "advocate" for some practice, and the zeitgeist often fosters iconoclasm, we have chosen to take some firm stands that support the assessment center method. We give our conclusions on such topics as: computerized assessment techniques, dual-purpose assessment centers, assessment centers as diagnostic techniques, and research findings related to the old-fashioned term *construct validity*.

ACKNOWLEDGMENTS

We wish to express sincere acknowledgment of the many contributions to our thinking from many sources. Our colleagues have stimulated us to clarify our logic and defend our positions on controversial issues. Reviewers have made suggestions for improvements in the coverage and presentation. Practitioners have provided accounts of their practices. Clients have provided the test-bed for practices in field settings. Students have challenged us with in-depth discussion of theory, research, and practice, and have struggled with, and helped us clarify our early drafts of this text. To all those colleagues, who are too numerous to list, we express our deep thanks. In the end, we take responsibility for any remaining deficiencies and omissions.

—*George C. Thornton III*
—*Deborah E. Rupp*

Chapter 1

Assessment Centers in Human Resource Management

The assessment center method is a procedure used by human resource management (HRM) to evaluate and develop personnel in terms of attributes or abilities relevant to organizational effectiveness. Even though all assessment centers share common features, the process can be adapted in many ways to achieve different objectives. The theme of this book is that each assessment center must be tailor-made to fit particular HRM purposes. The use of assessment centers for three human resource purposes will be analyzed in detail: (a) deciding who to select or promote, (b) diagnosing strengths and weaknesses in work-related skills as a prelude to development, and (c) developing job-relevant skills. The human resource manager must design the assessment center with a specific purpose in mind and then make choices to build an assessment center that adequately serves that purpose. Throughout this book, alternative ways of setting up each element of the assessment center are discussed, and a rationale for deciding what procedures to follow is provided. Recommendations for assessment center practice are based on theory and research relevant to each element of an assessment center, as well as the experience of many assessment center practitioners.

In this chapter we describe the assessment center method and compare it with other assessment procedures. Then we briefly describe several human resource functions and show how assessment centers have been used to facilitate these functions. In chapter 2 we present three cases that show how assessment centers are used to solve three very different types of HRM problems.

CONTINUITY AND CHANGE

We have seen both continuity and change over the last several decades in assessment center applications. Assessment centers are being used for a broader variety of purposes than they have in the past, and technological advances in assessment and development are being incorporated into the method in new and exciting ways. In addition, changes in the nature of work and organizations have called for changes in the way human resource functions are carried out. We describe these changes in more detail later in the chapter and throughout the book. However, to begin our discussion of the assessment center method, we start with what has remained constant throughout history: the basic assessment center method.

An essential feature of the assessment center method is the use of simulation exercises to observe specific behaviors of the participants (International Task Force, 2000). Also referred to as simulations, these exercises can involve, for example, situations requiring participants to prepare a written report after analyzing a marketing problem, make an oral presentation, answer mail and memos in an in-box, or talk with a customer about a service complaint. In addition to individual exercises, group exercises are often used if group interactions are a part of the target job. Such exercises could involve a situation where several participants are observed discussing an organizational problem or making business decisions. Trained assessors observe the behaviors displayed in the exercises and make independent evaluations of what they have seen. These multiple sources of information are integrated in a discussion among assessors or in a statistical formula. The result of this integration is usually an evaluation of each participant's strengths and weaknesses on the attributes being studied and, in some applications, a final overall assessment rating. When assessment centers are used for development, individuals and groups can learn new management skills. We describe the effectiveness of assessment centers for these different uses later in this chapter. However, in order to understand the uses of assessment centers in modern organizations as well as the evolution of the assessment center method over time, it is necessary to understand the changing nature of work, workers, and organizations.

THE CHANGING NATURE OF WORK, ORGANIZATIONS, AND THE GLOBAL BUSINESS ENVIRONMENT

There are a multitude of changes occurring within and around the world of work. First, the job market is growing significantly, with 168 million jobs anticipated to make up the United States economy over the next 6 years (U. S. Department of Labor, 2003).

Second, the composition of the labor market is changing. The workforce will be made up of ever increasing percentages of minorities and women (Triandis, Kurowski, & Gelfand, 1993), many of whom will be entering nontraditional occupations. Research conducted in the United States has documented the special challenges women and minorities face when in roles more stereotypically "male" (Eagly, Makhijani, & Klonsky, 1992; Heilman, Wallen, Fuchs, & Tamkins, 2004) or "White" (Cheng, 1997; Tomkiewicz, Brenner, & Adeyemi-Bello, 1998) in nature. Human resource policies are needed to guard against potential biases that might occur in such situations, as well as the lowered job satisfaction and retention that might exist among these potentially marginalized groups (e.g., Burke & McKeen, 1996).

Third, there are changes occurring in the way in which organizations manage themselves. Many modern organizations are structuring jobs in order to create "high-performance work systems" that maximize the alignment between social and technical systems. Related to organizational changes are changes in how jobs are designed. Boundaries between jobs are becoming more and more "fuzzy" as organizational structures become more team-based and business becomes increasingly global (Cascio, 2002; Howard, 1995). Fourth, "knowledge workers" (i.e., individuals with very specialized knowledge) make up nearly half of current and projected job growth. The use of contingent workers continues to rise, in addition to the use of flexible work schedules to accommodate the complexities of employees' personal lives (U.S. Department of Labor, 2001, 2002). Fifth, the world of work has seen a marked change in the implicit work contracts formed between employees and employers. Expectations of life employment have been replaced with expectations of shorter term employment. Whereas employers once took responsibility for the career development of employees, organizational cultures have shifted this responsibility to individuals who now form much shorter term implicit contracts with their employing organizations (Cascio, 2002). These changes call for innovations in HRM generally, and in assessment and development practices specifically.

THE IMPORTANCE OF CAREFULLY CONSTRUCTED HUMAN RESOURCE "TOOLS"

So what do all of these changes mean for the management of human resources? First, the increases in the labor pool, coupled with the changing nature of the employee–employer implicit contract, puts additional pressure on HRM to develop tools that will best enable organizations to recruit, select, train, and retain the very best talent available. Because of the increased diversity within the workforce and the importance of complying with various employment laws, it is necessary that these tools are both *per-*

ceived as fair by applicants and employees, and *actually are fair,* that is, free of various forms of bias. Indeed, research shows that in the United States, women and minorities continue to be promoted at lower rates than their male, Anglo counterparts (Cheng, 1997; Lyness & Judiesch, 1999; Roberson & Block, 2001). This places a special challenge on human resource professionals to create assessment and decision-making tools that "level the playing field" for these various groups.

The changing nature of the jobs themselves creates additional challenges. For one, organizations must be able to measure the attributes necessary for success in these evolving jobs. Such attributes include adaptability, acculturation, readiness and motivation to learn, and other skills that are difficult to define, measure, and develop. Last, the globalization of business and the technological advances that have made remote business possible have created business structures requiring human resource tools that are also remote, portable, flexible, and secure. In sum, changes in the organizational environment have altered the needs for various human resource management tools and the attitudes of applicants and employees about such tools. There is a great need for organizations to take much care in developing, validating, and administering HRM practices, using the best tools to achieve their goals.

THE ASSESSMENT CENTER METHOD

The assessment center method offers a comprehensive and flexible tool to assess and develop applicants and employees in a modern work environment. Assessment centers have many strengths: (a) They can measure complex attributes, (b) they are seen as fair and "face valid" by those who participate in them, (c) they show little adverse impact, (d) they predict a variety of criteria (e.g., performance, potential, training success, career advancement; Gaugler, Rosenthal, Thornton, & Bentson, 1987). Additionally, recent technological innovations have been incorporated into the assessment center method to allow the method to adapt to the globalization and computerization of the business environment (Lievens & Thornton, in press). Such advances include computer-based simulations, web-based assessment center delivery, software programs for scoring writing, voice tone, and other relevant attributes, and other aids for automating the assessment center process (Bobrow & Schlutz, 2002; Ford, 2001; Reynolds, 2003; Smith & Reynolds, 2002).

It is important to note that we are not advocating assessment centers as the "best" or "only" tool for carrying out human resource applications. In fact, there are disadvantages associated with using assessment centers that we discuss later in the chapter. We stress that the assessment center method, which was originally conceived in the 1940s (MacKinnon, 1977), has been evolving along with the world of work and offers just one "tried and true," comprehensive method for assessing and developing a broad range of employee competencies.

A TYPICAL ASSESSMENT CENTER

Here is how one assessment center works. We hasten to emphasize that there is really no typical or universal way that assessment centers are set up or conducted. On Monday morning, 12 participants or "assessees" (e.g., supervisors being considered for promotion to higher level management), 6 "assessors" (e.g., third level line managers, human resource staff), and an administrator report to a site away from the organization, such as a hotel. Prior to this time, the assessors have been trained to conduct the assessments, and the assessees have been briefed about the program. At the assessment center, the administrator provides orientation, makes introductions, and reviews the schedule. Over the course of the day, the participants take part in a series of simulation exercises and are observed by the assessors. While six participants are engaged in a group problem-solving discussion, the other six are individually analyzing a case study of an organizational problem and preparing a written report. Each participant then conducts a performance review session with a problem employee (a role player), makes a presentation of ideas for improving operations, and responds to material that has accumulated in the in-boxes (email, voicemail, desk in-basket) of a manager of a simulated organization.

Assessors rotate from exercise to exercise with laptops connected via a wireless network. In the exercises they observe and type notes. After each exercise they type a report summarizing the types of decision making, interpersonal, and communication behaviors demonstrated by each individual they were assigned to observe. These reports are electronically sent to the assessment center administrator who combines and prepares reports for the integration session at the end of the day. The rotation of assessors is such that that each participant is observed by at least three assessors.

At the end of the day, the assessees go home for the night, but the assessors spend the evening, and possibly the next day, discussing their observations and evaluating each assessee's management potential. Each assessee is discussed at length. Assessors take turns reporting the behaviors they observed relevant to the performance dimensions. After all the reports are given, the assessors enter their ratings of the assessee on each performance dimension, using a 5-point scale. A spreadsheet is constructed to illustrate the ratings each assessee received from each assessor on each dimension. Using the spreadsheet, differences in ratings are discussed until assessors reach agreement. Next, individual ratings of the probability of success as a higher level manager (i.e., an overall assessment rating across dimensions) are entered for each assessee and discussed until consensus is reached. In many programs, the assessors then discuss the development needs of the assessee and make suggestions for what might be done to improve job effectiveness.

The following week, each assessee receives an oral and written report on how well he or she did. The detail and specificity of the feedback depends on the reason for using the assessment center. If the center is to be used for personnel decision making, reports may also be given to higher level managers who will be making such decisions. When the assessment center is used to diagnose development needs, feedback may be given to the assessee and his or her immediate supervisor to plan follow-up actions. These example events are depicted in Fig. 1.1.

It is important to note that this is just one example of assessment center operations. Chapter 2 describes how three other organizations designed their assessment centers. There are many variations on the basic theme. In particular, very different procedures are useful in integrating behavioral observations. In the example of Fig. 1.1, assessors discuss their ratings until consensus is reached. Another procedure gaining wider acceptance is the statistical integration of ratings. For example, some organizations compute an average of the individual assessors' ratings to derive the final dimension ratings; others use a formula to combine final dimension ratings into an overall prediction of success. The advantages and disadvantages of various data integration methods are discussed in chapters 7 and 8.

COMPARISONS WITH OTHER ASSESSMENT PROCEDURES

The assessment center method is similar to some assessment procedures but quite different from others. For the purpose of making personnel decisions, there are techniques such as individual assessment in which an assessment practitioner assesses the job-relevant characteristics of individuals one at a time to make inferences about potential (Prien, Schippmann, & Prien, 2003). Typically, a trained psychologist uses psychological techniques to make a holistic judgment about a candidate's fit with a job (Highhouse, 2002). For the purpose of developing employees, there are techniques such as multisource feedback which involves the collection of surveys from multiple raters (e.g., supervisors, co-workers, subordinates) about the effectiveness of an individual on a set of competencies. Typically, a feedback report is returned to the target individual (Bracken, Timmreck, & Church, 2001). Like assessment centers, these methods serve a variety of purposes, with in-

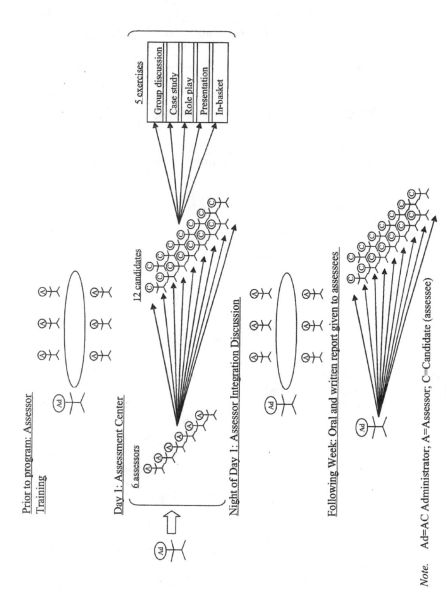

Prior to program: Assessor Training

Day 1: Assessment Center

6 assessors

12 candidates

5 exercises
- Group discussion
- Case study
- Role play
- Presentation
- In-basket

Night of Day 1: Assessor Integration Discussion

Following Week: Oral and written report given to assessees

Note. Ad=AC Administrator; A=Assessor; C=Candidate (assessee)

FIG. 1.1. A typical assessment center.

dividual assessment sometimes used for development (Prien et al., 2003) and multisource feedback sometimes used to make personnel decisions (Fleenor & Brutus, 2001). Alternative personnel assessment methods incorporate the use of personal history forms, ability tests, personality inventories, projective tests, interviews (Ryan & Sackett, 1998); work sample tests, integrity tests, biographical data measures (Schmidt & Hunter, 1998); interests, values, and preferences inventories (Heneman & Judge, 2003); weighted application blanks, as well as training and experience evaluations (Gatewood & Feild, 2001).

Each of these methods has strengths, and many have been found effective in predicting managerial success. Table 1.1 provides comparisons of some characteristics of assessment centers and other assessment techniques.

TABLE 1.1
Comparing Characteristics of Alternative Assessment
Methods and Assessment Centers

Alternative Assessment Techniques	Assessment Center Method
Individual assessment: • Holistic judgment made • Assessment conducted by a single person • One individual assessed at a time	• Specific judgments made, which may be combined into an overall rating • Judgments made by multiple assessors • Multiple individuals can be assessed simultaneously (e.g., 6–12)
Multisource feedback: • Raters receive limited to no training • Feedback is mostly written • Multiple raters used, e.g., supervisors, co-workers, subordinates, customers	• Assessors receive extensive training • Feedback is often oral and written • Multiple assessors used, but typically from upper management, HR, or outside the organization
Behavioral background interview: • Self reports of past behavior • Can be faked	• Observations of current behavior • Difficult to fake: candidate must demonstrate actual behavior
Situational interview: • Self report of intentions to behave *Cognitive ability tests:* • Abstract problems assigned • Abilities implied from responses to items • May cause adverse impact	• Observations of actual current behavior • Concrete, work-related problems assigned • Demonstration of overt behavior required • Little adverse impact caused
Personality questionnaire: • Easy to fake • Self description • Measures stable traits • Low face validity	• Hard to fake • Description by observers • Can measure both stable traits and developable skills • Participants respond favorably

What is special about the assessment center method is the way various individual assessment procedures are used in combination with each other. An assessment center can involve several different types of assessment techniques (e.g., tests, simulation exercises, interviews), more than one simulation exercise representing important elements of the target job, observation of complex behaviors relevant to managerial competencies, multiple trained assessors (often including higher level managers), and a systematic process of pooling observations and integrating the evaluations. The result of an assessment center is an evaluation of several managerial competencies and, in many cases, an overall evaluation of potential to succeed in the target jobs.

Simulation exercises are one of the distinguishing features of the assessment center method. Simulations provide the opportunity to observe complex behaviors of candidates as they interact with other people, solve problems, and act upon their analyses. These exercises need not be actual work samples. A work sample is a detailed replica of one segment of the actual work situation. For example, a typing test is a replica of one critical element of a secretarial job. An assessment center exercise for managers may be a work sample (e.g., an actual problem confronting the organization), but it does not have to be a complete replica of a job element. Instead, exercises may be only partial simulations of the job. The question of how similar assessment center exercises must be to actual work situations is explored in depth in chapter 6. At this point, it is sufficient to say that the most important characteristic of the individual simulation exercises is that they elicit overt behaviors relevant to the dimensions that are crucial for success in the job of interest.

ASSESSMENT CENTERS AND VARIOUS HUMAN RESOURCE MANAGEMENT FUNCTIONS

Assessment centers can contribute valuable information to a large number of functions that are carried out by any human resource management (HRM) system in an organization. These functions are designed to ensure that the organization recruits, selects, trains, compensates, evaluates, and retains personnel in ways that support the organization's objectives. Assessment centers are fair to individuals from racial, gender, and age groups and thus are useful in advancing diversity goals of organizations dealing with a changing workforce.

The following sections summarize many of the HRM functions carried out in most organizations (see Bohlander & Snell, 2004; Ivancevich, 2004). A brief example is given to show how assessment centers have been used in actual organizational settings.

Recruitment

Any organization must attract a steady stream of talented and motivated people ready to move into all positions in the organization (Rynes & Cable, 2003). The source of new personnel may be located outside the organization, in the form of applicants, or inside the organization, in the form of promotions and transfers. Diamond Star Motors, a joint venture between Chrysler and Mitsubishi, used the assessment center method to show applicants what they would experience in the Japanese management system (Henry, 1988). This orientation attracted many and led others to withdraw from the application process. The assessment center results were also used for making selection decisions. At Lawrence Livermore Laboratories, an assessment center was used to show engineers and scientists what management entails and to give them an opportunity to discover some of their own managerial strengths. This experience was helpful in attracting some of the participants to management positions.

Selection

Organizations must decide whom to select and whom to reject among the many applicants for a job opening (Gatewood & Feild, 2001). Selection procedures, therefore, should help the organization identify individuals who are likely to succeed on the job, and they should be nondiscriminatory. Assessment centers have been used to screen and select pilots (Damitz, Manzey, Kleinmann, & Severin, 2003), trainers for an automotive manufacturer's training program (Franks, Ferguson, Rolls, & Henderson, 1999), and police officers (Coulton & Feild, 1995).

Placement

There are often several possible jobs that can be assigned to a new employee. Ideally, the assignment results in a good match of job requirements to the individual's strengths. In a program for recruiting management trainees, Sears (Bentz, 1967) used an assessment center to not only select among applicants, but also to place new recruits in positions where there was an optimal fit. For example, recruits skilled in oral communication were placed in jobs requiring frequent presentations, whereas recruits who tested weak in planning were placed under managers with strong planning skills.

Training and Development

Training and development is the process of imparting the appropriate knowledge, skills, abilities, and other characteristics needed by an individual for effective organizational functioning (Salas & Cannon-Bowers,

2001). Assessment centers have been used to diagnose employee deficiencies and to provide skill training in selected areas (Lievens & Klimoski, 2001; Lievens & Thornton, in press; Thornton & Rupp, 2003). Throughout the book, we refer to centers used for these two purposes as *diagnostic assessment centers* and *developmental assessment centers*, respectively. For example, Tillema (1998) reported a developmental assessment center used to assess potential in Dutch companies. Other applications involve the use of development centers in large financial services organizations (Engelbrecht & Fischer, 1995; Shore, Tashchian, & Adams, 1997). Chapter 2 includes case studies of these two types of centers. Chapter 4 provides a more in-depth description of a developmental assessment center.

Performance Appraisal

Organizations need procedures for evaluating the job proficiency of employees. In most organizations, the immediate supervisor provides a performance appraisal on an annual basis. In other cases, assessment centers have been used to certify the competence of individuals to perform required technical skills. In these situations, the exercises are often work samples. For years the American Board of Professional Psychology (1988) used an assessment center to evaluate the skill of clinical psychologists in diagnosing a client's personal problems.

Organizational Development

Organizational development refers to a set of procedures that improve the effectiveness of a department or of an entire organization. Organization development is different from management development where the objective is to improve an individual's skills. Many organizations use large-scale, complex organizational simulations as a means of promoting organizational development (Iles & Forster, 1994). For example, Bobrow and Leonards (1997) reported on an assessment center developed for a large metropolitan service provider that was used to select the best-fitting candidates for positions that did not currently exist as part of a massive organizational restructuring. Thornton and Cleveland (1990) described the use of assessment centers for organizational development of leadership qualities.

Human Resource Planning

Effective organizations forecast future demand for particular skills and determine the supply of those skills in their current workforce (Heneman & Judge, 2003). Kodak's Colorado Division found that one by-product of its assessment center was the identification of a general deficiency among its first- and second-level managers in the skill of management control (i.e., the application of techniques to determine whether a work process or project was being completed in an accurate and timely manner). Kodak used this information to design a new training program to improve its employees' management control skills (Thornton, 1976).

Promotion and Transfer

Giving an employee a new and higher level of responsibility is a major decision for that individual and for others whom he or she will supervise. AT&T and many of the Bell Companies have used assessment centers for more than 40 years to identify individuals' potential for success in managerial positions in what was called their Advanced Management Potential Assessment Program (Bray, Campbell, & Grant, 1974; Bray & Grant, 1966; Ritchie, 1994). Of course, the candidate's performance on the current job is also considered very carefully. This type of program is described more fully in chapter 2.

Layoffs

When an organization must reduce its workforce for economic reasons or because of changes in its structure, it is faced with difficult decisions about whom to release and whom to retain. The security division of the Hoffman Company used an assessment center to simulate the job requirements of the restructured department. Each employee was given a chance to demonstrate his or her capabilities for the new assignment. Participants reported that they believed the assessment center provided a fair chance to demonstrate relevant skills. They preferred this process over one in which the decision was based solely on seniority or on their supervisors' performance evaluations of their current jobs. Cochran, Hinckle, and Dusenberry (1987) described the use of an assessment center in a mandated 50% reduction in force in a government agency. The assessment center helped identify training needs of employees left behind.

Summary

These brief examples show the wide variety of applications of the assessment center method. All this should not be interpreted to mean that all assessment centers are alike or that there is only one way to conduct an assessment center. Quite the opposite is true. The design of an assessment center depends on the purpose it will serve, and on the type of climate the organization wishes to create. The organization's human resource management system and its organizational climate are closely intertwined.

CONSIDERATIONS OF THE ORGANIZATIONAL ENVIRONMENT

To be sustainable, assessment centers are designed to fit with the organization's culture and environment. The organization's approach to human resource management and reactions of participants are important considerations.

Approaches to Human Resource Management

Organizations differ dramatically in the type of human resource management systems they use. Some are rigid and mechanistic; others are quite flexible and humanistic (Schein, 1970). Assessment processes are one manifestation of these different orientations to employees in the organization; they will differ from organization to organization, depending on the character of the organization, the demands of the context, and the image the organization wishes to project. Jackson, Schuler, and Rivero (1989) have shown that organization characteristics—such as industry sector, emphasis on innovation, the manufacturing technology, and the organizational structure—are related to several personnel practices in areas such as performance appraisal, compensation, employment security, and training.

Assessment Centers and Different Approaches to Human Resource Management

The assessment center is flexible enough that it can be adapted to varying human resource management philosophies. The assessment center can simulate the type of relationship the organization wishes to develop with its employees. For example, in line with a craft arrangement, Anheuser-Busch uses work sample procedures for assessing skilled craft positions, such as journey-level mechanics and plumbers. AT&T and a number of operating companies in the telephone industry follow a merit-based selection model by using an assessment center for making promotions to first-level supervisor. Kodak's Colorado Division followed a career growth model in implementing a series of assessment centers to foster career growth among technical personnel, first-level supervisors, and department heads. In seeking employees to work in its assembly plant, managed with a commitment-based philosophy, Diamond Star Motors used an assessment center to simulate a factory setting requiring close teamwork and constant improvement in methods.

Applicant/Employee Reactions

Every organization should also be aware that the human resource management practices and evaluation procedures have a strong effect on the attitudes and behavior of applicants and employees. Applicants and employees form psychological contracts with organizations as a result of the way they are evaluated in selection, training, and performance appraisal procedures (Schalk & Rousseau, 2002). If employees are treated in a routine and mechanical way, they may put forth only limited efforts, but if they are treated in a fair and individualized way, they are more likely to put forth extra effort on behalf of the organization (Ployhart & Ehrhart, 2002; Rupp & Cropanzano, 2002).

Applicants to an organization begin to form impressions of the organization on the basis of their first experiences with recruiting and selection practices (Bauer, Maertz, Dolen, & Campion, 1998; Ployhart & Ehrhart, 2002; Ployhart & Ryan, 1997; Thibodeaux & Kudisch, 2003; Truxillo, Bauer, Campion, & Paronto, 2002). Organizational brochures give information about policies and practices; interviewers treat applicants with respect or condescension; tests may appear relevant and fair or irrelevant and invasions of privacy; and contacts in the employment office may be supportive or demeaning.

All of these interactions with representatives of the organization form the basis of initial impressions. What is even more important is that these perceptions of the organization's personnel functions tend to generalize quite widely to other features of the organization (Thornton, 1993). The applicant begins to form an impression about other organizational policies, other members of the organization, and the general organizational climate. Even more importantly, these initial impressions form the basis of subsequent attitudes toward the organization and of the employee's commitment to that organization (Bauer et al., 1998). Ultimately, the employee's effort, job performance, and decision to stay or leave the organization are affected by attitudes that may have been formed during these early contacts.

There is much evidence to suggest that applicants and employees view the assessment center method quite favorably. Studies of participants' reactions to assessment centers used for a variety of purposes have been conducted (Dulewitz, 1991; Howard, 1997). Applicants for management trainee positions see the procedure as a fair selection process. Candidates for promotion believe the method gives them a fair chance to show their management potential. Both successful and unsuccessful assessment center participants have positive reactions. Minority applicants believe the method is unbiased. When used for developmental planning, high-rated as well as low-rated individuals use the information and engage in follow-up improvement activities.

CRITICISMS AND LIMITATIONS OF THE ASSESSMENT CENTER METHOD

In deciding whether an assessment center is an appropriate tool to meet the HRM needs of an organization, it is necessary to weigh the pros and cons of the assessment center method in light of why such a tool might be needed, as well as the resources the organization has available to meet these needs. Although there are many advantages associated with the assessment center method, numerous criticisms have been made as well. Some criticisms are practical in nature (e.g., the process is complex and requires time for key managers to serve as assessors). People have questioned whether the benefits outweigh the costs, especially in comparison with less costly assessment procedures. Other criticisms have arisen as a result of research that has not supported some of the typical assessment center procedures. For example, there is a mixture of support for the use of different procedures for observing, reporting, and combining behavioral observations. Still other criticisms are theoretical in nature; they challenge some of the basic assessment center assumptions about the perception of other people's behavior and the accuracy of social judgment.

Howard (1997), as well as Thornton and Mueller-Hanson (2004) have reviewed many of the frequently cited advantages and disadvantages to using assessment centers. These pros and cons are listed in Table 1.2. As we review in subsequent chapters, an assessment center in a useful method for measuring multiple competencies that are otherwise difficult to measure. Assessment centers predict future success, do not cause adverse impact, and are seen as fair by participants. They provide rich, behavioral information about a person and are very difficult to fake. Lastly, assessment centers are essentially "plastic"—they provide a standardized method that can be specially tailored to meet the specific needs of an organization (Howard, 1997).

At the same time, assessment centers are very complex undertakings, often difficult to develop and maintain. First, there is a significant cost associated with assessment centers, including labor, physical space, and a large amount of people's time. Given the shift in implicit contracts between employees and employers mentioned at the start of the chapter, organizations must consider if such an investment is justified if employees are not expected to stay with the organization for their entire career. Second, assess-

TABLE 1.2
The Pros and Cons of the Assessment Center Method

Arguments for the Use of Assessment Centers	Arguments against the Use of Assessment Centers
• predicts a wide range of criteria • highly accepted by applicants and employees • can measure many attributes that are otherwise very difficult to measure • the method can incorporate anything that can be measured • assessment center scores show little adverse impact • can measure developable attributes • reports are rich in behavioral detail • less restriction of range at high levels of management than cognitive tests • technological advances can offset many potential disadvantages • scoring and reporting advances can lessen load on assessors • allows for the measurement of multiple attributes • exercises are hard to fake • can assess both declarative and procedural knowledge • can be tailored to meet the specific needs of the organization	• expensive • cumbersome/difficult to manage • requires a large staff • requires a great deal of time • only a limited number of people can be processed at a time • may not be cost effective for initial screening of low-level jobs • cross-cultural/international adaptations may be difficult to design and standardize • much cognitive load on assessors • there may be confidentiality concerns • changes in implicit contracts may make the investment less justifiable

ment centers have been criticized for being cumbersome and very difficult to manage. Third, individuals cannot be put through an assessment center *en masse*, as is done with many paper-and-pencil assessments. Small groups go through, and spend from a half day to several days completing the exercises. Fourth, the quality of the assessment center ratings depends on the quality of the assessors, who must be trained and monitored. Even with adequate training, assessors face substantial cognitive load in carrying out their duties. Finally, as international business continues to rise, so does the need for culturally appropriate assessment and development techniques. Building assessment centers that are equivalent across cultures or building a single assessment center that is appropriate for candidates from varying cultures is a very complex undertaking.

In summary, it is important to understand the challenges surrounding the use of assessment centers. However, these challenges are often outweighed by the advantages of the assessment center method and the disadvantages of alternative methods.

One question that is often asked is "When and under what conditions should the assessment center be used, as opposed to other forms of evaluation and assessment?" This is not an easy question to answer. We can say with some certainty that when an organization needs a precise and defensible method for making promotion decisions, has adequate resources to commit to assessing and/or developing individuals in high-level positions, where a number of complex attributes are required, and when the goal is to obtain rich and detailed information about individuals' strengths and developmental needs, then assessment centers are appropriate. However, this is not to say that the assessment center method is not also useful in other situations. Throughout this book, we continue to address both the advantages and controversial issues surrounding the assessment center method. Arguments and research data on both sides of each issue are presented so the reader can form his or her own opinion.

ASSESSMENT CENTERS IN THE 21ST CENTURY: CONTINUITY AND CHANGE

We began this chapter by explaining that assessment centers of the 21st century are characterized by both continuity and change. That is, whereas there are some qualities of assessment centers that "are and always will be" (e.g., the use of multiple simulation exercises, trained assessors, and a pooling of ratings), there are many new and exciting issues capturing the attention of assessment center researchers and practitioners. These include more developmental applications of assessment centers, new construct validation strategies, the use of assessment centers in more international contexts, and technological innovations allowing for disassembled and web-based assessment center applications. Continuity and change will continue as a theme for the remainder of the book. We will present the basics of the assessment center method, the major issues surrounding the method, and the many uses of the method. In addition, we also point out areas of rapid change and growth within this field and discuss issues we feel will become especially relevant in the future.

Chapter 2

Case Studies of Assessment
Centers in Operation

This chapter presents case studies that show how three organizations have used assessment centers for very different purposes. Following our theme of *continuity and change*, the goals of this chapter are to (a) demonstrate the traditional components of an assessment center, and (b) illustrate the many ways in which organizations are incorporating innovations and new technologies into the method. We describe:

- a selection/promotion assessment center
- a diagnostic assessment center
- a developmental assessment center

In these case studies, we give special attention to technology used, the consideration of multinational/cross-cultural issues, the integration of assessment centers into the larger human resource management function, outsourced assessment centers, nonmanagerial assessment centers, and the assessment of abilities and personality within an assessment center. The cases chosen for this chapter are examples of how organizations have approached these issues for defined purposes. Alternative samplings of cases could have illustrated these issues in different combinations. The important thing is to remember that an assessment center is a general method which offers a great deal of flexibility in facilitating an organization's goals.

The first case describes an assessment center used by a city fire department to promote lieutenants to the rank of captain. The second case describes an organization's decision to outsource assessment center development to a major consulting firm. The purpose of this center is to diagnose the training needs of information technology (IT) workers, whose jobs are rapidly changing. The third case describes a developmental assessment center that is part of a comprehensive leadership development program used to train managers who will be taking overseas assignments. In each of these examples, the organization, target job, and specific features of the assessment program are described. The reader should note how each of the features of the assessment center has been designed to solve a particular human resource management problem.

PALMORE FIRE DEPARTMENT

The Palmore Fire Department (PFD) used an assessment center to help decide who to promote from the rank of Lieutenant to that of Captain. Over the years, PFD had not been pleased with the management talent of officers promoted into higher levels of the department. Often the lieutenants with the best fire fighting skills were promoted into higher management. These individuals may have been excellent performers as firefighters and as front-line ("working") supervisors, but that did not necessarily mean that they would excel in higher management positions where the job duties are quite different from basic operational duties. PFD also wanted to institute a method that would be fair, and be *perceived* to be fair, to minority and women candidates. Thus, the organization decided to set up a *promotional assessment center* to help identify those top-performing lieutenants who also had the talent to be developed into effective captains. Surveys of hundreds of assessment centers in the United States (Spychalski, Quinones, Gaugler, & Pohley, 1997) and Germany (Krause & Gebert, 2003) showed that 45% to 50% of the organizations sampled used assessment centers for promotion purposes.

The Organization

The PFD is considered a highly sophisticated department, consisting of more than 400 employees, working in more than 20 stations. The PFD owns a great deal of specialized equipment and has a budget exceeding 20 million dollars. The PFD provides services in fire fighting, emergency medical services, hazardous materials, rescue, fire prevention code enforcement, public education, and disaster preparedness. The Department is led by the Fire Chief. Fire Captains serve several managerial functions, including the supervision of lieutenants and entry-level firefighters. Figure 2.1 provides a simplified organization chart of the PFD.

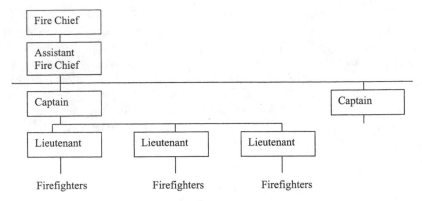

FIG. 2.1.   Simplified organizational chart of the Palmore Fire Department.

Target Job

The assessment center was designed to identify lieutenants who possessed the attributes needed to be effective captains. The job of captain involves managing an entire fire station. This middle-level management position involves the supervision of a company (i.e., a group of firefighters who work together on a shift), as well as the company officers who manage the other shifts within the station. The captain is in charge of all the day-to-day operations of the station, including the operation and maintenance of all equipment as well as all support services and personnel within the station. Support services include investigations, training, technical services, administration, and human resources. Therefore, the captain supervises firefighters, lieutenants, and administrative personnel.

The PFD had been concerned for some time that it did not have an effective mechanism for identifying lieutenants who make the best captains. Prior promotional decisions had been based on seniority, but the PFD realized that experience as a lieutenant did not necessarily equate to qualification as middle-level manager. Lieutenants mainly led teams of firefighters in fire suppression activities. The role of captain involved much broader tasks involving different types of personnel management and administration. The PFD wanted people who could be successful not only at first-level supervision where day-to-day operations are important, but also at skills such as training staff, resolving conflicts, counseling subordinates, managing personnel practices such as performance appraisals, scheduling, and writing detailed reports. Thus, in setting up the assessment center, PFD decided to analyze the attributes important for success as a captain and design an assessment center program to identify skills needed for long-range success as a captain.

Dimensions

A job analysis was conducted on the role of captain. Past job descriptions, training materials, and information from O*NET (U.S. Department of Labor, 2002) were collected and reviewed. Preliminary lists of tasks and knowledge, skills, and abilities were generated, and judgments of the importance of these factors were collected from subject matter experts (e.g., senior captains, assistant chiefs, and the fire chief). From this information, an updated job description and minimum qualification list were generated. It was decided that in addition to possessing the minimum qualifications (experience as a firefighter and lieutenant, and proper certifications), candidates must also show an adequate level of proficiency on the following dimensions: planning and organizing, decision making, conflict management, oral communication and written communication, and individual and group leadership.

Exercises

The job analysis identified several types of situations that captains must deal with on a regular basis, as well as the types of problems encountered in those situations. The job analysis information was used to build several assessment exercises that simulated important elements of the PFD captain job. It was decided that only individual exercises would be used, because of the possible lack of standardization associated with group exercises and the history of legal challenges of prior promotion decisions.

The first exercise was an in-box (formerly called the in-basket exercise). In this exercise, participants sat at a desk and carried out many of the tasks similar to those required of a captain in any given day. These tasks included approving/rejecting leave requests, scheduling lieutenants and firefighters to shifts, completing overtime logs, making entries into the station journal, completing incident reports, and sorting through other relevant and non-relevant information. This exercise was developed to assess planning and organizing, decision making, and written communication.

In another exercise, participants had to meet with two lieutenants (trained role players) who were experiencing conflict. These two individuals had very different personalities and very different philosophies regarding how firefighter teams should be led. They were currently in disagreement about how a particular policy should be carried out, and the disagreement was keeping the station house from completing routine duties. The participant met with these individuals and attempted to resolve the conflict. Decision making, conflict management, written communication, and group leadership were assessed in this exercise.

A third exercise required the participant to review reports and documentation about the performance of a subordinate, prepare a performance appraisal, and provide the employee (a role player) with performance feedback. This exercise assessed planning and organizing, oral communication, written communication, and individual leadership.

In a final simulation exercise, the participant prepared a short training presentation on how lieutenants should conduct safety checks on various pieces of essential equipment. A participant had time to prepare, was given access to various manuals and safety standards, and materials with which to prepare the presentation (i.e., note cards, flipcharts). Then, time was given for the actual training demonstration to be given to assessors who are playing the role of the trainees. This exercise assessed planning and organizing, decision making, oral communication, and leadership.

PFD also gave a set of cognitive ability and personality tests to assess whether candidates for promotion had the basic intellectual skills and personality traits necessary for effective performance as a captain. The three mental ability tests covered verbal reasoning, reading skills, and a measure of general intelligence. The two personality tests covered interpersonal styles and personality attributes such as dominance, sociability, and aggressiveness. Psychological testing was under the supervision of an industrial/organizational psychologist.

Participants

Candidates could self-nominate or be nominated by current captains. Self-nominations required approval from the chief. All nominations had to be approved by the department's human resource director, who verified that all minimum qualifications had been met. Those who had met the minimum qualifications were scheduled to complete the cognitive and personality assessments. The six individuals who scored the highest on these assessments were scheduled to participate in the full-day assessment center the following week. At this time they were given orientation to understand how the assessment center would operate.

Assessors

Chiefs, battalion chiefs, and assistant chiefs from other jurisdictions served as assessors. This practice is typical: Assessors usually come from management positions at least two levels above the participants (Spychalski et al., 1997). The assessors were trained and coordinated by an industrial/organizational psychologist, who had developed other assessment and validation projects. The assessors observed the candidates in the exercises and evaluated the dimension-relevant behaviors observed. The psychologist and her staff administered the exercises, led the integration discussion, presented the mental ability and personality test results, wrote reports, and gave oral and written feedback to participants and management.

Program

Administration of the exercises was completed in one day. The assessors then spent the late afternoon and evening preparing their evaluations and integrating the information they had collected. During this time, the assessors compared their observations with checklists and behaviorally anchored rating scales for effective performance in the exercises. Assessors made ratings on the performance dimensions, which were then compiled by the administrator. Assessors spent approximately 45 minutes discussing each candidate. Each dimension was discussed in turn. Where discrepancies occurred, the assessors discussed differences and came to agreement within 1 point on a 5-point rating scale. Once this level of agreement was reached, the administrator used a statistical formula to combine dimension ratings into an overall assessment rating of promotability which was used to rank order the candidates. If assessors disagreed with this prediction, they discussed the evidence more thoroughly and wrote a supplementary note to the chief. Statistical methods of integrating assessment results are employed in only about 15% of the assessment centers in Spychalski et al.'s (1997) survey, but the practice seems to be spreading, especially in fire and police jurisdictions.

Feedback

The following week, the psychologist gave each participant feedback about his or her performance in the assessment center. Feedback consisted of a verbal review of the findings and the recommendation regarding promotability. Soon thereafter the participant received a brief written report of the assessment results. The feedback given was not detailed. It simply laid out the decision-making process, the decision criteria, and how the candidates scored on relevant criteria. Throughout the book, we refer to this as *decision feedback*. We shall see examples of a second type of more detailed feedback (i.e., *developmental feedback*) in subsequent cases. A more detailed report of each individual's assessment was presented to the fire chief. This report also included a summary of the findings for the group who attended the program together, as well as a summary of all participants who had been assessed for the same target job in the past.

Other Elements of the Program

The results of the PFD assessment center, including the overall assessment rating of promotability, were only one set of information the fire chief had for making a promotion decision. The organization's policy called for the chief to seek out and use other information, such as past performance appraisals and safety violation and accident records. This information and a recommendation from the candidate's supervisor ensured that performance on the current job was carefully considered. Using all of this information, the fire chief made the final decision of whom to promote to captain.

Results

Five years after the assessment center was set up, PFD evaluated the effectiveness of the program. Responses to a survey questionnaire revealed that the captains, assistant chiefs, and the chief believed the assessment center had been providing valuable information about lieutenants' skills to be captains that had not been available previously. The fire chief was pleased that the new captains had better skills to run their individual stations and to carry out the roles they played in the broader department. Enough time had passed that some of these captains had even been promoted further in the fire department because of the competencies they demonstrated on the job. It appeared that a much better pool of leadership talent was being promoted from the ranks of the lieutenants.

Some problems with the assessment program were revealed by the evaluation study. In some situations the fire chief was not giving a great deal of weight to the overall assessment center rating (OAR). This was a problem in that research suggests that the OAR is a valid predictor of future success, and a far better decision-making tool than a more subjective judgment. Given the cost and difficulty in developing and maintaining an assessment center, it was especially problematic that the OAR was not being used to its full potential. The staff psychologist prepared several technical reports and presentations to illustrate to the fire chief the utility of giving more weight to the OAR in making final promotion decisions.

Summary

The PFD assessment center was designed to provide information for making promotion decisions. The dimensions and exercises were appropriate for identifying people with potential for long-range success in the fire department. The result of the assessment center was an evaluation of several managerial dimensions and a single overall assessment rating. Aside from feedback to participants, the findings were given only to the chief who made promotion decisions. The results were used in conjunction with other information relevant to the promotion decision.

TECHNOSOFT, INC.

Technosoft used an assessment center to diagnose the training needs of individual staff members working as computer software designers, developers, and engineers, called "techs" in this organization. Because each tech has a unique set of knowledge, skills, and experiences, as well as training needs, the assessment center served the purpose of creating a profile and training plan for each tech. Spychalski et al. (1997) showed that 51.2% of the organizations they surveyed used assessment centers for development planning, and 34.4% of the organizations used assessment centers to make decisions about training. By contrast, only 8% of the German assessment centers used the results for ascertaining training needs (Krause & Gebert, 2003). Technosoft used its assessment center for both of these purposes: to understand the skill gaps in each tech, and formulate a training plan to alleviate these gaps. Past experience had shown that training and development opportunities had not been provided to all techs in a consistent manner. Thus, Technosoft wished to institute a fair method of identifying training needs and providing appropriate experiences. Note that the "developmental" purpose was not to create a roadmap for promotion, but rather to identify the training needed in order for the techs to stay effective in their current positions.

The Organization

Technosoft, Inc. specializes in the sale of computer software and hardware. Its mission is to sell the very best computer parts and products. It has earned a reputation as an organization committed to a standard of excellence, and to guaranteeing customer satisfaction. Technosoft sells its products directly to individuals, as well as to schools, universities, and organizations. Technosoft strives to maintain its strong system of corporate values, including excellence in product development, internal relations, and customer service.

Target Job

A challenge Technosoft has encountered is keeping its techs up to date with the latest technology, which changes at a rapid rate. Just when it seems all the techs have mastery of a particular technique or application, there are new programming languages and protocols that must be learned. Technosoft has also discovered that within the tech workforce there is great variation in individuals' skills and experience. This has created many challenges in employee training. Specifically, different individuals are in need of training in different technologies in order for the workforce to keep up with rapid changes. A single training program for everyone would be grossly inefficient. What was needed was a program that would allow for unique training plans to be developed for each tech. In addition, there seemed to be an increased need for techs to be more flexible, adaptable, interpersonal, and team-oriented, so the program also needed to incorporate an assessment of these more "nontechnical" skills.

Dimensions

To meet these needs, Technosoft outsourced the project to a consulting firm to develop a *diagnostic assessment center* that assessed techs on both technical and nontechnical competencies. Because the knowledge, skills, and abilities of software techs change so quickly, a strategic job analysis (Schneider & Konz, 1989; Taylor, 1990) was conducted which sought to identify the technical knowledge and "soft" skills expected to be needed for the job over the next 5 years. The necessary dimensions clustered into 5 categories:

1. *technical knowledge* of specific applications that had been recently developed or were in the process of being developed;
2. *cognitive skills*, such as information seeking, critical thinking, complex problem solving, and decision making;
3. *communication skills*, such as active listening, writing, reading comprehension, speaking, and social perceptiveness;
4. *motivational dimensions*, such as active initiative, adaptability, and flexibility;
5. *project related skills*, such as project management and teamwork.

The assessment center was developed to assess techs' current level of proficiency in each of these areas.

The consultants also worked with Technosoft's training department to identify courses and other training opportunities currently offered by Technosoft, which could allow techs to develop in each of these areas. Training opportunities in these areas were modularized so that techs could participate in a very specific set of training activities depending on the skill gaps identified at the end of the assessment center.

Exercises

The diagnostic assessment center contained several components. The first component contained knowledge tests on specific technologies that were new and emerging. These tests changed each year depending on what new technology would have a large impact on Technosoft's competitive edge.

The second component consisted of a multistep exercise that focused on techs' motivation and ability to learn and adapt to new technologies and environments. Techs were presented with a new computer language and application (created for the purpose of the exercise) and asked to write a program using the language, troubleshoot a series of problematic code written in the language, and instruct a peer on using the application for a specific purpose. The programmer was timed carrying out these tasks, and cognitive, motivational, and communication skills were assessed.

In a third component, the tech was given the task to consult with an employee in the marketing department (a trained role player) who was having problems with a number of technical matters. The tech consulted with the employee, gathered enough information to understand the issues, decided on a best course of action, and communicated with the employee in nontechnical language what was wrong and what needed to be done. Both cognitive and communication dimensions were assessed in this exercise.

A fourth component required the techs to work together as a team. The group was given information about the software currently being used by the production department as well as a description of many shortcomings and problems associated with the current system. Techs also received information from a number of vendors proposing alternative systems. The group reviewed and discussed the pros and cons of each alternative, and together developed a proposal of what direction they felt the department should take. They also decided what needed to be done to implement the proposed changes, and divided the work among themselves. The exercise concluded with a group presentation to the department leadership (played by assessors) proposing the plan outlining what each team member would do. This exercise assessed cognitive, communication, and project-related skills.

Participants

Top management decided that all current techs would go through the diagnostic assessment center. Because the focus of the program was to update knowledge and enhance adaptability to change, the decision was made to put techs through in order of seniority, with the most tenured techs participating first. This served multiple purposes. First, the senior techs had been in the company the longest and therefore their training was likely to be more out-of-date than those programmers having just graduated from college. In addition, the consultants suggested putting the senior techs through the program first to build support and excitement about this new initiative among the less senior techs. Third, it was hoped that the senior techs would eventually rotate into roles of assessor and trainer, and therefore it was important for them to experience the program and get their skills up to date to prepare for such roles.

Assessors

Because the dimensions assessed in this program ranged from highly technical knowledge to highly psychological competencies, a varied panel of assessors was used. The panel consisted of trainers, members of the human resources department with psychology backgrounds, some members of the outside consulting team, and other subject matter experts internal to the organization. Initially, the consulting team played an active role in conducting assessor training, assessing, administering the center, conducting the integration discussions, and providing feedback, but over a period of 2 years, these responsibilities were transitioned to qualified and experienced individuals in the training and development department.

Program

Because this assessment center was built to assess "high tech" employees, it was important that the center itself to be very "high tech." The high level of complexity ensured that the center was perceived to be "face valid" to participants. These perceptions caused the participants to take the program seriously and approach the experience as a useful way to determine what training they needed. Therefore, many aspects of the assessment center were computerized, which led to reduced costs and increased efficiency of the program. The consulting team worked with Technosoft to create a web-based application that served as communication hub, assessment launch pad, and program management tool. The participants logged on to this system to register themselves into the program and schedule various activities. Once in the system, participants were required to take a web-based tutorial and orientation to learn about the program, the dimensions to be assessed, and the customized training plan that would result from their participation in the assessment center.

Techs first completed computerized, adaptive knowledge tests taken in a classroom with a proctor at the programmers' convenience in the 2 weeks prior to participating in the simulation exercises. The simulations occurred during half of each workday on two consecutive Fridays. The multistep exercise occurred one Friday morning, and the two additional exercises (the role play and the group discussion) occurred on the following Friday morning.

Assessors were equipped with wireless networked laptops that were logged onto the web-based application. Assessors typed notes and made ratings directly into the system, and ratings were integrated in real time as they were entered. Thus, a profile of each participant was initially built upon registering in the system and then added to following each assessment activity.

Assessor reports were automatically created after each exercise. Prior to integration, assessors logged into the system and reviewed each participant's profile. The profile contained scores on the knowledge tests and exercise-specific dimensions ratings made by each assessor. The assessors met for a half-day to discuss all profiles and come to a consensus on each participant's overall dimension scores. No overall assessment rating was derived. Through "webcast" technology, the laptops and the web-based application further helped facilitate this process by allowing assessors to view and point to specific things within the profiles using separate computers. Video and web conferencing also allowed remote assessors to be active in the discussion.

Feedback

During integration, the administrator entered final dimension scores for each tech. The system then generated a training needs profile for each participant, and the participant was automatically sent an email indicating that his or her assessment results and training profile were available to be viewed. This report not only suggested what training classes to take, but also listed the days and times each class was available and allowed participants to register on-line for the classes. In the following week, each participant met with his or her supervisor to discuss the training plan generated and to set goals for completing all necessary training.

Other Elements of the Program

Participants continued to use the web-based application to track their training progress. They could log on and see what training they had completed and what remained incomplete. The system also included scores on training exams and other success measures. Additional training or certification exams taken that were outside the training plan were also logged here, as well as any promotions or recognitions received by the employee. This tool was also used to notify the techs about new training courses. When these courses were particularly relevant to one of the program dimensions, participants who assessed low on this dimension were automatically sent an email notifying them of opportunities that were especially relevant to meeting developmental needs.

Results

Because of the extensive amount of data stored in the web-based system, the consulting firm was able to come back in the years following the launch of the program to determine if it was meeting its goal of diagnosing needs and prescribing the needed training to keep the Technosoft's techs current and effective. One noticeable improvement was that since the assessment center and training planning tools were implemented, the techs had been far more active in training than they had been. The techs themselves often commented on the efficiency of the program: The assessment center allowed them to get right to the heart of their skill gaps, to seek training only in the areas where they needed it, and to avoid wasting their time in training they did not need. Management also reported marked improvement in the extent to which the techs adapted to change, worked as a team, and consulted with nontechnical employees. Lastly, program data indicated that those who completed their training plans in a timely manner were more likely to be promoted to higher paying positions.

Summary

The purpose of the Technosoft assessment center was to diagnose training needs. In addition, it was deeply integrated into the broader training and development functions, in that assessment center results were used to develop training plans. The use of a common web-based implementation system allowed this integration to be completely seamless, and provided techs with the information and tools needed to be successful, up-to-date, and adaptive.

AUTO-MANUFAC WORLDWIDE

Auto-Manufac Worldwide (AMW) built a *developmental assessment center* as the foundation of its leadership development program. As a company dedicated to high-quality selection and development, AMW had been striving for innovative ways to create a "talent pipeline" rich with developmental opportunities that allowed high potential employees to continually upgrade their skills to be successful future leaders. AMW is also a global organization, and therefore designed the program to prepare managers for overseas appointments. Staffed with an internal team of industrial and organizational psychologists, AMW built a comprehensive leadership development program with the developmental assessment center at its core. The purpose of the assessment center was not to assess overall potential (as was the purpose at the Palmore Fire Department) or to diagnose (as was the purpose at

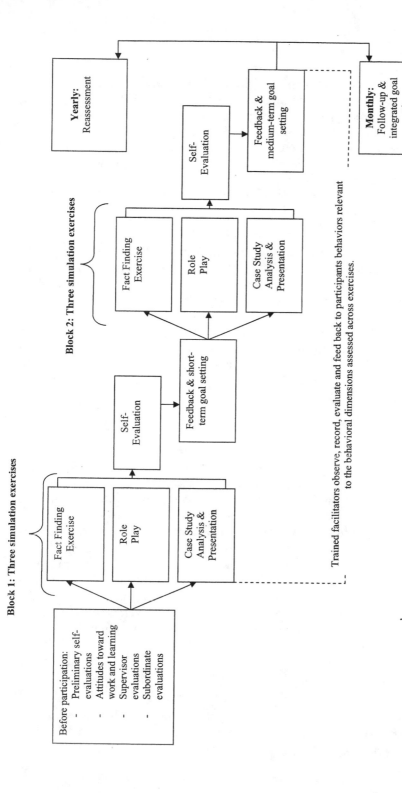

Block 1: Three simulation exercises

Block 2: Three simulation exercises

Before participation:
- Preliminary self-evaluations
- Attitudes toward work and learning
- Supervisor evaluations
- Subordinate evaluations

Fact Finding Exercise

Role Play

Case Study Analysis & Presentation

Self-Evaluation

Feedback & short-term goal setting

Fact Finding Exercise

Role Play

Case Study Analysis & Presentation

Self-Evaluation

Feedback & medium-term goal setting

Yearly: Reassessment

Monthly: Follow-up & integrated goal setting

Trained facilitators observe, record, evaluate and feed back to participants behaviors relevant to the behavioral dimensions assessed across exercises.

FIG. 2.2.   Diagram of AMW's Leadership Development Program (adapted from Gibbons & Rupp, 2004).

Technosoft), but to use the assessment center as an actual training experience in and of itself. This application involved several modifications to the traditional assessment center design. Figure 2.2 outlines the components of the AMW leadership development program. Only about 16% of the organizations in the survey by Spychalski et al. (1997) use assessment centers for this purpose. This may be an underestimate, though, because many organizations use complex behavioral simulations for training purposes, but do not call them assessment centers.

The Organization

AMW produces products used by manufacturing companies to automate their production process. These products include assembly line systems, warehouse and inventory systems, as well as technologies to automate shipping and receiving. AMW maintains production plants, warehouses, and sales offices in more than 50 countries, with a budget exceeding 3 billion U.S. dollars. The organization is led by the President/CEO and a number of vice presidents. Middle-level management consists of site managers, who are responsible for all site operations and personnel. These individuals directly supervise department heads and shift managers. In total, AMW employs more than 15,000 employees.

Target Job

AMW was committed to doing everything it could to prepare its site department heads and shift managers for positions as site managers. Because of the uniqueness of the industry, the complexity of the company, and the many products offered by AMW, the organization preferred to "grow" its site managers rather than hire external candidates. However, through experience, AMW learned that department heads and shift managers do not necessarily gain experiences in their current jobs that allow them to develop the skills they need to be leaders. Therefore, AMW decided to build a comprehensive leadership development program especially for these individuals. Because the purpose of the program was to develop skills needed in the next level of management, it was the site manager position that was the target job.

Dimensions

A job analysis was conducted to find a common set of performance dimensions necessary for effectiveness as a site manager worldwide. This analysis involved subject matter experts in all of the geographic regions in which

AMW conducted business. It is important to note that only dimensions that lend themselves to development are appropriate for a leadership development program or developmental assessment center. This is because the purpose of the program is to improve proficiency on the dimensions, as opposed to screening and selecting managers. Therefore, although some ability and personality dimensions were identified in the job analysis, only modifiable knowledge and skills were incorporated into the program. These included: cultural adaptability, conflict resolution, oral communication, information seeking, problem solving, and planning/organizing.

Assessment Exercises

In the developmental assessment center, the purposes of the exercises were twofold: to elicit dimension-relevant behaviors that could be observed by assessors as a basis for feedback and coaching, and to offer participants active, experiential learning opportunities in which to experiment and develop themselves on the dimensions. Therefore, two parallel blocks of three exercises were developed. In each block the participant took the role of a site manager and engaged in a role-play exercise, a fact-finding exercise, and a presentation exercise. The parallel exercises simulated different sites with similar yet different combinations of issues and challenges. The participant engaged in the first block and received feedback. Then, he or she participated in the second block of simulations and attempted to improve performance. Finally, a second round of feedback and coaching was given.

The role-play exercise challenged participants' cultural adaptability skills. In this simulation, some shift supervisors were transferred to the participant's site from a site culturally distinctive from the participant's site. Due to cultural differences, the shift supervisors were interacting with employees in very different ways, and this was causing conflict among employees, among supervisors, and between employees and supervisors. The participant was given a file of memos, emails, and personnel action documentation in addition to detailed information about the cultures of the two sites. The participant had the task of gathering additional information from the parties, and then meeting to resolve the conflict and set up policies to keep plant employees working effectively together as a team.

The second type of exercise was a fact-finding exercise. This exercise provided the participant with a small amount of information and a decision to be made. A resource person, usually one of the assessors, had a large amount of relevant information that the participant could obtain by asking the right questions. Following the question-and-answer period, the participant had to make a recommendation and provide a rationale in support of his or her decision. The resource person then provided additional information, challenged the initial decision, and tried to get the participant to change his or her mind. This exercise required participants to seek information, solve problems, manage conflict, and communicate effectively.

Finally, an oral presentation was required in which the participant presented recommendations for a new product line after studying marketing and financial data. Planning and organizing, problem solving, and oral communication were assessed in this exercise.

Participants

AMW's goal was to "grow" site managers from its pool of high-potential site department heads and shift supervisors. The purpose of the assessment center was not to identify high-potential persons, but rather to take those already believed to have great potential and equip them with the additional skills needed for higher level leadership positions. Therefore, those individuals identified as high potential through the performance appraisal process were invited to participate in the leadership development program.

Assessors/Facilitators

The assessors in this program took on very different roles from the assessors in the assessment programs described earlier in this chapter. Here they were called "facilitators," and they were responsible for making observations of effective behaviors and giving immediate feedback so that the participants could learn from the simulations. They were considered trainers and coaches rather than evaluators or judges. Thus, the integration session required facilitators to not only agree on each participant's strengths and developmental needs with regard to each dimension, but also to agree on the specific feedback and coaching to be given to each participant. In addition, since feedback occurred twice within the course of the assessment center, the administrator and facilitator team had to work quickly and efficiently. The assessor panel contained individuals from the corporate HR office, the training and development office, as well as vice presidents representing the different geographic regions within which AMW conducts business.

Feedback

Unlike the other two assessment center cases described in this chapter, AMW's developmental assessment center incorporated feedback that was more in-depth, incorporated specific short- and long-term goal setting, and occurred at multiple occasions throughout the leadership development program. As mentioned earlier, we refer to this type of feedback as *develop-*

mental feedback. The first feedback session occurred after the first block of simulation exercises was completed. Here the facilitators fed back the dimension-relevant behaviors observed over the first block of exercises and worked with the participant to develop goals to improve on areas of weakness in the second block of exercises. The second feedback session came after the second block of exercises. Here, the facilitator reported on the dimension-relevant behaviors elicited in the second block as well as improvement observed by the facilitators from the first to the second block. In addition, there was a discussion about ways in which the participant might continue improve on the dimensions in the context of his or her job. As is illustrated in Fig. 2.2, the facilitators continued to coach the participants on a monthly basis, and the participants came back to participate in additional simulation exercises each year.

Other Elements of the Program

Before the participants attended the program, multisource data were collected about each participant's proficiency on the dimensions using a standardized questionnaire. Input was gathered from the participants themselves, as well as their supervisors, peers, and subordinates. Additional self-reflection questionnaires were completed after each block of exercises during the assessment center. Multisource ratings were collected again four times a year to track the effectiveness of the developmental assessment center for improving participants' skill on the crucial site manager dimensions. Results from the multisource questionnaires were also fed back to the participants as part of their monthly coaching session to provide additional developmental feedback.

Results

There have been some complaints made by the shift supervisors about the leadership development program invitation process. Although the program policies clearly state that the program is purely developmental, and no personnel decisions are made on the basis of individuals' participation or success in the program, there are strong beliefs within the organization that the leadership development program is the "royal road" to middle management. Many have complained that there are politics inherent in the performance appraisal system, and since it is the performance appraisal data that are used to make decisions about whom to invite to participate in the leadership development program, the perception is that many are unfairly excluded from participating.

Despite the valid criticism, the program has seen great success among those that have participated. Longitudinal multisource ratings show significant increases in dimension proficiency after participating in the developmental assessment center, and these increases continue over time. Furthermore, participants who have been promoted to site manager have expressed that they felt well prepared due to all the practice they had received in the leadership development program.

Summary

AMW used an assessment center to actually develop employees. Used within a broader leadership development program, the developmental assessment center used blocks of exercises and multiple, in-depth feedback and goal-setting sessions to provide participants with practice and instruction on skills necessary for the next level of management. Results showed this was an effective means for growing talent within the organization and maintaining a talent pipeline.

Because developmental assessment centers are relatively new, a fuller description of them is included in chapter 4.

REVIEW OF CASES

The three case studies described in this chapter illustrate the several common features of all assessment centers, as well as many variations. All assessment centers involve observation of behavior relevant to dimensions of employee effectiveness in simulation exercises. Evaluations by multiple assessors are integrated and fed back to participants and others who need the information in order to make personnel decisions (if applicable). On the other hand, assessment centers for different purposes—promotion, diagnosis, or development—are designed somewhat differently. Elements of the method that are adapted include:

- dimensions to be assessed
- types of exercises
- content of exercises
- observation and evaluation procedures
- type, nature, and frequency of feedback
- support activities

All of these elements are designed to ensure that the assessment center meets the specific objectives of a given human resource management function. This theme is explored in more depth in subsequent chapters.

Chapter 3

Basic Requirements of an Assessment Center

As we look at the history of assessment centers in nonmilitary settings since they were launched in the late 1940s in British civil service organizations and in the mid-1950s in the United States by AT&T, we see an interesting combination of continuity and change. Continuity is evident in the requirements that assessment centers include a number of essential common features. Change is evident in the many variations of these features. Changes have been instituted as a result of changes in the nature of work, organization structures, demographics of the workforce, and technological advances. In addition, variations are seen in assessment centers that are designed for different purposes. Variations in assessment center features are seen in:

- the dimensions being assessed
- exercises used to simulate organizational situations
- the type of assessors used to observe and evaluate behavior
- methods to integrate data across exercises and assessors
- the type and level of detail in feedback provided to the participants, managers in the organization, and HR staff

One of the reasons variation in these elements has appeared is the changing demographics of the workforce, including increasing involvement of minorities and women, persons with diverse ethnic backgrounds, and older workers. In addition, variations in assessment center practices have been seen in cross-national applications. Throughout this book we explore many of these variations.

In spite of these variations, a number of basic requirements of the assessment center method have remained stable. In this chapter we discuss the central, core features of the assessment center method. These essential features have been stated and reinforced in three editions of the key document defining the method: *Guidelines and Ethical Considerations for Assessment Center Operations* (International Task Force, 2000). The *Guidelines*, which are reproduced in Appendix A, were written by a task force of experienced researchers, consultants, and practitioners, and endorsed by nearly 200 people at the 2000 International Congress on the Assessment Center Method. After describing these key features of the assessment center method, we present the theoretical foundations for assessment centers designed for different purposes. These principles are then translated into practical applications to show how the various elements of an assessment center are designed for a specific purpose. Congruent with the different theoretical underpinnings for different types of assessment centers, we see variations in the design and implementation of assessment centers. What remains constant in all of these rich variations are the set of key features that distinguish assessment centers from other methods. We conclude the chapter with a defense of why the assessment center community has taken steps to clarify the term *assessment center* and to monitor its use in the field of human resource management.

The three case studies presented in chapter 2 showed how assessment centers have been used to help organizations make promotion decisions, diagnose development needs, and develop managerial skills. These reports revealed that there are several common features among assessment centers, as well as several differences among them. When assessment centers are devised to meet other human resource management objectives, there are even more variations.

ESSENTIAL FEATURES OF AN ASSESSMENT CENTER

There are several basic requirements for an assessment process to legitimately be called an *assessment center* according to the *Guidelines*. Over the years, proponents of the assessment center method have insisted that this term should be applied to only certain methods. The reason for this protectiveness is that there is considerable research supporting the consistency and accuracy of the method. Individuals developing other assessment methods sometimes wish to benefit from the good publicity given the assessment center method without establishing the same level of empirical support. Therefore, proponents of the assessment center method have taken steps to ensure that the term be reserved for those procedures that contain the following basic features.

Job Analysis

Analysis of job requirements is the first step in developing any human resource management procedure (Brannick & Levine, 2002); it is particularly important for ensuring that a selection procedure is fair to all candidates. When applied to assessment centers, job analysis necessitates the collection of a wide variety of information about the job and organization situation, including the dimensions to be assessed (i.e., skills, qualities, attributes, motivation, knowledge), competency levels expected, tasks performed, and organizational context (Thornton & Mueller-Hanson, 2004). The dimensions serve as the framework for building simulation exercises, observing behaviors of candidates, evaluating effectiveness of performance, and giving feedback. (Different types of dimensions are more or less appropriate for assessment centers designed for different purposes. For example, dimensions for developmental assessment centers must be "developable"—a concept explored in more depth in chapters 4 and 10.) Capturing examples of tasks provides substance for the problems and issues to embed in the exercises. Understanding the competency levels expected provides guidance in how complex and difficult to make the exercises and what standards are built into the evaluation. Understanding the organizational context is essential for building exercises that have fidelity to the target job and face validity for participants. If an adequate job analysis has not already been carried out, a new analysis may be necessary. If the job does not currently exist, parts of the new job may already exist and can be analyzed to discover relevant dimensions. In recent years, competency modeling (Schippmann et al., 2000) has been used to complement the more traditional job analysis methods with information about how the job fits with organization strategies. Procedures for performing a job analysis as a preliminary step to assessment center operations are described in chapter 5.

Multiple Assessment Techniques

A variety of assessment techniques can be used to evaluate participants in assessment centers. These include interviews, tests, questionnaires, and simulation exercises. The techniques must be designed to provide multiple opportunities to observe complex behavior related to the dimensions identified in the job analysis. When cognitive ability and personality tests are used, persons properly trained in their administration and interpretation should be involved as assessors. Recently, there has been a trend in the

United States to limit the assessment center process to observations of behavior in multiple simulation exercises, and keep test data separate.

Simulation Exercises

One of the distinguishing features of the assessment center method is the simulation exercise (Bray & Grant, 1966). Simulation exercises portray important aspects of the target job. Job analysis reveals the most common tasks, problems, and situations that job holders must face. Simulation exercises are then created that closely resemble these important features of the job situation.

A simulation exercise presents the participant with a complex set of stimuli to deal with. For example, the "test" materials may include a complicated written case describing the economic conditions in a small town and call for the participant to perform a financial analysis to decide whether or not to open a branch bank. In a group discussion, the participant might interact with other participants to formulate a set of recommendations for higher management. In a role play simulating one-on-one interactions, the assessee might be required to talk with a person who is playing the role of a problem employee or an irate customer. The common feature of these exercises is that the participant is faced with a complex set of conditions representing a situation that may actually occur on the job. The advantage of simulation exercises over other assessment methods is that they require the participant to demonstrate complex, overt behaviors.

Certain types of exercises have been used less frequently in recent years. For example, group discussions and interaction simulations with a role player have been used less frequently in selection and promotional programs in the United States, because they may be vulnerable to charges that they can be somewhat unstandardized (i.e., the dynamics of one group can be quite different from another, or a role player may interact slightly differently from candidate to candidate).

In recent years, some assessment exercises have utilized various forms of technology (e.g., video, computer) to present stimulus materials to participants. The advantages and disadvantages of "high-tech" assessment will be explored in chapter 6.

Behavioral Responses

Simulation exercises are performance tests (Anastasi & Urbina, 1997) requiring the participant to display complex behavior in a situation resembling some critical scenario in the organization. To be successful, the participant must display some overt behavior consistent with the behaviors required on the job. For example, in a group discussion, the participant must offer suggestions about a new program or procedure; in a written case study, he or she must write a critical analysis, a recommendation, or a proposal. Such responses are quite different from the responses a person gives when taking a test that calls only for choices among alternative answers or ratings on Likert-type scales, where the participant may have to make several complex *covert* responses (in other words, think), but the only *overt* response is the simple motion of making a mark on a piece of paper. The test interpreter is then required to make an inference about the covert responses. In contrast, participants in a group discussion must not only think, but speak and act in ways that influence others. In exercises such as these, the assessor is not required to make such large inferences about the participant's skills or abilities.

Another distinguishing feature of some simulation exercises is that there is interaction: Other people in the group discussion talk and the participant must respond; in a presentation, the audience may ask questions; and in a simulation involving the problems of an employee, the verbal exchange may be intense. These sets of complex and dynamic interactions elicit a rich display of behaviors that are indicative of complex competencies that cannot be assessed by most multiple-choice tests.

In some recent assessment methods that approximate the assessment center method, the participant does not display overt complex behavior, but rather (a) makes choices from predetermined alternatives or (b) states what he or she would intend to do or say. Three examples illustrate the difference between these "low-fidelity" methods and "high-fidelity" simulation exercises that require complex overt behaviors. Computerized in-baskets often call for the participant to choose among alternative actions in response to a memo on the screen. Situational interviews call for the interviewee to state what he or she would do if faced with a situation. Video-based assessments sometimes present a scenario on tape or screen, then stop and ask the participant to fill out a questionnaire to indicate what action he or she would take. The advantages and limitations of these methods are explored in chapter 6.

Behavioral Observations

Behavior of the participants in simulation exercises is observed by trained assessors. Assessors take detailed notes of what the participants say and do. An example of a behavioral observation during a group problem-solving discussion might be: "Tim pounded his fist on the table and said, 'That's too little, too late,' when Bob offered to raise the travel allowance." Behavioral observations give a specific statement of observable actions and even actual words. They do not contain inferences, such as "he was angry," or interpretations, such as "he made a bad impression on other participants."

A behavioral observation can also entail a description of the assessee's failure to say something or to take action. The *absence* of overt behavior, when the situation calls for behavior, is often a relevant behavior. Examples include: "Lara failed to reply to an email request from her boss to provide information he needed for a meeting the next day," "Jeff did not address a critical point in his marketing report to upper management," and "Bob failed to discuss a serious safety violation in his performance review session with his subordinate." It is often difficult to train assessors to make note of and use the absence of behavior in their evaluations.

Multiple Assessors

In the assessment center method, more than one individual is involved in evaluating the participant. Observations from multiple assessors help ensure that inaccurate idiosyncratic biases from any one assessor will not unduly influence the final outcome of the assessment process. For example, one assessor may hold the false assumption that all written reports must follow a certain format. When we solicit several points of view, we are acknowledging that (a) we must make judgments about professional competence, (b) judgments, per se, have some subjectivity in them, but (c) adverse effects of biases of any one assessor can be minimized by pooling observations of more than one assessor.

Assessors with several different points of view can make valid contributions to the evaluation of professional competencies. Assessors bring different backgrounds and experiences to the assessment task and contribute a rich variety of perspectives. Such diversity means that assessors may not always agree on the evaluation of a participant. Each of the different evaluations may be accurate and include valuable information; in fact, such differences are expected and welcomed as a part of the principle of multiple assessors. The staff of an assessment center may consist of managers and/or human resource personnel from within the organization, outside consultants, or a variety of other individuals familiar with the target job. Research has indicated that a variety of different types of assessors can make valid contributions to assessment (Gaugler, Rosenthal, Thornton, & Bentson, 1987). There is no common agreement about how many assessors are necessary for adequate evaluations in the assessment center context. In a typical assessment center, three or more assessors make independent observations of each participant's performance.

Trained Assessors

Assessors are trained to carry out complex assessment functions. They must be able to observe behavior, record those observations in some manner, classify behavior into the dimensions being assessed, make judgments about the level of performance displayed by the candidate, describe these observations to other assessors, integrate behavioral observations from different sources and exercises, and in some cases, make an evaluation of overall success and give suggestions for development in the future (Thornton & Mueller-Hanson, 2004; Thornton & Rupp, 2003). To carry out these functions, assessors must be trained thoroughly, and then evaluated and monitored to determine that they carry out these functions accurately. Some of the elements of assessor training include discussion of the meaning of the dimensions to be assessed, practice in observing and evaluating behavior, integration of the information in the assessor team, and giving feedback to participants. Recent assessor training techniques have incorporated many of the principles of frame-of-reference training developed for performance appraisal raters (Schleicher, Day, Mayes, & Riggio, 2002). The *Guidelines* state that the organization should examine all assessors to certify that they are competent to observe, classify, and rate behavior. More details on assessor training can be found in several sources (e.g., Byham, 1977; Thornton & Byham, 1982; Thornton & Mueller-Hanson, 2004; Thornton & Rupp, 2003) and in chapter 7.

Integration of Observations

Here we introduce a very controversial aspect of the assessment center process and about psychological assessment procedures in general, namely, how to integrate pieces of assessment information. Traditionally, assessment centers have relied on judgments of assessors integrated in a group discussion among assessors. The results of individual exercises are observed and classified in a judgmental way. In addition, when the assessors integrate their observations across exercises and then integrate evaluations of dimensions to derive an overall rating, they do so judgmentally. The judgmental integration process has been called the "clinical method" (Dawes, 1979; Sawyer, 1966) because it is the method often used by clinical psychologists to combine information from different sources to diagnose an individual's personality makeup or predict the success of various forms of therapy.

There is an alternative to the judgmental method of integrating information, namely "statistical" or "mechanical" integration. Many people favor this method and it may be more appropriate for some assessment situations, for instance, when large numbers of candidates are being screened for low-level jobs or when the potential for employment litigation looms large. In the statistical method of combining information (Sawyer, 1966), pieces of information are assigned predetermined weights and then combined using a formula. For example, to arrive at an overall assessment rating of promotability, the rating on the dimension "decision-making ability" may be given twice the weight as the rating on "leadership." These different weights are selected to show the relative importance of the dimensions for the success of individuals in the target position. The statistical formula is an alternative to the assessors' judgment about the relative importance of the dimensions.

There is an unresolved debate over the best integration method to use. There is empirical evidence to support each method; at this time there is no definitive answer as to which is the best method. A much more thorough review of this debate is presented in chapters 7 and 8, where research from the assessment center domain and from the broader domain of psychological assessment is discussed. Traditionally, the assessment center method has used the judgmental integration process; that process is a legitimate part of an assessment center and has been demonstrated superior in some studies we review later. The reader should be aware, though, that some assessment center proponents strongly advocate the statistical integration process and can marshal clear evidence to support their position (Feltham, 1988b; Sackett & Wilson, 1982; Tziner, Meir, Dahan, & Birati, 1994). The previous discussion might suggest that assessment centers use *either* a judgmental *or* a statistical method to integrate their results. In fact, the two methods can be used jointly to complement each and to improve assessor decision making.

What Is NOT Addressed in the Guidelines

Although the *Guidelines* cover many features of this assessment method, the reader will see that several important considerations have not been addressed. We name just a few topics here, and then return to an exploration of areas of needed development in the last chapter of this book. We suggest future task forces carefully consider the following areas: cross-cultural considerations; types and levels of fidelity and technology; qualifications of assessor trainers; qualifications of assessment center developers and consultants; and the responsibilities of an organization to have support systems in place to complement diagnostic and developmental assessment centers.

THEORETICAL FOUNDATIONS FOR ALTERNATIVE ASSESSMENT CENTER PROGRAMS

Chapter 2 illustrated three very different ways of carrying out an assessment center program. The special features of these programs were designed to accomplish very different purposes. The objective of a long-range promotion program is to assess potential for managerial success and to predict the success of candidates for higher level jobs. The objective of a diagnostic program is to identify the relative strengths and weaknesses in the individual's job-related competencies. The objective of a development program is to teach a new set of skills to individual participants and to develop teamwork skills in groups. To accomplish these quite distinct objectives, very different assessment centers are needed. In the past, some assessment centers have been designed for one purpose and used for another. The results are usually disappointing. For example, an assessment center designed to aid in long-range predictions of management potential may not yield a good diagnosis of training needs, since the dimensions may not be amenable to development and the feedback may not be helpful in giving direction for change.

This section explores the theoretical foundations and general principles underlying different uses of the assessment center. Why should the student and practitioner of human resource management care about these theoretical foundations? Understanding the theory helps in very practical ways when the time comes to design an effective assessment center. As Kurt Lewin (1951), a famous psychologist in the 1930s, so simply and eloquently stated: "There is nothing so practical as a good theory" (p. 167). Following our discussion of principles of prediction, diagnosis, and training, several practical examples of assessment center design are given.

Principles of Prediction

We can look to the principles of measurement in the field of psychometrics for the theoretical foundations of good prediction (Ghiselli, Campbell, & Zedeck, 1981; Guion, 1998; Nunnally & Bernstein, 1994). Some key measurement principles are *standardization, reliability,* and *validity.* Standardization refers to the uniformity of the procedures for evaluating participants. A procedure is standardized if every person is provided the same instructions, the same questions, the same rules and time limits, and the same chance to respond fully. Several potential threats to standardization can occur in the administration of an assessment center. Simulation exercises can be unstandardized: participants may be given different amounts of time to complete a written case analysis; role players depicting a problem employee may act with different degrees of cooperation; and participants in a group discussion may get quite excited or remain rather calm. Usually, the impact of these threats can be minimized by careful administration of the program. Uncontrolled variations should be documented and reported along with assessment results.

Reliability refers to the consistency of scores for two measurements taken on two equivalent samples of behavior, or for two measurements taken at two points in time. Reliability also refers to agreement among scores given by different examiners. A test is reliable if we get a similar score no matter which form of the test is used, when it is administered, who administers it, who observes it, and who scores it. Unreliability in assessment center ratings may arise if different topics are assigned in a leaderless group discussion, if assessors differ in the behaviors they observe and record, or if the assessor team is somewhat lax in integrating the behavioral information. Fortunately, most of these potential sources of unreliability are controlled by thorough training of the assessors, clear scoring standards, and faithful adherence to the procedure of sharing and evaluating information in the integration discussion for each participant. In the end, the research evidence shows that assessment center ratings are highly consistent.

Validity refers to the ability of the test to achieve its aims and objectives. Establishing the validity of a test is a complex process (American Educational Research Association, American Psychological Association, American Council of Measurement in Education, 1999; Binning & Barrett, 1989; Guion, 1998) that involves the accumulation of evidence that the assessment procedure is measuring the targeted concepts and will contribute information relevant to the decisions that must be made. For example, in the case of a promotional assessment center, the most relevant validity information is the accuracy with which assessors could predict long-range success in the jobs in question (Society for Industrial and Organizational Psychology, 2003). Validity comes when the jobs have been carefully analyzed, critical components have been identified, and measures carefully constructed. Validity of the assessment center can be diminished if it includes components not critical to the job. There is much theoretical (Wernimont & Campbell, 1968) and empirical evidence (Asher & Sciarrino, 1974) to support the use of behavioral samples, as distinguished from signs, of effective performance on the job. Signs can be thought of as indicators of important behaviors. Examples of signs include paper-and-pencil tests of mental abilities and personality characteristics, interviews that cover a person's work experience, and biographical information forms that cover background and educational experiences. Behavioral sampling procedures are quite different; they require that the person demonstrate complex behaviors that are very much like on-the-job behaviors. Behavioral sampling is provided by the simulation exercises introduced in chapters 1 and 2; it is explained in more depth in chapters 5 and 6. Assessment centers have the potential for high accuracy in predicting future success. Numerous individual studies and meta-analyses of sets of studies show that the overall assessment rating predicts a wide variety of criteria over periods of time up to 25 years. Details of these studies are summarized in chapter 10.

Principles of Differential Diagnosis

The theory of diagnosis of differential strengths and weaknesses is similar to the theory of prediction of long-range success but is based on some additional principles of good measurement. Diagnosis requires clear and discrete measurement of separate characteristics (Wiggins, 1973). By contrast, for prediction of long-range success, we evaluate the dimensions as a way to ensure representative coverage of important elements in job performance, but our real interest is in predicting overall potential. For diagnosis, the measurement must give accurate measures of each of the separate dimensions in and of themselves. More than that, the measurement procedure must give measures of these attributes that are not highly related to each other (Guion, 1998). For example, if everyone who scored high on leadership also scored high on oral communication, having these two dimensions would not allow unique profiles of different individuals' strengths and weaknesses. In other words, the assessment process would not provide a diagnosis of different skill levels on these two dimensions.

The result we are seeking from a diagnostic assessment center is differential diagnosis. To achieve differential diagnosis, an assessment center must provide accurate assessment of separate dimensions of managerial competence. For example, the assessment must evaluate decision-making ability independently of other dimensions, such as negotiation. To accomplish this "nondependent" evaluation, the assessment center must be designed with certain features: The dimensions must be conceptually distinct, the exercises must allow assessors to detect variations in an individual's performance relevant to the different dimensions, and assessors must be trained to make the appropriate distinctions among behaviors relevant to the dimensions. Guidance on how to achieve these ends can be found in Lievens (1998) and is discussed in chapters 7, 8, and 10.

Principles of Training Relevant to a Developmental Assessment Center

If an assessment center is to be used to train skills, a very different set of principles is involved in the design. Whereas the emphasis in promotion or diagnostic programs is on evaluation and measurement of behavior, here the emphasis is on *change in behavior*. As illustrated in chapter 2, AMF used the assessment center to enable managers to learn new interaction skills. The exercises, feedback, and practice provided opportunities for each participant to develop in areas where he or she is weak.

Principles of learning and development provide guidance in the design of several aspects of the assessment center, including the selection of dimensions to be developed, the way exercises are run, how and when feedback is given, and the general climate of the program. We review all of these points after we present some key principles of training and development.

For a long time, psychologists have known about the conditions that foster learning (Goldstein, 1986). Early studies of learning patterns showed that new responses become associated with more basic responses after repeated pairings. From other learning studies, we know that people learn new behaviors that are followed by reinforcements. In the personnel development arena, a person will learn new skills if he or she gets positive feedback from the new behavior or if there is an indication that the new behavior leads to the effective completion of a project, profitability for the organization, or career progress.

Two additional areas of theory and research have contributed to the development of employee training programs: adult learning (Knowles, 1970, 1973) and social learning (Bandura, 1977, 1986, 1997; Goldstein & Sorcher, 1974). Adult learning theory (Knowles, 1970) is built on the premise that adults learn differently from children because they have a large amount of experience to draw on, are more ready to learn, and want to learn skills that will help them carry out important roles in life. In view of these particular characteristics of adults, Knowles (1973) derived several suggestions for how training programs should be set up. The training should be organized around real-life problems rather than abstract disciplines. Also, adults need a safe environment in which to unlearn old modes of behavior. In addition, adults learn better if they are provided an opportunity to be actively involved in the learning process.

Social learning theory provides different insights into how an employee training program should be set up. Bandura (1977) has shown that we learn many important behaviors vicariously, that is, by watching others learn. We ourselves need not engage in the behavior: When we can observe the behavior of others, we see which actions are effective and reinforced and which are ineffective and not reinforced. This principle is exemplified in the simulation exercises of assessment centers that involve interacting with others. Bandura has also shown that people become more self-confident in their skills when supportive conditions prevail: when there are multiple opportunities to *be* successful, when the learner can observe other people *being successful,* when credible people *support success,* and when the situation does not produce so much anxiety that the person questions his or her own *ability to succeed.* These conditions give us many practical suggestions about how an assessment center should be set up to foster actual learning and real skill development.

APPLICATION OF PRINCIPLES TO ASSESSMENT CENTER DESIGN

We turn now to the application of these principles to the design of an assessment center. In what ways do the three organizations described in our case studies utilize the principles we have just described? Does PFD's promotion assessment center use good principles of measurement and prediction? Does Technosoft's diagnostic program use good principles of differential measurement? Does AMW's managerial development program use good principles of training and learning?

Table 3.1 summarizes the different ways that assessment centers have been implemented, as illustrated in chapter 2. It shows how several features of the assessment center procedure are varied in the specific case examples. What should be apparent is that there is no such thing as a typical assessment center. These studies demonstrated that there is wide variation in the way all facets of an assessment center are set up and administered. What is not so obvious, and what forms the basic theme of this book, is that the characteristics of the assessment center must be matched with the purpose of the program. All too often in the past, assessment centers for diagnosis looked just like assessment centers for prediction of long-range potential. This may not be surprising because, in the early years, when organizations initiated assessment centers, they often wished to follow the excellent ex-

TABLE 3.1
Comparison of Assessment Centers for Different Purposes

	Promotion or Selection	Diagnosis of Training Needs	Development of Skills
Participants	High-potential employees or applicants	All interested employees	All interested employees
Position to be analyzed	Job to be filled now or in future	Current or future job	Current or future job
Number of dimensions	Fewer (e.g., 5–7), more global	Many (e.g., 8–10), more specific	Fewer (e.g., 5–7)
Nature of dimensions	Potentialities, traits	Developable, conceptually distinct	Trainable skills
Number of exercises	Few (e.g., 3–5)	Many (e.g., 6–8)	More than one of each type
Types of exercises	Generic	Moderate similarity to job	Work samples
Time required for assessment	Relatively short (e.g., .5–1 day)	Relatively long (e.g., 1.5–2 days)	Relatively long (e.g., 1.5–2 days)
Observation methods	Highly controlled		
Integration methods	Objective, quantified	Individualized for each participant	
Type of report	Short, descriptive	Long, diagnostic	Immediate verbal report
Who gets feedback	Participant, manager two levels up	Participant and supervisor	Participant, possibly supervisor
Who gives feedback	HRM staff	HRM staff or assessor	HRM staff, trainer, or facilitator
Important outcome	Overall assessment rating	Dimension ratings	Behavioral suggestions

ample set by AT&T and the Bell operating companies (Bray, 1964; Bray & Grant, 1966). What was often not recognized was that the features of a program like AT&T's might not be appropriate for a program in another organization, used for a completely different purpose. The bigger lesson to be learned by human resource managers is that excellent programs should not just be copied. The faddish adoption of techniques that work for someone else has been the curse of the human resource management field.

To be clear about our position on imitation and innovation, we should emphasize that it is entirely appropriate to benefit from the sound research and development done by prior organizations and to use the same procedures they have used, provided the new program has similar purposes. In fact, we would argue strongly that the same procedures *should* be used so that the earlier research results are applicable in the new setting. There is no need to "reinvent the wheel." On the other hand, the "wheel" may not be the apparatus you need for the vehicle you are building. That is, an organization may need an assessment center that is very different from the ones designed previously. Sackett (1982) observed that in the early 1980s, few job analyses had been reported in the development of assessment centers; organizations often used the same dimensions and exercises as their predecessors. Fortunately, the present situation seems to be different: Surveys by Spychalski et al. (1997) in the United States and Krause and Gebert (2003) in German-speaking countries, found that more than 90% of the organizations conducted a job analysis as a basis for their assessment centers.

Table 3.1 makes it clear that any one feature can be implemented in different ways. The job or jobs being simulated can be either *current* jobs, as in Technosoft's diagnostic program, jobs at the *next higher levels* as in PFD's promotion program, or a *set of jobs* that a variety of participants hold, as in the development program at AMW. The dimensions being assessed also differ markedly from one program to another. For promotion purposes, the assessment should be done on dimensions that reflect potentialities to grow over a long period of time, whereas for diagnosis and development, the program should assess skills or competencies that can be developed either during the program itself (in the case of a development program) or in the future (in the case of a diagnostic program).

There are also differences in the exercises used for the three types of programs. The basic types of exercises need not differ; all programs might use in-boxes, group discussions, and simulations of interactions with others. The differences are in the content of the exercises and the types of demands placed on the participants. For a selection or promotion program, we would assume that the participant had little experience with the problems being presented. Thus, we would not require any specific knowledge or technical skill to be displayed. By contrast, for a diagnostic or development program, we would assume the participants had relevant experience and we would be assessing the level of skills or trying to enhance those skills. Thus, in these latter programs the exercises can involve technical material relevant to the target job.

The process of observing, classifying, and evaluating behavior is quite different in the three programs also. Recall that the purpose of the promotion program is to predict potential for success in the future. The final overall assessment rating is based on the accumulated information about performance on several dimensions. There may be many paths to this result in terms of the types of behavior observed and the dimension ratings given. But in the end, the particular qualities of any one dimension rating are not as important as the predictive accuracy of the overall rating. In contrast, for a diagnostic program, each dimension rating must be quite accurate. Thus, the way that assessors are trained, and the ways they are required to observe, record, and judge behavior must be designed specifically to provide accurate measures on the separate dimensions. In fact, an overall assessment rating may not even be given. Chapters 7 and 8 go into more detail on the alternative ways that observation and judgment is carried out in various types of programs. For now, suffice it to say that the observation procedures must be designed to provide the types of information needed to fulfill the objectives of the program.

The results and feedback generated from the three types of programs certainly differ. In all programs, the participants should be given feedback about their performance. The *Guidelines*, provided in Appendix A, emphasize that participants should receive feedback on their performance and be informed about recommendations made by the assessment team. When psychologists are involved in designing and implementing assessment centers, they follow this practice because it is a part of their code of ethics (American Psychological Association, 1992), which states that a client has the right to know the results and interpretations from assessment techniques. Beyond feedback to the individual, the results of a promotion program should be presented to managers two levels above the participants, because in most organizations these are the people making final decisions about promotions. In order to preserve the privacy of the participants, the assessment results should not be given to other people, especially the supervisory level directly above the participants. These supervisors are in the target position being assessed, and they can give evaluations of current on-the-job performance of the participants, but they will probably not be making decisions about whether others will be promoted into a position like their own. What the higher level decision makers need to receive is an unbiased prediction of the likelihood of success if the candidate is promoted.

By contrast, in a diagnostic program, detailed information about performance on separate dimensions is provided to the assessee and, possibly, to the immediate supervisor. The detailed feedback often includes specific behaviors illustrating components of a dimension, for example, the person's leadership skill was considered weak because he or she never asked subordinates for their help in solving problems. Such information forms the basis of developmental planning and subsequent training and development activities. Some of these follow-up activities can be initiated by the individual, but the immediate supervisor is typically involved in many development activities. In summary, the feedback must be much more thorough than the feedback in promotion programs.

Feedback in a developmental assessment center program is different still. Two features are crucial: First, the feedback must be specific and give guidance for alternative actions to improve performance; second, the feedback must be provided soon after the behavior has been performed. Whereas results of a promotion or diagnostic program may come days or weeks later, it is most effective to give feedback in a training program immediately so the person can learn and have the chance to improve in subsequent exercises. This is why there must be two or more exercises and the facilitators must record their observations quickly and provide feedback to the participants in a helpful manner.

REASONS FOR LIMITING THE USE OF THE TERM *ASSESSMENT CENTER*

Why is there any need to insist that the term *assessment center* is used to refer only to assessment methods that include the essential features codified in various documents and described in this chapter? Isn't there common agreement on what is meant by the term? Unfortunately, the term is sometimes used in a way that does not conform to the *Guidelines*. One large human resource management association offered an assessment process that included only cognitive ability tests and personality questionnaires. A large consulting firm advertised in print that it had an assessment center, but in actuality it was using an individual assessment process conducted by one psychologist. A large municipality described its promotional examination process for police administrators as an assessment center when in fact only background interviews were conducted. A large organization described its testing and development facility as an "assessment and development center." We hasten to clarify our position: There may be nothing wrong with these assessment practices. They may be quite effective. Our point deals with the *term* used to describe these practices.

Over the years, assessment center researchers and practitioners have attempted to limit the use of the term *assessment center* to the set of assessment practices described in the *Guidelines* and in this chapter. There are several reasons for this concern. Persons working the field need consistency in the

use of terms to facilitate communication. When reading professional literature or hearing someone speak about a procedure, persons need an agreed-
upon language to discuss topics of common interest. Within a profession,
words take on important connotations. For communication to be effective,
professionals need to have some assurance that words are being used in a
consistent manner. Terms with commonly accepted meaning also make
communication efficient. When a human resource manager wants to say her
organization uses an assessment method that involves simulations, multiple
assessors, observations of overt behavior, and so forth, she does not have to
use all those words; she can instead say the organization uses an *assessment
center*, and knowledgeable colleagues will know what is meant.

Practitioners also need to use the term *assessment center* consistently when
invoking transportability claims about the method. Small organizations seldom have the resources to validate an assessment center with their own criterion-related validity studies. It is often necessary to validate the local process by demonstrating that the job and performance domain are comparable
to other situations where the assessment center has been proven valid. For
this argument to hold up, the assessment process in the new organization
must comply with essential features of the assessment process in the settings
where it was validated.

Researchers also need to have a standardized term in order to conduct
original research and aggregate findings across different studies. Recognizing the limits of any one study of a HRM practice, researchers often look
for common themes and consistent findings in diverse studies. For example, they often compute averages of statistical criterion-validity coefficients
to summarize the effectiveness of one technique and make comparisons
across techniques. One method for aggregating research findings is validity
generalization (Hunter & Schmidt, 1990; Hunter, Schmidt, & Jackson,
1982). This meta-analysis method involves aggregating the evidence, for example, of all studies of assessment centers. Errors of inclusion and exclu-
sion of relevant studies can occur if the terminology for the assessment
method is not consistent.

We also have concern that the occasional, unscrupulous practitioner pur-
posely misuses the term to take advantage of the long history of validation research and wide-spread adoption of assessment centers. He or she may be using some other method that does not have such a background of support.

IS THERE A SINGLE ASSESSMENT CENTER?

Is there such a thing as "The Assessment Center" with those capital letters?
The answer is "No," not in the sense that we can point to "the Wonderlic"
(Wonderlic, 1992) or "the NEO" (Costa & McRae, 1992). In the assessment

center field, there is no single set of dimensions that are assessed, no single set of published exercises, no single method of recording behavioral observations, and no single method of integrating the data. At the same time, there is a set of essential features of the assessment center method. In this chapter we have described both the set of features that are the defining characteristics of the assessment center method, and have hinted at the many variations of how these features are carried out in the diverse field of practical assessment center applications. In subsequent chapters we explore in more depth what has remained constant and what has changed in the dimensions (chap. 5), exercises (chap. 6), processing and integrating observations (chaps. 7 and 8), and methods of giving feedback (chap. 9).

CROSS-CULTURAL CONSIDERATIONS

Two sets of factors must be considered in applying assessment centers across different cultures and countries. First, there may be different sets of essential features that some country wishes to implement in its application of the assessment center method. For example, additional procedures for protecting the privacy of individuals, maintaining records, or uses of the assessment results may be articulated. Second, the same essential features may remain, but the manifestation may differ. For example, the same label for a dimension, say Leadership, may be used but the definition may change; simulations may be required but not the same type that has been used most frequently in the United States and Europe; different behavior anchors for performance levels of good and poor Leadership may be specified. Initial steps along these lines have been taken to write guidelines for assessment centers in Europe and Indonesia (Pendit & Thornton, 2001).

SUMMARY AND CONCLUSIONS

Two issues were raised at the beginning of this chapter: Are there distinguishing features of an assessment center, and can a single assessment center be used for more than one purpose? After reading about assessment centers so far, you might conclude that this method is not really different from other personnel evaluation procedures. After all, each one of the features of an assessment center is used elsewhere: Multiple interviewers are commonly used to select professionals and managers; situational interviews and in-baskets are used as stand-alone techniques; multiple sources of data are commonly combined to predict job success. What is unique about the assessment center is the way these procedures are used in *combination* with each other. Thus, we can look at an assessment procedure and say whether or not it is an assessment center.

To be called an assessment center, the process must have all the required elements of job analysis, multiple assessors, multiple simulation exercises, behavioral reporting, and integration by a team of trained assessors or by some statistical method that has been properly developed. Each of those elements can be varied somewhat to fit the specific purpose of the assessment program set forth by the human resource manager. Theories of measurement, differential diagnosis, and learning provide valuable practical suggestions for how each type of assessment center should be constructed.

The issue of whether or not an assessment center can be used for multiple purposes is a bit more complex. As an example, let us first consider whether an assessment center program designed primarily for promotion purposes can also be used for diagnosis and development. On the one hand, one might argue that during the assessment process the assessors have gathered a wealth of information, and it would be a good idea to use that information to help the individual develop. It would take only a little more time during the feedback session to give the participant suggestions about things he or she could do to improve. Even if the organization does not plan to do any systematic training, the participants might benefit from personal insight into their weaknesses and engage in self-improvement. Finally, talking about how the person can improve just seems to be a good thing to do.

On the other hand, it may be difficult and misleading to talk about developing many of the dimensions typically assessed in selection and promotion programs. Characteristics such as energy level, impact on others, adaptability, motivation, and integrity are not easy to change in the context of organizational life. There are those that would argue that organizations do not have the obligation to provide follow-up training to everyone who is considered for promotion. If the candidate does not have the motivation to manage others or to move upward in the organization, it may be unethical for the organization to try to change those basic values, even if it could.

Next, consider whether a program designed primarily for diagnosis or development can be used for promotion decisions. On the one hand, the organization may see that much valuable information has been gathered in the course of diagnosis or training that would indicate whether the person should be promoted to a position of more responsibility. The argument is that if a participant shows faults that are not likely to be changed easily in the short run, it would be irresponsible to the organization as a whole to promote the person.

On the other hand, if participants know that the assessment information might be used for decision making, they may not be willing to reveal weaknesses (even if we call them "developmental needs"), to explore alternative managerial styles, and to take the risks that are often required for learning. In essence, many aspects of the climate of a selection program are not compatible with the climate of a development program.

In summary, we believe that it is very difficult to use one program for multiple purposes. In our opinion, the many adaptations of the assessment center method that must be made to attain different goals imply that a program set up to accomplish one goal may be incompatible with the needs of another program. One final thought: Participants in an assessment center should be told how the information will be used (see *Guidelines*). For example, if the program is publicized as developmental, but higher level managers will have access to the results (and thus may use them for making promotion decisions), then the participants should be informed of this.

Chapter 4

Taking a Closer Look at Developmental Assessment Centers

In this chapter, we take a closer look at assessment centers developed exclusively for employee development. These centers, termed developmental assessment centers, or DACs, are unique. Whereas selection and diagnostic centers are designed to assess competence in order to make a judgment or decision about an individual (i.e., selection/promotion decisions, the preparation of an individualized development plan), a DAC serves the dual purpose of *both* assessment *and* development (Iles & Forster, 1994; Joiner, 2002; Kudisch, Ladd, & Dobbins, 1997). That is, learning and improvement are expected to take place over the course of the center. We have devoted an entire chapter to the DAC method for multiple reasons.

First, DACs are being used more frequently in organizations (Kudisch et al., 2001). A survey by Spychalski et al. (1997) revealed that nearly 40% of the assessment centers being used in organizations serve the purpose of employee development. Povah and Ballantyne (2004) reported data from assessment centers in the UK which show that 43% of a sample of 414 organizations were using DACs (Constable, 1999). The UK Industrial Society (1996) reported results from a survey of 201 UK HR professionals showing that 68% of respondents had either run or were considering running a development center. However, some of the assessment centers from these samples are closer to what we define as a diagnostic assessment center. We believe this trend will continue and we encourage the expanded use of DACs where organizations wish to foster skill development in targeted employee groups.

Second, there is no consensus on what constitutes a DAC. Povah and Ballantyne (2004) outlined an evolution of development centers with a gradual trend toward the DAC design we describe in this chapter. We believe that researchers and practitioners need to agree on a general set of DAC characteristics so that we can be sure we are talking about the same things when surveying organizations and evaluating the validity of DACs. Indeed, in reviewing the literature in this area we see that not only are there different terms being used to refer to this process (e.g., DACs, development centers or DCs, self-insight assessment centers, learning centers, leadership training with simulations), but also the elements of these programs vary considerably. Therefore, combining all programs together to assess their general effectiveness becomes problematic. In this chapter, we present a model of DACs which has been formulated recently (Gibbons & Rupp, 2004; Rupp, Gibbons, Runnels, Anderson, & Thornton, 2003; Rupp & Thornton, 2003) and which we hope will provide a general structure for the DAC method. This model draws heavily from work in the United Kingdom (Povah & Ballantyne, 2004).

A third reason we have added this chapter is that the *Guidelines* (International Task Force, 2000) offers limited guidance on how to develop, implement, and validate DACs. This chapter provides some additional detail on the method itself as well as important factors that need to be considered when designing and carrying out DACs.

Fourth, there is a paucity of empirical research evaluating DACs. As discussed in this chapter, although there exist decades of research evaluating assessment centers for selection, promotion, and diagnosis (e.g., Gaugler et al., 1987; Howard, 1997; Spychalski et al., 1997), DACs are too different in purpose and design to generalize the research on traditional assessment centers to DACs (Rupp et al., 2003). Thus, we encourage more research into the factors that lead to effective DACs, including characteristics of the participants, features of the assessment and development process, and support in the host organization.

In the sections that follow, we provide our definition and general model of DACs, discuss the major differences between traditional assessment centers and DACs, explore the effectiveness of DACs as training interventions, and provide a set of guidelines for developing, implementing, evaluating, and validating DACs.

DEFINITION OF DEVELOPMENTAL ASSESSMENT CENTER

A developmental assessment center, or DAC, is a collection of workplace simulation exercises and other assessments that provide individuals with practice, feedback, and developmental coaching on a set of developable behavioral dimensions found to be critical for their professional success

(Thornton & Rupp, 2003). A DAC is not merely the preliminary diagnostic step at the start of an employee development program, but rather it is a training intervention and therefore an integral component of the development process (Carrick & Williams, 1999; Jones & Whitmore, 1995; Rupp & Thornton, 2003; Thornton & Rogers, 2001). To facilitate learning throughout the process, a DAC incorporates elements such as training on the dimensions, exercises designed to maximize experiential learning, self-reflection activities, as well as feedback and coaching/goal setting sessions at multiple points throughout the center.

Dimensions are made completely transparent to the participants, and great care is taken to create a nonthreatening learning environment where experimentation and exploration are encouraged. Assessors are trained not only in observing and rating behavior but also in providing feedback and coaching to participants in setting goals to improve themselves on the dimensions (Thornton & Rogers, 2001). Participants also take part in self-reflection activities before, during, and after the DAC to develop their understanding of the dimensions, to come to know their strengths and developmental needs, to set improvement goals, and to identify ways in which they can transfer the skills acquired within the DAC experience to their workplace. Finally, participants may engage in further development activities following the DAC to continue improving themselves on the dimensions, to track their progress over time, and to increase both the maintenance and generalizability of transfer of training (Baldwin & Ford, 1988; Rupp & Thornton, 2003).

A Model of the DAC Process

In chapter 2, we described a DAC used by Auto-Manufac Worldwide to develop leaders in the organization and prepare them for overseas appointments. That case followed the DAC model proposed elsewhere (Gibbons & Rupp, 2004; Rupp et al., 2003; Rupp & Thornton, 2003; Rupp et al., 2004). A generalized version of this model is provided in Fig. 4.1.

The model, which is based on the work of other assessment center scholars (Boehm, 1985; Carrick & Williams, 1999; Engelbrecht & Fischer, 1995; Goodge, 1997; Griffiths & Goodge, 1994; Jones & Whitmore, 1995; Lee, 2000, 2003; Lee & Beard, 1994; Povah, 1986), contains a variety of assessment and development activities before, during, and after the DACs. Each step of the model is illustrated by describing the Managerial Development Program at the International Laboratory for the Study of Developmental Assessment Centers (DACLab; Rupp & Thornton, 2003). We then provide an in-depth discussion of specific elements of DACs, such as the dimensions assessed, assessor training, the simulation exercises, feedback, and validation.

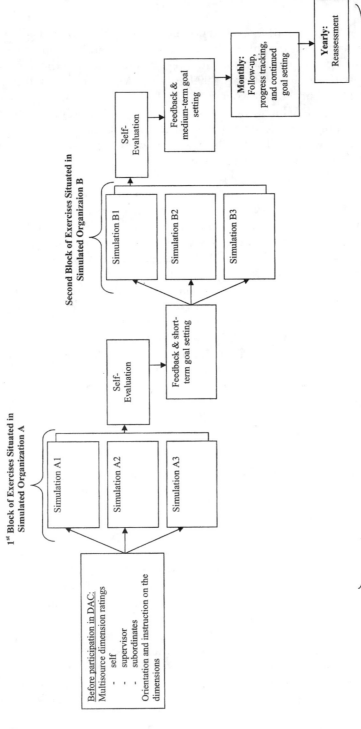

1st Block of Exercises Situated in Simulated Organization A

Before participation in DAC:
Multisource dimension ratings
- self
- supervisor
- subordinates
Orientation and instruction on the dimensions

Simulation A1

Simulation A2

Simulation A3

Self-Evaluation

Feedback & short-term goal setting

Second Block of Exercises Situated in Simulated Organizaion B

Simulation B1

Simulation B2

Simulation B3

Self-Evaluation

Feedback & medium-term goal setting

Monthly:
Follow-up, progress tracking, and continued goal setting

Yearly:
Reassessment

Trained facilitators (assessors) observe, record, evaluate and feed back to participants behaviors relevant to the behavioral dimensions assessed across exercises

FIG. 4.1. DAC process model.

60

Pre-DAC Activities

Before the DAC, information is collected about participants' proficiency on the dimensions to be assessed and developed. This is a necessary step in that it provides a baseline measure of dimension competence with which to track improvement on the dimensions over time. This information can be obtained using a variety of methods. DACLab collects multisource dimension ratings from the participants, their immediate supervisor, and their subordinates. Depending on the nature of the job, ratings might be collected from clients or customers as well, or the organization may already have data on file which assesses the participants on constructs similar to the assessment center dimensions. Two things are important with regard to preratings. First, it is essential that whichever method is used, the focus is on the dimensions that will be developed within the course of the DAC. We talk more about these dimensions later in the chapter. Second, it is critical that the same method used to collect preratings on the dimensions is also employed to collect postratings. This becomes important for program evaluation and DAC validation, which are also discussed in later sections.

Another important step of the DAC process includes orienting participants to the DAC process, the dimensions to be assessed, and background on the organization(s) to be simulated in the DAC. This might take place prior to the DAC, right at the start of the DAC, or both. For example, in the weeks prior to the DAC, DACLab participants are provided with a general summary of the DAC process, tips for getting the most out of the program, the list of dimensions with detailed definitions, and background readings on the two organizations simulated in the DAC. Then, when participants arrive for the DAC, the first hour is spent in a formal orientation which reviews these materials, the layout of the program, and the day's activities. Care is also taken to create a learning environment, where participants are encouraged to use their time in the DAC as an opportunity to try new techniques, experiment, and even make mistakes. Edison (2003) provided guidelines for conducting a "developmental planning workshop." This is a similar type of orientation where DAC participants are coached to take advantage of the experiential opportunities offered in the DAC by hearing, accepting, and acting on feedback.

Participants then spend the second hour completing a computerized assessment battery where additional information is collected with the goal of obtaining a holistic picture of the participants, which includes their interests, experiences, and personality characteristics. This information is used by assessors as a context for interpreting participants' improvement (or lack thereof) on the dimensions over time. This method follows the original method employed by AT&T in the Management Progress Study (Bray, 1964; Bray & Grant, 1966).

First Block of Exercises, Self-Reflection, and Feedback

Upon completion of the preliminary activities, participants take part in a set of simulation exercises designed to elicit behaviors relevant to the dimensions of interest. The simulations might include any of the exercises mentioned thus far. For example, DACLab uses a leaderless group discussion, a case study analysis and presentation, and a role play. All three of these simulations are based in an organization that is facing many employee relations problems. Some development programs have assessors provide participants feedback after each exercise (Goodge, 1991), but the DACLab employs a "blocked" approach, in which feedback follows the completion of multiple exercises, because this allows multiple assessors to observe participants in multiple situations prior to providing feedback. This approach is in line with the original conceptualization of the assessment center method, and should consequently provide reliable indicators of performance upon which to base feedback.

To give this initial feedback to participants, assessors (often called "development facilitators" in DACs, because they serve the role of both assessor and development coach) must conduct a quick and condensed integration session to develop the feedback report for each participant. Chapter 2 described ways in which technology can be used to facilitate this process.

While development facilitators are integrating their observations, participants take part in a self-reflection activity (Cochran, Hinckle, & Dusenberry, 1987; Griffiths & Allen, 1987) in which they contemplate their competence on the dimensions as shown across the first block of exercises. The report that they complete is then used during the feedback session as a tool for development facilitators to generate a discussion about the participant's experience in the DAC thus far. Also, because this activity requires reflection and critical analysis of one's behavior, it may lead to greater acceptance of the assessor feedback, since (if the training was successful) the two assessments should be similar (Edison, 2003).

As we discuss later in the chapter, the nature of the feedback provided is quite different than that given in assessment centers serving other purposes. That is, feedback is detailed and behavior specific (i.e., it includes specific behavioral examples of how the participant showed a strength or developmental need on each dimension). It also is forward-looking: In addition to feeding back what was observed, development facilitators also work with participants to develop goals and strategies for improving themselves on the dimensions in the second block of exercises. Notice that the focus is not yet on transferring learning back to the job, but merely improving oneself in a second round of practice.

Second Block of Exercises, Self-Reflection, and Feedback

At this point, participants might take a lunch break or go home for the day. Upon return they take part in a second block of exercises. It is essential that the same set of dimensions be assessed in both blocks. The second block allows participants further practice in improving on these dimensions and achieving the goals set in the first feedback session. The same "types" of exercises are used in the two blocks. See the notation in Fig. 4.1 showing exercises of the same type across block (e.g., A1/B1). This way, participants do not have to experience the discomfort of a whole new set of demands coming from a different exercise, and the same exercise by dimension matrix can be used for all exercise blocks.

Despite this alignment of exercise types across blocks, exercises are not the same level of difficulty across blocks. In fact, the "bar is raised" in the second block to present the participants with new challenges with which to further develop their proficiency on the dimensions. For example, the second block of exercises used by DACLab is situated in an organization which has recently experienced a merger with another organization that has a drastically different organizational culture. In each exercise, participants have to deal with complex issues of acculturation and adaptability as they work through several important issues facing the company during its transitionary period. The exercises are more difficult than those in the first block, although they require completion of the same sort of tasks (group discussion, presentation, meeting with role players) and assess the same dimensions.

After completing the second block of exercises, participants again take part in a self-reflection activity and development facilitators have a second integration session. Both of these events focus not only on the participants' performance on the dimensions in the second block of exercises, but also on improvement and attainment of goals from the first to the second block. Thus, the second feedback session is comprised of 6 major components:

- dimension performance on the second block of exercises;
- improvement on dimension performance from the first to the second block of exercises;
- review of whether or not goals set in the first feedback session were met;
- a final list of strengths and developmental needs relevant to the dimensions;

- a discussion of how the learning obtained over the course of the DAC can be transferred to the participant's specific job;
- agreement on a set of preliminary goals for further development on the dimensions; these goals will be reviewed with the participant's supervisor in a development meeting in the weeks following the DAC participation.

The DAC then concludes with a group wrap-up session, conducted by the DAC administrator, where any remaining questions are answered, the steps following the DAC are reviewed, and a program evaluation is completed by participants.

Follow-Up Activities

Although a critical assumption of DACs is that development takes place over the course of the DAC itself, the developmental power of the DAC program will be strengthened by the extent to which it is integrated into a larger training and development program. Thus, regular follow-up meetings are held with participants to track goal attainment, set new goals, and monitor career progress. Regularly scheduled meetings between the participant and a development facilitator provide an opportunity for a variety of follow-up activities.

For example, participants meet quarterly. In the first meeting we finalize the development plan, which has been approved by the participant's supervisor. To further enhance training transfer, participants generate examples of situations they have encountered since participating in the DAC, which required one or more of the dimensions, and where they attempted to use the skills and strategies learned in the DAC program. In the second follow-up meeting, in addition to further follow-up on learning and progress toward goals, participants are provided materials specifically geared toward the dimensions they are seeking to improve. These include books, online references and tutorials, and training modules being offered by their organization or the local community. The third follow-up meeting is a multisource feedback meeting in which multisource ratings received over the course of the year are reviewed. The meeting covers:

- overall ratings of the participant's proficiency on each dimension (across raters and time);
- differences in ratings across sources (assessors, self, subordinates, supervisor);
- change/improvement of dimension ratings over time;

- how the participant has come to a deeper understanding of the dimensions as a result of the DAC experience and the multisource feedback.

The final follow-up meeting is forward-looking in that it immediately precedes the participants' returning to the DAC for reassessment. Participants are prepared for the second DAC experience, conduct self-assessments, and set DAC performance goals.

Reassessment and Continued Development

After 9 months to a year, participants go through the DAC a second time. This reassessment, which follows the original AT&T longitudinal research model (Bray, 1964; Bray & Grant, 1966), allows for both a detailed assessment of each participant's development on each dimension, and also serves as an intensive follow-up training intervention. Whereas the AT&T managers repeatedly went through the same assessment process, the DACLab has participants go through a *parallel* version of the DAC. Such a DAC consists of the same dimensions and exercise types, and each block is matched for difficulty across forms. Whereas the deep structure remains the same across the two DACs, elements of the surface structure are varied (Clause, Mullins, Nee, Pulakos, & Schmitt, 1998). Therefore, the organizations simulated, the characters depicted, and particular details of the situation are varied. Creating parallel simulation exercises is no easy task (see Brummel & Rupp, 2004), but if developed correctly, they provide a "cleaner" measure of dimension improvement, free of the confounds common to test-retest situations.

MAJOR DIFFERENCES BETWEEN TRADITIONAL ASSESSMENT CENTERS AND DACS

DACs are similar to traditional assessment centers in some ways and quite different in other ways (see Table 4.1). The following sections describe some of the differences.

Dimensions

Dimensions in a DAC should be *developable*. Developable means that the dimension should be a knowledge, skill, ability, or other characteristic that can be developed either in the DAC or in a reasonable amount of time with a reasonable amount of effort following the DAC. In contrast to the general consensus about the set of dimensions needed for management success (see Borman & Brush, 1993; Tett & Guterman, 2000), and the dimensions

TABLE 4.1
Comparing DACs to Traditional Assessment Centers

	ACs	DACs
Purpose	• assessment • HR decision making	• assessment & development • transfer of training
Experience	• diagnostic	• experiential learning, self-reflection, performance improvement
Assessee's role	• assessee	• active learner
Focus	• overall performance	• dimension performance • improvement
Dimensions	• not always transparent • stable abilities	• extremely transparent • developable knowledge & skills
Feedback	• pass/fail, given upon completion	• extensive, given at multiple time points; detailed, behavior-based, high-quality action plans
Predictive Validity Evidence	• overall rating or dimension rating predict future success on the job	• dimension proficiency increases over time as a result of the DAC and subsequent developmental activities

Note. Table modified from Rupp and Thornton (2003).

commonly used in traditional assessment centers (Arthur, Day, McNelly, & Edens, 2003), there is less guidance on which dimensions are appropriate for DACs. What has not been systematically explored is (a) which dimensions are *developable*, and (b) if they are developable, whether DACs are effective interventions for developing these dimensions (Jones & Whitmore, 1995; Thornton & Rogers, 2001). Furthermore, since the majority of AC research has focused on selection or promotion centers, the emphasis has been on more stable characteristics (Howard & Bray, 1988). DACs, however, incorporate dimensions on which performance can reasonably be expected to change with reasonable time and effort (Thornton & Rogers, 2001). Therefore, DAC architects must think critically about the developability of the dimensions.

Rupp et al. (2003) were the first to systematically analyze what dimensions might best serve as the basis for managerial DACs. This research involved a comprehensive review of academic and practitioner articles, presentations, and reports in the areas of management, performance, assessment centers, training, and development. A database of dimensions was formed and reduced using both quantitative methods and subject matter expert ratings. A content validation survey was developed and distributed to a sample of U.S. and Korean managers. The combined results gave evidence for a model of 20 behavioral dimensions that are suitable for inclu-

TABLE 4.2
Dimensions Rated by Managers and Subject Matter Experts
as Amenable to Development in DACs

Leadership	Fairness
Conscientiousness	Persuasiveness
Problem Solving	Listening
Teamwork	Creativity
Relationship/Interpersonal Skills	General Adaptability
Planning & Organizing	Oral Communication
Motivation	Emotion Management
Readiness to Develop	Stress Management
Conflict Management/Resolution	Written Communication
Information Seeking	Cultural Adaptability

Source. Rupp et al. (2003).

sion in DACs. These dimensions are listed in Table 4.2. Now that DAC dimensions have been proposed, future research is needed to (a) test whether these dimensions can be developed over the course of a DAC program or with reasonable effort after the DAC, and (b) if development on these dimensions leads to career advancement among participants. Additional discussion of the validity of dimensions used in developmental assessment centers is presented in chapter 10.

Assessor Roles and Training

In a DAC, assessors are more appropriately termed development facilitators. Development facilitators have a far larger responsibility than observing, recording, classifying, reporting, and evaluating behaviors (Atchley, Smith, & Hoffman, 2003; Poteet & Kudisch, 2003). That is, development facilitators provide feedback to participants about strengths and developmental needs on each dimension, and engage in coaching, action planning, and goal setting.

This brings up a very complex issue with regard to who might be best suited to carry out these duties. Indeed, to be a competent assessor requires skills in observation, analysis, and evaluation. On the other hand, to be a competent development facilitator, one must have additional skills in communication, have a charismatic personality, and have the ability to motivate participants to strive to reach their goals. Table 4.3 lists assessor/development facilitator characteristics shown by Edison (2003) to predict participants' acceptance of feedback. Researchers have discussed whether or not the same group of people should carry out these two very distinct sets of duties (i.e., assessment vs. development; Atchley et al., 2003; Rupp & Thornton, 2003). Whether it is the same or different individuals providing feed-

TABLE 4.3
Feedback Giver Characteristics That Predict
Participant Feedback Acceptance

Experience giving feedback
Shows skill in reducing anxiety
Checks to ensure understanding
Demonstrates trustworthiness
Has good understanding of target job
Conveys warmth through nonverbals
Shows politeness/pleasantness

Source. Edison (2003).

back and follow-up coaching, it is essential to impart them with quality training to carry out these roles.

Simulation Exercises

The DAC exercises, which simulate realistic workplace challenges, are one of the features that make DACs effective training tools. Not only do the exercises elicit dimension-relevant behaviors that can be observed, evaluated, and fed back to the participants, but the exercises themselves also provide opportunities for experiential learning, practice, self-reflection, and performance improvement (Goodge, 1991). Participants are afforded opportunities to try out and practice new behaviors in a "safe" environment designed to be very similar to their actual job environment (Thornton & Cleveland, 1990). The requirement of active participation inherent to all DACs, an element shown to be crucial for adult learning (Mehta, 1978), also helps make the benefits of the DAC process apparent to the participants.

Furthermore, transfer of training is maximized when the exercises are designed to present challenges and situations similar to those participants face in their everyday jobs. The use of realistic exercises affords more confidence that the strengths and developmental needs uncovered over the course of the DAC will be an accurate representation of the participants' *actual* strengths and developmental needs on the dimensions.

In addition, lifelike simulation exercises have the potential to increase the extent to which dimensions are internalized and skills acquired. This was shown empirically by Schmitt, Ford, and Stults (1986), who found that participants perceived significant improvement on the dimensions following participation in realistic simulation exercises, even in conditions where no feedback was provided. Lastly, in group exercises, such as leaderless group discussions, participants might learn and develop via behavioral modeling (Bandura, 1986; Smith-Jentsch, Salas, & Baker, 1996). That is, they observe the effective behavior of other participants and imitate them.

Feedback

The feedback provided to DAC participants is very different from the feedback provided to participants in selection, promotion, or, in some cases, diagnostic centers (Griffiths & Allen, 1987). In traditional assessment centers, the term *feedback* often means simply indicating to participants the outcome of their performance in the center. This could take the form of a pass–fail judgment, a numerical score, or an organization-specific rating system (e.g., "top box," "bottom box"). In a diagnostic assessment center, feedback may include dimension-level judgments, but it only includes descriptions of past behavior. Diagnostic feedback typically does not provide guidance on how participants might actually modify their behavior to improve the dimensions of interest, both over the course of the DAC, and in the time following it (Arnold, 1987).

The purpose of feedback in DACs is to catalyze development (Joiner, 2002). Therefore, the feedback sessions are often longer and more detailed than sessions in traditional assessment centers. Developmental feedback provides rich, detailed, behavior-based, and forward-looking information as opposed to simply a global evaluation (Tillema, 1998). At multiple times during and following the DAC, participants are told in great detail about the behaviors elicited relevant to the dimensions across exercises that illustrate highly proficient, proficient, and/or nonproficient performance on every dimension assessed.

In addition, developmental feedback is much more conversational than feedback in other types of centers. Participants are encouraged to be active in the session, such that the participant and the development facilitator jointly generate a set of strategies and goals for the participant to improve on each of the dimensions. Depending on when the feedback is given (e.g., midway through or at the end of the DAC), these goals and strategies might focus either on subsequent simulation exercises or on the participant's actual work environment (Cochran et al., 1987; Griffiths & Allen, 1987). Whenever feedback occurs, it is essential that it is detailed, behaviorally specific, high quality, and that it provides the participant with knowledge of how his or her efforts will lead to enhanced proficiency on the dimensions. This type of feedback ensures that developmental learning is maximized (Boehm, 1985; Francis-Smythe & Smith, 1997; Kluger & DeNisi, 1996).

TABLE 4.4
Assessor/Development Facilitator Strategies for Increasing Feedback
Acceptance and Use

Foster open discussion and shared dialogue
Provide practical help, teaching, and follow-up support
Establish trust and identity needs and interests
Give recipient ownership and accountability for change
Demonstrate concern, interest, and empathy
Link feedback and coaching to outcomes
Provide specific, behavioral feedback
Establish credibility
Discuss themes
Create realistic, actionable development plans
Avoid being judgmental, inattentive, over-convincing,
    confrontational, and overly prescriptive

Source. Poteet and Kudisch (2003).

Poteet and Kudisch (2003) suggested many techniques for assessors/development facilitators to use when giving feedback. These strategies, which are summarized in Table 4.4, are designed to maximize participants' acceptance of feedback.

The Development Plan

Another important component of the DAC feedback process is the establishment of a development plan. This plan, which is based on quantitative (dimension ratings) and qualitative data (assessor comments and feedback), lays out specific opportunities that the participant can pursue following the DAC for further development in areas of weakness. The plan also includes sections that assist participants in transferring the knowledge and skills learned in the DAC to their everyday work life (Engelbrecht & Fischer, 1995). As a result, assessment and development are closely linked. DACs measure proficiency on the dimensions, provide a training opportunity for improvement on the dimensions, and initiate a long-term development plan with which participants' continued progress on the dimensions can be measured, tracked, and maximized. The development plan might also include a formal agreement between the participant, the development facilitator, and the participant's supervisor, in which the participant commits to making an effort to improve themselves in their areas of weakness, the supervisor pledges continued support of the employee's development, and deadlines are set for the attainment of goals (Thornton & Cleveland, 1990). Goodge (1991) suggested that all development plans include future learning objectives, methods for implementing these objectives, and a timetable.

Summary

DACs are different from traditional assessment centers in a number of ways: They are a training intervention in and of themselves; they provide experiential and participative learning environments; they incorporate realistic and relevant simulation exercises; the staff execute roles of both assessors and development facilitators; and they incorporate in-depth feedback, coaching, and development planning. These features differentiate DACs from selection, promotion, and diagnostic centers. Although DACs may be used in different ways depending on the purpose behind the program (e.g., for general training and development, Engelbrecht & Fischer, 1995, Griffiths & Allen, 1987; or as part of a succession planning program, Cochran et al., 1987), their developmental nature makes them unique and complex.

Although DACs are certainly a special application of the assessment center method, it is important to note that despite these differences, DACs are still true assessment centers in that they conform to the requirements laid out by the *Guidelines*. That is, they measure behavioral dimensions, require participation in multiple simulations, employ multiple trained assessors, and the results (i.e., feedback and development plans) are based on information that is integrated across exercises and assessors.

EVALUATING DACS AS TRAINING INTERVENTIONS

It has been suggested that it is the intervention quality of DACs that has led to their popularity in organizations (Hollenbeck, 1990). Because a major goal of DACs is to train participants in becoming more effective on the dimensions of interest, it is necessary to look to the broader training literature to ensure that the DAC contains elements shown to be effective for fostering adult learning. There are several models that can inform this exploration. For example, Hezlett, Ones, and Kuncel (2000) identified 5 components that are crucial to any development program:

1. the assessment or diagnosis of development needs;
2. development planning and the setting of learning objectives;
3. the opportunity to participate in development activities;
4. a mechanism for transferring learning to new situations;

5. the availability of outcome or rewards stemming from performance improvement following training.

Furthermore, McCauley and Hezlett (2001) proposed 5 elements that should be in place to maximize individual development:

1. awareness of developmental needs;
2. self-efficacy for learning;
3. new experiences;
4. self-reflection;
5. support from others.

Other training research has identified several characteristics that all training programs should possess (Salas & Cannon-Bowers, 2001). These include:

1. a presentation of the information or concepts to be learned;
2. a demonstration of the skills or dimensions to be learned;
3. the opportunity to practice what has been learned;
4. the provision of feedback during and after practice.

The DAC model proposed in Fig. 4.1, and the program implemented in the Illinois DACLab, incorporates all of these elements. The assessment and feedback aspects of the DAC give participants an indication of their developmental needs and allow for the setting of performance goals. The exercise blocks provide participants with new experiences within which to practice honing and developing their skills. The self-reflection activities allow participants to internalize the dimensions and really come to understand their own strengths and developmental needs. The establishment of a development plan and continued follow-up meetings maximize transfer of training.

In addition to these elements, these training and development models suggest that care should be taken to ensure that participants' supervisors and employing organization provide support for the learning experience and continuing process, and that the participants feel supported by various parties (which might also include HR, peers, and subordinates). Moreover, participants should also be reminded that the dimensions assessed and developed in the DAC program are indeed amenable to development and that it is in their reach to improve on them. This information could easily be provided to participants in the orientation packet given to them ahead of time, or in the orientation session at the start of the DAC.

The training literature offers some further suggestions that DAC architects and administrators may want to bear in mind. For example, research shows that using simulations for training purposes is more effective when combined with other training methods, such as lectures, demonstrations, and readings (Manz & Sims, 1981; Pinolli & Anderson, 1985). Thus DACs may benefit from including other components in addition to blocks of simulation exercises. The prework, participant orientation, and multisource feedback components utilize such alternative training methods. However, research may want to consider if additional components using training techniques other than simulations might lead to increased improvement on the dimensions. Griffiths and Allen (1987) provide evidence that combining lecture and discussion has proven effective in developmental assessment center programs.

Are DACs Valid Training Interventions?

It is necessary to mention another issue relevant to establishing DACs as effective training interventions, which is discussed in greater depth in chapter 10 where evidence supporting the validity of the DAC method is presented. In selection and promotion centers, criterion-related validity evidence is established by showing a relationship between performance in the AC and future success on the job (Nunnally & Bernstein, 1994). The focus in that application case is *prediction*. Conversely, in the case of DACs, the focus is on *change* (Carrick & Williams, 1999; Jones & Whitmore, 1995). An effective DAC is not one that predicts future performance, but rather a method that leads to *improvement* on the dimensions of interest. Therefore, effectiveness is established longitudinally, by comparing dimension proficiency before, during, and following DAC participation. Said differently, whereas traditional assessment centers are validated as assessment tools, DACs are validated as training interventions. Such validation evidence may be marshaled in a number of ways, such as:

- tracking multisource dimension ratings over time;
- comparing assessor ratings of dimensions taken at various points within the DAC;
- reassessing participants over time and tracking development;
- comparing the development of participants over time to those of a control group not having participated in the DAC.

In addition to focusing on individuals' development on the dimensions over time, validity evidence is also provided by considering the impact of the DAC experience on participants' well-being, self-esteem, growth, and learning. This is discussed in more detail in chapter 10.

A paucity of research exists which provides empirical evidence supporting the validity of the DAC method but this chapter provides researchers and practitioners alike a basis upon which to conduct research and publish their DAC data. We will return to this issue in chapter 10, where the research to date is reviewed.

SPECIAL CONSIDERATIONS WHEN USING/STUDYING DACS

This chapter has outlined the complexity of the DAC method, provided a general DAC model that might inform future work in this area, and shown the fundamental difference between traditional ACs and DACs. We conclude this chapter with some general guidelines for researchers and practitioners conducting work in this area (see Table 4.5).

TABLE 4.5
DAC Guidelines

- Dimensions should be both relevant for career success and amenable to development over the course of the DAC and in the period following participation.
- Dimensions should be completely transparent.
- Participants should be thoroughly oriented in the dimensions, made to understand their meaning, and instructed on how they are manifested behaviorally at varying levels of proficiency.
- The DAC administrator should instill self-efficacy for learning in participants. This can be done by stressing the developability of the dimensions in the prework and participant orientation.
- The DAC should employ multiple blocks of simulation exercises, with feedback in-between in order to provide multiple opportunities for practice and improvement.
- Exercises should be built to maximize experiential learning.
- The same types of exercises should be used and the same dimensions assessed in each exercise block.
- The DAC should culminate in a development plan that the participant uses to maximize continued development and transfer of training following the DAC.
- Dimension-related performance measures should be taken at multiple times during the development period. This includes prior to participating in the DAC, at multiple times during the DAC, and periodically following the DAC. This could take the form of multi-source dimension ratings, or reassessment using a parallel DAC some time later. A control group should be used when possible.
- When collecting validation evidence, remember that the purpose of the DAC is to foster change (as opposed to predict success), and validation strategies should therefore match this purpose.
- The DAC program should ensure buy-in from the organization and participants should be made aware that they are supported by their colleagues, supervisors, and the organization.
- The DAC program should be integrated with the broader training and development program, as well as other HR functions and organizational strategies.
- DACs require a long-term commitment and are costly undertakings. Hence, all practical considerations should be made prior to moving forward with a DAC.

These guidelines include the use of developable dimensions, training participants on the dimensions, providing participants multiple opportunities to practice new behaviors via blocks of simulation exercises, multiple feedback sessions during and following the DAC, intensive follow-up, development tracking and coaching, and the use of formal development plans.

In addition, it is important to remain cognizant of the assumption about experiential learning inherent to DACs. Because DAC activities are meant to offer participants opportunities to learn, explore, and experiment, exercises must be designed to provide as much practice trying out new behaviors as possible. Also, the effectiveness of DACs as a training intervention will be maximized to the extent to which the DAC program is integrated in the larger training and development function (as well as other HR functions within the organization; Wilkinson & Byham, T., 2003). This is discussed in more detail in chapter 11.

Related to this, the purpose of the DAC is not to predict success, but to make success a reality. That is, the main goal of DAC programs is development, so the focus is on change, development, learning, and improvement. This is one of the reasons we advise against the use of "hybrid centers," where the organization simultaneously attempts to use an assessment center to develop employees and make personnel decisions. The focus on development has implications for the design of the DAC program, the dimensions assessed, the validation evidence collected, the feedback provided, the assessors employed, as well as how assessors are trained.

Lastly, DACs are very expensive to develop and maintain and require a long-term commitment on the part of the organization, the participants, and those that manage them. The DAC model proposed in Fig. 4.1 could certainly be simplified, for example, by using only one block of simulation exercises. Whatever steps are taken, it is important to evaluate the DAC to ensure its effectiveness (International Task Force, 2000). Chapter 10 provides additional information about how an organization might assess the utility (the benefit compared to the cost) of an assessment center program. In some organizational contexts, such as environments where turnover is high and employee loyalty is low, an organization may find itself helping its competition by developing employees who are not likely to stay. On the other hand, having a DAC and a rich training and development department may be a recruiting and retention tool for an organization, may lead to development of women and minorities who may be overlooked in the normal development activities of organization life, may allow management to show its commitment to its employees, and consequently may increase company loyalty, teamwork, and employee citizenship. All of these things should be carefully considered when deciding whether or not to implement a DAC.

CONCLUSION

Having dedicated the first four chapters to defining assessment centers, discussing their different purposes, providing illustrative case studies, and outlining the basic requirements inherent in all assessment centers, we now take an in-depth look at the dimensions assessed, the exercises typically used to assess them, and the psychological processes underlying assessment and feedback.

Chapter 5

Behavioral Dimensions:
The Building Blocks
of Assessment Centers

This chapter analyzes the various behavioral dimensions that can be evaluated in assessment centers designed for different purposes. The chapter defines terms, clarifies the importance of thorough job analysis, describes the basic elements of traditional and nontraditional job analysis techniques, and then discusses the nature of dimensions to be assessed in selection/promotion, diagnostic, and development programs. Finally, some alternatives to behavioral dimensions as the focal constructs measured in assessment centers are discussed.

BEHAVIORAL DIMENSIONS DEFINED

In the last four chapters, we have made many references to the behavioral dimensions assessed in an assessment center. We have mentioned that a job analysis must be conducted to determine the dimensions, assessors must be trained in the meaning and scoring of the dimensions, and the dimensions will differ depending on the purpose of the assessment center. We also provided some examples of dimensions assessed in assessment centers in the case studies. In this chapter, we focus more directly on what exactly dimensions are and how they are selected and defined.

In short, behavioral dimensions are the units of analysis within an assessment center. Whereas the simulation exercises are the tools of measurement, the dimensions are what are actually measured. Thornton and Byham (1982) defined a behavioral dimension as a logically homogeneous cluster of observable behaviors. Dimensions are also referred to as proficiencies, competencies, and KSAOs (knowledge, skills, abilities, and other characteristics). However, the term *dimension* is the traditional term used by assessment center researchers and practitioners. The key to an assessment center dimension is that it is defined behaviorally, since it is actual behavior that can be observed to make judgments of levels of proficiency on the dimensions.

Later in this chapter, we discuss some alternatives to using dimensions as the focal constructs within assessment centers. However, because the practice of measuring dimensions is historically a defining element of any assessment center program, and because most assessment centers are organized around dimensions, we continue to take a dimensions perspective throughout the book.

Examples of Common Dimensions

The dimensions assessed in any assessment center should be based on a thorough job analysis, and different assessment centers will logically assess different dimensions depending on the organization, the particular job or position for which the assessment center is being designed, and, of course, the purpose of the assessment center. Despite this variety, there are common dimensions that are used across many assessment centers, especially at the managerial level where a more consistent set of attributes is required across jobs and organizations. For example, Arthur, Day et al. (2003), for the purpose of conducting a meta-analysis, identified a set of 168 dimensions from 34 empirical assessment center research studies. These dimensions were systematically collapsed into seven dimensions, which are listed in Table 5.1.

Similarly, in a study which sought to identify dimensions for developmental assessment centers, Rupp et al. (2003) assembled a list of dimensions used in assessment centers reported in published research, conference papers, unpublished manuscripts, assessment center tech reports, O*NET, and performance models used by major human resource management consulting firms. In all, 1,095 dimensions were identified from 65 sources. These authors used both an automated data reduction technique and subject matter expert ratings to reduce their list to 16 behavioral dimensions that were grouped into four clusters. These dimensions are listed in Table 5.2. There is much overlap in the Arthur et al. and Rupp et al. lists. The commonalities reflect the fact that many dimensions come up repeatedly when conducting managerial job analyses. Additional discussion of the validity of developable dimensions is included in chapter 10.

TABLE 5.1
Common Assessment Center Dimensions
Identified by Arthur, Day et al. (2003)

Communication: The extent to which an individual conveys oral and written information and responds to questions and challenges

Consideration/Awareness: The extent to which an individual's actions reflect a consideration for the dealings and needs of others as well as an awareness of the impact and implications of decisions relevant to other components both inside and outside the organization

Drive: The extent to which an individual originates and maintains a high activity level, sets high performance standards, and persists in their achievement, and expresses the desire to advance to higher job levels

Influencing others: The extent to which an individual persuades others to do something or adopt a point of view in order to produce desired results and takes action in which the dominant influence is one's own convictions rather than the influence of others' opinions

Organizing and planning: The extent to which an individual systematically arranges his/her own work and resources as well as that of others for efficient task accomplishment; and the extent to which an individual anticipates and prepares for the future

Problem solving: The extent to which an individual gathers information; understands relevant technical/professional information; effectively analyzes data and information; generates viable options/ideas/solutions; selects supportable courses of action; uses resources in new ways; generates and recognizes imaginative solutions

Tolerance for stress/uncertainty: The extent to which an individual maintains effectiveness in diverse situations under varying degrees of pressure, opposition, and disappointment

TABLE 5.2
Common Assessment Center Dimensions
Identified by Rupp et al. (2003)

Cluster	Definition
Problem Solving	
Problem Solving	After gathering all pertinent information, identifies problems and uses analysis to perceive logical relationships among problems or issues; Develops courses of action; Makes timely and logical decisions; Evaluates the outcomes of a problem solution.
Information Seeking	Gathers data; Identifies and finds relevant and essential information needed to solve a problem; Effectively analyzes and uses data and information.
Creativity	Generates and recognizes imaginative solutions and innovations in work-related situations; Questions traditional assumptions and goes beyond the status quo.
Approach to Work	
Planning & Organizing	Establishes procedures to monitor tasks, activities, or responsibilities of self and subordinates to assure accomplishment of specific objectives; Determines priorities and allocates time and resources effectively; Makes effective short- and long-term plans; Sets and uses appropriate priorities; Handles administrative detail.
Adaptability	Remains effective by modifying behavioral style to adjust to new tasks, responsibilities, values, attitudes, or people; Shows resilience in the face of constraints, frustrations, or adversity.

(Continued)

TABLE 5.2
(Continued)

Cluster	Definition
Stress Tolerance	Maintains composure and performance under pressure, opposition, tight time-frames, and/or uncertainty; Directs effort to constructive solutions while demonstrating resilience and the highest levels of professionalism.
Conscientious-ness	Works efficiently and consistently toward goals with concern for thorough-ness; Consistently meets deadlines and expectations; Displays concentra-tion, organization, and attention to detail; Thinks carefully before acting.
Motivation	Originates action rather than passively accepting or responding to events; Demonstrates capacity for sustained effort over long time periods until the desired objective is achieved or is no longer reasonably attainable; Ex-presses a desire for advancement through self-development efforts.

	Communication
Oral Communi-cation	Expresses thoughts verbally and nonverbally in a clear, concise, and straight-forward manner that is appropriate for the target audience whether in a group or individual situation.
Written Commu-nication	Expresses ideas clearly and succinctly in writing, using appropriate grammati-cal form for both formal and informal documents; Adjusts writing style, tone, and language as indicated by the needs of the audience.
Listening	Actively attends to and conveys understanding of the comments and ques-tions of others in both group and individual situations; Hears, pays atten-tion to, and determines important information and ideas presented through spoken words and sentences; Performs active listening by asking questions when appropriate.
Persuasiveness	Uses written or oral communication to obtain agreement or acceptance of an idea, plan, activity or product; Demonstrates keen insight of others' be-havior and tailors own behavior to persuade or influence them; Gains sup-port and commitment from others.

	Relational
Relationship/ Interpersonal Skills	Initiates and maintains effective relationships by presenting oneself to others in a positive manner, even in the face of conflict; Responds to the needs, feelings, and opinions of others; uses relationships appropriately to accom-plish personal or organizational goals.
Leadership	Guides, directs, and motivates subordinates toward important and challeng-ing work in line with their interests and abilities as well as the needs of the organization; Gives regular, specific, and constructive feedback to sub-ordinates in relation to their personal goals; Commands attention and re-spect; Promotes positive change by setting goals and priorities that are in line with the common vision of the organization.
Teamwork	Works effectively with others by cooperating and contributing to the pursuit of team goals; Communicates decisions, changes, and other relevant infor-mation to the team in a timely manner; Develops supportive relationships with colleagues and creates a sense of team spirit.
Conflict Man-agement/ Resolution	Recognizes and openly addresses conflict appropriately; Arrives at construc-tive solutions while maintaining positive working relationships.

THE IMPORTANCE OF JOB ANALYSIS

The first step in designing any assessment center program is determining the dimensions to be assessed and/or developed. This step is typically done by conducting some sort of job analysis. Job analysis for assessment center development is somewhat broader than traditional job analysis methods, which simply seek to determine job tasks and KSAOs. Thornton and Mueller-Hanson (2004) referred to this broader process as situational analysis, because it involves analyzing several components of the job situation, such as the dimensions required, the relative competency required for each dimension, the job tasks, and organizational environment. We advocate this broader analysis at the beginning of the development of an assessment center because it provides such a rich variety of information for many aspects of the development, implementation, validation, and defensibility of an assessment program.

There are five major reasons job or situational analysis is a crucial first step in developing assessment centers. First, the results of the job analysis produce information that is useful for many aspects of building assessment centers. Analyzing the job situation allows us to determine the dimensions to be assessed. Identifying the relative proficiency level expected in the organization gives us an indication of the difficulty level to build into the simulation exercises. Knowing the job tasks gives us information about the content and types of the simulation exercises to be used. Finally, a thorough understanding of the organizational environment allows us to determine the setting of the assessment center and the general orientation of the exercises.

A second reason for conducting a job analysis is to ensure good measurement, that is, to achieve accurate personnel decisions. In order to hire, promote, and train the best people for a job, an organization has to know what a job entails. Through job analysis, job-relevant dimensions can be selected and used to identify the employees with the highest potential.

Third, job analysis provides us with crucial information used to train assessors. That is, job analysis provides detailed information about the nature of the dimensions, the necessary level of proficiency on each dimension, and the behaviors that are commonly displayed relevant to each dimension. In assessor training, assessors must come to a common understanding of the meaning of the dimensions. In order to accurately rate the performance of participants, the assessor team must develop a common frame of reference. We talk more specifically about frame of reference training in chapter 7.

A fourth reason for conducting a sound job analysis is legal defensibility. That is, any legal challenge to the use of an assessment center for selection or promotion must be answered with evidence of thorough job analysis (Thompson & Thompson, 1982). There are laws in many countries that prohibit personnel decisions based on race, color, sex, religion, national origin, age, or disability, unless the characteristic has been explicitly shown to be required for the job. In the United States, these laws include Title VII of the Civil Rights Act of 1964, the Civil Rights Act of 1991, the Americans with Disabilities Act of 1990, and the Age Discrimination in Employment Act of 1967 (Landy, 2005). Much of what is done in human resource management involves a set of inferences. Assessment center developers infer the behavioral dimensions from current job information or organizational objectives; they infer what simulation exercises will elicit behavior-relevant behaviors; they train assessors to infer performance effectiveness based on observed behavior. Each one of these inferences can be challenged legally, and the role of job analysis is to provide an organization with enough evidence to be confident about the inferences themselves as well as the legal appropriateness of the entire human resource process (Gatewood & Feild, 2001).

A final reason for conducting a job analysis is to develop exercises that are face valid in the eye of the users and participants. For obvious psychometric and legal reasons the exercises should, in fact, simulate relevant work contexts. In addition, the exercises should have perceived relevance because the content of an assessment center can impact applicants' attraction to the organization, employees' perceptions of fairness, and trainees' motivation to learn, develop, and pursue follow-up training. Assessment center participants expect organizations to evaluate them based on their job-relevant skills and experiences, rather than other characteristics, such as popularity or demographic characteristics. Perceived relevance of the assessment or development program begins with complete and accurate information about job and organizational requirements derived from job analysis.

All of these reasons take on heightened importance in light of the increasing diversity of the workforce. Thorough job analysis, competency modeling, and situational analysis ensure that the selection and developmental interventions such as assessment centers are based on actual job requirements and not stereotypical assumptions. Thus, these preliminary analyses help organizations develop practices that are both *in fact* fair and *perceived to be fair* by diverse individuals and groups.

BASIC ELEMENTS OF A JOB ANALYSIS

A wide variety of different techniques are available for conducting a job analysis (see Brannick & Levine, 2002; Chen, Carsten, & Krauss, 2003; Sanchez & Levine, 2001). Some methods focus on the job activities themselves, whereas others focus more on the characteristics of the people who

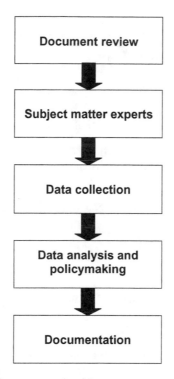

FIG. 5.1.   The building blocks of job analysis.

carry out job activities. Some methods start at a very basic level of task information and move up to organizational effectiveness; others start with very broad organizational values and work downward to expected employee behaviors. Despite the variety of job analysis methods available to assessment center developers, there are some basic elements common to many methods. These elements are illustrated in Fig. 5.1.

Document Review

During the document review stage, the assessment center developer gathers information about the job being analyzed to develop a preliminary list of the tasks and KSAOs required for the job. Table 5.3 lists many sources of job information. One source is written material about the job and industry. This material could come in the form of organizational charts, existing job descriptions, policy/procedure manuals, training manuals, textbooks from the discipline, technical manuals, and design specifications for the equipment used on the job. Another excellent source of information about some jobs is the Occupational Information Network, or O*NET (Peterson et al.,

TABLE 5.3
Sources of Job Information

Observational Methods
  Direct observation
  Video recording
  Audio recording
  Actually do the job for a period of time
Relevant Documents—Internal to the Organization
  Job descriptions
  Organizational charts
  Policy & procedure manuals
  Training manuals
  Equipment specifications
Relevant Documents—External to the Organization
  O*NET
  Occupational Outlook Handbook
  Trade journals
  Textbooks
  Research literature
Other Activities for Obtaining Information
  Attend industry conferences or conventions
  Talk with other job analysts
  Interview SMEs
  Interview job incumbents
  Have job incumbents complete work diaries
  Interview trainers, instructors, and educators

2001). The O*NET is an online database (www.onetcenter.org) made available by the U.S. Department of Labor to provide information about industry, work, and worker characteristics of many jobs in the U.S. economy.

There are numerous ways that assessment center developers can obtain preliminary information about the job. For instance, he or she can conduct observations of people carrying out the job. This process could be in person or via an audio or video recording. In some instances, an assessment center developer might even do the job for a period of time to get a real sense of what "a day in life" is like for people in the position. If doing or observing the work is unrealistic, the assessment center developer might interview job incumbents individually or in groups. Employees can complete work diaries over a period of time. In addition, assessment center developers might attend the technical/professional conferences people in the job often attend or read the profession's trade journals. The key idea is to use a variety of sources of information about any job being studied. Each source of information may provide a different picture of the job. This does not mean that a given source is not valid; in fact, all provide accurate information from different perspectives.

Use of Subject Matter Experts

Many job analysis methods rely on subject matter experts, or SMEs. SMEs are individuals with experience or insight into the job of interest. SMEs assist the assessment center developer in understanding the tasks and KSAOs required for a particular job. SMEs can be job incumbents, supervisors, training specialists, or anyone who knows the job. The assessment center developer might hold a workshop with a diverse panel of SMEs to verify the accuracy of the initial list of tasks and expand them into more formalized task statements. The assessment center developer then works with the SMEs to determine the relative importance of the job tasks, and what specific KSAOs are required to complete each task.

Data Collection

After the job analyst has a refined set of information, data are often collected using a much larger sample of job incumbents. The most common method for collecting additional information is a survey instrument. The survey may be created using the tasks and KSAOs generated from the SME panel in the specific organization, or may be purchased "off the shelf" from a consulting firm. Regardless of the method used, it is important that certain information be obtained about the tasks, the KSAOs, and how the tasks and KSAOs are related to one another.

Although not all the job analysis methods collect all the information reviewed here, research (Goldstein, Schneider, & Zedeck, 1993), case law (see Thompson & Thompson, 1982), and the *Uniform Guidelines* (Equal Employment Opportunity Commission, Civil Rights Commission, Department of Labor, & Department of Justice, 1978) all suggest that diverse information should be obtained, because it provides the basis for developing and defending many aspects of an assessment center.

Data Analysis and Policymaking

The next step of the job analysis process involves synthesizing all of the information collected to determine (a) the dimensions to be assessed, (b) the types of exercises that will be developed to measure the dimensions, (c) the level of difficulty required and the degree of proficiency required for each dimension in each exercise, and (d) the general context or setting in which the assessment center will be set. At this point, the assessment center developer may construct a dimension by exercise matrix, which specifies which dimensions will be assessed in which exercises. This matrix may be revisited as the assessment center is developed.

Documentation and Maintenance

A final step to any job analysis is documentation. It is essential for all information obtained during all steps of the job analysis process to be well documented and carefully filed. In addition, the job analyst should document the process by which the job analysis was conducted, how the data were analyzed, and how the final dimensions and exercise content were selected. Moreover, it is important to re-evaluate the job analysis results regularly. This is especially true when the job has recently undergone a change, the job has been redesigned, the organization's mission or values have shifted, or the job's boundaries may have shifted. It may be necessary to hold additional SME panels or collect additional job incumbent data to ensure that the original tasks and KSAOs are still essential.

Summary

The foregoing procedures provide a systematic means for analyzing a job as it is currently being carried out by its incumbents. These procedures are effective in capturing existing behaviors, activities, important dimensions, and types of problems encountered. If the job remains stable, the analysis of existing behaviors may be adequate for the development assessment procedures to select and develop new employees for that job. In fact, many jobs do remain stable over a period of time, and the basic attributes required for success also remain stable in the short term.

Despite these facts, all too often the pressures to start an assessment center make it difficult to adequately carry out these basic yet necessary steps. It is important to note that job analysis provides valuable information that will be used at several stages of assessment center development: the dimensions to be assessed, examples of behaviors that clarify the dimensions, suggestions for the types of simulation exercises, suggestions for the content of problems to be put into the exercises, an indication of the level of proficiency required on the dimensions, standards for scoring assessee performance in the exercises, and documentation of job-relatedness of the assessment process. The effort required for a thorough job analysis, therefore, yields many payoffs.

SOURCES OF JOB ANALYSIS METHODS

There are more job analysis methods than we are able to cover in this chapter. These methods include the Task Analysis Inventory, the Position Analysis Questionnaire (McCormick, Jeanneret, & Mecham, 1989), the Critical Incidents Technique (Flanagan, 1954), Fleishman's Job Analysis Survey

(Fleishman & Reilly, 1992), Functional Job Analysis (Fine & Cronshaw, 1999), the Job Elements Method (Primoff, 1975), the Job Components Inventory (Banks, 1988), and Tasks and Demands Analysis (Rohmert, 1988). We refer readers to the most recent papers and texts on this topic for a complete overview (see Brannick & Levine, 2002; Chen et al., 2003; Gatewood & Feild, 2001; Sanchez & Levine, 2001). Table 5.4 compares these many methods.

Although many different job analysis methods can contribute valuable information, usually no single method will suffice. Surveys by Spychalski et al. (1997) and Krause and Gebert (2003) showed that the vast majority of assessment center developers used several job analysis techniques. Regardless of the method employed, for the purpose of developing assessment centers, special attention should be given to identifying and validating the behavioral dimensions to be assessed, defining the dimensions in behavioral terms, and collecting a large amount of rich information in order to inform the development of the simulation exercises as well as the general assessment center context.

NONTRADITIONAL METHODS OF JOB ANALYSIS

The job analysis methods just described are helpful in understanding certain aspects of work: activities currently being done in specific jobs; KSAOs that are currently important; the stable aspects of jobs that change little over time. Traditional methods reflect a bottom-up approach, in the sense that they carefully examine the specific, existing elements of work and make inductions about important dimensions of work. However, these techniques may not be completely adequate, because many jobs today are not simple and stable. Many jobs are characterized by vagueness, complexity, and change. In addition, boundaries between jobs are becoming more and more "fuzzy" as organizational structures become more team-based. Some have argued that because of this, traditional methods for conducting job analysis may not always be appropriate (Howard, 1995). In this section, we explore two nontraditional approaches to understanding work behavior: competency modeling and strategic job analysis. These techniques may be viewed as top-down approaches, because they start at the level of current and future organizational objectives.

Competency Modeling

An alternative to traditional job analysis is a top-down, deductive approach known as competency modeling (Schippmann, 1999). In this approach, rather than starting with the job as a point of analysis, the organization is

TABLE 5.4
Comparison of Job Analysis Methods

Evaluation Factor	Task Analysis	Position Analysis Questionnaire (PAQ)	Critical-Incidents Technique	Fleishman Job Analysis Technique (F-JAS)	Functional Job Analysis (FJA)	Job Element Method (JEM)	Job Component Inventory (JCI)	Task & Demands Analysis (T&DA)	Competency Modeling (CM)	Strategic Job Analysis (SJA)
Off-the-Shelf Availability?	No	Yes	No	In-Part	In-Part	In-Part	Yes	Yes	No	No
Standardization?	Yes	Yes	No	Yes	No	No	Yes	Yes	No	No
User/Respondent Availability?	Moderate/High	Low/Moderate	Moderate	Moderate/High	High	Moderate				
Required Amount of Analyst Training?	Low	Moderate	Low/Moderate	Low	High	Moderate/High				
# of People Required?	Large	Small	Small	Small/Moderate	Moderate	Small				
Cost?	Moderate/High	Low/Moderate	Moderate/High	Low/Moderate	Moderate/High	Low/Moderate	No			
Focus on Organization Goals/Mission/Values?	No	No	No	No	No	No	No	Somewhat	Yes	Yes
Considers the future of the job?	No	No	No	Nc	No	No	No	No	No	Yes

Source. Modified and expanded from Gatewood and Feild (2001).

first considered. That is, the analyst first identifies what the organization needs to be effective. Then KSAOs are identified that allow an employee to be effective in a number of jobs within the organization (Lawler, 1994). Such an approach has become popular in organizations, especially with the current trend for organizations to identify their core competencies, or the characteristics that the organization (as opposed to the employee) needs to be successful (Prahalad & Hamel, 1990).

Despite the concept's popularity in the business world, a precise method for conducting competency modeling has yet to be well defined (Schippmann et al., 2000). Table 5.5 lists some of the major differences between traditional job analysis and competency modeling. Competencies are often

TABLE 5.5
Job Analysis Versus Competency Modeling

Characteristic	Job Analysis	Competency Modeling
Purpose:	Used more as a basis for selection and performance appraisal programs	Used more as a basis for training and development programs
Focus:	Work-focused	Worker-focused
Rigor of methods & measurement:	Rigorous	Not so rigorous
Variance of source/type of information depending on purpose:	Combination of methods often used; specific combination heavily dependent on purpose of job analysis	Same method typically used regardless of purpose
Reliability of ratings and judgments evaluated:	Almost always done	Seldom done
Effort to understand the broader business context; strategy; alignment of business goals:	Seldom considered	Substantial effort taken
Level of analysis/focus:	Focus is on specific jobs and the characteristics that differentiate them from one another; focus is on differences	Focus is on individual-level competencies that cross occupational categories or jobs or the entire organization; focus is on similarities
Level of detail:	Highly detailed	More broad
Orientation toward time:	Oriented toward shorter-term job descriptions	Oriented toward long-term organizational fit
Face validity:	Little consideration given to the "flavor" of the organization	Methods produce results that capture the language and spirit of the organization
Focus on personality and values:	Not so much	Yes

Note.   Based on results presented in Schippmann et al. (2000).

nothing more than the traditional KSAOs, but sometimes competencies are much broader than KSAOs. For example, a competency may be a broad organizational objective such as "customer service." Breadth in competencies reflects fundamental differences between the two approaches: Whereas traditional job analysis seeks to identify the things that make jobs unique, competency modeling seeks to find similarities among jobs; whereas the results of traditional job analysis are often used to establish selection criteria, which are used to make distinctions among applicants, the results from competency modeling are often used to determine aspects of development programs, which encourage a set of common skills across many jobs.

Competency modeling has been criticized for not being as rigorous as traditional job analysis in terms of its methods and measurement techniques. However, competency modeling pays attention to an important element often ignored by job analysis techniques: the spirit, culture, and climate of the organization. That is, competency modeling approaches often start with the job analyst interviewing the top management team of the organization in order to understand the organization's core values, mission, goals, and strategic outlook. Only after understanding the organization's broader business context does the job analyst seek to identify individual-level competencies. At this point, the analyst works "down from the top" to validate the competencies and KSAOs in specific jobs.

Although the level of detail typically provided by a competency modeling project is far less than the level of detail generated by a more traditional job analysis approach, the results are much more future-oriented and aligned with the organization's long strategy. In addition, organizational members who participate in competency modeling projects tend to see the project as important and exciting because the methods produce results that capture the language and spirit of the organization, as well as workers' personalities and values. Traditional job analysis methods, on the other hand, have far less face validity and are often perceived as tedious to participants. Organizations should be careful when employing competency modeling approaches for identifying assessment center dimensions (especially for selection or promotion centers—where there are more legal constraints), because competencies are seldom linked to tasks. Also, applicants or employees may feel uncomfortable being evaluated based on competencies that do not seem to be linked to their jobs (Sanchez & Levine, 2001).

Strategic Job Analysis

Strategic job analysis accounts for the reality that job requirements change. Activities may be added, responsibilities may increase, new skills may become necessary, and expectations of performance may increase—all due to environmental pressures, technological innovations, organizational restructuring, or changes in management philosophy. For example, the recent emphasis on customer service as a means of increasing revenues has caused many organizations to ask employees to show more skills in such areas as listening, responding with empathy, and helping clients solve problems. A traditional job analysis that examines how current employees carry out their jobs may not capture the kinds of behaviors and dimensions that are expected in the future.

To understand future job requirements, strategic job analysis (Campion, 1994; Schneider & Konz, 1989; Taylor, 1990) may be helpful. Strategic job analysis is a process of thinking about the future goals of the organization and determining what implications these changes will have for performance on specific jobs. It is a process of looking into the future as opposed to looking into the past. It is a deductive process of inferring job requirements from organizational goals, rather than an inductive process of examining how people currently behave. For example, we might start the analysis by noting that a new organizational objective is entrepreneurship. For middle managers, this means that risk taking and innovation become relevant dimensions. These attributes might go undetected if we analyzed how managers are currently doing their jobs. Murphy and Kroeker (1988) pointed out the several advantages of taking this approach when defining the criteria and skills needed for effective performance. The approach allows us to assess the adequacy of measures of performance effectiveness, to avoid missing important determinants of performance effectiveness, and to consider a wide range of important dimensions unrestricted by how we might ultimately measure them. A deductive approach also helps to ensure that broad organizational goals are considered and that work on individual jobs is linked to these goals.

In summary, we advocate employing a combination of the methods encompassed by the processes of job analysis, competency modeling, and strategic job analysis. Each method provides valuable information in the development, implementation, validation, and defense of an assessment center.

When developing assessment centers, we have traditionally translated job-analysis information into the attributes needed for job success. Now we need to look in more depth at the various types of human attributes we can assess.

SELECTING THE APPROPRIATE DIMENSIONS

Organizations may be legally vulnerable if they do not have a clear rationale for the dimensions assessed in any human resource management procedure that affects the employment status of applicants or employees. We sometimes see mismatches between the purpose of the assessment center and the dimensions assessed. For example, some assessment centers used for selection or promotion decisions assess knowledge and skills that can be readily learned on the job. This practice is not only inefficient, but also inadvisable in light of the *Uniform Guidelines* (Equal Employment Opportunity Commission et al., 1978) that are a set of regulations that describe the way organizations should develop, evaluate, and use procedures for selecting and promoting people in organizations. The *Uniform Guidelines* have served as the basis for many court cases where unfair discrimination against minorities and women has been charged. They admonish organizations against making selection decisions based on the results of tests of characteristics that can be learned in the initial training for a job.

The purpose of the assessment center should guide the selection of the dimensions to be assessed. This basic principle seems quite logical but all too often it has not been followed in the design of assessment centers (Spychalski et al., 1997). The assessment center developer should formulate a clear statement of the purpose of the assessment center and should specify the ways in which the information will be used. Then, when analyzing the target job, the developer should select only appropriate dimensions for assessment.

Theory and research on social cognition show that the purpose of the observation process affects the way in which behavior is observed, encoded, stored in memory, and retrieved (Fiske & Taylor, 1984; Wyer & Srull, 1986). For example, if the purpose is to form a general impression of an individual, the observer will notice different behaviors and store them in memory in a different manner than if he or she is observing specific behaviors. Thus, in the assessment center context, the purpose of the program and the types of dimensions must be made compatible so that the observation and judgment tasks of the assessor are guided properly.

Selection and Promotion Centers

For selection and promotion programs, organizations are usually interested in using an assessment center to help higher level managers identify candidates who have the abilities and potential to learn and grow in a new position. Therefore, these assessment programs should assess attributes related to the person's abilities and potential to learn (e.g., basic interpersonal and problem-solving skills). Thus, the job analysis effort is designed to identify those attributes that the assessors should be focusing on in the exercises. These attributes must be clarified for all assessors so they have a common frame of reference for their observations.

In contrast to the previous situation, there are some selection programs that are designed to assess current levels of skills and competencies. For example, a government agency may want to know if an applicant has knowledge of certain rules, regulations, and procedures, or a manufacturing company may want to know if a welder has the skill to use certain equipment and materials. In such cases, actual work-sample procedures are appropriate for assessing present knowledge and skills.

Diagnostic Centers

For diagnostic programs, the goals, and thus the dimensions, are much different. Here the assessment center should measure only developable skills. A developable skill is one that can be improved in a relatively short time with a reasonable amount of effort by the individual and the organization. Thus, the organization must think carefully about what feedback it can give to the participant, what training programs are available to improve weaknesses if they are diagnosed, and what support can be given to the participant's immediate supervisor to help overcome deficiencies. If the organization is unwilling or unable to provide follow-up resources to remedy weaknesses on a given dimension, then that dimension should not be assessed in a diagnostic program.

Some assessment centers designed to diagnose training needs make assessments of characteristics that cannot be developed in any reasonable amount of time through organizational training activities. Examples of such dimensions are intelligence and deep-seated personality characteristics. Two points of view are held about the place of such stable traits in assessment centers. Our point of view is that it makes little sense to assess these characteristics and to give someone feedback about a deficiency in these areas when there is little that can be done in the short run to change it. It makes much more sense to assess and provide follow-up training for deficiencies in dimensions such as problem analysis and decision analysis, because these dimensions are more conducive to change. Another point of view is that assessment of stable traits provides meaningful information about the whole individual, including strengths and weaknesses that bolster or hinder development in the future. Assessing stable traits in a diagnostic center may be beneficial if everyone understands that follow-up development in these areas is not expected.

Developmental Centers

Developmental assessment centers should be built around a somewhat different set of dimensions. Like the dimensions in a diagnostic assessment center, the dimensions here should be developable, but more specifically, they should be trainable in the context of the current assessment center or with reasonable follow-up efforts. In this type of center, the dimensions must be readily observable. It would make no sense to ask facilitators to try to observe and give feedback on "customer service orientation" if the exercises had no content that provided opportunity for behaviors in that dimension. It is also helpful if the dimensions are qualities that can be observed by the participant's supervisor, coworkers, and subordinates, as it is a common practice to ask these people to provide descriptions of on-the-job behavior prior to the participant's attendance at the assessment center. Feedback from these other sources can then be combined with feedback from the assessment exercises. If the purpose of the developmental assessment center is also to facilitate organizational development, the dimensions should be clearly related to the functioning of a group or the organization as a whole. For example, in the context of most team-building programs, it would serve little purpose to assess and give feedback on the individual's written communication skills, unless these skills were central to the team's functioning.

Broad Versus Narrow Dimensions

Byham (1990) offered another useful way to organize dimensions. His arrangement includes four categories of dimensions, moving from general to specific: classes of dimensions (e.g., communications and decision making); dimensions (e.g., oral communication and problem analysis); situational dimensions (e.g., quantitative analysis and staffing analysis); and subdimensions (e.g., technical translation and fact finding). Byham suggested that the level of specificity employed in defining dimensions depends on how the information will be used. For general selection programs, classes of dimensions are appropriate; for selection or placement into a specific position, situational dimensions are often useful; for diagnostic programs, subdimensions help give direction to trainable components of a dimension.

DETERMINING THE NUMBER OF DIMENSIONS

Historically, assessment centers have involved 12, 15, or more dimensions. In their survey of more than 200 organizations, Spychalski et al. (1997) found that the average number of dimensions assessed was 11, but 15% of the organizations assessed more than 18 dimensions, and at least one organization assessed 100 dimensions! Krause and Gebert (2003) found that in assessment centers in German-speaking countries, more than 50% assessed more than 8 dimensions, and 12% assessed more than 15 dimensions. The assumption has been that assessors can reliably observe and classify behaviors into the chosen dimensions. An argument for using several dimensions is that it forces assessors to note a wide variety of behaviors, all of which may be relevant to professional effectiveness. In this light, there is no assumption that the several dimensions are unrelated to each other, or even conceptually distinct. Proponents of the practice of assessing many dimensions argue that multiple dimensions yield a healthy redundancy in assessment.

In contrast, recent research (summarized in chap. 7) has shown that assessors may not be able to adequately distinguish among a large number of dimensions. With large numbers of indistinguishable dimensions, assessors often give ratings that are interdependent and thus not meaningfully different from each other. We must consider the heavy cognitive load placed on assessors when they are asked to observe, record, recall, and report on a large number of dimensions. Research has shown that assessment center ratings show enhanced validity when a smaller set (3 to 6) dimensions are used as opposed to a large set (more than 9; Gaugler & Thornton, 1989; Sackett & Hakel, 1979; Schmitt, 1977; Woehr & Arthur, 2003).

We argue that future assessment centers should not attempt to assess more than about seven dimensions unless the designers are willing to go to great lengths to assess a larger set of dimensions by including many exercises, giving extensive assessor training, and spending a long time in the integration discussion.

A CONTINUUM OF BEHAVIORAL DIMENSIONS

Assessment center developers should use different types of dimensions for different assessment purposes (Gibbons, Rupp, Kim, & Woo, 2005; Rupp et al., 2003; Snyder, Gibbons, Woo, & Kim, 2005). This section offers a way to conceptualize types of dimensions. The term *dimension* has been used in the literature on assessment centers to refer to a cluster of behaviors that can be defined with specific behaviors and observed with some consistency (Thornton & Byham, 1982). A good definition of a dimension includes a statement of the behaviors that make up the dimension, the conditions under which the behaviors are demonstrated, and the level of effectiveness on the dimension expected of someone in the target job.

Examination of the dimensions that have been used in the past shows that the term dimension usually refers to some form of human attribute. In this section, we present alternative ways of thinking about different types of human attributes. Human attributes can be arranged along a continuum, as illustrated in Fig. 5.2.

Potentialities

On the right-hand side of the chart are basic human attributes that are deeply ingrained in an individual. Two examples are intelligence and shyness. Attributes of this nature are characterized by stability, consistency, and

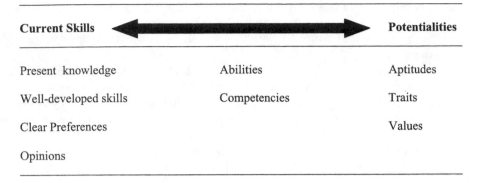

Current Skills		Potentialities
Present knowledge	Abilities	Aptitudes
Well-developed skills	Competencies	Traits
Clear Preferences		Values
Opinions		

FIG. 5.2.   A continuum of human attributes.

generality, and are therefore termed potentialities because of their great potential to influence behavior consistently in a wide variety of situations.

Potentialities are stable in the sense that they have taken a long time to develop in adult individuals and will likely take a long time to change. This does not mean that attributes of this type are unchangeable and it certainly does not mean that they are in-born and genetically determined. In fact, we do see evidence of the developability of traits over the lifespan (Fraley & Roberts, 2005; Robins, Norftle, Trzesniewski, & Roberts, 2005). It does mean that these characteristics will not change over a period of a few weeks or months. Second, consistency means that the characteristic manifests itself in a wide variety of situations. A person who is shy in classroom situations tends to be shy in other group settings as well. The point is that there is considerable consistency in the behavior of people in these types of human attributes.

Also, potentialities are widely pervasive in their effect on many different tasks or human endeavors. A person's basic values serve as a guide or motivator for a variety of activities (Rokeach, 1973). Similarly, a person's level of intelligence allows him or her to solve a variety of different complex and abstract problems. Generality does not mean that the trait affects all other related activities. A person whose general intelligence level is high may not be very good in solving abstract mathematical problems. A person who consistently values hard work and advancement may not be interested in working on a project for which he or she holds no interest.

Examples of basic human attributes commonly assessed in promotional assessment centers include:

- decision-making ability;
- impact on others;
- motivation to work.

Each of these attributes meets the criteria for potentialities and will affect a wide variety of managerial functions. A person with a high level of decision-making ability who has a positive effect on others and is highly motivated will probably have a high potential for success in a variety of managerial and professional positions.

Skills

At the left end of the continuum (see Fig. 5.2) lies a set of human attributes that are specific, developed as a result of recent educational, work, or life experiences, and subject to change more quickly than potentialities. These attributes are specific in that they refer to a limited area of knowledge or a circumscribed skill. To cite two examples, knowledge of how to calculate a rate of return on an investment would be a technique learned in a course on financial analysis or in a bank job. Similarly, a person's opinion about an alternative way to dispose of nuclear waste might be a function of knowing the relative risks involved; as such, it might be subject to change over time with further information. Such opinions are not pervasive in that they may be unrelated to opinions about how the U.S. trade deficit should be handled. In the assessment center context, examples of dimensions that fall on the left-hand side of the continuum include:

- knowledge of agency regulations;
- financial analysis skill;
- orientation to company values.

These attributes would be relevant to a specific job in a specific organization. Krause and Gebert (2003) found that skills such as communication and cooperation were assessed in more than 85% of the German-speaking centers, in comparison with rarely assessed personal characteristics such as tolerance for ambiguity and charisma.

Other Attributes

In the middle of the continuum lies a set of dimensions that varies between the two extremes. These dimensions vary in terms of the major characteristics defining the continuum (i.e., specificity and stability). Terminology is not uniform here, but we can refer to these dimensions as abilities, competencies (McClelland, 1987), or general skills (Fleishman & Quaintance, 1984). What these dimensions have in common is that they are attributes that are relevant to performance in a well-defined area of work. Also, although they are learned, they are relatively stable over time. In the assessment center context, examples of dimensions that fall somewhere in the middle of the continuum include:

- planning and organizing;
- management control;
- sensitivity.

These dimensions can be made more explicit in several different ways. One way might highlight the more generalized characteristic, whereas a second might highlight the specific skill. For example, "planning and organizing" can be conceptualized as a general ability to lay out work in a deductively logical manner showing the sequential relationships among a variety of activities; alternatively, it can be conceptualized as a specific set of techniques including charts, diagrams, and symbols for displaying a manufacturing process. The former is more similar to a general characteristic; the latter is more similar to a developed skill. It is instructive to note that a significant number of assessment centers use dimensions falling all along the continuum represented by Fig. 5.2. Table 5.6 shows the percentage of assessment centers assessing various types of dimensions, as revealed in Spychalski et al.'s (1997) survey of more than 200 organizations. Unfortunately, the survey results do not tell what types of dimensions are used in what types of programs.

A Continuum of Developability

The extent to which a dimension is learnable, trainable, or developable is especially important for designers of developmental assessment centers (DACs). That is, dimensions used in DACs have to be not only relevant to

TABLE 5.6
Percentage of Assessment Centers Assessing Various Dimensions

Dimensions Assessed	*Percentage of Centers Using Dimension*
Current skills	
Sales ability	21
Development of subordinates	17
Abilities	
Planning and organizing	86
Oral communication	91
Potentialities	
Judgment	74
Creativity	18

Source. Spychalski et al. (1997).

the job of interest, but also amenable to develop within a DAC program like that described in chapter 4. Gibbons and colleagues (Gibbons, Rupp, Kim, & Woo, 2005; Rupp et al., 2003; Snyder et al., 2005) have presented a "continuum of developability" on which they place many common assessment center dimensions according to the extent to which they are developable and which types of training methods might be suitable for developing the dimensions.

A third criterion offered by these authors for choosing DAC dimensions is a function of participants' subjective perceptions of the developability of the dimensions. Research on implicit theories has shown that individuals vary in their beliefs about the malleability of various human attributes (e.g., intelligence, personality), and these perceptions predict development attitudes and activities (Dweck & Leggett, 1988). For example, Dunning (1995) found that both the importance of traits and their perceived modifiability affected the degree to which people displayed self-assessment versus self-enhancement preferences for receiving feedback. In addition, Potemra (2005) found that beliefs about the improvability of dimensions related to academic success were related to learning oriented attitudes toward attaining specific goals in a university context. This research suggests that developability beliefs of DAC dimensions may influence development behavior, and therefore DAC developers should consider the job relevance, the true developability, and developability beliefs on dimensions to be included in the DAC program.

An Alternative to Dimensions: Tasks

Up to this point, when discussing the dimensions to be observed in an assessment center we have referred to them as human attributes of one type or another. In the language of most assessment center proponents, the term *dimensions* has become synonymous with characteristics describing human beings. But these are not the only categories that can be used to classify behaviors. We can also group behaviors into categories representing tasks. Tasks are statements of activities involved in work that has been accomplished (Brannick & Levine, 2002). Examples of tasks include writing a report or solving a performance problem with an employee. Each of these tasks can be broken down into subtasks, which require several behaviors. A task can be thought of as a sequence of activities carried out to accomplish some goal.

What are the arguments in favor of using tasks as dimensions in an assessment center? Some researchers (Klimoski & Brickner, 1987; Lance, Foster, Thoresen, & Gentry, 2004; Lowery, 1997; Sackett & Tuzinski, 2001; Thoresen, 2002) have suggested that because of evidence that brings into question the ability of assessors to consistently rate behavior related to the same attribute in different exercises, we should ask assessors to use tasks as the categories for observation rather than human attributes. Task statements tend to be more job-specific than general human attributes and thus may provide assessment categories that are more clearly related to any one job. Tasks also may provide categories that are more conducive to observation.

It remains to be determined whether task categories provide a better classification scheme for assessors and, more importantly, whether task categories overcome the problems noted when assessors rate human attributes (Lance, Foster et al., 2004). Along these lines, Adams (1990) has provided some preliminary laboratory data that shows that assessors can classify behaviors more accurately using task categories than attribute categories. Ultimately, the test of these new proposals is whether or not the purposes of the assessment center are better achieved using human attributes or tasks (or some other set of categories). A more thorough discussion of these issues is presented in chapter 10. For now, let us note, there has been no published research on an assessment center using tasks as the only assessment framework. So, we are left to speculate about whether this method would really work. We are aware of no comparative studies that have been carried out to evaluate the relative effectiveness of these two approaches to assessment center design (i.e., tasks vs. dimensions) in field settings.

There are several arguments in favor of using human attributes as dimensions in an assessment center. There is evidence to suggest that people naturally think in terms of human traits when evaluating others (Mischel, Jeffry, & Patterson, 1974). Attributes also provide meaningful information when assessors provide feedback to participants. In addition, feedback about attributes can be applied more generally to numerous job situations in comparison with tasks that apply to a specific job. Furthermore, job performance can be described with relatively few skills, whereas task lists tend to be relatively long and detailed. Worker-oriented job analysis systems using human attributes as the framework have been proven valuable in many other personnel assessment and training applications (Gatewood & Feild, 2001). Finally, we have the long history of developing effective assessment centers using attribute dimensions. By contrast, there is no published, empirical research demonstrating the effectiveness of an assessment center using tasks as the organizing principle. It remains to be seen whether an alternative framework would be effective. There is no full description in the published literature of an assessment center following this method and no published evidence of reliability and validity of assessment center results using this framework. Until that evidence is provided, we recommend continuing to use human attributes as the dimensions in an assessment center.

Diversity in the population being assessed or developed presents a challenge to specifying the behaviors that are considered effective or ineffective performance on certain dimension. This challenge is present no matter what type of variable is used for observation and evaluation of performance: potentialities, skills, competencies, tasks, exercises, etc. Leadership in a group may be accomplished by different behaviors by men and women; oral communication may be accomplished in different ways by persons in different ethnic groups; younger and older workers may complete tasks in different ways; interpersonal effectiveness may be demonstrated in different ways in different ethnic groups; the behaviors that lead to effective decision making may differ across national cultures. These and many other examples demonstrate that assessment center developers must be sensitive to subgroup differences in accomplishing work in complex organizations with diverse populations. The label and definition of assessment center dimensions are only initial steps in designing an assessment center structure. Subgroup differences must be considered in specifying the behavior that reflects effective performance in the dimensions in the simulation exercises.

SUMMARY AND CONCLUSIONS

The dimensions used for assessment centers should be carefully chosen on the basis of detailed information gathered by a variety of job analysis and competency modeling procedures. Different types of dimensions should be used for selection/promotion, diagnostic, and developmental assessment centers: More trait-like attributes are appropriate for applications involving long-range prediction of success, whereas developmental applications should be built around specific skills. In most assessment centers, only about five to seven dimensions can be assessed with any great precision. In order to make finer distinctions, a much more extensive assessment program must be used. To facilitate the assessors' job, dimensions must be defined clearly, in specific behavioral terms that distinguish each dimension from the others. A wide variety of different human attributes can be assessed accurately in this manner, including knowledge, skills, abilities, motivations, interests, and interpersonal styles. In the future, tasks may provide meaningful categories for assessment observations, but evidence to support their usefulness has yet to be provided.

Chapter 6

Simulation Exercises

An essential element of any assessment center is the observation of behavior in simulation exercises. Simulation exercises are situations that present participants with complex stimuli and call for complex behavioral responses. The complex stimuli may include any of the following:

- financial, demographic, and community data available to a bank executive considering a new branch in a suburb;
- a set of personnel problems including alleged safety violations, absenteeism, and thievery being reviewed by a disciplinary committee; or
- a set of letters, emails, and memos in a manager's in-box.

The corresponding complex responses may be:

- financial analyses and written rationale in favor of and in opposition to opening the new bank branch;
- decision making and leadership actions to help the committee find solutions; or
- written responses, assignments, and directions to subordinates or others.

Each simulation exercise represents some important aspect of the job for which the participant is being considered or trained. Each simulation affords assessors the opportunity to observe and evaluate the participant on a number of predetermined dimensions, such as written or oral communication, problem analysis, leadership, or initiative.

The purpose of this chapter is to present examples of several types of simulation exercises that have been used in assessment centers and to evaluate their effectiveness for different assessment purposes. The chapter explores several issues relevant to the design, selection, and implementation of simulation exercises. Based on the premise that each type of exercise can be used for different purposes, the content, level of difficulty, and similarity of the exercises to the target job must be chosen carefully to achieve the goals of different assessment center programs.

This chapter also explores similarities and differences between present-day and traditional simulation exercises. Many traditional exercises continue to be used quite successfully. For example, in-baskets contain memos from supervisors, peers, and subordinates, a one-on-one interview simulation may require a discussion with an employee whose performance has declined, and case studies call for analyses of complex operational and personnel problems. At the same time, the following sections show that significant changes have taken place over the past 50 years. Exercise materials are being presented through a wider variety of sophisticated media (e.g., video, computer displays). Responses are being captured on audio and video recorders to allow evaluation at other locations. There has been a decline in the use of certain exercises in some settings. For example, group discussions, which call for interaction among candidates for promotion, are used less often in police and fire promotional examinations, because of concern about standardization. In addition, integrated sets of exercises are being presented in the "day in the life" arrangement. These and other examples of continuity and change in assessment exercises are explored in this chapter.

TYPES OF ASSESSMENT EXERCISES

Many different types of assessment techniques have been used in assessment centers, including mental ability tests, personality questionnaires, projective techniques, and background interviews, but the mainstay of the assessment center method is the simulation exercise. There is a wide variety of simulation exercises, each of which has been described in detail elsewhere for the reader who wishes more information. Thornton and Byham (1982) provided a detailed summary of the early research on various simulation exercises used in assessment centers. Thornton and Rupp (2003) provided a more recent evaluation of research on simulations and their psychometric properties. Thornton and Mueller-Hanson (2004) describe how to build various types of simulations for the purpose of assessment, development, and research. This section emphasizes special characteristics of different types of exercises, analyzes their strengths and weaknesses, and lists various considerations in choosing among them.

Table 6.1 lists the percentage of assessment centers using the most common simulation exercises, based on three surveys. The first survey included 215 organizations in the United States (Spychalski et al., 1997). The second survey included an international sample of 114 organizations (Kudisch et al., 1999). The third survey included 281 organizations from German-speaking countries (i.e., Germany, Switzerland, and Austria; Krause & Gebert, 2003). The next several sections describe the types of exercise, in terms of the problems presented and behavior expected of the participant. This order is somewhat arbitrary, since even the simplest type of exercise can be made quite complex with special instructions or content. In addition, information about the use of other assessment methods is shown for comparison purposes.

The reader will want to keep in mind that (a) not all exercises are relevant to all jobs. For instance, an in-basket may be critical to an office supervisor, but relatively meaningless to a lead person on an assembly-line, and (b) the content of the exercise may or may not resemble the target job. For instance, in a case where the target job is supervisor in an insurance office, the contents of the in-box may closely replicate that of an insurance office, or it may replicate the in-basket of a government organization or a research laboratory. Job analysis tells us what the target job is like, but we may or may not choose to closely replicate that situation in the assessment center.

Written Case Analysis

In a written case analysis, the participant is given material to read that describes an organizational problem and is then asked to prepare a set of recommendations for higher management as to how the problem should be addressed. The problem may require financial, system, or process analysis. For example, in one case analysis, each participant was asked to review record-keeping procedures in a community blood bank. About 50% of the assessment centers use a written case study.

One advantage of this exercise is that it is quite flexible and can be tailor-made to assess or develop general attributes, such as the ability to organize an operation, or specific skills, such as calculating a rate of return on investment. The output from this exercise is typically a written report, but this can be supplemented with an oral presentation, as described in the next section. When a written report is submitted, assessors can evaluate both its form and its substance. A poorly written report may suggest the need for remedial training in business correspondence. Superficial or faulty analysis of the case material or unsystematic evaluation of alternative solutions may be

TABLE 6.1

Types of Assessment Techniques: Frequency of Use as Reported in Three Surveys

	Type of Simulation	U.S. Organizations[a]	International Sample[b] Administrative/Developmental Assessment Centers	German-Speaking Countries[c]
More complex simulation	Business game	25%		53%
	In-basket	82%	82%	
	Group tasks (not in survey)			
	Group discussion			
	Assigned roles	44%		
	Not assigned roles	59%	46%/37%	95%
	Information not available on type			89%
	Oral presentation	46%	62%/48%	
	Case study/Analysis problem	49%	46%/51%	65%
	Fact finding	38%		
Less complex simulation	Interaction simulation	47%	53%/42%	3%
	Background interview	57%	71%/48%	87%
Other assessment techniques	Cognitive ability test	31%	58%/44%	
	Personality test		43%/51%	
	Some form of test			31%

Source. [a]Spychalski et al. (1997); [b]Kudisch et al. (1999); [c]Krause and Gebert (2003).

indications of the need for training in decision-making skills. A difficulty in using written exercises is developing objective scoring guidelines for the assessors. Jacobsen and Sinclair (1990) have shown that methods can be developed to reliably assess the quality of written responses through the use of multiple assessors and objective standards.

Oral Presentation

In an oral presentation exercise, participants are asked to make a short, extemporaneous speech about a simple topic or a longer, formal presentation about a case study like those described earlier. The presentation is usually given to an assessor who then asks questions intended to challenge the participant. Where it is relevant to the target job, the assessor may even put the participant under stress by opposing his or her conclusion and pointing out its limitations and flaws. In another format, several participants give their presentations, then discuss their recommendations and choose the best solution. Thus, the written case analysis and oral presentation can be preliminary steps before a group discussion exercise, which is described next.

A presentation exercise is a relatively easy exercise to construct and administer. Participants can be asked to talk on virtually any topic. Administrators can have a list of topics and use this exercise to fill time when other exercises move ahead of schedule. This exercise provides an excellent opportunity to assess or develop a particular facet of oral communication skill (i.e., the ability to make formal or semiformal presentations). In some assessment centers, the participants are provided materials such as flip charts, markers, and transparencies to use with an overhead projector. In more technologically advanced situations, the participant may be provided with a computer, presentation software, and an LCD projector. If the assignment for preparation is given before the assessment center, participants may be expected to prepare much more formal presentation material. Assessors can then see how participants use these devices to enhance the effectiveness of their communications. An oral presentation is used in about 50% of assessment centers in the United States and other countries, except in German-speaking countries where usage is around 90%.

Leaderless Group Discussion

In a leaderless group discussion, or LGD, four to eight participants are given several problems to resolve in a fixed period of time, say one hour. They are asked to discuss the problems and to prepare written recommendations that have been endorsed by all the participants. For example, the problems may involve a set of recommendations on how to handle personnel issues that have arisen in the organization. In one form of the group discussion exercise, there are no roles assigned, and everyone cooperates in developing the best solution for the organization as a whole. In contrast, a more competitive situation can be simulated in which each participant is assigned the role of a head of a department or special interest group trying to get a share of a federal grant or other sources of revenue.

The LGD is particularly effective for assessing and developing teamwork and emergent leadership skills, such as the ability to contribute good ideas and guide the discussion process (Harris, 1949). Problem analysis and decision analysis abilities can also be assessed (Bass, 1950, 1954). Group discussions are used in virtually all assessment centers in German-speaking countries, but to a lesser extent in the United States and other countries. In the United States, nonassigned role discussions (59%) are used more frequently than assigned role discussions (44%).

Several potential limitations of LGDs should be mentioned. First, differences in behaviors and interactions are possible, depending on the composition of the group of participants. The climate and tone of the discussion can differ from one group to another, ranging from quite lively and challenging to quiet and subdued, depending on the composition and mood of the group. This potential lack of standardization across groups means that assessors sometimes have a difficult time knowing whether the behavior they observe in a particular individual is a function of the individual or the group dynamics.

Demographic composition may have an impact on LGD performance as well. For instance, Fenwick and Neal (2001) studied the effects of gender composition on group performance on a simulation task. They found that the number of women per group was positively related to team performance on the simulation. The authors argued that the women's cooperative work styles complemented the analytical, competitive work styles of men, with mixed gender groups showing the highest levels of performance on the task. Assessment center administrators should take the demographic composition of the group into consideration when group exercises are part of the assessment center design. This is especially the case for selection and promotion centers, where it is imperative to create a level playing field for all candidates.

We also must consider whether this exercise is a valid simulation of job situations, because few organizational settings are truly "leaderless." In most situations, there is a designated supervisor, task leader, or project coordinator who has some formal leadership assignment. Ideally, we want to know how well the individual executes the leadership functions he or she has been given. In a few assessment centers, each participant is asked to lead a meeting of a group of persons playing the roles of subordinate staff members. Although this format simulates many actual organizational situations, few assessment centers have the time or resources to provide all the role players needed. It may be more appropriate to design an exercise that involves an assigned leader in a one-on-one situation. This type of exercise is discussed in the next section.

Interview Simulation or Role-Play Exercises

An interview simulation is a simulation exercise in which the participant talks with one or more persons playing the roles of a subordinate, colleague, or customer. Interview simulations are adaptations of the role-playing technique developed in the 1950s to foster attitude change (Fishbein & Azjen, 1975). These exercises are sometimes called *role plays*, but the term may have inappropriate connotations, because in an assessment center, we do not want participants to be playing a role. We want them to be displaying authentic behavior representative of behavior on the job. Interview simulations are used in approximately 59% of assessment centers in the United States and international samples, but by only 3% of the German-speaking programs.

The examples in Table 6.2 show the variety of situations that can be simulated for different types of jobs. The "interviewee" in all these situations is a role player trained to act in a standardized manner. The role player might ask questions, make suggestions, answer questions, and even act upset, depending on what the situation calls for. The participant must talk with the role player and resolve the problem while being observed by one or more assessors. The interview simulation is particularly effective in revealing behaviors related to dimensions such as oral communication, empathy and tact, and problem-solving ability.

An advantage of this exercise is that it is relatively short, requiring 15 to 30 minutes to prepare and only 8 to 10 minutes to execute. Thus, several different interview simulations can be incorporated in an assessment program. Interview simulations are particularly appropriate for assessment centers for inexperienced supervisors, because they provide controlled situations for

TABLE 6.2
Examples of Interview Simulations

Target Position	Interviewee	Situation Simulated
Middle-level executive	Telephone reporter	Investigation of environmental violations
First-level supervisor	Subordinate	Discussion of a performance problem
Telephone sales	Client	Selling a product or service
Customer service representative	Irate customer	Complaint about a faulty product
Financial supervisor	New financial planner	Soliciting a client on the phone

assessing and developing rudimentary communication and problem-solving skills (Thornton & Cleveland, 1990). One disadvantage of the interview simulation is the need for a role player, which increases staffing needs. A solution is to have an assessor play the role of the interviewee, but this in turn causes another problem for the assessor who must then carry out two difficult functions simultaneously. Another potential problem with interaction simulations is that the role player may not play the role consistently from one participant to the next. This problem can be controlled through proper training of role players and careful monitoring by assessors.

Technological innovations, including computer-adaptive stimuli and computerized feedback, are being employed in interaction simulations used in developmental assessment centers. For example, the FBI Undercover Training School uses computerized interview simulations to train agents in cultural sensitivity (Crudup, 2004). In these simulations, the agent must question a foreign person about various matters. The agent is live, sitting in front of a video monitor, but the various situations occur in several different locations, that are presented on the screen. The agent may have to go to an individual's home, knock on the door, and engage in a questioning session. The screen presents a real person responding to the agent's questions. The program incorporates both voice recognition and computer adaptive software such that the video images of the foreign person actively respond to the questions asked by the agent.

In-Basket or In-Box

Originally, the exercise known as the in-basket was a simulation of the paperwork that arrives in the mailbox of a typical manager (Fredericksen, Saunders, & Wand, 1957; Lopez, 1966). In modern organizations, information comes to managers through various electronic media, including voice mail, fax, computer in-box, etc., and thus technologically advanced assessment centers present the information in these forms. For continuity with prior literature on this technique, in this chapter we continue to use the term *in-basket* in full recognition that few managers get their information only through a physical object on the desk. In whatever form the exercise takes, the information might include memos, letters, reports, announcements, requests, and irrelevant information that present personnel, financial, accounting, or procedural problems for the participant. The participant is given a calendar, background information, general instructions, and alternative means of responding (e.g., paper and pencil or email), but usually no access to a secretary or telephone. The participant must write out instructions, draft letters, make decisions, and set up meetings, all within a relatively short time period. The time pressures force the participant to set priorities and make decisions. A vast majority (80%) of U.S. assessment centers, but only about half in German-speaking countries, use an in-basket.

When adequate staff personnel are available, a secretary or "assistant" may be assigned to each participant to help with routine work, such as making phone calls or arranging meetings. This procedure is used in the Israeli Air Force assessment center, where each officer candidate is assigned a lower level enlisted person to supervise during the exercise (S. Haboucha, personal communication, July 16, 1990). Assessors evaluate the resulting written work and also observe how the candidate uses the assistant; the assistant, in turn, later provides information to the assessor about the candidate's supervisory effectiveness.

The written or typed responses to the in-basket materials can be the sole output scored by the assessors. More frequently, an assessor conducts a follow-up interview in which the participant explains the reasons for action taken. Whereas the written material provides recorded evidence of how the action will be seen by others, the verbal explanations provide valuable insight into the participant's thought processes. Assessors must be trained to be somewhat skeptical of the participants' ability to retrospectively describe their thinking during the exercise, because people tend not to have accurate insight into their own judgment and decision-making processes (Hammond, McClelland, & Mumpower, 1980). The actual records of responses probably provide the most relevant assessment data.

The in-basket exercise allows the assessment of a wide variety of dimensions and has a high degree of face validity for many managerial jobs, features that may explain why the vast majority of assessment centers use an in-basket. Dimensions such as delegation, planning and organizing, management control, and judgment can be assessed with an in-basket. Many studies have been conducted to investigate the relationship of performance on in-basket exercises and success in management (Schippmann, Prien, & Katz, 1990; Thornton & Byham, 1982). The evidence shows that in-basket scores are related to ratings of actual managerial performance, progress in management rank, and on-the-job performance of tasks similar to those assessed in the in-basket. Both Schippmann et al. and Thornton and Byham concluded that the research evidence supports the use of in-baskets for making promotion decisions, but Schippmann et al. warned that in-basket content varies considerably and research evidence is quite fragmented. Human resource managers are cautioned to seek evidence of the effectiveness of any individual in-basket exercise they are considering for an assessment center. This is sound advice for all assessment techniques.

One limitation of the in-basket exercise is time: It usually requires 2 to 3 hours to complete and then almost that much time to score. Additional time is required for a follow-up interview and evaluation of interview performance. Scoring can be difficult because the assessor must consider the complex set of responses given to several items, as well as the person's rationale for these responses. Brannick, Michaels, and Baker (1989) have shown that if assessors are allowed to make inferences about several dimensions on the basis of one "red hot" item, there are likely to be artificially high relationships among dimension ratings. Problems such as this can be minimized by developing clearer scoring standards for assessors. Scoring can be standardized by providing assessors with examples of behavioral responses to each item and by showing the relevance of the behavior to a specific dimension. With adequate training, assessors appear to be able to rate in-basket performance with high levels of consistency (Schippmann et al., 1990; Thornton & Byham, 1982).

To reduce time requirements and to standardize scoring procedures, computerized in-baskets have been developed to present stimuli and score responses (Heine & Struth, 1989; Thornton & Mueller-Hanson, 2004). In one form of this method, participants are presented the items on a monitor and asked to choose from several alternative courses of action. Each alternative has been predetermined to indicate effective or ineffective performance on the dimensions being assessed. The computer can then score the responses and give ratings on the dimensions. The time saving is indisputable, but the accuracy of such a method has not yet been demonstrated. Allowing the participant to pick from among several alternatives is quite different from requiring the participant to generate and execute the response in his or her own words. This sort of test may predict managerial success, but in our thinking does not qualify as an assessment center exercise because complex, overt behaviors are not required.

Oral Fact Finding

In this exercise the participant reads a small amount of information about a problem and then is given the chance to acquire additional information by directing questions to a resource person. The resource person can be a trained role player or an assessor. The fact-finding exercise is a variation of the incident process (Pigors & Pigors, 1961) originally designed to train managers in analytical thinking, practical judgment, and social awareness (Pigors, 1976). Vague questions result in general answers; specific questions yield valuable information. After the question-and-answer period, the participant is asked to make a recommendation and provide a rationale. The resource person may then challenge the participant, supplying new information in an attempt to elicit a change of position. This type of exercise is used in nearly two thirds of assessment centers in German-speaking countries, but only about one third of U.S. programs.

Table 6.3 illustrates various examples of fact-finding exercises. The fact-finding exercise is particularly effective for assessing and developing the

TABLE 6.3
Examples of Fact-Finding Exercises

Target Position	Situation Simulated
Middle-level executive	Budget proposal has been turned down
First-level supervisor	Faulty product coming off assembly line
Telephone sales representative	Customer seeking help in identifying appropriate product to order
Computer analyst or accountant	Request from client department for a new information system

skills involved in soliciting information from customers, peers, and other sources who might not be willing or able to provide complete information. Assessors can also use fact-finding exercises to evaluate decision-making skills and tolerance for stress. One disadvantage of fact-finding exercises is that they are somewhat difficult to construct and administer. In order to be challenging, the resource material must be very thorough, and the assessor must anticipate many questions from assertive participants. In addition, the resource person/assessor must be familiar with the material in order to provide responses in a timely fashion. Also, as in an interview simulation, the resource person might have difficulty providing a standardized situation to all participants.

Assigned-Leader Group Task

In the assigned-leader group task, the administrator of the program assigns one participant to act as the leader of the group and then gives the group some task to accomplish. For middle-management positions, the person may be assigned to head a team of staff assistants and build a piece of equipment using Lego blocks. In assessment centers in fire or police departments and in the military, the assigned leader may be put in charge of a group faced with a physical challenge, such as using ropes and boards to move the team over a barrier.

The obvious advantage of this type of exercise is that it simulates one aspect of the job of many managers, namely leading a group of subordinates. Like the group discussion exercise, the group task provides a means to assess a variety of leadership skills. Its disadvantage is that it is time-consuming to give all participants a chance to act as the assigned leader. To be fair, the assessment center would have to have one such exercise for each participant. Because most programs assess six or more people at a time, there would need to be at least six of these exercises to give everyone a turn in the leader role. Some programs overcome this problem by changing the leadership assignment part way through the exercise. Other programs provide four role players who act as subordinates for one participant (Slivinski, Grant, Bourgeois, & Pederson, 1977). This arrangement provides more standardization, but requires several role players for an extended period of time.

Business Games

Business games vary in level of complexity. The following are typical examples:

- a 2-hour simulation of a manufacturing operation run by a team of six department heads;
- a 4-hour simulation of stock trading by three four-person teams;
- an 8-hour computer-driven game for 20 managers running a large multidivisional organization.

The common denominator of these games is the relatively unstructured nature of the interactions among the participants and the variety of actions that can be taken by any or all participants (Jones, 1972). As a complex game unfolds, it often resembles a sequence of simulation exercises: A leaderless group discussion takes place, a number of one-on-one interactions occur, someone makes a presentation, others engage in fact finding, the group convenes again to make decisions, and so on.

The interactive nature of business games provides opportunities to assess dimensions such as strategic planning, teamwork, and leadership. The content of the game can also be geared to the assessment of financial analysis, marketing, or production control. The complexity of business games, even the simple ones, creates advantages and disadvantages. On the positive side, games come closer to representing reality in the organization than more simple exercises. Games look more realistic to participants than less complex simulations, and they can help experienced managers learn skills. Games can also be exciting and fun for the participants. On the negative side, assessors often have difficulty observing behavior of participants as participants move around to different rooms and huddle in small groups. When used for training purposes, the situation may be so complex that no one has the skills to function very well and, consequently, little learning may take place (Thornton & Cleveland, 1990). Games are difficult to develop, expensive to purchase, and seldom customized for a specific organization. It is interesting to note that complex business games are used in only about 25% of the assessment centers covered in the survey by Spychalski et al. (1997), suggesting that games may present some administrative difficulties. A variety of computer-assisted games have been developed in German-speaking countries (Kleinmann & Strauss, 1998). They have been used infrequently in assessment centers and few validity studies have been reported in this context.

Integrated Exercises: "Day in the Life"

Up to this point, most of this chapter has presented the exercises as though they were separate and distinct from each other. An alternative arrangement is to relate two or more exercises to one another. This can be done in several ways. First, the results of one exercise can be used as the input for another. For instance, the recommendations that a candidate generates in the written report for a case study can be used as the starting point for a group discussion. Second, one set of background materials about the company and its policies, industry, and environment can be presented at the beginning of the assessment program and then used for all exercises. In each individual exercise, the participant can draw on information from the general background information, plus additional information presented at the beginning of subsequent exercises. With this arrangement, the separate individual exercises can be administered in any order, and the order can be different for different participants. Bycio and Zoogah (2002) found that the order in which participants completed exercises had a trivial (< 1%) effect on ratings.

By contrast, in a third arrangement, the exercises can build on each other as the person works through a typical "day in the life" in the simulated organization. For example, after the general background information, the person may begin to work on the in-basket. The background information in the in-basket then provides additional operational procedures and problems relevant to the items in the in-basket. In the next exercise, say the group discussion, all the information from the general background and in-basket may be relevant to the problems being discussed. In turn, in a subsequent performance review meeting with a problem subordinate, all the previous information can be used.

There is much that remains constant from one integrated exercise to the next: the description of the organization, the rules and regulations for operation, the people in various positions, job descriptions, and so on. What someone learns in the initial exercises may be useful in subsequent exercises. When Spychalski et al. (1997) surveyed more than 200 assessment centers, they found that 20% used an integrated exercise, typically composed of four definable segments. Smith and Reynolds (2002) described a complex, automated, integrated set of exercises for executives.

Advocates of integrated exercises argue that this arrangement is more realistic. People in real-life organizations familiarize themselves with their environment over time; they gain information in one interaction that helps in the next. In fact, integrated exercises may actually test the candidate's ability to capitalize on this accumulation of information in ways that disjointed exercises do not. Integrated exercises may also test the individual's ability to bounce back if he or she does poorly in an early exercise; that skill may be very important on the job. It can also be argued that integrated exercises have high face validity, that is, they closely resemble the actual job and the actual organization. This feature means that employees may be more willing to participate in the assessment center and have more confidence in the results and feedback.

What, then, are the arguments against integrated exercises in assessment centers? One argument is that the manager's job is very fragmented and made up of short, disjointed interactions (Mintzberg, 1975). The manager may be talking on the telephone about a financial matter one minute, responding to a memo about a production problem the next minute, and advising a supervisor on a disciplinary problem a few minutes later. And, none of these interactions may be connected. The relevant background information, the people involved, and the skills required may be very different from one task to the next. Thus, a set of disconnected and unrelated assessment exercises may actually resemble a very important part of the manager's life.

A second argument against integrated exercises has to do with motivation. When exercises are discrete, unrelated activities, participants are given a "fresh start" in each exercise. If an individual does poorly in the in-basket exercise, for example, he or she has a chance to start over in the group discussion. A lack of understanding of the information in one exercise will not penalize the person in the next exercise.

Related to this second argument is the idea that separate exercises give independent measurements of the dimensions being assessed. This is good, because measurement principles tell us that an evaluation is more consistent and accurate if it is based on several different observations that are not artificially related to each other (Nunnally & Bernstein, 1994). Integrated exercises may lead to some "contamination" of performance from one exercise to the next. Separate exercises minimize this possibility.

We are not taking a firm stance on whether or not exercises should be integrated. If the program requires an accurate assessment of management skills, the exercise content might best be kept separate to provide several independent measurements. If it is important to have a high level of acceptance of the program among participants and others in the organization and the situation allows all individuals to work through the exercises in the same order, an integrated set of exercises that resemble a day in the life of the organization may be appropriate and feasible.

EVALUATION OF RELATIVE CONTRIBUTIONS
OF EXERCISES

The data to support the value of each of the types of exercises discussed so far in this chapter has been described in other sources (Thornton & Byham, 1982; Thornton & Mueller-Hanson, 2004; Thornton & Rupp, 2003). As pointed out earlier, the content, difficulty, and similarity of the exercises to the actual job must be determined carefully to make them appropriate to different types of assessment centers. Although they have all been used successfully in a variety of assessment centers, there is little data to evaluate the *relative* merits of different exercises. It is not possible to say with any authority which one is *better* or *worse* than the others.

The relative merit of simulation exercises depends on the job being studied, the purpose of the assessment center, and the resources available to conduct the assessment activities. The question may be partially answered by a thorough job analysis, which shows not only the dimensions to be assessed but also the types of situations the participants face on a regular basis. For example, a first-level supervisor may spend considerable time in one-on-one discussions with subordinates solving work-related problems, but seldom meet with other supervisors in unstructured groups. Thus, in this situation, interview simulations may be more appropriate exercises than leaderless group discussions. On the other hand, staff professionals, such as engineers and cost accountants, may work regularly on teams and task forces. These activities may require leadership skills in situations that are frequently unstructured. Such skills readily emerge and can be assessed in leaderless group discussions.

The relative merit of the types of exercises is also a function of the willingness of the organization to properly administer them. In-baskets, fact finding exercises, and business games require careful and time-consuming preparation, thorough training of assessors, and considerable time to properly observe, review, and evaluate the complex behavior they elicit. If the organization is willing to develop and carry out these complex exercises properly, they are likely to be quite powerful; if not, the organization may be better served by the simpler exercises.

EXERCISE BY DIMENSION MATRIX

A somewhat simplified summary of the effectiveness of different types of exercises is presented in the exercise by dimension matrix in Table 6.4. It shows the dimensions that typically can be assessed in each exercise. The matrix is simplified in several ways. Not all possible dimensions are listed. For example, a case study may be constructed to evaluate financial analysis skills. In ad-

TABLE 6.4
Dimensions Observable Matrix

Dimension	Written Case Analysis	Oral Presentation	Leaderless Group Discussion	Interview Simulation	In-Basket	Oral Fact Finding	Assigned Group Task	Game
Problem Analysis	X		X	X	X	X	X	X
Decision Making	X	X	X	X	X	X		X
Leadership			X	X	X		X	X
Empathy				X	X			
Administrative Skills				X	X			
Delegation				X	X			
Planning and Organizing	X				X			X
Stress Tolerance		X				X		
Teamwork			X					X
Oral Communication		X	X	X		X	X	X
Written Communication	X				X			

dition, instructions may direct the participant to carry out a certain set of tasks and thus ensure that a dimension not normally measured can, in fact, be observed. Finally, the content of the exercise can be altered to elicit behavior relevant to a dimension not normally assessable. For example, although the typical leaderless group discussion does not afford the opportunity to assess behaviors relevant to the dimension Planning and Organizing, it is quite conceivable that the problems presented to the group could call for in-depth discussions about how to plan for various work activities.

A theoretical explanation of the relative effectiveness of an exercise to measure different dimensions comes from trait-activation theory (Tett & Guterman, 2000). The principle of trait activation states that "the behavioral expression of a trait requires arousal of that trait by trait relevant situational cues" (p. 398). The theory helps reconcile trait and situational explanations of behavior, by emphasizing the interaction of these behavioral determinants. In the context of assessment centers, the theory helps us understand how different exercises provide opportunities for individuals to display different skills, abilities, and other dimensions of performance. The content, instructions, and type of exercise combine to provide situations in which individual differences in performance can be observed and evaluated. Haaland and Christiansen (2002) demonstrated that ratings from exercises judged to be high on trait-activation potential for a given dimension showed more convergent validity than exercises judged to be low in trait activation for that dimension. Additional application of trait-activation theory to assessment centers was provided by Lievens, Chasteen, Day, and

Christiansen (2004). They found that correlations of assessment ratings for extraversion and conscientiousness were higher between exercises that provided opportunities to observe behavior related to those traits than for exercises not eliciting those behaviors.

A MODEL OF ASSESSMENT EXERCISES

An examination of assessment exercises suggests that there are two features of the exercises that determine their complexity: (1) the standardization of the stimulus material and (2) the structure imposed on the responses required of the participant. *Standardization* refers to the formality and uniformity of the assessment procedures. In a highly standardized test, all participants are presented with exactly the same instructions, questions, and conditions. For example, a written multiple-choice test is highly standardized, whereas observation of behavior in field settings is usually unstandardized. *Structure* refers to the latitude the participant has to respond in a unique and individualized way. In an unstructured test, the participant can decide how he or she will respond. For example, a leaderless group discussion is unstructured. By comparison, a high level of structure can be imposed on a written case study by instructing the participants to write a three-page report, list three alternatives, specify the benefits and costs of each, and so forth.

Often standardization and structure go together. In other words, standardized tests (e.g., a multiple-choice test of police procedures) require clear and structured responses, and unstandardized tests (e.g., a business game) provide little structure for required responses. However, the complexity of the test stimuli and that of the required response are not directly linked. For example, a simple and standardized one-sentence printed question may require complex and unstructured decision making and written responses, whereas a complex in-basket exercise may require a relatively simple choice or action.

Table 6.5 depicts a wide variety of existing assessment techniques in terms of standardization and structure. The table provides suggestions for new devices that have not typically been used in assessment programs. Blank cells represent assessment procedures that could be constructed. For example, the upper right portion of the table (i.e., structured response, unstandardized stimulus) suggests an exercise in which the participants are asked to fill out a questionnaire about some complex social interaction in which they have participated. On the other hand, the lower left portion of the table (unstructured response, standardized stimulus) suggests an exercise that might involve some verbal response to social stimuli presented on a video. Examples of early efforts along these lines were described by Frank (1990), who developed computer simulations of interactions with subordi-

TABLE 6.5

Model of Assessment Center Exercises

| | Level of standardization of the Stimulus Material — Standardized ←———→ Unstandardized | | | | | | | | |
| | | | | | Role Players (Subordinate, Peer, Supervisor, Customer) | | Other Assessees in: | | |
Structure of the Response Mode	Written	Videotape	Administrator	Assessor	One Role Player	Two or More	Assigned Roles	Nonassigned Roles	Other Teams
Structured:									
Completion of form	Ability test Personality questionnaire Background information form								
Handwriting	Case study In-basket		In-basket						
Verbal presentation	Case study			Fact finding	Problem employee		Analysis/ discussion		
Verbal response to questions				Background interview Interview after in-basket or analysis	Irate customer				
Participant-controlled interview		Interview simulation		Fact finding	Interview simulation				
Group discussion		Case study LGD				Staff meeting	LGD	LGD	Game
Multi-group discussion									Game
Combination of verbal, written, and physical behaviors									Game
Unstructured:									

119

nates and customers. An innovative exercise using video technology that fits in the upper left-hand corner (structured response, standardized stimulus) was developed by Cascio (1989) to simulate job learning among firefighters. An experienced firefighter is shown training on a piece of equipment, the tape is stopped, and participants are asked to indicate on paper whether or not they think the trainee took the correct action. More advanced, computer-adaptive techniques were described in the section on interaction simulations and role-play exercises.

MAJOR CONSIDERATIONS IN SELECTION
AND CONSTRUCTION OF SIMULATION EXERCISES

The types of exercises (e.g., individual or group, oral or written) used in an assessment center should be based on a thorough analysis of the job situation that the organization wishes to represent. Many other factors, other than the type of exercise, should be considered in developing the exercises.

Number of Exercises

Guidance about the appropriate *number* of exercises to use in an assessment center comes from prior research studies. Assessment centers that use a larger number of exercises and a wider variety of exercises tend to show more accuracy (Gaugler et al., 1987) than centers with a small, narrow set of exercises. A survey of more than 200 assessment centers showed that the typical assessment center used approximately five exercises, but some centers used 10 or 11 exercises (Spychalski et al., 1997). This first finding must be tempered with the seemingly contradictory finding that the length of the assessment center does not affect its predictive accuracy (Gaugler et al., 1987). These two findings are reconcilable. It is reasonable to conclude that a variety of *types* of exercises is needed, but little is gained from having more than two of the same type. For example, it would be better to use two group discussion exercises and an in-basket and interview simulation than to use four group discussions.

   To our knowledge, research has not been conducted to investigate what mixture of types and numbers of exercises is optimal, but theoretical support for the use of multiple types of exercises comes from correspondent inference theory (Jones & Davis, 1965). This theory states that we explain other people's behavior by searching for stable qualities in individuals that are discernible across different situations. When we see that an individual behaves the same way in several different situations, we infer that the behavior is a function of stable attributes of the individual and not of the external situation. For example, if I observe that Tom gets confused and cannot explain his decisions when speaking to another individual, to a small group, and also to a large group, I can reasonably conclude that Tom lacks oral communication skills.

The implication of this principle is that we should use several, shorter exercises of different types—some oral, some written, some individual, some group—rather than a few exercises of the same type. With a complex blend of exercises, inferences we make about attributes of people allow us to understand and predict their behavior in the future. Multiple exercises give assessors a chance to make these interpretations about dimensions, evaluate strengths and developmental needs, and predict future managerial success.

Fidelity of Exercises

The question of fidelity of assessment center exercises, that is, "To what extent should exercises resemble actual job situations?" is complicated. One reason the question is complicated is that fidelity includes many different features of the simulation:

- the industry in which the simulation is depicted;
- the content of the problems in the case material;
- the importance of the tasks;
- the medium for presenting the stimulus material;
- the response mode called for from the participant.

The first response to the question is often that the exercises should be very detailed and faithful representations of the job. Taken to the extreme, this would mean that the exercises should be an exact duplication of part of the job: Such exercises are often known as work samples (Anastasi & Urbina, 1997) or job replicas (Cronbach, 1970). A work sample test duplicates one small segment of the actual job performed. For example, a welder can be given actual equipment and materials and asked to weld together two pieces of metal; a typist can be given handwritten material and asked to type it on a computer like the one used on the job; or a managerial applicant might be given financial information relevant to a business deal and asked to perform some computation of return on investment.

Work samples are particularly appropriate when the purpose of the assessment center is to assess the current level of skill or the ability to perform a specific job. For example, a work sample would be appropriate for testing a mechanic's ability to repair the brakes of an automobile. Work samples are more appropriate when the assessment is targeted at one specific job, rather than a range of jobs or job levels.

For certain assessment purposes, there are several disadvantages of having a high level of fidelity in the exercises. If the purpose of assessment is identification of potential rather than assessment of present skills, the exercises should measure the basic aptitudes necessary to acquire job skills and not those skills per se. Job replicas often give inappropriate and unfair advantage to individuals with certain job experiences. People who know the specific practices of the organization usually perform better than outsiders on an in-basket that replicates their own office setting. At the same time, the outsider may have better basic decision making and leadership skills. A solution to this problem—and one that we favor—is to design exercises that depict the same type of industry or business but not the exact organization. For example, a fictitious government agency might be depicted for use in assessment of candidates for promotion in government positions. A generic supermarket depicted in an in-basket exercise and leaderless group tasks might be used to assess candidates for a wide variety of different grocery stores and other retail stores (Fogli, 1985).

The approach advocated here is a compromise between generalized exercises that have little fidelity and therefore appear to be unrelated to the job, and exact replicas of the target job and organization in each new assessment center. Fidelity (or face validity, as it is sometimes called) is important and will affect not only people's reaction to the exercises but also the accuracy of the responses they give (Nevo, 1989; Nevo & Jager, 1986). On the other hand, there are strong arguments against using work samples that may in fact penalize those people who do not have certain organizational experiences.

TECHNOLOGY IN ASSESSMENT EXERCISES

Assessment center exercises have historically been presented in paper-and-pencil format. The instructions, case materials, in-basket items, and other materials have been presented on paper, and are often supplemented with verbal comments. In addition, when written responses are required, participants have typically written responses by hand. This format is still appropriate and widely used. Furthermore, there are sound reasons to do so, as we describe later. On the other hand, many technical advances have been incorporated into assessment center exercises in some settings. High-tech means of presenting stimulus material (i.e., the instructions and case material) and recording responses (verbal and nonverbal behaviors and outputs of work) are increasingly being used.

With the advent of computers, there have been creative innovations in assessment center exercises. In the typical computer-driven exercise, the computer presents a video display of an employee talking about a job situation. The video stops and a narrator asks the participant what he or she would say next. Four alternatives are presented on the screen, and the participant makes a choice by pressing a key on the keyboard. In some applications, a branching takes place so that Choice A results in one response from the employee on the screen, whereas Choice B results in a different response, and so on. After further comments by the employee, the participant makes more choices of actions. The choices have been determined to reflect more or less effective actions related to dimensions of managerial performance. The computer then computes scores for the participant's performance.

This mode of presentation is an example of a high level of both standardization and structure. The standardization of the video-recorded employee's responses eliminates some of the problems role players can cause if they do not treat individual participants equally. But the way participants respond to computer-driven exercises is quite different from typical assessment center exercises. One of the essential features of an assessment center is that participants display complex and overt behaviors. In the computerized exercise, the response is often just the press of a key. Computerized exercises might have very high predictive accuracy, and if they do, they might have a place in the total set of evaluation techniques available to human resource managers.

There are three obvious limitations to many computerized exercises. First, the participant is given multiple choices and does not have to generate his or her own response. Second, the participant does not have to actually demonstrate the behavior, thus the exercise may be more a measure of opinion or knowledge than a measure of skill. Third, the exercise is not truly interactive the way an interview simulation or group discussion is, in which participants interact with one another or with role players.

In our opinion, computerized assessment techniques are exciting and can be efficient in assessing many applicants and can be effective in developmental applications. Exciting possibilities can be envisioned and initial applications are being tested. A new program at the FBI shows the potential for using computer-adaptive presentation of stimuli, individualized feedback, and coaching on a real-time basis. Still, much more research needs to be done and published in the professional literature before the human resource manager can be confident these techniques provide accurate assessments of attributes, predictions of future success, and effective developmental outcomes.

BEHAVIOR SAMPLING VERSUS BEHAVIORAL INTENTIONS

Assessment center exercises elicit a sample of overt behavior that resembles the behavior that the participant would demonstrate in the work setting. Behavior sampling is quite different from asking the person what he or she would *intend* to do. In this regard, the assessment center method is different from the situational interview method (Maurer, Sue-Chan, & Latham, 1999). The situational interview is based on the theory that intentions predict behavior, it asks people to state what they would do in the future if faced with certain situations, and uses a behaviorally anchored scoring guide to evaluate responses (Maurer et al., 1999). Two of these features, namely the presentation of situations and the use of scoring guides, are similar to assessment center practices. Two other features are quite different. Assessment center exercises typically present more extensive stimulus materials (e.g., a variety of materials in an in-basket; financial and production data in a case study; a human being playing the role of newsreporter challenging an executive) than is presented by the interviewer conducting a situational interview. In addition, the assessment center method is based on the theory that *actual* behaviors, rather than intentions to behave, are predictive of future behavior. Whereas the situational interview might ask the candidate for promotion to supervisor to state what he or she would intend to say to a problem employee whose work performance has deteriorated, an assessment exercise presents the candidate with a variety of background information about the employee and the organizational setting, and then asks the candidate to actually conduct a performance review session, face-to-face, with a role player trained to depict the problem employee. The candidate has to actually talk to the simulated employee, react to questions and recalcitrance, and overtly demonstrate the skills involved in diagnosing the employee's problems, motivating change in behavior, and gaining commitment.

STRUCTURING EXERCISES TO MEASURE
ABILITY OR MOTIVATION

Many assessment exercises can be constructed to provide *either* a measure of ability or a measure of motivation. For an exercise to measure a participant's motivation or preferred style of behavior, the participant should be given a choice of taking action or refraining from action. Jones and Davis (1965) provided a theoretical explanation of how we make inferences about other people's behavior. They said that we can infer less about a person if behavior is a required part of the person's social role. Voluntary behavior is more informative about the person's motivation than required or role-related behavior. This principle can be applied to the construction of different assessment center exercises to ensure they measure the dimensions one wishes to assess.

First, consider the leaderless group discussion: In most group discussions, a participant can make suggestions or remain silent, defend his or her position or let counterarguments go unchallenged, attack the positions of others or passively accept them. These actions reveal levels of assertiveness and provide a means to assess assertiveness. The freedom to be nonresponsive provides a measure of assertiveness, but if the participant chooses to be nonresponsive, there is no opportunity to assess ability to communicate. To make the exercise a measure of communication ability, the instructions should not give the participant a choice of taking action. For example, the instructions might specify that each participant must make an initial 2- to 3-minute presentation of recommended solutions, thus ensuring the opportunity to assess verbal presentation ability.

The in-basket provides another example where the participant can be given choices or where actions can be "forced." For example, the instructions can be silent on the question of whether or not to delegate work to an assistant, and thus provide an assessment of willingness to give responsibility to others. By contrast, some items can be structured so the participant is directed by a higher level manager to assign work to someone so that the task is completed during the assessee's absence from the organization. Thus, the skill of delegation can be assessed.

The structure of a written case study provides a third example. The materials can be vague on what the participant is to do, stating only to "make recommendations." As a result, the written report may or may not show how the participant came to the conclusions. Alternatively, the instructions can very explicitly state: "List the three most significant issues facing the company and provide supporting evidence for your diagnosis. For each issue, list at least two alternative courses of action and give advantages and disadvantages for each. Recommend actions to be taken, the negative consequences that may ensue from each choice, and what preventive steps should be taken." These instructions leave no doubt about the decision-making process to be used, and thus provide an opportunity to observe behaviors relevant to the person's ability to carry out the process. Thus, assessors have a chance to assess the quality of problem-analysis and decision-analysis abilities.

As a final example, in an assessment center exercise designed to select instructors for an industrial training program, role players (pretending to be trainees) asked scripted questions to seek specific feedback from the instructor candidates. The objective was to find out if the participants had the skill to give the feedback, not whether they had the interest in doing so voluntarily.

In summary, if we wish to use simulation exercises as standardized measures of abilities, the exercises should not give the participants many choices about whether or not to act. By giving clear instructions that each person is expected to take action, motivation to act is eliminated as an explanation of behavior, and inferences about *abilities* are then possible. On the other hand, if we wish the assessors to evaluate motivation, interests, and styles, the participant *should* have many choices.

FOCUSING ON THE PURPOSE OF THE ASSESSMENT

Throughout this book we have emphasized that the design of an assessment center should be based on the purpose of the assessment activity. Anyone involved in designing an assessment center should focus on this principle when considering the appropriate type and level of exercises. The purpose of exercises in selection/promotion programs, diagnostic programs, and development programs are very different, as well. Just as other elements of the assessment center must be designed according to its purpose, so should each individual exercise.

Table 6.6 provides a summary of considerations for selecting exercises for different assessment purposes. In programs designed to identify people with long-range potential, the purpose of the exercises is to assess basic aptitudes and characteristics that indicate the person will develop over time. The exercises should provide opportunities to observe behavioral information relevant to predicting long-range success in a variety of higher level positions. As such, the exercises should be designed to tap basic attributes that will allow the person to benefit from enriched experiences provided by the organization over the course of many months and years. These exercises can be general in nature, in other words, not models of any specific job or organization. For this purpose, fidelity to any job or organization is not important because the purpose is to predict success in a wide variety of jobs, some of which may not even be known at time of assessment.

In most selection programs, the participants are relatively inexperienced and thus do not have a basis for engaging in exercises that require specific knowledge of a particular organization. By necessity, therefore, the exer-

TABLE 6.6
Comparison of Exercises for Various Assessment Purposes

Exercise Characteristic:	Identification of Potential	Selection	Diagnosis	Training
Target job(s)	Range of jobs	Specific job	Current job	Current job or higher-level job
Number of exercises	3–6	3–6	7–10	7–10
Level of fidelity	Low	Moderate	High	High
Complexity	Simple	Moderate	Complex	Depends on skill of participants

Purpose of Assessment Center spans the four purpose columns.

cises cannot be replicas with a high level of fidelity. Work samples are not appropriate for this type of program unless the job requires specific skills that will not be trained upon entry into the job. Instead, exercises that enable the person with the basic set of attributes to perform well without penalty due to some lack of experience are most appropriate. At the same time, the exercises should have a moderate degree of fidelity, so that candidates see their relevance to the job they are applying for. For some selection programs, the organization must single out people who have fully developed skills. In those cases, work-sample exercises are appropriate. For example, a welding task that involves the use of actual tools and materials for the job site may be appropriate for screening skilled welders.

For diagnostic assessment centers, the exercises serve a very different function. Here the exercises must be designed to provide accurate assessment of several distinct attributes. Whereas in most selection programs the dimensions serve as intermediate steps in the process of evaluating overall potential, in a diagnostic program the dimensions are the end-products of assessment. Therefore, the exercises must provide detailed evaluation of each separate dimension. This means that the assessment must be thorough for each and every dimension and that low correlation among the dimensions should be possible.

To be effective, a diagnostic center needs a relatively large number of exercises. For instance, in assessing participants' ability to lead groups, the assessors need to make more than one observation of group interactions. Unlike the selection program, in which group leadership is just one of many attributes needed for successful performance, a diagnostic program must pinpoint deficiencies in the various facets of the individual's group leadership skills. For example, we would like to know if an individual is unable to clearly state ideas or if he or she lacks the assertiveness to make contributions heard. The exercises in diagnostic programs must have a much higher level of fidelity than selection programs. The exercises should be more like work-sample tests and measure present levels of skills.

For a developmental assessment center, considerations are different still. To ensure transfer of training from an assessment center to the job situation—a perennial problem for any training program—the exercises must have several special features. They must be highly relevant to the job (current or future, depending on the purpose of the assessment center) to bring out the best efforts of the participants. They must provide opportunities for successful practice in a nonthreatening environment, and they must provide situations that can be observed by assessors or facilitators who can later provide feedback and guidance for continued improvement. There must be enough exercises so that participants can solidify their new skills in the program before having to use them on the job.

OFF-THE-SHELF VERSUS HOME-GROWN EXERCISES

Organizations face the decision to "make or buy" exercises. There are advantages and disadvantages to each of these choices (see Table 6.7). Both options can result in both "good" and "bad" exercises.

There are not many options for buying ready-made exercises, but some exercises are offered by consulting firms. In certain circumstances, there are clear advantages to purchasing "off-the-shelf" exercises sold by professional organizations. Often such organizations have experienced staff members with extensive background in developing and implementing simulation exercises. The exercises they offer have usually been tried out and refined in other settings. Such pretesting is one suggestion in the *Guidelines* (International Task Force, 2000). If the new user has only a few persons to assess, it may be cost effective to purchase an exercise, but he or she must recognize that an off-the-shelf exercise may lack face validity.

On the other hand, in other circumstances, a tailor-made exercise may be fashioned to model the user organization, and if the organization anticipates a large-scale operation, it may be able to justify the expense of developing its own, new exercise. It is not easy to develop high-quality simulation exercises. Poor simulations may result in negative reactions from participants and difficulties for assessors to observe relevant behaviors. Flaws in exercises may make them indefensible if challenged by low-scoring candidates for selection. An advantage is that the home-built exercise being developed for one-time use, say for a promotional assessment center, can be kept confidential from candidates. A potential disadvantage is that the exercise may not be thoroughly pretested with a wide sample of respondents, and there is the possibility that minor flaws are not detected and eliminated. The decision to make one's own exercise may be appropriate if the exercise is a relatively simple one (e.g., a nonassigned role leaderless group discussion), and the organization has the time and expertise. Thornton and Mueller-Hanson (2004) provide guidance on how to construct simulation exercises. More complex exercises (e.g., complex case studies, in-

TABLE 6.7
Advantages and Disadvantages of Off-the-Shelf
and Home-Built Exercises

	Advantages	*Disadvantages*
Off-the-shelf	May be less costly for small AC May be higher quality Norms are sometimes available	May be more costly for large AC May have less face validity

Home-Built	Can have high fidelity to specific job
	  and organization
	Can be kept secure from participant
		May not be pretested thor-
		  oughly

baskets, and organizational games) are much more difficult to construct, and the organization may wish to contract with an outside consultant to build this sort of tailor-made exercise.

COMPLYING WITH PROFESSIONAL STANDARDS

There are several steps the assessment centers developers can carry out to ensure that the exercises are valid, job-relevant, fair, and legally defensible. These actions will help ensure that the exercises comply with professional standards and guidelines that apply to tests in general, and assessment centers in particular.

The following documents provide guidance for developing and using any personnel assessment technique:

- American Educational Research Association, American Psychological Association, American Council on Measurement in Education. (1999). *Standards for educational and psychological tests.* Washington, DC: American Psychological Association.
- Society for Industrial and Organizational Psychology. (2003). *Principles for the validation and use of personnel selection procedures* (4th ed.). Bowling Green, OH: Author.
- Equal Employment Opportunity Commission, Civil Rights Commission, Department of Labor, & Department of Justice. (1978). Uniform Guidelines on Employee Selection Procedures. *Federal Register, 43*(166), 38290–38309.
- International Task Force on Assessment Center Guidelines. (2000). Guidelines and Ethical Considerations for Assessment Center Operations. *Public Personnel Management, 29*, 315–331.

The guidance in these documents regarding the design, development, evaluation, and implementation of personnel assessment techniques can be summarized into three categories—standardization, reliability, and validity:

- Standardization refers to the consistent administration of an assessment technique so that all participants have the same instructions, environment, stimulus conditions, and consistent scoring, such that any given response behavior receives the same score.
- Reliability means that the score from the assessment is consistent and repeatable.

- Validity is demonstrated by accumulating evidence that the assessment technique measures the intended attributes and that inferences from the scores are supported by evidence.

Full descriptions of how to build in and then confirm these properties are beyond the scope of this chapter, but we summarize some of the steps that can be taken. Thornton and Mueller-Hanson (2004) provide a general model and a set of specific steps for the construction of simulation exercises. In addition, they provide details on how to comply with professional and legal requirements when building and using simulation exercises. Actions can be taken when (a) building the simulation exercise, (b) pilot testing the exercises before implementation, (c) conducting the assessment and scoring, and (d) evaluating the exercises after they are used.

Compliance begins with a clear specification of the purpose of the assessment center, thorough job analysis or competency modeling, inclusion of only relevant tasks, avoidance of irrelevant content, and editing the materials to make the instructions and substance clear and purposeful. General and specific guidance on how to build each of the types of simulation techniques covered in this chapter are provided in Thornton and Mueller-Hanson (2004).

Pilot testing the exercises with persons similar to the target group provides the opportunity to obtain feedback on the instructions and exercise materials. Participants at this stage can comment on the clarity of instructions and the processes they used in solving the problems. Timing can be checked to see if it is feasible to complete the exercise. The solutions given by the pilot subjects provide suggestions for behavioral anchors on rating scales. The adequacy of the support materials for assessors can be assessed. The level of performance provides a framework for discussing expectations with assessors in subsequent training programs.

The defense of the adequacy of any simulation exercise is partially established by confirming that the exercise was implemented properly. Administrative consistency, in terms of instructions, time allowed, freedom from disruptions, etc. is rudimentary. During an assessment program, the administrators should make a detailed plan for administration, adhere to the schedule, and keep a careful record of how the assessment activities progressed. A list of any "incidents" that occurred should be kept, along with notes on how the situation was handled and whether there was any apparent effect on the participants.

Follow-up evaluation should always be carried out. Evaluation can begin with the administration of simple feedback questionnaires to participants and assessors. The raw descriptive data for the ratings in exercises and the dimension ratings should be tallied and examined for unexplained high or low scores, group differences, and other rating errors. If there are enough data, more formal, psychometric evaluations of reliability and validity should be conducted. Traditional indices of item statistics and reliability (e.g., coefficient alpha) are difficult to compute because simulation exercises do not have a set of discrete test items in the same sense as multiple-choice test questions. On the other hand, the user may have the data to study the relationship of dimension and exercise ratings to other measures of performance.

SUMMARY

This examination of simulation exercises continued our theme of continuity and change. With few exceptions, present-day assessment centers continue to use the same types of exercises used for the past five decades: case studies and presentations, group discussions and games, one-on-one interaction simulations. Changes have emerged in the way simulations are conducted; they currently involve more "high-tech" elements such as video presentation of stimulus material and computer-assisted administration and scoring. Simulation exercises continue to provide a rich source of data for the evaluation of candidates' potential for long-range success, for diagnosing current skill levels, and as vehicles for developing managerial skills. Most assessment centers still include a variety of different types of exercises, ranging from simple one-on-one simulations to written case analyses and complex organizational games. Recent applications of diagnostic and developmental programs tend to involve a large number of shorter simulations rather than a small number of complex simulations. Information from interviews and paper-and-pencil tests, which was commonly a part of early assessment centers, can still provide valuable information, but such information is now frequently kept separate from assessments of behavior observed in the exercises and integrated in different ways after the assessment center. In recent years we see that any given exercise is implemented in different ways to serve a variety of purposes.

Chapter 7

The Role of Individual Assessors: Observing, Recording, Classifying, and Scaling Behavior

In the last two chapters, we discussed two main elements of the assessment center method: the types of dimensions that are appropriate for different assessment centers and the types of exercises that elicit behaviors relevant to those dimensions. In this chapter and the next, we discuss the process of evaluating behaviors to assess competence on the dimensions. This chapter describes the steps that *individual* assessors take to observe, classify, and evaluate behavior in separate exercises. Chapter 8 takes us beyond individual processing to discuss how the *group* of assessors work together to share their evaluations, determine final dimension ratings, and derive overall assessment ratings (as well as how statistical processes are used to aggregate ratings).

We begin by reviewing the general steps taken by individual assessors. We then review theory and research on cognitive processing which are relevant to how assessors carry out their duties. After gaining a clearer understanding of the assessors' processing abilities and limitations, we examine the assessor training literature. We discuss common practices and past research findings, and make recommendations as to how both assessment centers and assessor training programs might be designed to optimize assessor accuracy.

THE PROCESSES CARRIED OUT BY INDIVIDUAL ASSESSORS

In this section, we explore the processes carried out by individual assessors in assessment centers (AC). Assessment centers may vary in the specific steps carried out by assessors. That is, individual assessors may or may not assign ratings to participants on each dimension, and if they do assign ratings, this may occur at different times in the assessment process. This is discussed further in this chapter as well as in chapter 8. What is important to understand here is, despite these differences in design, there are processes common to all assessment centers. These processes are illustrated in Fig. 7.1.

As is shown, the first duty carried out by trained assessors is to observe the assessees as they participate in the simulation exercises. While observing, assessors take detailed, nonevaluative notes of the behaviors displayed by assessees. After the simulation has been completed, assessors classify the behaviors listed in their notes into the dimensions being assessed in that particular exercise. Then, the assessor might prepare a summary sheet to be used to report to the assessor group or, alternatively, the assessor may assign ratings for each dimension assessed in the exercises. The left half of Fig. 7.1 illustrates what is known as the "behavioral reporting method," which was originally devised by AT&T (Bray & Grant, 1966). The right side of the figure illustrates what has been termed the "within exercise dimension rating" or "post exercise dimension rating" method (Sackett & Tuzinski, 2001). Whichever process is used, it is repeated by assessors for each simulation exercise the assessor is assigned to observe.

After all assessees have completed all exercises, either assessors come together to discuss and determine final ratings, or the ratings are combined statistically. This part of the AC process is discussed in chapter 8. Depending on the purpose of the AC, assessors might provide assessees with oral or written feedback on their performance (this could alternatively be carried out by the AC administrator). Feedback is discussed in chapter 9. In what follows, we discuss each of the individual assessor processes in turn.

Observation and Recording of Behavior

Virtually all assessment centers follow the practice of having assessors take notes during exercises (Spychalski et al., 1997). These notes may be recorded while watching a video recording of behavior captured at a remote site. Assessors record behaviors while participants engage in group discussions, interview simulations, or other exercises. Assessors often use a blank form, similar to the one shown in Fig. 7.2, to write down details of what they observe. Behavioral observations can include overt actions that the assessee takes, and the failure to take action when it is clearly warranted.

Usually the assessor has only one chance to observe the behavior as it unfolds in the exercise. Some assessment centers video record the assessees participating in exercises (Ryan et al., 1995). This practice allows the assessors to watch the video at a convenient time and even to replay it in order to pick up subtle details. Videotaping also enables an assessor to view an exercise in which he or she was also a role player or resource person. Under nor-

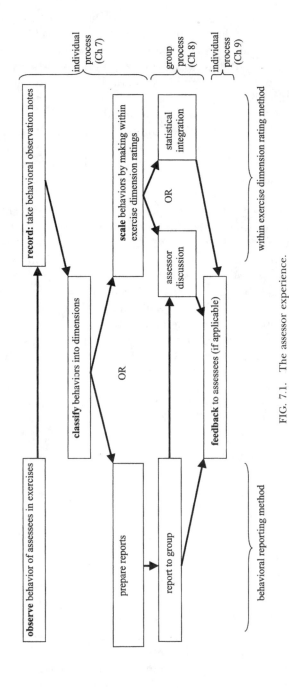

FIG. 7.1. The assessor experience.

134

Briefing Exercise
Assessor Report Form

Assessor's Name___I. Sharpe_____Date:___10-20-87_____
Participant's Name___Bob_____Assessor's Name_____

Greeted Bob warmly and shook his hand

-Sen Asked if housing arrangements were satisfactory
      Said he could understand Bob missing his family
         during training.
+Head Being alone will help you concentrate on training
         where high performance is required
      Clearly stated objectives of this briefing session
      Asked if Bob had questions
-Sen Did not answer question about second objective
      Stated "practice makes perfect"
+Head Said I want to reinforce your good skills
         and correct your weaknesses
-OC   Fumbled with words when describing first
         objective in some detail
-OC   Had poor eye contact - looked across the room
      Stated that Bob had to over-learn so as
         to handle emergencies
      Asked if there were questions
      Described second objective in more detail
      Asked if there were questions
+Head Stated that he would expect Bob to learn
         exact procedures
-OC   Looked down at table most of time
      Stated he had confidence in Bob
      Said "let's get on with it"
      Didn't ask for Bob's cooperation

FIG. 7.2.   Example of behavioral observation notes.

mal circumstances, videotaping is not recommended for most organizations because some participants feel increased stress or may even "play act" for the camera. In addition, reviewing the tape increases the time required by the assessors, and research has shown that although the practice may increase assessors' behavioral accuracy, there is only a slight increase in their rating accuracy (Ryan et al., 1995). However, videotaping is a necessity for "remote assessment centers" where assessors are not actually present to observe the assessee in real time (Bobrow & Schultz, 2002; Kudisch et al., 2001; Lovler & Goldsmith, 2002; Reynolds, 2003; Richards, 2002; Smith & Reynolds, 2002).

In the case of written exercises, such as the in-box or a case study analysis, there is a permanent record of the overt behaviors of the participant that can be scrutinized for evidence of dimension-related behaviors. In such exercises, the assessor can easily re-examine the written work to confirm what action was taken. Still, there is no substantiated difference in the reliability of assessments of written responses and overt behavior.

Few studies have directly examined the observation process of assessors. Both McIntyre and Vanetti (1988) and Lievens (2001) found that behavior observation training (in comparison with no training) led to greater accuracy. Furthermore, warnings that the candidate was generally "good" or "bad" did not interfere with observation accuracy. An in-depth study was conducted by Gaugler and Thornton (1989), who investigated the accuracy of assessors' observations of videotaped exercises. Observational accuracy was measured by calculating (a) the ratio of good observations (i.e., specific and behavioral records) to the total number of dimension-relevant behaviors actually displayed by participants (determined by experts after a careful review of the tapes) and (b) the ratio of good observations to the total number of observations made. Results showed that assessors recorded approximately 50% of the observations made by the experts and that approximately 75% of the assessors' observations were actual behaviors rather than inferences or impressions. Assessors observed a smaller percentage of the behaviors when asked to look for 9, as opposed to 6 or 3, dimensions. Research suggests that although assessors can and do make many good observations, they do not record all of the dimension-relevant behaviors that participants exhibit. Because the assessors in this study were trained for a limited amount of time, we can assume that experienced assessors would observe a larger percentage the behavioral events. The results also show that assessors have trouble making behavioral observations when asked to observe larger numbers of dimensions.

Classifying Behaviors and Preparing Reports

In addition to observing and recording the dimension-relevant behaviors displayed by assessees, assessors also *classify* these behaviors into the dimensions categories. While the assessors are observing behaviors, they may actually start the classification process by making notes that signify the dimension to which a particular behavior belongs. Figure 7.2 shows a few examples: "+OC" means effective oral communication; "-Sen" means poor sensitivity. The thorough classification process takes place very soon after the exercise is completed. Assessors look back over their notes and identify all the behaviors observed relevant to each dimension. They then record these behaviors on a separate form, shown in Fig. 7.3, to facilitate reporting to the other assessors in the integration discussion, which may take place after all the exercises have been completed.

Briefing Exercise

Oral Communication

Effective expression in individual and group situations.

+ *Clearly stated objectives*
+ *Said "practice makes perfect" to make his point emphatically*
- *Fumbled with words when describing first objective in detail*
- *Had poor eye contact*
- *Looked down at table*

Leadership

Ability to influence others, through direction and personal guidance, to achieve goals.

+ *Stated being alone will help Bob concentrate on good performance in training*
+ *Said "I want to reinforce your good skills"*
+ *Stated he expected Bob to learn exact procedures*
- *Failed to ask for Bob's cooperation*

FIG. 7.3. Example of classification of behaviors.

The classification process of assessors is an undeveloped area of research. Gaugler and Thornton (1989) calculated the ratio of good observations correctly classified by assessors to the total number of good observations classified by experts (28%) and the ratio of the total number of good observations the assessors correctly classified to the total number of good observations the assessors made (40%). Assessors were able to correctly classify far more behaviors when they had to deal with 3 dimensions than when they had to deal with 6 or 9 dimensions. The relatively weak classification accuracy scores found in this study suggest that these subjects were not making "clean" distinctions among the dimensions, but they did better when they had a small number of clearly defined dimensions. Well-trained and experienced assessors may be more effective at this task.

At the end of this process of observation and classification, the assessors have detailed narrative reports of behaviors classified into the appropriate dimensions. Assessors typically complete each of these reports soon after they view the candidates participating in the exercises. Scheduling time for assessors to complete these reports is difficult, but it must be done so that the notes and observations are fresh in assessors' minds. Research in the area of social perception shows that specific behavioral information fades quickly unless there is some record made immediately after the events take place (Fiske & Taylor, 1984; Wyer & Srull, 1986).

At this point, the assessor may take one of multiple courses of action. If following the behavior reporting method, the assessors would attend a meeting and orally present reports from each exercise. If following the within-exercise dimension rating method, the assessor would, after each exercise, rate each dimension measured in that exercise.

Presentation of Reports

If the assessors meet to integrate their observations, they discuss the performance of one participant at a time. Each assessor reads the narrative report of behaviors observed. Assessor A may report on the group discussion, Assessor B on the one-on-one simulation, Assessor C on the in-basket, then Assessor A on a fourth exercise, and so on. As illustrated in Fig. 7.3, in each narrative report, the assessor describes the behaviors he or she observed relative to the various dimensions. In their reports, assessors consider several points relevant to each dimension, for example, did the participant set a follow-up date to review performance improvements discussed in a performance appraisal simulation? While the reports are being read, the other assessors listen and may take notes on a dimension summary form similar to that shown in Fig. 7.4. There is usually one page for each dimension. This format provides a place to accumulate behavioral evidence relevant to a dimension across all exercises.

**Scaling of Behaviors: Within-Exercise Dimension
Rating Method (After Each Exercise)**

In the within-exercise dimension rating method, assessors are asked to provide a rating on each dimension that can be observed in an exercise. After they have observed and classified behaviors, assessors typically use a 1 to 5 rating scale to evaluate the participant's performance on each dimension. This very task of recording these ratings may affect individual judgments

Oral Communication   Effective expression in individual and group situations (include gestures and nonverbal communications).

1. Briefing   Overall
                                                                       <u>4</u>
2. Training
3. Debriefing

Notes

1. Briefing	+	greeted John with smile and handshake
	+	"pleased to work with you" + warm, support
	+	spoke firmly yet quietly
	-	fumbled for right words to state objective, then gave clear description
	+	maintained good eye contact
	+	slowed down his speech to make a point
2. Training	+	gave clear, brief description of objectives
	+	made small jobs about an exchange in the briefing
	+	gave overview of procedure
	-	stumbled over description of 2 steps John didn't understand
	+	showed energy and enthusiasm
	+	used hand gestures to get John involved
	-	didn't directly answer a question by John
3. Debriefing	+	stated that these were strengths and weaknesses in John's training performance
	-	didn't give clear example of poor performance
	+	reviewed positive steps in performance
	+	showed enthusiasm
	+	summarized objectives, performance, and continuing strengths and weaknesses
	+	ended on up-beat note—confidence in future

FIG. 7.4.   Example of dimensions summary form.

and the group dynamics in the assessor discussion, a topic pursued more fully in the next chapter.

Our interest now is in the quality of these within-exercise dimension ratings. What evidence is there that they are adequate measures of the attributes they supposedly measure? One way to answer this question is to compare the independent ratings given by two or more assessors. These comparisons are called estimates of interrater agreement and can range from .00 to 1.00. Ladd, Atchley, Gniatczyk, and Baumann (2002) found that the average interrater agreement of two assessors observing behavior and rating performance on the same dimensions was .83. The authors concluded that the finding suggests independent raters agree on the degree to which dimensions are exhibited by an assessee. A detailed review of the research on within-exercise dimension ratings is presented in chapter 10. We argue that the question of the reliability and validity of within-exercise dimension ratings should not be assessed at the exercise level, because exercise-specific ratings are not used to make decisions about assessees, but rather overall dimension ratings or perhaps overall assessment ratings. Likewise, how these higher level ratings are determined will depend on the integration method utilized by the assessment center program. The various integration techniques are discussed in chapter 8.

Scaling of Behaviors: Behavior Reporting Method (After All Exercises)

After all the exercise reports have been read during the assessor integration discussion in the behavioral reporting method, each assessor takes a few minutes to review the accumulated behavioral evidence and determines a rating for overall performance on that dimension. Table 7.1 illustrates the ratings determined for one participant by a group of three assessors over five dimensions.

After they have heard the preliminary reports of other assessors, but prior to any discussion, do the assessors agree on the overall dimension ratings? Here again, evidence of interrater agreement is informative of the accuracy of overall dimension ratings. Table 7.2 shows that in past assessment center studies, the level of agreement among assessors on preliminary overall dimension ratings has been found to range from *relatively low* (.50), to *moderate* (.67), to *quite high* (.94). Thomson (1970) found high levels of agreement for both psychologist assessors and management assessors. As shown in chapter 8, the levels of agreement are even higher after the integration discussion, but it should be clear that agreement could be fairly high from the start.

TABLE 7.1
Preliminary and Final Overall Dimension Ratings

Dimension	Preliminary Overall Dimension Ratings			Final Overall Dimension Rating
	Assessor A	Assessor B	Assessor C	
Leadership	4	4	4	4
Decision making	2	2	3	2
Assertiveness	2	3	3	3
Oral communication	3	4	4	3
Planning and organizing	2	2	4	4

TABLE 7.2
Studies of Agreement Among Assessors
on Preliminary Overall Dimension Ratings

Authors	Estimates of Agreement Among Assessors (average reliability)
Lievens, 2001	.62–.91
Konz, 1988	.81
Tziner & Dolan, 1982	.50
Schmitt, 1977	.67
Borman, 1982	.76
Kehoe et al., 1985	.82
McConnell & Parker, 1972	.83
Neidig & Martin, 1979	.94
Sackett & Hakel, 1979	.69

TOOLS USED TO AID OBSERVATION, CLASSIFICATION, REPORTING, AND SCALING

In this section we review some of the common tools used to aid individual assessors in various stages of the assessment process, namely, behavioral checklists and behaviorally anchored rating scales (BARS).

Behavioral Checklists

Behavioral checklists provide assessors with a checklist of behaviors that assessees might display during the course of a simulation exercise. The assessor uses the checklist by marking which behaviors occur. Figure 7.5 shows an example of some items on a behavioral checklist for a leaderless group discussion. If the assessor sees the participant start the discussion and direct its course, he or she can simply make a mark by the entry "Effectively leads the discussion." If the checklist is used to aid the behavior recording process, the assessor completes the checklist while the exercise is taking place (in lieu of or in addition to taking behavioral observation notes). Behavioral checklists might also be used as scaling or rating tools, with the behaviors listed by dimension, and scaled by proficiency, such that a score for each dimension can be computed from each checklist. This would typically occur following each exercise, but could also be used as a tool during the assessor integration session to aid discussion or for assessors to rate dimensions after all reports have been given.

The supposed advantages of a behavior checklist are that it reduces the assessors' writing time, allows the assessors freedom to watch more carefully, and can reduce the number of judgments the assessor must make

Leaderless Group Discussion Exercise

Initiative

_____ Proposes a viable method to organize the meeting

_____ Proposes to the members that an opinion be ruled out if all agree

_____ Proposes that the options initially chosen be discussed later

_____ Proposes various methods of organizing the discussion

_____ Proposes to the members that they begin by eliminating options

_____ Proposes that each member identify their priorities

_____ Proposes that each member choose one option they most prefer

_____ Keeps the discussion active by moving on to other options

_____ Proposes revisions of an option

_____ Introduces a vote before discussion has ended

_____ Proposes that if the members cannot decide between two options, they can choose the third option

_____ Introduces points that have already been mentioned

_____ Introduces the voting procedures

_____ Effectively leads the discussion

_____ Controls the discussion by speaking frequently

FIG. 7.5.   Example of behavioral checklist.

(Reilly, Henry, & Smither, 1990). The potential disadvantages of checklists are that assessors have to look through lists of behaviors to find the correct entry and may miss subsequent behaviors. Assessors still have to make judgments as to whether the listed behavior actually matches the behavior demonstrated. Furthermore, the entries on the list must be, to some extent, abstractions of specific behaviors rather than what the person actually does. Also, it is not feasible for the list to be long enough to include all behaviors that might be displayed, and thus the assessor is faced with making additional narrative notes anyway. Finally, when behavioral checklists are used after each exercise, the behaviors on each list, relevant to each dimension, will differ from exercise to exercise. These differences, in essence, redefine the dimensions each time (Joyce, Thayer, & Pond, 1994).

Although behavioral checklists are used a great deal in practice (Boyle, Fullerton, & Wood, 1995; Spychalski et al., 1997), research on the effects on convergent and discriminant relationships of within-exercise dimension ratings is mixed. There is some evidence that behavioral checklists improve assessment center ratings (Hennessy, Mabey, & Warr, 1998). Reilly et al. (1990) found that a behavior checklist (in comparison with the conventional 1 to 5 rating scale) led to greater agreement in ratings of the same dimensions across exercises, although there was no reduction in correlations of dimensions within exercises. Donahue, Truxillo, Cornwell, and Gerrity (1997) found their use to increase only discriminant validity; Fritzsche, Brannick, and Fisher-Hazucha (1994) found their use to improve construct validity very little. Research has also argued and found evidence that the effectiveness of behavioral checklists is increased when the number of behaviors on the checklist is limited to between 6 and 12 (Reilly et al., 1990; Lebreton, Gniatczyk, & Migetz, 1999), when only key behaviors are listed (Hauenstein, 1994), and when behaviors are clustered naturally as opposed to randomly (Binning, Adorno, & Kroeck, 1997).

Given a list of behaviors that might take place in an exercise, the process of designating which dimensions they reflect is a fairly logical one. Hypothetical behaviors (or behaviors observed in prior assessment centers) can be "preclassified" into the appropriate dimensions. In instances where such preclassification has taken place, computer programs in which the assessor indicates which behaviors have been displayed generate dimension scores automatically. The advantages are obvious—the assessors' task is immensely simplified. Once the behavior is checked off, it is automatically classified and the dimension score produced instantaneously. Some caution is needed, though, because this process may compound complexity at the observation stage. Assessors must still make inferences about the similarity of the demonstrated behavior to the available entries on the list. Any deficiencies in the list will be compounded in the classification process.

Behaviorally Anchored Rating Scales (BARS)

Behaviorally anchored rating scales (Smith & Kendall, 1963) are used as a tool for collecting the assessors' ratings on each assessee's performance on each dimension. There is a scale ranging from, say *not at all proficient* to *highly proficient*, and along the scale are behaviors that are illustrative of different levels of performance on that dimension. Depending on the design of the center, BARS may be completed by assessors following each exercise (this in done in the within-exercise dimension rating method). Or, they may be used by assessors to make preliminary dimension ratings after all assessor reports are given in the integration session (this is done in the behavior reporting method).

Figure 7.6 provides an example of BARS used to collect postexercise dimension ratings for one dimension. In this particular assessment center (a developmental assessment center), computerized BARS are used, and each dimension has subdimensions, which provides a "multi-item" measure of each dimension. Assessors also use this form to classify the behaviors written in their notes into the subdimension categories by typing in relevant behaviors above each BARS. These are then used in the feedback session as behavioral examples. In many assessment centers, assessors complete just one BARS per dimension.

As is shown in this example, there are behavioral anchors along the continuum of proficiency. It is important to note that, unlike behavior checklists, the behaviors that serve as anchors on BARS are not necessarily behaviors that will or should be displayed by all candidates. Instead, these behaviors are only to be used as a guide to assist assessors in their scaling of the behaviors they actually observed in the exercise relevant to the dimension of interest.

Like the research on behavior checklists, the research on BARS is also mixed. Baker (1986) and Campbell (1986) each compared the construct validity of within-exercise dimension ratings obtained from the use of a behavioral checklist to those obtained from the use of BARS. Baker (1986) found that the within-exercise dimension ratings obtained with the behavioral checklist had greater discriminant validity for the nonassigned-role leaderless group discussions, whereas the within-exercise dimension ratings resulting from the BARS format had greater discriminant validity for the assigned-role leaderless group discussions. In addition, the checklist had lower correlations among the dimensions within an exercise for both types of leaderless group discussions than the BARS format. Campbell (1986) found that the BARS format demonstrated superior discriminant validity, but neither format exhibited superior convergent validity.

Summary

Taken together, these studies point to the differential effect various rating formats may have on subsequent judgments. Unfortunately, the data lack consistency and are too limited to determine if there is one "superior" rating format. This same conclusion, that is, no single format is superior to the others, has been drawn from research on performance appraisal (Bernardin & Beatty, 1984; Murphy & Cleveland, 1991).

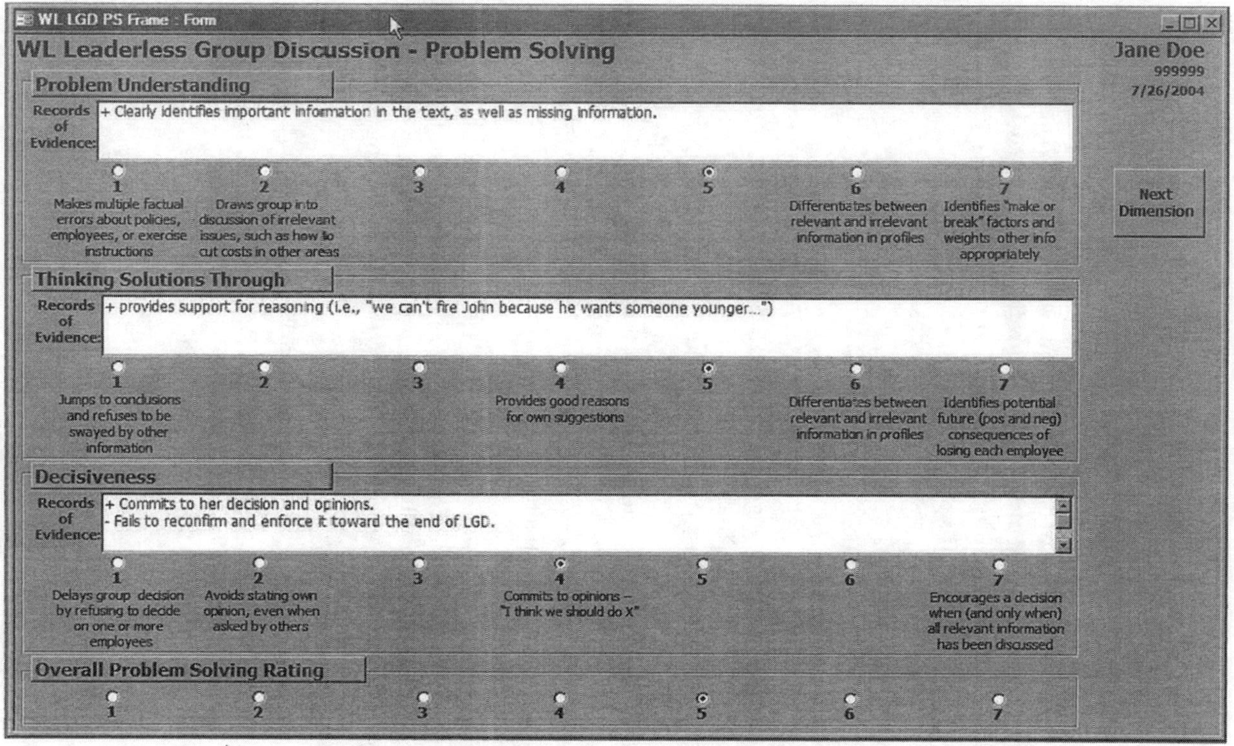

FIG. 7.6. Example of behaviorally anchored rating scales (BARS).

145

SOCIAL COGNITION AND ASSESSOR PROCESSING

Now that we have described the procedural steps individual assessors carry out, we turn our attention to the internal, cognitive processes required to observe, record, classify, and scale assessee behaviors. The literature on cognitive processing reminds us that assessors are not necessarily "superheroes." Their cognitive and attention resources are finite, and they may be prone to assessment errors. In this section we review two major approaches to social cognition that inform our understanding of assessor cognitive processing: schema-driven approaches and behavior-driven approaches (see Fig. 7.7). Then, in the subsequent section, we discuss how thorough assessor training and the procedures of the assessment center method maximize assessor accuracy.

Schema-Driven Theory

Schema-driven theories suggest that we have limited capacities to attend to the vast array of environmental stimuli to which we are exposed (Fiske & Taylor, 1984), and thus, we must selectively attend to only some events (Alba & Hasher, 1983). The direction of this selectivity is shaped by the schema we hold in our mind. A schema is a mental picture, model, or belief about the topic we are observing. According to schema theory, also termed a top-down approach, a cognitive categorization model (Nisbett & Ross, 1980), and a limited capacity model (Lievens & Klimoski, 2001), this selective perception operates in a predictable way: We tend to undersample relevant observations (Cooper, 1981; Major, 1980). That is, we make relatively few observations that are pertinent to the judgments we must make. In social perception more specifically, according to schema-driven theory, our prior knowledge of an individual influences our subsequent observations of

	Behavior-Driven Theory	**Schema-Driven Theory**
Alternate terms	Bottom-up approach Behavioral model Data-driven approach	Top-down approach Cognitive categorization model
Basis of evaluation	Behavior displayed by person	Behavior beliefs and stereotypes about person
Memory storage	Specific actions	General impressions
Quality of judgment	Objective	Subjective

FIG. 7.7.   Comparison of two theories of social judgment.

that person's behavior. The prior knowledge might be information about the person's lack of education or poor job performance, or it might be an initial impression formed in the first few minutes of interaction. According to this view, the observer has a difficult time withholding judgment until all the evidence is in. Thus, there may be a process of selective perception that filters out details not consistent with the existing knowledge (Cooper, 1981). The processes proposed by schema theory have implications for each step carried out by assessors (Burrus, 2004).

The processes of observing and classifying behaviors may be influenced by a schema. With regard to observing behaviors, assessors' observations may be biased due to faulty classification schemes. Schema theories emphasize that the classification schemes we use are often just devices to help us simplify our observations and may not be meaningful categories. The categories we use, the associations we make among specific behaviors within categories, and the associations we make among categories may be artificially created by the implicit personality theories we hold about people (Cooper, 1981). An implicit personality theory is the set of beliefs and assumptions we have about which traits go together. For example, you may believe that people who speak fluently are intelligent. According to schema theory, these systems of beliefs may be artificially created and not based on real behavior. If assessors use such classification schemes and implicit personality theories when observing assessees, they are at risk of observing, recording, and reporting behaviors in a biased or inaccurate way.

It is also important to remember how quickly exercises pass before assessors. That is, assessors must observe and record behaviors at a very fast rate (Lievens & Klimoski, 2001). In such situations, they are at risk of relying more on their schemas than every single behavior that unfolds in the exercise. We are also reminded by Lievens and Klimoski of the inferential leaps that the assessors must make when classifying behaviors. Schema-based cognitive processing may evolve as a method of reducing the cognitive load sometimes experienced by assessors.

The process of reporting behaviors to other assessors in the integration may be influenced by schema. When presenting their reports, assessors rely heavily on the notes they have taken while observing the exercises. However, because they cannot write down every detail, assessors must frequently rely on their memory. To what extent can assessors recall the actual events that take place? According to the schema theory, memory is predominantly composed of abstract representations or interpretations of events we have witnessed (Cooper, 1981; Fiske & Taylor, 1984). This perspective says that while *short-term* memory may consist of accurate details, *long-term* memory consists largely of general categories lacking in detail (Wyer & Srull, 1986). Furthermore, any detail transferred to long-term memory remains there only for a limited period of time. Decay takes place, and this decay is selective: According to this theory, we tend to retain only those bits of information that are consistent with the general impressions we hold about the person.

An even more extreme process, called reconstruction, is proposed by other theorists (Cooper, 1981). In this process, observers reconstruct events that never took place; in other words, they believe that events took place that are consistent with their initial impressions, when, in fact, those events never actually happened. In an assessment center we would be troubled if an assessor falsely recalled that his or her favored participant summarized the group's final conclusions when, in fact, another person had done so.

Finally, the process of scaling behaviors may be influenced by schema. Schema-driven theory proposes that people develop and use simple guiding principles for making judgments about others. The theory says we make judgments on the basis of very little information instead of the abundant information that is usually available. This position holds that because of selective memory decay, integration and judgment will depend more on information that is consistent with our general impression of the participant. Fiske and Taylor (1984) summarized much research suggesting that internal impressions, rather than detailed episodes in memory, are easier for people to recall and thus will dominate our evaluations. Feldman (1981) suggested further that we will "reconstruct" or invent events that will fill in empty spaces in memory in order to substantiate and support our judgment. Lievens and Klimoski (2001) argued that assigning ratings to behaviors which have been classified by dimensions also requires an inferential leap, which may lead assessors to rely on schema-based processing.

One simple schema that assessors may use is their first, general impression of an assessee. Lance, Foster et al. (2004) provided evidence to support the notion that assessors initially form a general impression of an assessee's performance that then influences ratings on specific dimensions. This effect may have been due to the requirement that assessors in this study were asked to rate the candidate's overall performance before assigning the dimension ratings, although Lance, Foster et al. refute this explanation.

The most thorough criticism of human inferential processes is provided by Nisbett and Ross (1980). They claim that humans use several heuristic procedures, or "rules of thumb," which introduce errors in the decision process. Research has shown heuristic-based processing is common in situations where there is time pressure to complete a task, and the use of such processing often leads to errors in judgment (Goodie & Crooks, 2004). In assessment center contexts, where assessors are forced to make judgments under time pressure, several different cognitive heuristics might be used.

The *anchoring and adjustment heuristic* (Tversky & Kahneman, 1974) is often used by individuals who are judging others. This involves looking for some sort of quick reference point to anchor evaluations, and then adjusting one's ratings around that anchor (Fiske & Taylor, 1984). Research has shown that people often overestimate their abilities relative to others on simple tasks, and underestimate their abilities relative to others on complex tasks (Kruger, 1999). Assessors falling prey to such a phenomenon may inaccurately rate assesses when they anchor to themselves, or even to the first of multiple assessees they have to evaluate (Burrus, 2004).

Other similar heuristics may be used as well. The *representativeness heuristic* (Nisbett & Ross, 1980) is used when objects are assigned to categories after one observation, and we proceed to make judgments based on presumed category membership. The problem with this cognitive shortcut is that this initial classification may be inaccurate, and will cloud all subsequent judgments. In an assessment center context, this becomes a problem when assessors have misclassified behaviors into dimensions, because regardless of what additional evidence emerges counter to this categorization, assessors will use the original categorization as the main point of judgment, which could lead to inaccurate ratings.

The *availability heuristic* is used when individuals use information that is readily available in memory to make judgments about frequency, probability, and causality. The problem with the use of availability is that if the most readily accessible information is invalid or uncharacteristic, faulty judgments will result. It is possible for something to occur in the course of a simulation exercise that remains prominent in the assessor's memory. This single bit of information may be used to rate the assessee on dimensions rather than all of the rich behavioral information available to the assessor. Related to this, the *salience and vividness* heuristic involves putting put more weight on readily available, visible, and outstanding information. The use of this heuristic is problematic because vividness is not usually relevant to the value of the information on which assessors should be basing their judgments.

These and other shortcomings in our judgment processes make it particularly difficult for us to make accurate predictions about future events. All hope is not lost, though, as we see later. Nisbett and Ross (1980) pointed out circumstances when human judgment is quite adequate to accomplish great feats. These circumstances are established by assessment center procedures.

Behavior-Driven Theory

A very different view is provided by behavior-driven theories, which emphasize that observers are able to observe and remember specific behaviors (Hintzman, 1986, 1988). The behavior-driven approach has also been called a data-driven approach (Abelson, 1981), a bottom-up approach (Fiske & Taylor, 1984), a behavior model of human judgment (Borman, 1977, 1978), and a rational model (Lievens & Klimoski, 2001). These terms convey the idea that we are capable of attending to the detailed behavior of other people, storing memories of specific events, and forming objective judgments based on what actually takes place (Wegner & Bargh, 1998). Research has shown that when observing others, people perceive and remember most of the social interactions that take place (Hastie & Kumar, 1979; Locksley, Borgida, Brekke, & Hepburn, 1980). Each observation becomes represented in memory by several different features (Kintsch & vanDijk, 1978; Linville, Fischer, & Salovey, 1989); for example, a segment of a leaderless group discussion is stored in memory in terms of who was speaking, what was said, nonverbal gestures that accompanied the words, and what reactions were elicited from the audience. Summarizing much of the literature on social cognition, Higgins and Bargh (1987) concluded "people apparently encode environmental information fairly accurately without supplementing the original information with previous knowledge" (p. 373).

There is much theoretical support for the assumption that observers can make and retain careful observations of the complex behavior that takes place in the exercises. Furthermore, there is both direct and indirect experimental evidence from studies in numerous areas of psychology that specific behavioral observations can be made and retained. Direct observation of behavior is widely used in behavioral assessment (Foster & Cone, 1986), behavior modification, and behavior therapy (Kazdin, 1984). There is a long history of these procedures (all based on the ability to observe and give feedback about specific behaviors) being used for the treatment of alcoholism, eating disorders, depression, and mental retardation (Leitenberg, 1976). All these examples illustrate that people can and do make objective observations of specific behaviors.

Hintzman (1986, 1988) argued that *all* experience is recorded in human perceptual processes. Likewise, Johnson and Raye (1981) argued that all perceptual events produce persistent memory traces. Such claims may seem exaggerated, and few would claim that humans perceive and store in long-term memory literally all of the stimuli hitting our senses. But, the primary issue is whether we can record details of observations if we are asked to do so. Theory and research suggest we can. This view also has obvious implications for various steps in the assessment process, which we discuss next.

In terms of behavioral observation, the two different views of social perception (schema- and behavior-driven) may both be true under certain circumstances. The question then is, when and under what conditions is one or the other process likely to operate. Fiske and Taylor (1984) maintain that more detailed records of experiences will be stored in memory and can be remembered if the observer takes the task seriously. In addition, Nathan and Lord (1983) have shown that when observers can see how behaviors fit into meaningful mental patterns, there will be a direct record of specific details stored in long-term memory. Other research shows that the purpose of observation determines what is observed and selected (Higgins & Bargh, 1987). In most everyday social interactions, individuals need to form only general impressions of other people. Thus, we tend to extract and retain overall impressions, a fact that supports the schema-driven approach. On the other hand, when people are told that the purpose of observation is to note details in what they observe, they can in fact do so. Furthermore, if accuracy is stressed, and raters are held accountable for their judgments, details are noted, selected, and retained quite thoroughly (Alba & Hasher, 1983; Mero & Motowidlo, 1995). These are the very conditions that exist in assessment centers: assessors take the task seriously, dimensions provide meaningful categories, assessors are responsible for reporting behaviors, and accuracy is stressed.

Next we consider the relevance of this theory to the processes of classifying and scaling behaviors. In contrast to the notion that attribute dimensions may be artificial categories, other theory and research suggest that these dimensions are meaningful and "real" categories. Support for the idea that dimensions are meaningful categories comes from work by Rosch, Mervis, Gray, Johnson, and Boyes-Braem (1976) on physical objects, and by Hampson, John, and Goldberg (1986) on social activities. According to these researchers, natural categories exist in various areas of our thinking, and these categories are perceived quite generally across samples of people. Furthermore, we are able to perceive information about objects that allows us to categorize objects and behaviors into the natural categories. In the assessment center context, these ideas support the notion that there are meaningful categories, such as "leadership" behaviors and "decision-making" behaviors. Furthermore, it implies that assessors can observe behaviors such as "the participant suggested that the group spend 15 minutes on each of four problems and the suggestion was followed by the group" and distinguish it from the behavior "participant stated three reasons why he would not put sales representatives on commission." The first is an example of leadership, and the second is an example of decision making.

The theory underlying the development of behaviorally anchored rating scales (Smith & Kendall, 1963) provides another bit of support for the belief that observers can meaningfully classify behavior. This technique assumes that work behaviors can be sorted consistently into meaningful categories. Using this technique, supervisors observe work behaviors, classify these behaviors into categories, and over time accumulate evidence to support ratings of meaningful areas of work performance.

In the context of performance appraisal research, Nathan and Lord (1983) provided further evidence that observers can classify behaviors into separate categories and make ratings based on actual behaviors displayed. In an experiment, they found that poor behaviors of the "good performers" and good behaviors of the "poor performers" had a clear impact on the ratings. General impressions of overall effectiveness had some effect on the ratings of dimensions, but the raters were clearly able to distinguish among the behaviors and dimensions they were rating.

Conclusions Regarding Assessor Cognitive Processing

We have seen two clear and well-developed points of view about how interpersonal perception and judgment unfolds: the schema-driven and behavior-driven theories. We have seen theoretical and empirical research support for each one. A logical question is, "Which point of view is most accurate in an assessment center context?" It is probably inappropriate to seek a definitive answer to this question. Neither of these approaches explains what happens in all instances of interpersonal judgment in all assessment centers. A better approach is to try to understand *when* each process occurs, *what conditions* foster behavior-based or schema-based evaluation, and *what can be learned* from each theoretical position that will foster better assessment.

The research contains some hints about the conditions governing the two opposing approaches. If people are simply forming general impressions of others, then schema are more likely to affect observations, memory, and judgments (Fiske & Taylor, 1984). On the other hand, if people are told to observe details, they can and do perceive and retain a vast amount of specific information (Sherman, Judd, & Park, 1989). If observers must rely on memory, implicit personality theories may come to mind, and artificially high relationships among the dimensions may result (Cooper, 1981). But if some device—such as a diary—is used to record observations, halo error in the form of artificially high relationships among rated dimensions is reduced (Bernardin & Walter, 1977). Nathan and Lord (1983) have shown that if behaviors fit into clear cognitive dimensions, observers are able to put observations directly into long-term memory, but if observers do not have a clear understanding of the categories, they will not recall real behaviors and may in fact reconstruct events to fit the general schemata they hold (Alba & Hasher, 1983). Nisbett and Ross (1980) contend that when individuals are given instructions to engage in careful problem solving, they use more systematic, scientific strategies for making inferences. Swann (1984) suggested that accuracy in human perception is greater when the judge is making situation-specific predictions than when he or she is making global or transsituational predictions. Accuracy is greater because the observer is examining only a limited set of behaviors and can be more familiar with the specific situation and with the surrounding situations to which inferences are being made.

The schema- versus behavior-driven distinction is similar to and often overlaps with the controlled versus automatic processing distinction in the realm of social information processing (see Fiske, 1993; Wegner & Bargh, 1998). Controlled processing is conscious and systematic, whereas automatic processing occurs unconsciously and also involves the use of heuristics as discussed earlier. What is important for our purposes here is that decades of experimental research show that although social judgment can often occur quickly, offline, and involve the use of many stereotypes, attributions, and cognitive heuristics, in many situations, social judgment occurs in a much more controlled manner. In the words of Wegner and Bargh (1998):

> If one is motivated to form an accurate, fleshed-out impression of an individual, the control process will attend to and pick up individuating details about that person, so that the impression will not be based only on the automatically supplied input (largely stereotypic assumptions based on easily observable features). (p. 478)

Given that cognitive biases are reduced when the judgment-maker is motivated (Kunda & Sinclair, 1999), the question is: Are assessors motivated? We answer with a resounding yes! When assessors are members of the organization conducting the assessment center, they may have volunteered for the position or have been nominated to serve as an assessor in recognition of their managerial competence and reputation as good judge of people. Furthermore, there is a great deal of structure within an assessment center program, which serves to guide assessors' judgment processes. Assessors are provided multiple opportunities to observe assessee behavior and given multiple tools to aid in the judgment process. These include behavioral observation note sheets, behavioral checklists, BARS, and other resources. Likewise, assessors are also held accountable for their judgments, such as in the integration discussion and feedback sessions (Lievens & Klimoski, 2001; Mero & Motowidlo, 1995). And finally, as discussed in detail in subsequent sections, assessors are trained in their roles. Such a situation causes far more motivation than the typical laboratory conditions where much of the social cognition research takes place.

This line of reasoning is akin to Lievens and Klimoski's (2001) *expert model* of assessor judgment. This model posits that, assessors are professionals in their roles. They have been trained and have gained experience. Therefore they have developed and utilize well-established cognitive structures when evaluating assessees. This model also argues that assessors abstract from their past experience and training in order to observe, recall, record, classify, and scale behaviors with accuracy (Sagie & Magnezy, 1997). We discuss the empirical evidence for assessor accuracy in more detail in our chapter on assessment center validity (chap. 10).

All of these bits of evidence suggest there is good reason to have confidence that assessors can make effective judgments about managerial competencies if the conditions are right. We have seen how many of these conditions are built into the assessment center method:

- Assessors are given time to make specific observations and take notes.
- Assessors make ratings soon after observations and do not have to rely on long-term memory.
- Dimensions for effective performance are clearly defined.
- Assessors often have no vested interest in the outcome and can look at behavioral evidence objectively.
- Assessors are making predictions about success in specific jobs that are familiar to them.

The question now becomes one of training. That is, how might assessors be trained to make accurate judgments? We now turn to this topic.

TRAINING ASSESSORS TO OBSERVE, RECORD, CLASSIFY, AND SCALE BEHAVIORS

Assessor training typically covers a combination of knowledge, skills, abilities, and general information (International Task Force, 2000):

- knowledge of the organization and setting;
- knowledge of the purpose of the assessment center;
- information about how participants were informed of the assessment center;
- discussion of and practice in avoiding common errors of observation and rating;
- description and discussion of the dimensions to be observed and assessed;
- description of, participation in, and observation of mock participants in the exercises;
- study of and practice with assessor support materials, including checklists, rating scales;
- frame of reference training to develop common expectations of performance and the meaning of levels on the rating scales.

Taking Advantage of Behavior-Driven Processing:
Process Training

The most classic form of assessor training takes a behavior-driven approach.
This technique, which is also known as behavior-driven rater training (Lievens & Thornton, in press), is by far the most common training method
used by organizations. Proponents of this method argue that since research
has shown that individuals have the ability to systematically carry out the
judgment process, training should be designed to impose the prescribed assessment process onto assessors. That is, assessors are trained in the steps of
the assessment process (i.e., observe, record, classify, rate). The sequence
of steps is strictly enforced such that assessors can learn to distinguish the
assessment stages from one another and learn to only carry out the assessment process sequentially.

Process training often includes both lectures and practice with exercises
focused on the facilitation of each step in the assessment process. The training can also include a full example at the end of the training session, where
assessors watch a videoed simulation exercise and carry out the individual
assessment process start to finish. A key to success in this type of training is
practice. Training should focus on providing assessors experience in the
process such that they learn to use a systematic judgment process that is
free of observation and rating biases, stereotypes, false attributions, and
faulty cognitive heuristics. Such practice appears to help, in that research
has shown that experienced assessors outperform inexperienced assessors
(Kolk, Born, Van der Flier, & Olman, 2002). Process training gives assessors
such experience. Given the increasing rate at which women and minorities
are entering managerial positions (Triandis et al., 1993), and the potential
for bias members of such groups face in performance evaluation situations
(see Burke & McKeen, 1996; Cheng, 1997; Dipboye, 1985; Eagly, Makhijani, & Klonsky, 1992; Heilman, 1995; Heilman et al., 2004; Perry, 1997;
Swim, Borgida, Maruyama, & Myers, 1989; Tomkiewicz et al., 1998), it is
also necessary to train assessors to guard against the demographic stereotypes tied to both individuals and job tasks when observing and evaluating
behaviors.

Taking Advantage of Schema-Driven Processing:
Frame of Reference Training

All of the process training in the world won't keep assessors from using automatic processing. We are, after all, "cognitive misers" (Fiske & Taylor,
1984). To simplify our lives, we often rely on schema when processing our
observations of others. In particular, being an assessor is a highly demand-

ing task cognitively. Assessors must complete multiple tasks at once and work under strict time pressure. Therefore, to say that we can remove schema-driven processing from the assessment processing would be an impossible goal. What we can do, however, is take advantage of the benefits of schema-driven processing.

This is exactly what schema-driven training does. Although not always labeled as such, elements of the schema-driven training have long been a part of assessor training (Thornton & Byham, 1982). Assessors have been informed about the target job and organization, instructed in the dimensions to evaluate, trained to recognize behaviors demonstrating effective and ineffective levels. In recent years a method commonly referred to as *frame of reference training* came out of the performance appraisal literature (Arvey & Murphy, 1998; Bernardin & Buckley, 1981; Woehr, 1994; Woehr & Huffcutt, 1994), and has been gaining popularity among assessment center researchers and practitioners (Lievens, 2001; Schleicher & Day, 1998; Schleicher, Day, Mayes, & Riggio, 2002; Thornton & Rupp, 2003). The essence of the technique is to impose an accurate implicit theory of performance on the assessors. To do so, a great deal of effort is placed on training the assessors on the nature of the target job as well as the performance dimensions being assessed. What emerges is a common frame of reference, or a shared schema of what high and low proficiency on each dimension actually looks like. In other words, the focus is on the behaviors likely to be displayed by assessees with varying degrees of proficiency on each of the dimensions. As such, the administrator is ensuring that the assessors are acting as if they were of one mind—every behavior would be observed, recorded, and evaluated the same way by each assessor. By imposing a performance schema on assessors, it is, in fact, appropriate to use automatic processing during times of cognitive overload. Assessors are being trained to be automatically accurate.

In addition to spending a great deal of time discussing the nature of the job and the meaning of the dimensions (at various levels of proficiency), this method might also include practice activities where assessors practice assessing a videoed exercise individually, and have discussions about any difference in ratings assigned by individual assessors. This allows assessors to "calibrate" themselves with one another, hence strengthening the common frame of reference.

Research has shown the benefits of training assessors to work from a common schema. That is, assessors who are trained in this way show more agreement in their assessments of candidates, they are better able to differentiate between the dimensions being assessed, they are more accurate in their judgments, and their ratings are more predictive of the candidates' future performance (Goodstone & Lopez, 2001; Lievens, 1999, 2001; Schleicher et al., 2002).

Which Type of Training Is Best? (Answer: Both!)

Given we have argued that both behavior-driven and schema-driven processing occur in the context of assessment centers, and that both training techniques are helpful for increasing assessor accuracy, the question remains of which training method organizations should actually use. The major difference between the two methods has to do with the implicit approach to information processing (Thornton & Rupp, 2003). Process training takes a bottom-up approach, whereby assessors are trained to start by observing discrete behaviors and proceed sequentially to classify and evaluate them. Frame of reference training on the other hand takes a top-down approach in that assessors are trained to start with the performance schema and scan the array of behaviors displayed by an assessee for behaviors that fit with the schema. One of the more difficult skills for assessors to develop is the recognition that the failure to act, when action is appropriate, may be a "behavior" that is evidence of poor performance on a dimension. Two examples illustrate this principle. In an in-box exercise, if the assessee fails to request that a subordinate notify him of the results of a meeting attended in his absence, this is evidence of poor management and supervision. In a group discussion, if the assessee fails to correct an obvious error in information presented by another discussant, this is evidence of poor decision making and judgment.

Lievens (2001) conducted an experiment that compared the effectiveness of process training, frame of reference training, and minimal training (consisting of information and an exercise about the organization, job, assessment center, dimensions, and rating scales). Results indicated that both the process training and the frame of reference training led to significantly better interrater reliability, rating accuracy, and dimension differentiation than the minimal training. In other words, careful training helped. Furthermore, the frame of reference training outperformed the process training on each of these factors. However, those assessors who had received the frame of reference training generated fewer descriptive behaviors than those who had undergone process training, an outcome that is very important for developmental centers, where detailed behavioral feedback is often more important than evaluation of specific levels of dimension performance.

So where does this lead us? Due to the differences between these two training strategies in approach, orientation, theoretical foundation, and impact, one might suggest that maybe frame of reference training should be used for selection/promotion and diagnostic centers, and process training should be used for developmental centers. However, we argue, as we have in the past (Thornton & Rupp, 2003), that assessment center architects should build assessment centers based on a mixed theory of observation (Ebbesen, 1981) that pulls from both of these approaches. That is, assessors can be trained to *both* carefully and sequentially carry out the process, *while at the same time* remain cognizant of the performance model and dimension definitions adopted by the assessment program. Assessor training programs should also provide training on common behavioral observation and rating errors (e.g., halo, leniency, severity, stereotypes), the assessment center *Guidelines*, and the ethics of being an assessor.

SUMMARY

This chapter has presented a large amount of information dealing with the practice, theory, and research related to the processes individual assessors carry out in observing, classifying, and evaluating behavior in an assessment center. There is mixed support for each step in the assessment process: Some theory and research supports the accuracy of these processes, and other theory and research does not. The nonsupportive evidence suggests a need to improve the assessment center method, and many innovations have been proposed.

The review of theory and research in this chapter leads to the conclusion that the proclivities for assessors to use both schema-driven and behavior-driven processing while assessing can be capitalized on and incorporated into the assessor training program. Assessors can be trained to follow a very systematic process for observing, recording, classifying, and scaling behaviors. They can also be trained to form a shared schema of how a competent person in the job of interest should act in different situations. Based on this information, we argue that the characteristics inherent to an assessment center, coupled with a thorough training program (involving process- and schema-based training) can lead to reliable and valid assessor judgments.

WHAT HAPPENS NEXT: INTEGRATION, REPORT GENERATING, AND FEEDBACK

Now that we have discussed at length the behavioral and cognitive processes carried out by *individual* assessors, we turn to the *group* processes required of the assessor panel. Returning to Fig. 7.1, we are reminded that individual assessors observe, record, classify, and scale behaviors. Looking at the middle of the figure, we see that after individual assessors carry out these functions, there may be the opportunity for the assessors to come together to discuss their individual experiences and come to a consensus on each assessee's performance on each dimension and/or their performance across the entire assessment process. Chapter 8 walks us through this process, as well as the host of *group processing* phenomena that are relevant to these activities. Then, in chapter 9, we talk more specifically about the process of giving feedback in assessment center contexts.

The Role of the Group of Assessors: Integration of Assessment Information

Chapter 7 covered the processes each *individual assessor* carries out to observe behaviors in individual exercises and classify behaviors into performance dimensions. Up to this point, the process is essentially one of individual judgment. That is, behaviors are recorded and ratings are possibly made by individual assessors as they watch participants in the exercises. We now turn to the processes by which the observations and evaluations of the *group of assessors* are integrated across assessors, exercises, and dimensions to determine ratings and feedback, as applicable. We trace the historical trend of integration procedures and see a movement from judgmental and holistic processes to statistical and molecular processes. A return to pure behavioral feedback is evidenced in some developmental assessment centers.

The journey we take through this chapter exposes us to many new paths that have been forged by assessment center practitioners since the 1960s. The ways in which observations of multiple assessors have been integrated are probably more diverse than any feature of the assessment center method. A full picture of these many changes in integration processes requires an elaborate and lengthy presentation. The patient reader will be rewarded with a full understanding of the many ways assessment centers can be adapted to meet the specific needs of organizations with diverse goals.

PROCESSES CARRIED OUT BY THE GROUP OF ASSESSORS

A variety of different practices are followed in integrating observations and evaluations from individual assessors. A continuum of integration processes ranges from pure judgmental to pure statistical:

- Judgmental integration methods: Assessors discuss their observations of behavior, and come to consensus on behaviors to be fed back and/ or ratings to be given.
- Statistical integration methods: Ratings by individual assessors after each exercise are combined quantitatively with a statistical formula.

Table 8.1 depicts a representative sample of the methods that have been carried out in various assessment centers. At the far left is what can be called the purely judgmental method. This method is often utilized in developmental assessment centers. Assessors observe and integrate behavioral observations, but no numerical ratings are given because the sole purpose is to give developmental feedback on behavioral performance. The example of the developmental assessment center in chapter 4 described the operation of one such program utilizing a judgmental method of integrating the information from different assessors. (That program also calls for assessors to make ratings but the numerical data are for research purposes and not operational feedback.)

Next in line is the integration method carried out by the early adopters of the assessment center method such as AT&T, Standard Oil of Ohio, IBM, and Sears (Thornton & Byham, 1982); it has been called the behavior reporting method. A single assessor observes and then reports behavior to the other assessors, who listen and take notes on a dimension summary form illustrated in Fig. 7.4 (see p. 139). Assessors then render independent dimension ratings after hearing all behavior relevant to each dimension. Discussion and consensus follows to produce final dimension ratings. Optionally, assessors then derive final overall assessment ratings.

A hybrid method, depicted in the middle of Table 8.1 and called the within-exercise dimension rating method, has been used extensively in recent years. It calls for individual assessors to provide ratings on each dimension after observing behavior in only one exercise. These ratings have been called postexercise dimension ratings (Sackett & Tuzinski, 2001), and have been the subject of much research. They were originally recorded as a way for assessors to tentatively supplement and summarize the behavioral observations that were reported; they were never meant to be used for any decision making. Assessment center designers and users recognized that any within-exercise dimension rating was a product of one observer evaluating behavior in one dimension in one exercise. Statistical analyses of the within-exercise dimension ratings have led to extensive controversy about the construct validity of assessment centers, a topic we explore in chapter 10. After agreement on the dimension ratings is achieved, overall assessment ratings are sometimes given and consensus reached.

Moving toward the more statistical approaches of combining ratings is the method we label the modified statistical method. This procedure is car-

TABLE 8.1

Various Methods of Integrating Assessment Center Observations and Ratings

Purely Judgmental: Development Centers	Modified Judgmental: Behavior Reporting Method	Hybrid Methods: Within-Exercise Rating Method	Modified Statistical: Public Jurisdictions	Purely Statistical
One or more assessors observe, record, and classify behaviors in each exercise.	A single assessor observes, records, and classifies behavior in each exercise.	A single assessor observes, records, classifies, and scales behavior in each exercise.	Two or more assessors observe, record, classify, and rate behaviors in an exercise, providing initial, independent, within-exercise dimension ratings.	Two or more assessors observe, record, classify, and rate behaviors in an exercise. There is no discussion.
Assessors meet and share observations across exercises.	Assessors meet and share observations across exercises.	The assessor renders within-exercise dimension ratings.	If the ratings are no more than one point apart (on a 5-point scale), these ratings are recorded as final. If there is more than one point difference, the assessors discuss until they come to adequate agreement.	The ratings are averaged across the two or more assessors, then across the several exercises to yield overall dimension ratings, and finally across the dimensions to yield the overall assessment rating.
The feedback to be given to each participant, in terms of behaviors demonstrating effective and ineffective behavior.	Assessors give independent ratings of overall dimension performance.	Assessors meet and share observations and dimension ratings for the exercises.	No meeting is held; the ratings are averaged across the two or more assessors, then across the several exercises to yield the overall dimension ratings, and finally across the dimensions to yield the overall assessment rating.	
	Assessors discuss dimension ratings and come to consensus on final dimension ratings.	Assessors give independent ratings of overall dimension performance.		
	Optional: Assessors give independent overall assessment ratings, then discuss to consensus.	Assessors discuss dimension ratings and come to consensus on final dimension ratings.		
		Optional: Assessors give independent overall assessment ratings, then discuss to consensus.		

ried out by many fire and police jurisdictions in promotional examinations where a high degree of formality is needed. Two or more assessors watch each exercise and render independent within-exercise dimension ratings. If the ratings are within, say, one point of each other on a 5-point scale, the assessors need not have a discussion. If the ratings are more than one point apart, the assessors discuss observations to clarify what took place, then re-rate until the difference is reduced. Subsequently, the ratings are aggregated across assessors, exercises, and dimensions to yield an overall assessment center rating. Dimensions may be given different weights to reflect their importance in the job.

The purely statistical integration method eliminates any discussion among assessors. After observation, assessors record within-exercise dimension ratings which are then aggregated across exercises and dimensions. Again, dimensions may be given different weights to reflect their importance on the job.

Advantages and Disadvantages of Judgmental and Statistical Integration Methods

These and other variations of integration methods are discussed in this chapter. Table 8.2 summarizes some of the advantages and disadvantages of judgmental and statistical integration procedures, as becomes apparent as the chapter unfolds. Judgmental methods have the potential to yield deeper insights into each individual's pattern or configuration of strengths and weak-

TABLE 8.2
Comparison of Statistical and Judgmental Integration Methods

Method of Integration	Advantages	Disadvantages
Statistical	Appearance of objectivity	May not account for meaningful configurations among information
	Takes less time	
	Supported by some evidence	Large samples are needed for stable weights
Judgmental	Provides unique insights into each candidate's strengths and weaknesses	Takes more time
		May be subject to biases of assessors' judgments
	Can take into account idiosyncratic information	May not be consistent over time
	Supported by some evidence	

nesses at the level of specific behaviors. These insights are in line with the original purposes of the holistic assessment center methods pioneered by the Office of Strategic Services (OSS, 1948) and early industrial adopters of the assessment center method (Thornton & Byham, 1982). In contrast, the statistical methods have the potential to yield more precise, quantitative differentiations among individuals when direct interindividual comparisons are called for (e.g., police and fire promotional examinations).

THEORIES OF JUDGMENT

Now that the general processes and the steps of some of the various integration methods have been described, we turn to theories of judgment and group decision making to understand the integration processes of the assessment center method. Even though considerable research has been conducted on the assessment centers using various integration methods, it is virtually impossible to form conclusions about the relative effectiveness of these methods because various studies have used different variations on each method, different criterion measures taken at different points in time, and different combinations of dimensions, exercises, and assessors. Lievens and Klimoski (2001) noted the lack of research on group processes in assessment centers, but it is easy to understand the reluctance of organizations to experiment with variations in assessment practices in operational assessment centers.

In the following sections, we review two sets of theories relevant to the integration processes. First, we discuss theories relevant to the judgments made after assessors hear information presented by the individual assessors. Second, we discuss theories relevant to the processes of groups working together to form judgments and evaluations. Each of these theories is discussed as they apply to selected steps in the assessment center integration discussion.

BEHAVIOR RECALL, SHARING, AND JUDGMENT

We now explore two theories and principles from schema-driven and behavior-driven theories as they relate to sharing information in the integration process.

Schema-Driven Theory

When presenting their reports, assessors rely heavily on the notes they have taken while observing the exercises. However, because they cannot write down every detail, assessors must frequently rely on their memory. During an integration discussion, assessors may ask each other questions about a candidate's behavior. To what extent can assessors recall the actual events that take place? As discussed in chapter 7, according to the schema theory, unaided memory may be predominantly composed of abstract representations or interpretations of events we have witnessed (Cooper, 1981; Fiske & Taylor, 1984). This perspective says that although *short-term* memory may consist of accurate details, *long-term* memory consists largely of general categories lacking in detail (Wyer & Srull, 1986). Furthermore, any detail transferred to long-term memory may remain there only for a limited period of time. Decay takes place, and this decay is selective: According to this theory, we tend to retain only those bits of information that are consistent with the general impressions we hold. If the more extreme process of reconstruction (Cooper, 1981) takes place, an assessor may falsely report that an event took place when in fact that event never actually happened.

Behavior-Driven Theory

A very different view of how memory will operate in the integration discussion comes from other sources. As described in chapter 7, theory and research on interpersonal perception provide support for our ability to remember a vast amount of detail about observations we have made. Some memory theories (Hintzman, 1986, 1988; Smith & Medin, 1981) suggest that our memory consists of traces of all the perceptions we have ever experienced. These memory traces include records of detailed episodes we have observed. Johnson and Raye (1981) even maintain that we can distinguish between the traces in memory that were created by actual external events (e.g., we met someone who criticized his wife, complained about the food in the cafeteria, and derided the president of the United States) versus inferences that we have created internally (e.g., "that new employee is a negative person"). They also argue that the externally generated memory traces (all those complaints) are actually more specific and fixed than the internally generated ones (i.e., "negative person").

Even if we accept that memory consists of extensive and detailed information, we must also recognize that people have difficulty locating and recalling the information when involved in the integration discussion. The retrieval of assessment observations is made easier by training assessors thoroughly in typical actions that participants may display in each exercise, requiring behavioral notes, providing support tools, and, most importantly, training assessors to challenge each other in the assessor discussion. Assessors can help each other recall details by asking whether expected behaviors were displayed, and if a team of two or three assessors observed an exercise, team members can help each other recall actual events.

RATINGS ON DIMENSIONS

In the within-exercise dimension rating method, when all the exercise reports have been read, each assessor takes a few minutes to review the accumulated behavioral evidence and determines a preliminary overall dimension rating for each of the dimensions. These preliminary ratings are made independently and written on the dimension summary form. The ratings might be displayed electronically or posted on a large display. Table 8.3 illustrates the ratings determined for one participant by a group of three assessors over five dimensions. The assessors then discuss the ratings in order to resolve differences. There are several possible patterns of ratings that might be generated. When there is total agreement, for example, all three assessors give a "4," then the integration is straightforward and the participant gets a "4."

On the other hand, if there are differences among the ratings, discussion takes place. One might think that agreement at this stage of the integration process is desirable. After all, wouldn't that be an indication of consistency? Some research on the group judgment process shows that disagreement at this stage can be beneficial and can lead to increased levels of accuracy in the final group decision (Libby, Trotman, & Zimmer, 1987; Rohrbaugh, 1979; Sniezek & Henry, 1989). Disagreement may reflect a diversity of valid opinions that leads to better decisions in groups than by individuals (Wanous & Youtz, 1986). Group decision processes are discussed more thoroughly later in this chapter. The traditional assessment center method calls for group consensus. In this context, consensus means that each assessor can accept the agreed-upon rating as an adequate representation of the performance. Consensus does not mean that there is total agreement by each assessor that the rating is exact.

Schema-Driven Theory

According to this theory, people develop and use simple guiding principles for making judgments about others. In chapter 7 we saw how these principles

TABLE 8.3
Preliminary and Final Overall Dimension Ratings

Dimension	Assessor A	Assessor B	Assessor C	Final Overall Dimension Rating
Leadership	4	4	4	4
Decision making	2	2	3	2
Assertiveness	2	3	3	3
Oral communication	3	4	4	3
Planning and organizing	2	2	4	4

may affect assessors observing in individual exercises. We now consider how these principles may be operating in the integration discussion. The theory says we make judgments on the basis of very little information instead of the abundant information that is usually available. This process of simplification is one of two alternative theoretical explanations for the processes of integration and judgment that take place at this stage of assessment.

The integration discussion takes place sometime after the exercises are completed. Each assessor has observed other assessees before the integration discussions. It may be difficult to remember details of which assessee exhibited which specific behavior in which particular exercise. Accurate memories of details may be difficult to call up. It may be true that the assessors' judgments are based on fallible and selective memory. This position holds that because of selective memory decay, integration and judgment will depend more on information that is consistent with our general impression of the participant. The general impression held by Assessor A about one assessee may be a function of the behavior observed in Exercise 1. That initial general impression may color A's understanding of the behavior reported by Assessor B about that assessee in Exercise 2. Furthermore, an initial impression may induce halo in ratings at this stage of the discussion. Cooper (1981) emphasized that there will be considerable "halo error" in ratings, that is, artificially high relationships among attribute ratings caused by the broad effect of a single bit of strong information on the evaluation of several characteristics. Alternative interpretations suggest that many of the observed relationships among dimension ratings may be due to actual relationships among similar attributes (Murphy, Jako, & Anhalt, 1993). Fiske and Taylor (1984) summarized much research suggesting that internal impressions, rather than detailed episodes in memory, are easier for people to recall and thus will dominate our evaluations. The heuristic devices, or "rules of thumb," described by Nisbett and Ross (1980) and reported in chapter 7, may induce errors at this stage of the integration discussion. Examples of these rules include:

- *Representativeness*—Objects are assigned to categories after one observation, and we proceed to make judgments based on presumed category membership. Problem: The information about the category is not always accurate and is overused. Example: Assessor reports that an assessee emerged as the clear leader of the group discussion, and subsequent assessors inflate their reports and evaluations of leader behaviors.
- *Availability*—Information that is readily available in memory is used to make judgments about frequency, probability, and causality. Problem: Available information may not be valid. Example: Assessors may discuss at length observations about how an assessee handled a single prominent incident and then generalize to other incidents.

- *Salience and vividness*—We put more weight on readily, visible and out-standing information. Problem: Vividness is not usually relevant to the value of the information to our decision. Example: One spark of creativity from an assessee in one exercise may override memories and evaluations of numerous inane comments.

These and other shortcomings in our judgment processes may make it particularly difficult for us to make accurate judgments after hearing the evidence from the team of assessors. Another point of view about the discussion provides more hope for the value of the group discussion.

Behavior-Driven Theory

According to behavior-driven theory, people use the objective and detailed information available to them and combine this information in a logical manner. Hintzman (1986, 1988) maintained that the judge will recall and use actual behaviors to form an evaluation. Anderson (1974, 1981) has shown that people use a simple mental algebra to combine information through adding or averaging to form an overall evaluation. Along these lines, Nathan and Lord (1983) have shown that ratings of specific dimensions are based on performance demonstrated, not just general impressions the observer has formed. Alba and Hasher (1983) reviewed much research on human perception and concluded that the distortions in judgment emphasized by the schema-driven theories are actually quite infrequent. Hastie and Dawes (2001) described how people can make rational choices in an uncertain world. And finally, Murphy et al. (1993) have argued that the supposedly pervasive halo error may not be all that pervasive, but rather a reflection of actual relationships among performance dimensions.

Summary

Given the point of view about social perception and human judgment held by the schema theorists, we might wonder if there is any hope for the accurate assessment of employee performance. The answer is clearly "yes" because the integration discussion in the assessment center method is very different from most of the processes studied by social judgment researchers. Researchers in social judgment have dealt mostly with everyday experiences of human interaction. They have studied these phenomena in temporary groups of subjects in laboratory situations where people have limited information. As Bernardin and Beatty (1984) observed in their review of performance appraisal research and practice, *performance* appraisal is different from *personal* appraisal. They see reason to be optimistic that many of the obstacles to good judgment that plague daily human judgments can be overcome in the controlled performance appraisal situation. Improvements in judgments about job performance can be expected when managers are systematically trained to rate performance using clear standards for judgment, when behaviorally anchored rating scales are used as originally intended, when diaries are kept, and when managers are properly motivated to provide accurate ratings. Whether or not this is overly optimistic is debatable. However, in the case of assessment center evaluations, where many of the everyday pressures to distort appraisals (Murphy & Cleveland, 1991) are absent, there is even more reason to be optimistic. Is there data to support this optimism?

Assessment Center Research

One way to determine if some of the aforementioned problems are a risk for assessment center programs is to ask whether, after assessors have heard the preliminary reports of other assessors in the within-exercise rating method but prior to any discussion, assessors agree on the overall dimension ratings. The findings reported in Table 7.1 suggest high levels of interrater agreement. The levels of agreement are even higher after the integration discussion, but it should be clear that agreement can be fairly high after all assessors have the reported information available to them.

In a slightly different analysis, Smith (1989) investigated interrater agreement on dimension ratings for two types of assessment center methods (the behavioral reporting method and the within-exercise method) by examining the agreement of the dimension ratings across teams. Regardless of whether final dimension ratings were obtained via consensus discussion or by averaging individuals' preliminary ratings, the level of agreement was greater for the teams using the within-exercise method.

These studies demonstrate that assessors are consistent in determining their across-exercise dimension ratings. Additionally, evidence suggests that some assessment center methods, such as those where assessors give and report within-exercise dimension ratings, may lead to greater assessor reliability and agreement than other methods, such as those where assessors report only behaviors before assigning their individual across-exercise dimension ratings.

OVERALL ASSESSMENT RATINGS

After the assessors have agreed on the final overall dimension ratings, they may derive an overall assessment rating for each participant. An overall assessment rating is appropriate if the purpose of the assessment center is to provide a recommendation for selection or promotion. If this is the case, decision makers in the organization want a clear indication of the final conclusion of the assessment: a prediction of success or failure in the new job. Such an overall assessment rating is usually not warranted in assessment centers used for diagnosis of development needs or those used for individual and organizational development. In the latter programs, the end products are the dimension ratings or the feedback on areas needing improvement. The next section, then, is relevant only to programs where an overall assessment rating is warranted.

To arrive at an overall assessment rating in any of the judgmental integration methods, each assessor looks over the final dimension ratings and makes an individual judgment on whether the participant is likely to be successful in the target job. This overall assessment rating is a combination of all information presented to this point. The assessor must use his or her judgment on how to combine the dimension ratings. No formal equation is used for weighting the various dimensions. However, during assessor training, the assessors are presented with job analysis findings that typically indicate the importance of the dimensions and have developed some common frame of reference for combining the dimension ratings into an overall assessment rating. It is expected that each assessor will consider the job requirements and the accuracy of the information regarding the participant, and will combine the dimension ratings based on that knowledge and on training received in the assessment center process.

The overall assessment rating can take several forms. For a selection program, the rating might be "probability of success." For a promotion program, the rating might be "probability of success in the next level" or "probability of success in middle management." In the Management Progress Study launched in 1955 (Bray & Grant, 1966) the assessors made two predictions: "probability of promotion" and "whether the person should be promoted." The first was a prediction of whether the person had the qualities the organization was currently seeking for promotion, whereas the second was an evaluation of whether the person had the qualities that *should* be recognized and rewarded in the organization.

Prediction of the Overall Assessment Rating

Correlations between various dimension ratings and the overall assessment rating (OAR) provide some insight into how assessors form OARs. These correlations tend to be fairly large. Hinrichs and Haanpera (1976) found that the average correlation between each across-exercise dimension rating and the overall assessment rating in eight countries ranged from .25 to .82. Hinrichs (1978) and Mitchel (1975) also reported high correlations between dimension ratings and the overall assessment rating. Lastly, Huck and Bray (1976) found correlations between scores on groups of dimension ratings and the overall assessment rating to be high for both White and Black assessment center participants. These findings suggest assessors have used the various final dimension ratings to form judgments of overall performance.

Research has suggested that even though assessors are often told to use all the dimension information, only a few dimensions, that is, three to seven, are needed to support assessors' overall assessment ratings (e.g., Bray & Grant, 1966; Hinrichs & Haanpera, 1976; Kehoe, Weinberg, & Lawrence, 1985; Konz, 1988; Neidig, Martin, & Yates, 1978; Russell, 1987; Schmitt, 1977). Because a large portion of variation in overall assessment ratings can be accounted for by a statistical combination of the final dimension ratings, some have suggested there is no need for the assessor discussion (Herriot, Chalmers, & Wingrove, 1985; Wingrove, Jones, & Herriot, 1985). This suggestion is premature, though, because it is quite possible that the integration discussion yields an overall assessment rating that is more accurate than the statistical combination of dimension ratings. We explore this issue in chapter 10.

After the assessors independently give their overall assessment rating, the ratings are sometimes posted on a display and compared. If there is total agreement, that rating is final. If there is disagreement, the assessors discuss their differences and come to a consensus, much the way they do in deriving overall dimension ratings. By this point, there is seldom need for extensive discussion. In the majority of cases, disagreement is minimal, and this part of the integration discussion goes very quickly. There have been suggestions that this part of the integration process is eliminated (Feltham, 1988b; Sackett & Wilson, 1982), but little time would be gained by doing so. In addition, assessors often wish to see closure in the process; elimination of the integration discussion would deprive them of a meaningful final step. The vast majority of assessment centers currently in operation use consensus discussion to derive final ratings: 84% of U.S. companies (Spychalski et al., 1997) and 92% of companies in German-speaking countries (Krause & Gebert, 2003). On the other hand, alternatives have been proposed, and we must ask whether some other methods of combining the data would improve predictive accuracy. This issue is explored later in this chapter and in chapter 10.

THEORIES OF GROUP DECISION MAKING

Anyone who has participated in a group discussion, either to solve a problem or to accomplish a task, has probably noted that the group can be either the source of valuable ideas and a vehicle for progress, or the group can suppress creativity and progress and lead to erroneous conclusions.

Even the briefest reading of the theoretical and research literature on group decision making reveals these same two sharply contrasting views (Aronson, Wilson, & Akert, 2002; Levine & Moreland, 1998). One view, which we might call pessimistic, notes that the group discussion process interferes with good decision making and results in what Steiner (1972) called "process losses." Hinsz, Tindale, and Vollrath (1997) concluded their extensive review of the literature on information processing in groups by saying "Groups generally decrease variability in the way information is processed, compared to individuals" (p. 53). They give examples of narrowed focus of attention, failure to share, store, and remember information, and pressures to conform and accentuate limited information. The more optimistic view holds that groups follow an orderly process of forming decisions (Laughlin, 1999), they have the potential for "process gains" (Steiner, 1972), and they generate good ideas and sound solutions (Argyris & Schon, 1974; Hill, 1982).

DISADVANTAGES OF GROUP DECISION MAKING

There are many potential problems with group decision making (Laughlin, 1999; Moscovici, 1985). For one, the final decision of the group may not be better than the decision of the best individual in the group (Einhorn, Hogarth, & Klempner, 1977). Similarly, the group discussion process may dilute the good information contributed by the most accurate person. This problem may arise because one person, for example someone with poorer judgment, unduly dominates the discussion and leads others to focus on poor information. Processes of conformity may operate such that a more passive member of the group, yet one who could make a valuable contribution, simply follows the suggestions of the other group members. One solution to this problem is to identify the best member and dismiss the others (Libby et al., 1987). This is usually not practical though, because even if the researcher can identify the best member after the experiment, the group itself cannot identify the best person during the discussion (Miner, 1984). Another reason the rest of the group cannot usually be dismissed is that this practice meets with great resistance in practical situations.

Another dynamic that may distort group decisions is the group polarization process (Kameda, Tindale, & Davis, 2003; Lamm & Myers, 1978; Myers & Lamm, 1976). Group polarization means that the initial position of the majority of the group is strengthened following group discussion. Members may move toward the dominant position in the group for any number of reasons. Ideally, this would only happen when the substance of the majority's position is sound, and this often happens (Lamm & Myers, 1978; Myers & Lamm, 1976). Unfortunately, other less desirable processes occur also.

For example, group members may adopt the majority position because of some artificial rule (such as "the majority rules") or because members want to be seen as agreeable to other group members. One form of group polarization is the "risky shift" phenomenon (Kameda et al., 2003; Kogan & Wallach, 1967; Laughlin, 1999), in which the final group position is more risky than the initial position of some individual members. For example, it has been found that under certain conditions, the group will endorse a stronger statement of opinion on an issue after the discussion process. One interpretation of this dynamic is that there has been a diffusion of responsibility to all members of the group in comparison with the responsibility that might fall on any one individual (Latane & Darley, 1970). This interpretation makes sense when there is some negative effect of the group's decision on another person (Lamm & Myers, 1978), a situation that often exists in assessment centers when the results will be used in promotion or hiring decisions. Herriot et al. (1985) found a negative bias operating in judgments about candidates for officer training school. Individual assessors tended to lower their preliminary ratings to match the majority's rating, especially if the majority was already giving a low rating. In this assessment center, a low rating resulted in the rejection of the candidate's application for an officer training school. Thus, movement toward the majority position in this group represented a shift toward a risky position.

"Groupthink" (Aldag & Fuller, 1993; Janis, 1982) is another potentially dangerous process that may undermine the quality of group decisions. Cohesive groups may inhibit differences of opinion and promote conformity to informal, unspoken norms of agreeableness. Members in a cohesive group may strive for unanimity at the expense of appraising alternative actions and positions. Groupthink becomes "a deterioration of mental efficiency, reality testing, and moral judgment from in-group pressures" (Janis, 1982, p. 9). There may be a tendency for this dynamic to operate in assessor groups. Assessors who work together in the organization or serve together in an assessment center for a long time may feel pressure to be "nice" and agree with each other.

Aldag and Fuller (1993) critiqued, refined, and expanded the groupthink model into a more inclusive general group problem-solving model. This model includes other variables that may determine group decision processes, including the nature of the decision (e.g., its importance, and time pressures), features of the group (e.g., its cohesiveness and stage of development), and the content of the decision (e.g., political, degree of stress), all of which may affect how the group perceives its vulnerability and whether its decision processes will deteriorate. Given this inherent complexity in whether a group will succumb to "groupthink," Aldag and Fuller (1993) are skeptical that specific remedies will be effective. Rather, they suggest the potentially negative consequences of group features may be overcome by altering the culture and rewards surrounding the decision-making discussion. The context and process of the assessment center integration discussion typically includes elements that mitigate the group dynamics described by Janis, and may in fact, create a climate suggested by Aldag and Fuller.

The assessment center integration method incorporates many features that may combat groupthink: Assessors are taught to be critical thinkers, and to challenge the ratings of other assessors; everyone is assigned the role of devil's advocate and asked to challenge ratings, and assessors are given a chance to review all data and change their minds as the integration discussion unfolds. In addition, assessor groups are often not stable groups that work together over time. Thus, the negative dynamics of a cohesive group may not operate in assessor integration discussions. In addition, the assessor team is typically removed from the normal pressures of organizational politics that may foster conformity and the rewards of assessors are not contingent on any specific assessment outcomes.

Another potential problem with group decision making is that groups have a tendency to fail to discuss unshared information. A "hidden profile" is said to exist in the situation where various group members have critical information that is not initially known by others (Laughlin, 1999; Stasser, 1992; Stasser & Stewart, 1992). Failure to focus more on information they share can lead to inadequate consideration of all critical information. This tendency can be minimized if groups are held accountable for their decision, a topic discussed in a later section of this chapter.

ADVANTAGES OF GROUP DECISION MAKING

The more optimistic view of group decision making emphasizes evidence that groups can work effectively together and produce decisions quite superior to those of any one individual (Argyris & Schon, 1974; Hill, 1982). Moscovici (1985) observed that the historical emphasis on conformity in groups has been replaced with recognition that the individual influences the group. In fact, Nisbett and Ross (1980) asserted that "assembly bonuses," that is, the gains that come from individuals working in groups, are the best hope for overcoming many deficiencies inherent in individual human judgment.

What support is there for the group judgmental process of combining information? McGrath and Kravitz (1982) concluded that one of the most robust findings in the literature is that groups tend to follow the pattern of "truth supported wins." This means that even though there may be some group process losses (i.e., the group decision is less effective than that of the best individual), if the good solution has support, the group will accept it. Laughlin and his associates (Laughlin, 1980; Laughlin & Ellis, 1986; Laughlin & McGlynn, 1986) have shown that the "truth supported wins" pattern is an accurate description of how groups operate when solving inductive reasoning problems. Laughlin, Bonner, and Milner (2002) summarized decades of research by concluding that "groups perform better than the average individual on a range of problem solving tasks" (p. 605). Furthermore, Laughlin (1999) concluded that given sufficient information and time, the decisions of groups are comparable to the decision of the best individual. In addition, many of the arguments that groups do not adequately process information are based on one of two reasons: The group is not motivated properly, that is, members do not put forth effort, or they have limited information-processing capabilities (McGrath & Kravitz, 1982). Neither of these two conditions seems to be present in the assessment center context: Assessors are typically hand-picked for their interpersonal skills and interest in human resource issues, and they are trained in and certified to have the required assessment skills.

Benefits come from group decision making when several individuals with heterogeneous skills and experience contribute to the decision. Of course, for the principle to operate, assessors must bring unique information to bear on the evaluation of participants. Here again, an assessor team is usually composed of managers with different organizational experience, and each has the opportunity to observe different exercises. For these reasons it is not surprising when there is a lack of agreement on dimension ratings across exercises. The advantage of diversity is that individuals can then pool their expertise to provide a wider variety of information. In addition, procedures in the typical assessor discussion provide "checks and balances" that prevent misinformation or poor judgment by any one individual.

Sniezek and Henry (1990) proposed and tested a decision-making procedure that parallels the one followed in the integration discussion of an assessment center. In this procedure, individuals make judgments that are then revised in the process of interaction with the group. These revised individual judgments are then evaluated and combined by the group in a discussion that requires group consensus. Two studies (Sniezek & Henry, 1989, 1990) provided support for the efficacy of this procedure. The group judgments were found to be superior to numerically averaged judgments of the individuals, when compared to judgments of experts. Furthermore, in the group process, the change in the group's judgment and the judgments of most of the individuals was in the direction of the more accurate judgment. The correction of the initial judgment was considerable. In fact, an improvement of more than 32% was demonstrated using Sniezek's decision-making approach. That improvement is far greater than the average of 12% improvement found by Hastie (1986) in his review of earlier group decision-making models.

Miner (1984) conducted research that clarified that the process used by the group in deriving the decision determines whether the group produces quality decisions. He found that if the individual group members make independent decisions before the group discussion, the group decision is better than when the decision is made without initial individual judgments. This finding implies that at any stage of the integration session, assessors should report behaviors, perform independent ratings, and only then proceed with discussions. Miner (1984) found that after the experiment, he could identify a "best individual" who outperformed the group, but the group itself could not identify the best individual at any better than chance rates.

Thus, even though there was some process loss in comparison with the best individual, there was no way for the group to identify the "best" or most accurate member during the decision process. In a practical sense, there was process gain in comparison with the decision that resulted from a statistical average of the individual decisions. The process Miner found most effective in this research is exactly the procedure used in the assessment center method: Preliminary independent ratings are made by each assessor, then the group makes the final assessment rating.

Summary

Which view of group discussion is more accurate, the one of process losses or of process gains? Both contain elements of truth; the challenge is to understand under what circumstances groups work well together. Although there is less definitive research in identifying the variables that determine group effectiveness, many clues exist to show what conditions make a difference. As this literature is reviewed, it will be apparent that the assessment center method creates many of the conditions that have been shown to lead to effective group decision processes. In fact, the assessment center integration discussion is an elaborate case study of how human behavior can be evaluated and predicted; it also shows the value of many of the principles that have emerged in lab and field research on group decision making over the past several decades.

FACTORS AFFECTING GROUP EFFECTIVENESS

Piecing together the fragments of research and theory provides some indication of the factors that make a difference in whether group processes improve or undermine the quality of decision making. Some of these factors include: knowledge and skills of group members, effort applied to the decision-making task, group accountability for decisions, consistent use of an effective decision-making strategy, the use of techniques to foster positive group dynamics and minimize the forces of conformity, and careful information processing to engender message-relevant thinking.

Knowledge and Skills in the Group

When group members have a high level of knowledge and skills relevant to the task at hand, they are more effective than if these skills are absent (Chaiken & Stangor, 1987; Kameda et al., 2003). Desired levels of knowledge and skill can be assured by selecting competent group members and by training them properly. These conditions are standard practice in the development of an assessment center. Higher level managers are frequently selected to be assessors because they are familiar with the target job or jobs. Further screening is done to select managers who have demonstrated judgmental and interpersonal skills relevant to the assessment tasks they must carry out. But that is only the beginning. Assessor training is then conducted to enhance the specific skills assessors need for the assessment center they are part of. The *Guidelines* (International Task Force, 2000) further specify that assessors should be tested and certified competent to carry out the assessment tasks.

Effort

A basic requirement for effective group information processing is that group members must pay careful attention to the information. Hinsz et al. (1997) suggested that attention to the task (rather than one's own role), examination of shared and unshared information, and moderate time pressures contribute to increased attention among group members. In addition, for a group to be effective, its members must be motivated to carry out the necessary judgment and decision making; ideally, the effort of the group must be at a high level and well coordinated. Barker, Wahlers, Cegala, and Kibler (1983) concluded that when a group is asked to achieve a high level of performance in terms of sound judgment and fast responses, it performs better than it would under less pressing conditions. Hackman and Morris (1978a, 1978b) suggested that the effort of group members can be improved by redesigning the group task to include the following features, all of which will elicit effort from workers: utilization of a variety of skills, the opportunity to accomplish a specific task, work on a significant task, autonomy, and feedback about group effectiveness.

Virtually all of these factors are present in an assessor integration discussion. Assessors are certainly under pressure to produce a lot of accurate work. Working as an assessor also requires a wide variety of skills: administering and evaluating exercises, preparing evaluations and suggestions for placement or development, and, in some cases, writing feedback reports and giving oral feedback to participants and their immediate supervisors. Clear and identifiable tasks are accomplished in the assessment in the form of recommendations for hiring, promotion, or development and these tasks are significant in the professional lives of the participants as well as in the life of the organization itself. Autonomy is experienced because there is no one else to overrule the judgments made by the assessor team. On the other hand, feedback on the effectiveness of the assessment center is often lacking: Assessors often do not know how their recommendations are used in the organization. Feedback of this kind might do much to improve assessor motivation, which is already at a high level.

All these conditions seem to minimize the possibility of "social loafing," a phenomenon in which people in groups "slack off" or reduce their effort. Social loafing seems to occur more frequently when the individual's effort within the group is not readily identifiable and people are not accountable for their individual contributions (Weldon & Gargano, 1985; Weldon & Mustari, 1988). The importance of accountability for decisions is explored further in the next section.

Accountability

Tetlock (1983, 1985) argued that individuals will engage in complex decision strategies, rather than simplified thinking, when there is a norm of structured, balanced debate within a group. If the social context makes the decision maker accountable to others whose positions are not known ahead of time, then individuals will use more thorough and vigilant information processing. According to Tetlock, complex decision making requires the willingness to be inconsistent in our thinking (i.e., to recognize good features in a rejected position and bad features in a preferred position), to engage in self-criticism, and to have more insight into the decision strategy we use. Although the effects of holding decision makers accountable are complex and depend on many factors, several conclusions emerge from the continued research in this area (Lerner & Tetlock, 1999). Accountability has beneficial effects when the audience's view is unknown, when decision makers are accountable for the process they used (rather than the outcome), when accountability is demanded by legitimate authorities, and when attention to the normal decision process has been low.

Making a group accountable for their decision may mitigate the problem of failure to fully discuss unshared information. If groups are held accountable, research shows they spend more time in the discussion, focus on critical information, and arrive at better solutions (Stewart, Billings, & Stasser, 1998).

Accountability is fostered in the assessor discussion as a result of several facets of the traditional assessment center method: the structured method of recording and reporting behaviors; the requirement to back up any evaluations with behavioral evidence; the detailed reporting of both positive and negative observations related to each dimension; the lack of personal connection between assessor and participant; and the separation and independence of the multiple assessments from different exercises. All these features of the group decision process perpetuate a climate of accountability in the assessor discussion.

Consistent Use of Strategies for Decision Making

Groups work most effectively when they utilize existing strategies that each individual has learned previously (Hackman & Morris, 1978a, 1978b). Any one of a number of decision-making strategies may work in a given situation. The point here is that group norms supporting the use of a strategy must be maintained or the strategy may be abandoned. The task of maintaining the proper strategy in assessment center discussions usually falls to the administrator leading the discussions. Experienced assessors sometimes need reminders because they may try to take shortcuts, and new assessors or assessors who assemble for only one or two programs often need careful guidance because they have not practiced the techniques often enough. One challenge organizations face is the maintenance of quality and integrity of the assessment center process when it is carried out in different departments and divisions (Schmitt, Schneider, & Cohen, 1990). Maintaining the "operational validity" (Byham & Temlock, 1972) of an assessment center includes careful scrutiny to ensure that decision-making strategies are being applied consistently. Assessment center administrators make it a practice to observe a sample of assessor discussions to see if the integration procedures specified for that program described earlier in this chapter, are being followed.

Group Dynamics

Groups must guard against the detrimental processes noted earlier in this chapter. Hoffman (1978a, 1978b) pointed out many of the factors that can inhibit effective problem solving in groups, including pressures toward uniformity, pressures toward conformity, and an informal structure that has no leader. Most assessor teams are temporary groups who meet only for the duration of a particular assessment center. Thus, there is little concern that ill feelings created in the discussion will carry over to the job. Furthermore, the assessor discussion process follows a procedure that Hoffman suggested actually promotes effective group problem solving: All ideas are laid out for consideration and evaluated, and conflict is exploited, that is, the group uses differences of opinion to better understand the participant.

An extensive body of research on group decision making suggests that unshared information (i.e., various bits of information that are known only to separate members of the group) is not discussed because group members put pressure on members to conform to its initial position (Kameda et al., 2003). New and different information is seen as disruptive and the group tends to ignore or not benefit from open discussion of distinctive information. Small-group research has shown the tendency of groups to neglect unshared information can be combated by making participants anonymous, providing a nonthreatening environment, providing a means to share information simultaneously, and providing a means to share information openly among all members.

The assessor discussion process follows many of these suggestions, and suggestions offered by others, about how to foster effective group dynamics in the decision process, such as assigning people the role of devil's advocate (Schweiger, Sandberg, & Rediner, 1989) and focusing on the data and not personal credentials of the person proposing the idea (Janis, 1982). It is heartening to know that research has shown that certain characteristics of the assessors do not affect the influence they have on the other assessors: for example, holding a line or a staff position (Neidig & Martin, 1979), being male or female, or being chair of the team (Sackett & Wilson, 1982).

Message-Relevant Thinking

Theories of persuasion also help us understand the conditions under which groups process information. According to Petty and Caccioppo (1986), the messages that come to us may be processed systematically (i.e., very carefully and thoroughly) or only peripherally (i.e., very quickly, using simple rules). Systematic processing will take place if people are motivated and able to engage in careful thinking about the relevance of the message to the problem at hand. Several factors motivate and enable individuals to engage in systematic thinking: relevance of the material, repeated exposure to the message, adequate prior knowledge about the topic, prior learning of ways to organize material, and concern for truth seeking, that is, a goal to seek a correct solution versus one that is accepted by others (Chaiken & Stangor, 1987). These are the very conditions present in the assessor discussion. Assessors are experienced managers, they have a clear understanding of the dimensions as mental frameworks, behavioral data are available for their consideration, and the goal is to derive an accurate evaluation of each participant without external pressures. In addition, assessors have the time to devote their full attention to the assessment effort.

Furthermore, when using the systematic style of thinking, people are less likely to be influenced by another person's status or appearance. This point is supported by the assessment center research cited earlier, which shows that the gender and status of assessors do not determine influence in the integration discussion.

Summary

There is much theoretical and research evidence to support the proposition that the judgmental processes of integrating information across assessors, exercises, and dimensions, and the group decision processes used in the traditional assessor integration discussion can foster good decisions. Many of the factors that have been acknowledged to lead to process gains in group decision making are present in the traditional assessment center process, but that is no guarantee that they will actually be followed. A poorly run integration discussion could succumb to the many conditions that lead to poor decision making. The alternative to the judgmental processes are statistical methods of data integration. These are discussed in the next section.

GROUP COMPOSITION/DIVERSITY CONSIDERATIONS

In addition to the decision-making literature, the relational demography (Riordan, 2000; Jackson, Joshi, & Erhardt, 2003) and workplace diversity literature also points out that the demographic composition of assessor groups may impact the quality of decisions reached about assessees. For example, relational demography research has shown that workgroups that are more heterogeneous in terms of race and age display more citizenship behaviors (Chattopadhyay, 1999). Fenwick and Neal (2001) found that the number of women per group was positively related to team performance in a computer simulation task. In contrast, dissimilar groups may encounter hindrances in decision making (e.g., Jackson et al., 2003) and experience less cohesion, although these effects may diminish over time (Carpenter, 2002; Chatman & Flynn, 2001; Earley & Mosakowski, 2000). These findings, albeit inconsistent, suggest that assessment center designers should carefully consider the effects of the demographic composition of the assessor team and discuss potential effects in assessor training and during the integration discussion. Whatever the actual effect of diversity in the assessor group may have on decisions about assessees, diversity in the assessor group will likely lead to an increase in the perceived fairness and accuracy of the assessment process.

STATISTICAL METHODS OF DATA INTEGRATION

Statistical methods involve the use of a mathematical formula to derive dimension or overall scores. Statistical combination of ratings can take place at the following stages of assessment:

- the within-exercise dimension ratings of two or more assessors after watching the same exercise;
- the within-exercise dimension ratings of assessors across several exercises;
- the dimension ratings of two or more assessors after hearing evidence of behavior on each performance dimension reported in the integration discussion;
- the final overall assessment rating for a candidate after assessors have agreed on dimension ratings;
- the final overall assessment rating for a candidate after each assessor gives an independent overall rating.

At each of these stages, the pieces of information may be weighted equally or differentially. Equal weights are often called "unit weights" because each piece is weighted "1." The ratings are simply averaged across assessors, exercises, or dimensions. Differential weights show the relative importance of pieces of information being combined. For example:

$$Overall\ Assessment\ Rating = (4\ x\ Decision\ Making)$$
$$+\ (2\ x\ Leadership) + Sensitivity + Company\ Orientation$$

In this example, differential weighting of these dimensions shows that decision making is weighted four times as important and leadership is two times as important as sensitivity and company orientation. These weights can be determined by several methods:

- rational preference of organizational decision makers who decree the relative importance of the dimensions;
- job analysis findings based on judgments of subject matter experts about the importance of task and performance dimensions;
- statistical methods, such as multiple regression.

To carry out a statistical study, the investigator needs data from a large sample of at least 100 to 150 people. The data from such a study would include the scores on the "predictors," which in this case would be the ratings on the several dimensions, and scores on some "criterion" such as progress in managerial rank or evidence of successful performance on the job. Statistical analyses of the relationship between the criterion scores and the predictor scores reveal the weights. Once these weights are determined, a formula is used to combine the dimension ratings and predict success.

There is much theoretical and empirical evidence from other areas of psychology to support the statistical method of information integration. Early reviews of studies comparing statistical and judgmental methods in clinical psychology (Meehl, 1954; Sawyer, 1966) and other fields (Dawes, 1979) showed that statistical methods provide more consistent and accurate predictions. Judgmental methods can be faulty when judges do not consistently use subjective weights to combine several pieces of information. In addition, accuracy is reduced when assessors do not have a clear understanding of what variables are most important. There is even some support in the assessment center literature that supports the statistical combination of dimension ratings (see chap. 10).

There may be advantages and disadvantages of combining information statistically or judgmentally at various integration steps. The following sections explore some of the arguments of each approach.

DERIVING POSTEXERCISE DIMENSION RATINGS

In some assessment centers, only one assessor observes each candidate in an exercise. For example, one assessor observes the interview simulation, another assessor observes the in-basket, and so on. In these arrangements, there is only one rating on each dimension for each exercise. In other arrangements, more than one assessor observes the candidate. For example, a group of three assessors may observe the candidate make a presentation in the case study exercise. The question then is, how do we combine the ratings of the three assessors? With the statistical combination method, the three ratings on each dimension would be averaged.

DERIVING FINAL DIMENSION RATINGS

Assume now that one or more assessors have observed behavior in several exercises. Assume further that within-exercise dimension ratings are made. What is the best way to combine the behavioral observation and rating information into overall dimension ratings? To date, no assessment center research study has investigated the best procedure for deriving final dimension ratings. To the best of our knowledge, no study has compared a purely judgmental method of reaching consensus on final dimension ratings to a purely statistical method. Assuming that within-exercise dimension ratings have been given, then the simplest approach would be to average these dimension ratings, with each rating carrying equal weight. Conceivably, ratings from certain assessors or different exercises could be weighted more heavily, although it would be difficult to establish before the assessment center which assessors are more accurate. Even if it were possible to determine during the discussion who was more accurate, the procedure would probably not be acceptable to assessees, assessors, or organizational members. We are left, therefore, with little more than speculation about any procedure other than the traditional ones of achieving final dimension ratings.

Conversely, results from three studies support the statistical method of data integration (although it should be noted that these studies did not involve cross-validation with new samples of subjects). Wollowick and McNamara (1969) found that the judgmentally derived overall assessment ratings correlated less with a measure of management success than the statistically derived overall assessment ratings correlated with the same criterion. In addition, the accuracy of the judgmentally derived overall assessment rating was lower than the accuracy of a summing of the overall exercise ratings, a summing of the across-exercise dimension ratings, and objective test scores. Higher correlations for the statistical method were also reported in Borman's (1982) study, which compared the ability of the two data combination techniques to predict three criterion measures. Lastly, Tziner and Dolan (1982) found the statistical combination of assessment ratings to be superior to the judgmental combination in predicting training performance. Again, we must be cautious about these results, since the studies were not cross-validated in independent samples. The results of Mitchel's (1975) cross-validation are quite revealing. Initially, the statistical method provided more accurate predictions of success than the judgmental rating. But, when the statistical formula was used on different samples over different time periods, the accuracy of the statistical method dropped considerably.

Silzer and Louiselle (1990) questioned the necessity of holding the discussion about dimension ratings at all. They compared the predictive validity of preconsensus and postconsensus discussion ratings and found mixed evidence for which was more predictive of managerial performance 2 years later: The ratings of two dimensions *before* discussions were more predictive, but the ratings on two other dimensions after discussion were more predictive. More studies along these lines are needed.

No firm conclusions about the superiority of one data integration technique over the other can be made on the basis of these studies. Until the data are more conclusive, we recommend, if time permits, retaining the process of having assessors combine assessment center data in the way it has been done in studies showing long-range accuracy. A statistical method may be appropriate when the ultimate purpose of an assessment center is to arrive at one final "select/don't select" decision for each candidate. Statistical integration techniques are not appropriate when the purpose of an assessment center is to generate developmental feedback or to identify development needs on each performance dimension.

DERIVING OVERALL RATINGS

What about the stage where assessors have posted their preliminary overall assessment ratings? Some researchers have questioned the usefulness of the integration discussion at this point (e.g., Sackett & Wilson, 1982; Wingrove et al., 1985). Specifically, they have argued that if integrated ratings can be predicted by individual ratings, then instead of the integration process, a statistical method can be used to arrive at a final overall assessment rating. Two equally logical points of view can be taken. According to Sackett and Wilson (1982), using a statistical method at this point would have several benefits, including the savings in time and money and the elimination of social influences that may adversely affect the final rating. On the other hand, Thornton and Byham (1982) argued that the integration discussion is a critical part in an assessment center, because it holds individual biases and stereotypes in check. An integration discussion ensures that individuals support their ratings with behavioral evidence; it also ensures that individuals have a chance to change their ratings after hearing alternative interpretations of a candidate's performance. Whether the integration discussion actually leads to a better or poorer decision depends on the nature of the discussion.

Some studies that have compared preliminary and final overall assessment ratings suggest that the integration process adds very little to this stage of assessment. Sackett and Wilson (1982) found that for a group of 719 participants, assessors' preliminary overall assessment ratings disagreed with the final ratings for only 1% of the participants. In addition, the final assessment ratings could be accurately predicted by a simple rule based on final dimension ratings. In addition, Wingrove et al. (1985) found that final assessment ratings were no more predictive of training performance than preliminary assessment ratings.

In ascertaining whether the integration discussion might result in poorer decisions, Herriot et al. (1985) examined what group dynamics characterized the integration discussion. They identified 2,640 cases where three of four assessors agreed on their preliminary ratings, then checked to see what the fourth assessor did with his or her final rating. In two thirds of the cases, the dissenting assessor did not move to the majority's position, but in one third of the cases, he or she did. Among the shifts from preliminary to final ratings, Herriot et al. found some predominant patterns. For example, they found that an individual was more likely to shift from a *high* preliminary rating to the majority position than to shift from a low preliminary rating. In addition, the individual was more likely to shift to the majority's low position, in comparison with shifting to a *high* position. In combination, these patterns of shifts suggest a negative bias in the group's decision process, that is, the group seemed to be trying to avoid giving high ratings, which in this assessment center led to a recommendation for officer training.

One conclusion we might draw from these studies is that the integration discussion at this final stage when deciding on overall assessment scores is unnecessary because assessors' final ratings typically do not differ from their preliminary ratings and, in fact, can be predicted from their overall dimension ratings. We might further conclude that these studies even suggest that the integration discussion may be harmful, as group dynamics may have a negative effect on discussions and because gains in predictive accuracy as a result of these discussions have not been shown.

Before such conclusions are warranted and the traditional assessment center method is modified in practice, far more research is needed. Studies must be done to establish that overall assessment ratings derived from a data integration method that does not include discussions about dimension ratings and preliminary overall assessment ratings have the same predictive accuracy already proven for the same ratings derived in the traditional manner. If assessors do not anticipate the integration discussion, their observations, categorizations, and ratings may be carried out quite differently. It is not appropriate to assume that the new data integration method will yield highly accurate overall assessment ratings.

SUMMARY

Should we follow the recommendations to discontinue the integration discussion at this final stage of the assessment center process? There are several problems with this recommendation. The statistical procedures used to develop a formula with differential weights for combining dimension ratings have several features that may impose limitations on the application of the results: (a) They give an optimal solution for a set of data and may overstate the typical relationships of the variables; (b) they are developed from *one sample* of assessees which is usually small and may not be representative of the entire range of candidates; and (c) they investigate the *linear* combination of dimension scores. In considering the statistical method as an alternative, we must recognize that the formula for one sample may not be appropriate for an independent sample, statistics derived from small samples are unstable, and special combinations of dimensions, which allow for the possibility that patterns of high and low dimension scores may be meaningful, may be important. Dugan (1988) argued that these statistical procedures may not capture the rich ways that assessors use information. She noted that prior research and informal discussions with assessors reveal the special combinations of assessment observations not captured with the statistical formulae.

INTEGRATING OTHER ASSESSMENT DEVICES
WITH SITUATIONAL EXERCISES

In addition to situational exercises, other measurement techniques can be used to evaluate individuals in an assessment center. The most frequently used of these are aptitude tests, questionnaires measuring personality characteristics (motivation, social interaction preferences, values, and so forth), biographical information forms, background interviews, multisource feedback systems, and interviews in which the participant is asked to describe how he or she would handle job situations. Occasionally, projective tests of personality (e.g., sentence completion tests, picture interpretations), current affairs tests, or measures of reading ability are used.

There are at least three ways other measurement techniques can be used. First, tests and interviews can be administered before the assessment center process begins as screening devices to select from among potential candidates (i.e., as a "hurdle" in the screening process of a selection or promotional program). For example, a knowledge test is sometimes used to screen candidates in a police and fire promotional system, prior to attending the behavioral assessment. Alternatively, a test of reading ability would select only those individuals who have the skill to comprehend the complex material presented in written case studies and in-basket exercises. Similarly, an interview might be conducted by a member of the human resource staff to assess the individuals' commitment to and interest in a management career, especially as some people may feel pressured by their supervisors into attending a diagnostic or developmental assessment center.

When tests and interviews are used within the framework of the assessment center, either of two procedures depicted in Fig. 8.1 can be followed: These other methods can be used in *parallel* with or in *series* with the situational tests. In the parallel processing method, tests and interviews are used in the same way as situational exercises to provide information that the assessors consider simultaneously when formulating their overall dimension

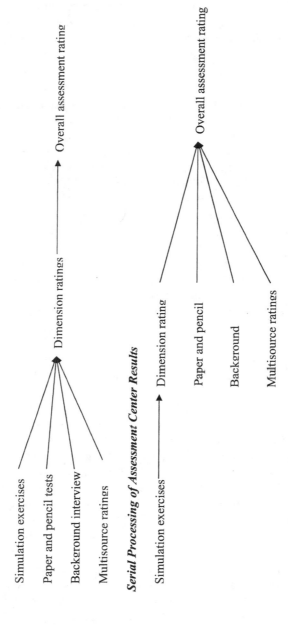

FIG. 8.1. Serial and parallel processing of information from simulations and other assessment results.

ratings. In this approach, the assessors learn about behavior in exercises and information from the tests and interviews, then give an evaluation on the dimensions. The rationale is that the score on an aptitude test, along with observed reasoning behaviors in situational exercises, may be relevant to the evaluation of dimensions such as problem solving and decision analysis. Assessors can gain a better understanding of success or failure in these behavioral dimensions if they have information about a participant's general reasoning ability as indicated by paper-and-pencil tests. A similar argument can be made for personality tests. The assertive behaviors shown in group discussion exercises might be understood more completely if the assessors have test scores measuring related personality characteristics. The tests may show that the individual describes him- or herself as quite assertive, but in actual group situations, that individual may be reticent because he or she lacks the skills to interact effectively or because he or she is not as outgoing as the personality test indicated.

The other way to use tests in an assessment center is to put them in series with the situational exercises. First, the assessors evaluate all the information from the situational tests and derive dimension ratings. Then the test scores and interview information are introduced. Then, either the assessors integrate all this information to arrive at an overall assessment rating, or other scores can be combined statistically.

A variant of this process is to have someone other than an assessor integrate all the information (i.e., dimension ratings from the assessment center, tests, interviews) at a later time. This might be done by a human resource staff member, a committee reviewing candidates for promotion, or a department manager examining the personnel files of people nominated for promotion.

There are advantages and disadvantages associated with each of these procedures. An advantage of parallel processing is that all information is used to formulate ratings on dimensions, and comparisons and contrasts can be made between the results of very different types of measurement. A disadvantage of parallel processing is that managers may rely too heavily on test scores, which can be deceptively "objective" in comparison with the sometimes conflicting reports of several assessors watching several exercises. An advantage of serial processing is that the major sources of information are kept separate in the early stages of assessment: The "here-and-now" behaviors of situational exercises are integrated before the information about "past" behavior from the interview and "test" behavior is examined. The disadvantage of serial processing is that it takes two separate integration meetings: one by the observers of situational exercises and one by people who review all available data. If someone else integrates the final set of information, the assessors may feel loss of control. Of course, assessors can perform both steps, as in some assessment centers, such as Standard Oil of

Ohio (Finkle, 1976; Finkle & Jones, 1970), but this is time-consuming. It should be emphasized that assessors do not have access to test or interview data in either of these methods before they observe behaviors in the situational exercises. There is too much potential for this other information to influence the behavioral observations. For an interesting counterargument, the reader may wish to refer to the classic book, *Assessment of Men*, which describes the program of the Office of Strategic Services (1948) for selecting espionage agents in World War II. This account of the first assessment center in the United States shows how a very holistic assessment can be carried out by mixing together all sorts of information at all stages of the assessment process.

Some practitioners favor the serial processing approach, in which assessments on the dimensions are based only on the behavioral observations from the exercises. Later, information from tests and interviews can be introduced by psychologists or other professionals trained to gather and interpret these data. Assessors can then modify dimension ratings or, more commonly, use the dimension ratings along with the other information to derive an overall assessment rating. This procedure keeps the different sources of data separate from each other for as long as possible. Other practitioners favor the parallel processing approach in which information from all methods (i.e., simulations, tests, multisource feedback) are integrated by assessors to derive assessments of the chosen dimensions.

ASSESSOR TRAINING

If the assessors are following some process that involves discussion among the assessors, assessor training will involve an explanation of the manner in which this should be conducted. Often assessors must be educated about the rationale for the requirement that behavioral notes must be recorded to document effective and ineffective behaviors, namely that assessees wish to see the supportive evidence for low ratings and clear documentation is needed in case promotion decisions are challenged in employment litigation. Assessors also will need an explanation for the requirement that independent ratings are to be recorded before any discussion, namely that this procedure helps to ensure independence of judgments and to minimize the potential negative effects of conformity pressures. Because some assessment centers do not have the resources to have an administrator present with each pair of assessors in each exercise, the assessors will need to practice the administration of the exercise, starting with any instructions to the assessee and continuing through the closing of the session, the period of recording notes and ratings, and the comparison of ratings and final resolution if large differences in initial ratings are present. The trainer will want to know that assessors can carry out these details and that assessors know how to proceed if the team of assessors has any disagreements.

If the integration process involves a discussion in which assessors report behaviors (and potentially, ratings) from different exercises, the assessors will need to practice the process of reporting to each other, taking any notes to integrate the observations, completing the preliminary and final dimension ratings, and completing the preliminary and final overall assessment ratings, if the latter are called for. At each stage of the integration process, a discussion may be held; assessors need to practice how to achieve consensus, or what to do in the worst-case scenario when consensus cannot be reached. Each assessment center program will need a policy to cover various contingencies involving conflict among assessors.

In addition to lectures about and practice with the procedural steps of the group discussion, assessor training should also describe the types of dysfunctional group processes that can occur and how they can be combated. From the opposite point of view, the training should emphasize the benefits of productive group decision-making processes and how the assessment center integration discussion incorporates the lessons learned about how to make group decision making more functional.

SUMMARY AND CONCLUSIONS

This chapter has taken us on a long journey through many theoretical, empirical, and practical considerations dealing with the integration of assessment information. What have we learned from this information? We can summarize our conclusions by addressing three questions.

Is the statistical process or the judgmental process better for integrating assessment center information?

We have seen support for both techniques. Statistical methods may be more appropriate if the organization:

- wishes to use a method that is less vulnerable to the accusation that it is subjective;
- has adequate research to establish reliable differential weights for combining the dimensions;
- does not have time and expertise to conduct thorough integration discussions to reach consensus when combining information across exercises and dimensions;

- wishes to have an accurate overall assessment rating but is not interested in diagnostic information about each individual's strengths and weaknesses;
- will not be giving detailed feedback to individual assessees.

Nearly twenty years ago, Peterson and Pitz (1986) summarized much research on individual decision making by saying:

> over twenty years of research on . . . decision aids has produced two clear conclusions. The first is that unaided predictions made by decision makers are not as accurate as predictions derived from a statistical . . . model. The second is that decision makers will probably not allow important decisions to be based only on the output of any mechanical method for combining information. (p. 163)

This conclusion is still appropriate in many organizations using assessment centers for some purposes. One innovation that holds promise is the combination of statistical and judgmental methods. For example, after the assessors agree on final dimension ratings, these ratings can be combined in a statistical formula to give a tentative overall assessment rating. The assessors can then discuss this rating to see if they agree with it or if it should be modified in light of special information regarding that participant. In support of this proposal, a related study of individual judgment by Peterson and Pitz (1986) found that when the predictions from a statistical formula were provided to the judges, their accuracy improved.

Do group dynamics have a negative impact on the integration discussion?

Group dynamics may play a part in assessment center integration discussions, just as they do in any group interaction, but to a lesser extent. In only a minority of integration discussions do we see evidence that the individual assessors are unduly swayed by judgments of the other assessors. The structured process of reporting behaviors and determining dimension ratings minimizes many of the detrimental group effects present in the typical group decision-making situation.

Does the group discussion process improve or degrade assessment center judgments?

Depending on the purpose of the assessment center and which research you consider, there is reason to believe that group processes may lead to losses in accuracy, to gains in accuracy, or have no effect at all. In our opinion, accuracy is enhanced if the assessors follow the procedures laid down for the traditional method of observing, classifying, reporting, and integrating the behavioral observations. Accuracy will be high because the evaluations are based on behaviors rather than general impressions, each assessor makes independent judgments before discussing those judgments with others, and the decision process is carefully designed to gather information about multiple dimensions from multiple exercises observed by multiple observers.

We turn now to the last major element of a complete assessment center program: feedback of the results to participants and organizational decision makers. In chapter 9 we explore the types of feedback that should be given in selection/promotion, diagnostic, and development assessment centers.

Providing Feedback of Assessment Center Results

The assessment center process of making behavioral observations, evaluating performance on dimensions of professional effectiveness, and predicting future success yields a vast amount of information about each individual. We have seen that these observations and evaluations can be made with a high degree of consistency and accuracy. However, whether the information has any practical value for the individual, managers in the organization, and the entire organization depends on how it is used. Just because the assessors are able to make accurate observations and judgments does not mean that the information will be helpful to anyone else. The value of the information depends on whether or not:

- feedback is given in a timely fashion to the appropriate people;
- reports are delivered sensitively by a creditable person;
- clear examples of both positive and negative results are included in the reports.

Organizations have many options when it comes to handling assessment information. The human resource manager (or other manager in charge of assessment center operations) must make many decisions that will have far-ranging implications about the process of supplying feedback. How such decisions are made depends on the purpose of the assessment center, as well as on ethical and professional considerations. The goals in planning a feedback procedure are to devise an effective system for both retaining

193

and disseminating the information and to achieve the original purpose of the assessment center. At the same time, the rights of the individual must be carefully protected.

MATCHING FEEDBACK TO ASSESSMENT PURPOSE

Assessment programs used for selection, promotion, diagnosis, and development all require different procedures for providing feedback to participants and management. The purpose of a selection or promotion program is to help the organization identify individuals who have potential for success in the organization, either in the near future or over a longer period of time; thus, feedback should be given to the individuals who are making selection and promotion decisions. For these purposes, assessment center information may not be given to other individuals. The organization may want to keep the assessment scores separate from other information provided by other individuals who are making independent evaluations of candidates for selection or promotion. Of course, each candidate should be told the results of the evaluation.

In a diagnostic program, the objective is to devise an individualized training program for each participant; thus, feedback should be given to the participant and to the participant's immediate supervisor so that they can jointly plan future developmental activities. One of the trends in recent assessment centers is the movement toward providing richer diagnostic feedback about strengths and weaknesses on each separate dimension, rather than just scores and numbers.

The purpose of a developmental assessment center is to foster skill development during the assessment center itself; therefore, feedback is most effective if given after the person participates in one or more exercises, so that the participants can learn new skills and practice them in subsequent exercises during the program. Results of developmental assessment center programs may not be supplied to the participants' immediate managers if the organization wishes to keep employee development separate from personnel decision making. On the other hand, some organizations insist that the participant's manager is closely involved with assessment and follow-up development. Another trend is the recent emphasis on an expanded concept of "feedback." Whereas, traditionally feedback was limited to an explanation of how the person performed in the assessment center (e.g., pass/ fail, a score), recently in developmental assessment centers, the term *feedback* has much more of a coaching component in which suggestions are offered about how to perform more effectively on the dimensions in future similar situations.

RIGHTS OF THE INDIVIDUAL AND RESPONSIBILITIES
OF THE ORGANIZATION

Each organization must work out a set of policies and procedures that strike a delicate balance. On the one hand, participants have a right to know the results of assessment and to benefit from participation in the program. On the other hand, the organization must protect against unethical use of the information and the threat of a lawsuit.

The need to provide feedback and the processes of doing so can be considered in the context of a broad set of duties that assessment center administrators have to several key stakeholders in the human resource management system of an organization. Caldwell, Gruys, and Thornton (2003) provided an analysis of the obligations of the assessment center administrator in public service contexts. This analysis of stewardship responsibilities can be generalized to other organizational settings. Caldwell et al. present an analysis that describes seven duties that are relevant to seven stakeholders in the assessment center process. One of the duties of the assessment center administrator is to inform the stakeholders about the process and findings. Of course, candidates need to be informed so they can be prepared and then to have the results explained. In addition, the administrator needs to inform the city administration (information about costs and benefits), the operational department (information about their involvement and the findings), the assessor (so they understand their roles and demands and the use of the findings), the public (so they know good employment practices are being followed), and human resource managers (so they see the role of assessment in the broader HRM system). Finally, an assessment center administrator needs to keep his or her family informed because running an assessment center is often a time consuming task requiring long work days. The ways in which information about and results of an assessment center are handled can serve to fulfill the multitude of obligations that organizations have to multiple constituents.

Rationale for, principles of, and professional guidance in providing feedback, and guidelines for alternative systems of feedback in an assessment center can be found in a variety of legal, professional, ethical, and research sources, shown in Table 9.1. The discussion of feedback in this chapter takes into account the many suggestions and requirements in these sources.

Employee Rights

The system of gathering, storing, and providing feedback must take into account the rights of the individual employee to access to personal information, to privacy, and to know the results of assessments. Employees often

TABLE 9.1
Sources of Regulations and Guidelines Relevant
to Feedback to Persons Being Assessed

- Federal and state laws regarding privacy: These statutes provide legal protection of individuals, and thus guidance to organizations.
- American Psychological Association. (1992). Ethical principles of psychologists and code of ethics. *American Psychologist, 47*, 1597–1611.
- American Educational Research Association, American Psychological Association, American Council on Measurement in Education. (1999). *Standards for Educational and Psychological Tests.* Washington, D.C.: American Psychological Association.
- Society for Industrial and Organizational Psychology (2003). *Principles for the validation and use of personnel selection procedures* (4th ed.). Bowling Green, OH: Author.
- Equal Employment Opportunity Commission, Civil Rights Commission, Department of Labor, & Department of Justice. (1978). *Uniform Guidelines on Employee Selection Procedures, Federal Register, 43*(166), 38290–38309.
- International Task Force on Assessment Center Guidelines (2000). Guidelines and Ethical Considerations for Assessment Center Operations. *Public Personnel Management, 29,* 315–331.
- Research on perceptions of distributive and procedural justice in organizations suggests principles and practices that lead employees to perceive fairness in organizational decision making (Folger & Cropanzano, 1998).

---

have access to their personnel records as a result of the Privacy Act of 1974, which governs federal employees (Bennett-Alexander & Pincus, 1998), state laws with similar provisions (Finkin, 2004; Schuler & Huber, 1990), or the policies of many large companies that voluntarily provide access to this information (Sovereign, 1984). The individual has the right to know the results of any evaluation that will affect his or her status in the organization. More specifically, if assessment center information is going to be used in making decisions about promotion, in evaluating performance, or in designing development plans, then the individual has the right to know what is in the assessment report (International Task Force, 2000).

Even without a law requiring access to the assessment report, it makes good sense to let the individual know how he or she did. The credibility of the system depends on individuals having confidence in its accuracy and fairness. Schuler (1993) pointed out that any evaluation must have social validity, that is, it must be acceptable to the participants. Social validity is based, in part, on the opportunity of the participants to receive information about how the program was conducted and how they fared in the evaluation. Perceptions about selection practices are especially important because applicants and employees generalize from these specific practices about a wide variety of organizational characteristics (Chan, Schmitt, Sacco, & DeShon, 1998; Rynes, 1991; Thornton, 1993).

Furthermore, giving individuals clear feedback about their evaluations can foster quality social exchange relationships between employees and the organization (Cropanzano, Prehar, & Chen, 2002). In such relationships, the individual and the organization have an open and reciprocal relationship with each other that is based on mutual trust. The organization treats the individual as a mature and responsible individual, recognizing his or her rights as an equal partner in the employment relationship. Research has shown that such relationships positively influence employee performance, citizenship, commitment, and satisfaction (Masterson, Lewis, Goldman, & Taylor, 2000; Rupp & Cropanzano, 2002).

Ethical and professional guidelines for industrial and organizational psychologists also require that assessment center participants receive feedback about their evaluations. *Ethical Principles of Psychologists and Code of Conduct* states that psychologists respect the rights of privacy and confidentiality of all people (Principle D) and explain the results of assessments in an understandable language (Standard 2.09). *Standards for Educational and Psychological Tests* (American Educational Research Association et al., 1999) states that when test scores are released to examinees and others, the administrator should provide interpretations of the meaning of scores in simple language (Standard 5.10). In addition, *Guidelines and Ethical Considerations for Assessment Center Operations* (International Task Force, 2000) states that there should be some provision for feedback of the results of an assessment center. Participants already employed by an organization should be allowed to read any written reports and recommendations; outside applicants for employment should be told the final recommendation if they request that information.

Organizational Interests

The organization also has many interests to protect when it devises a system to gather, retain, and disseminate information about employees. First, the organization must ensure that standardized procedures are being followed (American Educational Research Association et al., 1999) so that the system has *operational validity* (Byham & Temlock, 1972). Operational validity means that a selection procedure is being implemented in a consistent and fair manner across the various divisions and departments where it is being used. Schmitt et al. (1990) have shown that the effectiveness of a well-developed assessment center can vary quite dramatically if the program is not implemented in a consistent manner across different job sites.

Second, organizations must maintain control over the results of an assessment center to protect themselves in the event of a lawsuit or investigation by an equal employment opportunity agency. In light of the litigious nature of the United States and other societies, especially in the employment arena, organizations must have written policies about personnel decision making and take steps to ensure that these policies are being followed throughout the organization.

Finally, the organization must ensure that the information is used properly. Assessment centers can be very expensive operations that may involve the valuable time of management assessors. If the program is to benefit the organization and demonstrate its own usefulness for the expense involved, the results must be applied properly.

Other Considerations

The type of feedback given to current participants in an assessment center can influence the effectiveness of future assessments. For example, although it makes sense to give detailed feedback to participants in each specific exercise, a written report of this nature could easily be passed along to someone about to participate in the next assessment program. The advantage to the "informed" participant could alter the subsequent assessment. There is no clear resolution of this conflict. The organization must weigh the benefits and drawbacks of each practice. Most likely, the organization will want to be more protective of the integrity of the exercises in selection and promotion programs; thus, less detailed feedback will be given. In developmental programs, however, more feedback is needed to facilitate learning, and there is less harm if specific information about exercises is passed along to later participants. Leaks of information about the specific content of exercises can affect the integrity of the entire assessment program, but experience has shown that general knowledge of the exercises does not destroy the accuracy of assessments.

The organization must also have clear policies about feedback and information retention because practices in these areas determine whether the organization can conduct meaningful research and evaluation studies on the assessment center. It might seem that detailed information from the assessment center should be disseminated widely throughout the organization. The problem with this practice is that operational managers may base their subsequent performance appraisals on assessment center ratings rather than performance on the job. If the performance appraisals are contaminated with the knowledge of the assessment ratings, it is impossible to evaluate the true accuracy of the assessment center. Therefore, organizations must have clear policies about what information is given to participants and managers, where the reports are kept, who has access to reports, and how long the reports are retained.

THEORIES OF EMPLOYEE JUSTICE PERCEPTIONS

Providing feedback to an individual who has received a negative evaluation for promotion or selection is particularly difficult. One goal of the feedback session is to help the person see that even though the outcome was not favorable to him or her, the procedure for carrying out the center and making decisions based on the results, as well as the treatment received by the administrator, assessors, and other human resource staff was *fair*. Theory and research on perceptions of justice shows that individuals distinguish between *distributive justice, procedural justice, informational justice,* and *interpersonal justice* (Colquitt, 2001; Colquitt, Conlon, Wesson, Porter, & Ng, 2001). Distributive justice refers to beliefs about an outcome or decision that affects us; procedural justice refers to beliefs about the process used to arrive at the decision; informational justice refers to the adequacy and truthfulness of, or justification for, explanations provided for an outcome; interpersonal justice refers to the general dignity and respect with which individuals are treated by those in authority.

An individual's reaction to an unfavorable outcome may be lessened when the outcome is reached via fair procedures and interactions (see Brockner & Wiesenfeld, 1996; Cropanzano & Schminke, 2001; Skarlicki & Folger, 1997). For example, a sales representative may be disappointed that he was not promoted to district manager but may accept that outcome if he understands that his past performance was considered carefully, that he had ample opportunities to demonstrate his skills and aptitudes, and that his credentials were evaluated equally with those of other candidates. It is natural to be disappointed if a decision is not made in our favor, but we may or may not be satisfied with the procedure that led to that decision. If we believe the process, information, and interpersonal treatment is fair, we are more willing to accept the outcome even though we are not happy with it.

In summary, individuals will view a situation as fair when:

- the outcomes they receive reflect their efforts and performance;
- adequate information and feedback is given about an outcome;
- procedures are applied consistently to all individuals;
- neutrality and consistency is shown;
- actions toward the individuals convey kindness, trustworthiness, integrity, and concern;
- there is an appeal process for questioning bad decisions;
- information is conveyed accurately;
- there is a mechanism for providing individuals an opportunity to express their opinions about the process and outcomes;
- ethical standards are abided by;
- timely feedback is given following a decision;
- communications are honest, respectful, forthright, realistic, and accurate.

There is also strong evidence that fairness perceptions predict employee performance, citizenship behavior, satisfaction, trust in management, organizational commitment, and many other important outcomes (Cohen-Charash & Spector, 2001; Colquitt et al., 2001). Furthermore, research shows that perceptions of fairness are closely tied to employees' acceptance of performance feedback. That is, if feedback recipients feel they have been evaluated in a fair manner, they are more likely to believe the feedback is accurate and strive toward goals set based on performance evaluation (Cropanzano & Randall, 1993; Greenberg, 1986; Leung, Su, & Morris, 2001).

Many of the fairness elements listed earlier are built into the assessment center method (Rupp, Baldwin, & Bashshur, 2004). During the feedback session, the assessor or other feedback providers should review these practices so that the participant understands clearly that just procedures were practiced. For example, it is common practice for feedback providers to give a thorough description of the assessment center process. Information about the process usually includes a description of how the assessors took detailed notes of behaviors in the exercises, classified behaviors into performance dimensions using support materials (such as pre-established behavioral examples of each dimension), shared their observations with other assessors observing other exercises, and integrated their observations in a discussion before arriving at consensus ratings or in a mathematical formula. During this description, the feedback provider usually points out that the various assessors served as checks and balances on each other to avoid any idiosyncratic impressions on the part of a single assessor. Only after describing this process should the feedback provider give feedback on performance. It is also common to allow participants to provide *their* feedback on the assessment center program, and to ask questions.

CONSIDERATIONS OF WORKPLACE DIVERSITY

The justice literature reviewed in other sections speaks to how assessment center feedback may be perceived of by individuals *in general*. We can also look to the diversity and relational demography literatures to consider how different forms of feedback might be received by individuals of differing demographic groups, as well as how feedback acceptance might be impacted when feedback providers and recipients differ on various demographic characteristics.

The relational demography literature has called into question whether dissimilarity between feedback providers and recipients might lead recipients to question the accuracy or fairness of the feedback provided. With increased workforce diversity, there is an increased likelihood that assessment center participants will be assessed and provided feedback by someone demographically different from them. Although the research in this area is mixed (Jackson, Joshi, & Erhardt, 2003), some empirical findings suggest that this demographic dissimilarity may be detrimental to feedback acceptance. For example, Geddes and Konrad (2003) found that, in a performance appraisal context, employees reacted more favorably to feedback received from White managers than from managers of other races/ethnicities, and males responded less favorably to feedback received from female (as compared to male) managers. Theory to date (e.g., status characteristics theory, social identity theory) explains that when evaluated by someone one feels different from, one may feel misunderstood or stereotyped in some way. Likewise, if the evaluator is of a group that is not stereotypically associated with management or supervision, their competence may be questioned by the feedback recipient. A recent extension of the similarity–attraction paradigm by Riordan (2000), further predicts that individuals with similar characteristics would more quickly build rapport with one another, have smoother communication, and believe that one another's values and opinions would be validated (Geddes & Konrad, 2003).

This suggests that in developmental programs, designers might consider matching assessors and participants in terms of demographic similarity. However, this may not be possible in many cases, and may be inappropriate in selection, promotion, or diagnostic contexts. To our knowledge, the effectiveness of such a strategy has not been evaluated empirically and therefore should be approached with caution. However, there is evidence that leader–subordinate dyads that share demographic characteristics have more positive relationships, less conflict and role ambiguity, more trust, increased justice perceptions, and higher support, liking, effectiveness, attraction (see Geddes & Konrad, 2003 for a review of this literature).

This summary is simply meant to highlight the many factors that can influence feedback acceptance. With the workforce becoming increasingly demographically diverse, and the rise in women and minorities taking on roles more traditionally held by Anglo men (Cheng, 1997; Heilman et al., 2004; Tomkiewicz et al., 1998), fairness, and more specifically differential fairness perceptions among various demographic subgroups, needs to be paid very special attention when attempting to maximize feedback acceptance within AC programs.

OUTLINE OF ASSESSMENT FEEDBACK

Figure 9.1 provides an outline of topics usually covered in a feedback session. By necessity, this outline is somewhat general because, as we have mentioned, feedback is different for different types of assessment centers.

Introduction

    Establish rapport

    Describe your role as the feedback provider

    Encourage questions, comments, and note taking

Describe the process

    Explain the process and its results

    Review assessment center activities

    Describe assessment methodology: exercises, reports, team evaluation

Describe the results

    Describe performance dimensions

    Provide overall ratings (if applicable)

    Review results on individual dimensions

    Explain the meaning of results

Give developmental suggestions (if applicable)

Close on positive note

FIG. 9.1.   Outline of a feedback session. *Source.* Q New York Telephone Company 1989. Modified with permission of New York Telephone Company, authored by B. Savage.

FEEDBACK IN A PROMOTION PROGRAM

The main purpose of feedback in a promotion program is to give high-level managers information they can use in making promotion decisions. In addition, the participant should be given information so that he or she thoroughly understands the assessment process and results.

Feedback to the Individual Participant

In many assessment centers used for promotion decisions, the participant is given oral feedback by a member of the human resource staff. In fact, Spychalski et al. (1997) found that in 67% of the organizations that responded to their survey, a human resource administrator conducted the feedback session; in 30% of the programs, assessors gave feedback. Feedback in a promotion program usually consists of a statement of the overall assessment rating, a statement of strengths and weaknesses in the dimensions, and a few supporting examples from the various exercises. This feedback session is usually not very lengthy. The person giving feedback should be supportive and sensitive, but must guard against making commitments to the employee. When the overall assessment rating is favorable, the participant must be warned that this does not guarantee promotion. There may not be any immediate openings, and the decision maker may take into account other information that overrides the assessment center rating. If the assessment center evaluation is negative, the participant needs additional support to understand the reasons for the decision. He or she will probably ask many questions about what can be done next, whether there can be another assessment, if there is an appeal process, and so on. The person providing feedback must have a clear understanding of the organization's policy on all these issues.

Feedback to Management

When an assessment center is being used for promotion, the results should be given to the managers who make such decisions. The decision maker needs to know the results of each individual's assessment and to have some comparative data. The comparative data may be the results for the group as a whole (these candidates might even be ranked) or some larger norm group consisting of people assessed in the program in the past. The comparative information helps to give the decision maker some perspective on the overall assessment evaluation. For example, he or she might put more weight on the assessment information if it shows that the candidate in question performed at a higher level than most of the other participants in all past programs.

The decision maker is most interested in the final overall assessment as to the promotability of the individual. Assessments of strengths and weaknesses on the various dimensions might be useful, too. Of course, the assessment information should be presented in conjunction with other information about the candidate, for example, length of time with the company, types of experience, recent performance records, and recommendations from supervisors. All of these sources provide valuable information about the candidate's suitability for the job.

Figure 9.2 shows an example of a summary sheet for the evaluation of six candidates who were finalists for one position. Note that the overall assessment rating and the various dimension ratings are provided, along with the names of the assessors for that program. Of course, a complete definition of the dimensions would also be available. Knowing the assessors may help the decision maker interpret the results. Assuming the assessors are credible managers who have been trained well, the decision maker should be willing to accept the results as meaningful.

Knowing the dimension ratings may allow the decision maker to overlook a marginal overall assessment rating. For example, Gary Dutton was

	Gary Dutton	Rick Daves	Ken Lemon	Mary Armor	Steve Blake	Debra Stan
Written Communication	3	4	5	4	3	2
Planning and Organization	3	3	4	4	4	3
Interpersonal Sensitivity	1	4	3	4	4	3
Delegation	3	3	3	3	3	2
Decision Making	5	3	2	4	3	3
Intellectual Abilities	5	3	3	3	3	2
Assertiveness and Initiative	1	3	2	3	3	3
OVERALL ASSESSMENT RATING	2	3	4	4	4	2

Assessors: Martin, Bloom, Lawrence

FIG. 9.2. Assessment center summary sheet. *Note.* "3" is a passing score.

not recommended for promotion, presumably because he was rated low on interpersonal sensitivity and assertiveness and initiative. On the other hand, he received very *high* marks on intellectual abilities and decision making. If the decision maker is looking for someone with those particular strengths, he or she might discount the overall assessment rating and promote Gary.

A brief written report might also be prepared for the decision maker and for the assessment files. The report might describe each participant's strengths and weaknesses and include examples of behavior in a few of the exercises as supportive evidence. This report might also include ratings on the dimensions and other information not usually given to the participant.

For documentation purposes and for research, a complete file should be prepared with all exercise reports, ratings, and rankings, with demographic information on the participant's age, sex, race, date of hire, and so on. This record should be kept locked in the office of the human resource department. It should not be given to the decision maker or the participant, except in organizations governed by open-records laws that permit employees access to all public information, including records relevant to the employee's employment status.

FEEDBACK IN A DIAGNOSTIC PROGRAM

The feedback given to the participant and management in a diagnostic program is quite different from that given in a promotion or selection program. Here the purposes of assessment are to (a) provide a diagnosis of strengths and developmental needs, (b) foster effective developmental planning for the individual, and (c) motivate the individual to undertake follow up activities. Assessment should be only the first step in the planning of a series of developmental assignments that will lead to the growth and progress of the individual. The example in chapter 2 of the diagnostic assessment center at Technosoft illustrates one way that participants can be directed toward training classes that address specific training needs.

Because of the planning aspects of diagnostic feedback, feedback is often given to the participant's immediate supervisor by a human resource manager or a management assessor who is on the same level or higher than the supervisor of the participant. For example, in one assessment center, the participants were first-level supervisors and the assessors were third-level managers. These assessors then provided feedback to the participants and to their managers, who were second-level department heads. Because the assessors were at a higher level, they had considerable influence over the developmental planning efforts of other line managers.

One of the biggest challenges that organizations face is the difficulty of getting participants to follow-up participation—to engage in developmental activities following the assessment center. Thornton (1976) found that feedback interviews of the type just described (i.e., a midlevel manager/assessor giving feedback to the participant and his boss), in conjunction with support materials to help the participants' supervisors, led to better developmental planning for supervisors and technical personnel assessed in a large manufacturing organization. The support materials included a workbook in which the individual and his or her supervisor recorded dimensions in need of improvement, action steps to remediate the weaknesses, and target dates for reviewing progress.

These practices are just one example of the practices that have been found effective in identifying and developing leadership talent in organizations (Byham, Smith, & Paese, 2000). Byham described the necessity of having an integrated system of talent development which identifies a talent pool, diagnoses strengths and weaknesses, provides growth opportunities in assignments, short-term experiences, training, and coaching, and engages the chief executive officer in supporting the entire system.

Feedback to the Participant

In a diagnostic program, the participant is usually provided with a written report describing in detail the assessment evaluations. Figure 9.3, at the end of this chapter, shows an example of some portions of such a report. The report gives a clear statement of Bob's relative strengths and weaknesses on the dimensions, and then goes further to provide a thorough diagnosis of each dimension of his performance. For example, rather than just saying Bob is poor on delegation, the report states that he is willing to delegate, but does not give the subordinate any real responsibility and does not use any control mechanisms to determine whether the delegated work is carried out. For planning and organizing, Bob demonstrated a good theoretical approach, but he had difficulties applying the skills. For example, he tends to "live with things" rather than take some action to study an issue or lay out steps to correct a problem. The report includes examples of effective and ineffective behavior in several exercises.

Whereas the report for the promotion program may be only one to three pages long, a diagnostic report tends to be much longer. It may have one page for each of the 8 to 10 dimensions. A longer report is needed to provide more than just an evaluation on the dimensions; it provides an analysis of that individual's performance on the various facets of each dimension. The assessors may also compare and contrast behaviors relevant to a dimension displayed in different types of situations. For example, the participant's leadership skills might be quite effective in one-on-one situations, yet very poor in groups. The report also contains suggestions for developmental activities that the assessors believe would help the participant improve in the areas of weakness. Before the assessor prepares the final written report, he or she may meet with the participant to give oral feedback. This meeting, which often takes place soon after the integration discussion, gives the participant a chance to comment on the report and clarify any misunderstandings. During this meeting, the assessor wants to make sure the participant understands the reasons for the various evaluations and gain agreement from him or her regarding developmental needs. In a sense, the assessor is "selling" the participant on the accuracy of the report before it is presented to his or her supervisor. It is important for the participant to accept the report so he or she is willing to make a development plan and take follow-up action based on the findings. During the feedback meeting with the participant's supervisor, the assessor will then be able to help the participant get the types of developmental assignments needed for growth. The assessor thus takes on some of the roles of mentor (Arnold, 2001; Hunt & Michael, 1983) in supporting the participant in the advancement of his or her career.

Feedback to Management

After feedback is given to the participant, oral feedback and the written report can then be given to the participant's supervisor in a meeting between the supervisor, the participant, and the assessor. Here we can see the advantage of having the third-level manager serve as assessor and give the feedback. As a higher level manager, the assessor may have influence in ensuring that the assessment results will be used to foster the participant's development. Of course, many organizations prefer to have someone from the human resource staff deliver these feedback reports, because assessor/manager time is so valuable. And, in many cases, this is just as effective. On the other hand, it is a not-so-subtle pressure on the boss to know that a higher level manager is interested in the development of one of his or her people and will be watching as the follow-up efforts unfold.

FEEDBACK IN AN INDIVIDUAL AND ORGANIZATIONAL DEVELOPMENT PROGRAM

Whereas feedback in the promotion and diagnostic programs may be provided several days after the assessment center program, the feedback in a training program must be given immediately after participation in one or more exercises to have the most impact. The purpose of a development program is to help the participants develop new skills. The standard recommendation in the feedback and training literature is to provide immediate and specific feedback about performance (London, 1997), set specific and challenging goals for improvement (Locke & Latham, 1990), and then give the learner a chance to practice new modes of behavior (Salas & Cannon-Bowers, 2001). Little learning takes place if the participant goes through all the exercise activities with no guidance and then receives feedback at the end of the program with no opportunity to adjust behaviors in subsequent learning situations (Thornton & Cleveland, 1990). Some large-scale behavioral simulations, similar to assessment centers, are set up so that feedback is not given until the end of the 2-day program. Participants may gain some insight into their own ways of handling these situations, but little skill development can take place unless the person gets a chance to repeat the activity and receive reinforcement for correct behaviors. At IDS Corporation

(Braaten, 1990), daily feedback, along with suggestions for improvement, are given to participants so they can practice new skills in subsequent parts of the 3½-day program.

An example of how immediate feedback and subsequent practice are built into a development assessment center was shown in chapter 2's description of the leadership training program at AMW. Two blocks of exercises of the same type were included in the program. Feedback after the first block of exercises provided guidance for the participant to try out new actions in the second block of exercises and then get another round of feedback. This process allows the participants to not only develop skills during the program itself, but also to plan other feedback and follow-up actions to ensure that these skills are developed even further and transferred to the job.

Whereas the standard recommendation is to provide specific feedback on past performance and to provide guidance on alternative specific actions to take in the future, recent theory and research has questioned the value of being specific. Goodman, Wood, and Hendrickx (2004) have pointed out that an increase in specificity may lead to better immediate performance, but not to better performance over a longer time period. Increase in specificity may actually lead the person to engage in less exploration behavior, which is needed for true learning to take place. Thus, specificity in feedback may not lead to some of the behaviors that are most effective for long-term learning. A challenge for the feedback giver is to provide enough information so the participant understands performance deficits, and at the same time helps the participant generalize to other settings and explore future behavioral goals for his or her own improvement.

Assessors/Facilitators

The role of the staff members in a development assessment center is somewhat different from the role of assessors in a promotion or diagnostic assessment center. In a training assessment center, the staff members attempt to help the participants learn new skills or help the group develop better teamwork. Therefore, he or she is often called a facilitator, as opposed to an assessor.

Development facilitators should have many of the skills needed for other kinds of assessment centers. They must be able to observe and record behavior, to accurately classify behaviors into dimensions, and to articulate these observations to other facilitators and the participants. Some skills needed by assessors in evaluative assessment centers are not as important for facilitators. They may not be required to make overall judgments about the effectiveness of performance on the dimensions or to make predictions about long-range success in the organization. They do not have to have deep insights into organizational requirements. On the other hand, facilitators must have effective teaching skills, such as excellent oral communication, empathy, and listening ability. They must be able to provide effective feedback about behaviors displayed in the simulation exercises in a supportive manner. Some research has found that it is, at times, difficult to find individuals who have both of these diverse skill sets, and has suggested some individuals do the assessing and others do the coaching (Atchley, Smith, & Hoffman, 2003).

Facilitators can be managers or human resource staff members from the organization, or training and development consultants from outside the organization. Consultants can often give valuable insights into effective group dynamics. Because they have no ties to the organization, they can observe behaviors objectively, and they have experience in diverse organizations.

Peer Feedback

When the assessment center includes group exercises, such as a leaderless group discussion, problem-solving activities, or business games, the participants have a chance to observe the behavior of other participants relevant to job effectiveness. In some programs, the participants are asked to evaluate the performance of other participants, for example, by rating the creativity of others' ideas, rank ordering others in terms of their contribution to group accomplishments, or nominating someone to lead a project team. Surveys show that approximately 20% of the assessment centers in the United States and German-speaking countries use peer ratings, but they do not distinguish the relative use of peer ratings in promotional or developmental assessment centers. Krause and Gebert (2003) found that whereas 18% of promotional and developmental assessment centers in German-speaking countries used peer ratings, only 4% of assessment centers used for external selection did so. Interestingly, Coors Brewing Company makes peer feedback (and receptivity to such feedback!) a central part of its behavioral assessment process in screening new employees because it places high emphasis on teamwork in its production workers (J. Kane, personal communication, May 15, 2001).

Feedback of peer assessment information can be very powerful. Most organizations do not give feedback from peer evaluations in promotion programs, because even though peer descriptions might be valid for predicting success, participants in an assessment program often feel that competitive pressures make the evaluations inaccurate.

In contrast, peer feedback has proven helpful and acceptable in diagnostic and training programs in the United States (Thornton & Byham, 1982) and in Japan (Umeshima, 1989). In these situations, there is little competition and the climate promotes supportiveness and self-insights. Participants usually want to learn all they can about their own developmental needs and how they can improve their skills. Input from peers provides a valuable additional perspective to the feedback from management and staff assessors. In fact, some organizations find peer feedback so valuable and so readily acceptable that they have designed the entire assessment center around peer evaluations. Human resource management staff coordinate the program, and no higher level management personnel are used as assessors.

Computerized Feedback

Recent technological developments provide the means for immediate feedback following specific behavioral responses in assessment exercises. For example, in an interview simulation exercise developed for the Federal Bureau of Investigation, the participant engages in an adaptive interaction with a role player displayed on a video screen (Crudup, 2004). As the participant asks questions, voice recognition technology allows the virtual person on the video screen to respond appropriately, and the dialogue ensues. The program interprets the participant's responses and a small image either reinforces good responses or scolds bad responses.

RESPONSE TO FEEDBACK

Numerous surveys have been conducted of participants' reactions to feedback from an assessment center (Dodd, 1977; Kudisch, Lundquist, & Smith, 2002; Poteet & Kudisch, 2003; Thornton & Byham, 1982). The large majority of participants respond favorably, saying that the feedback interview is helpful in understanding their own strengths and weaknesses. They find the feedback provider supportive and willing to give clear examples of the reasons for the assessment results. Of course, feedback is handled very differently in different organizations and may be handled inconsistently by different staff members. Therefore, it is difficult to generalize about all feedback sessions.

There are some common ingredients that make feedback more acceptable to participants. For example, participants like to learn about specific examples of behaviors in more than one exercise that support the evaluations. In addition, they want the feedback to focus on evaluations that represent consensus among the assessors, rather than on the idiosyncratic reactions of one assessor. These characteristics of feedback have been found to be effective in a wide variety of organizational settings (Ilgen, Fisher, & Taylor, 1979; Taylor, Fisher, & Ilgen, 1984).

In an interesting study of the usefulness of an assessment center for developmental purposes, Fleenor (1988) found that both good and poor performers accepted feedback when it was presented by a knowledgeable source, when the feedback included performance-related information, and when the person giving feedback was interested in their development. Furthermore, both good and poor performers subsequently demonstrated improved performance on the job after receiving feedback.

A study by Fletcher (1991) provides a rare examination of the longitudinal effects of assessment center participation over a 6-month period. Even though immediately following assessment some attitudes increased (e.g., dominance and pursuit of excellence) and other attitudes declined (e.g., need for achievement and work ethic), all these attitudes returned to their initial levels after 6 months. Unsuccessful candidates appeared to experience the most negative effects over time, with declines in feelings of competitiveness and self-esteem. Fletcher concluded that organizations should give feedback quickly to exploit the learning potential that immediate changes in attitude provide and provide supportive counseling to those whose assessments are low.

THE ROLE OF THE INDIVIDUAL PARTICIPANT

The individual participant plays a key role in the success of diagnostic and developmental assessment centers. No matter how well the organization conceives, develops, and implements an assessment center, diagnostic and developmental assessment centers will not achieve their full potential if the individual participant is not motivated properly. In a diagnostic program, the individual must be actively involved in follow-up actions after learning about developmental needs. In a developmental program, the participant must be motivated to process the feedback and attempt to improve performance during the assessment center and later on the job.

Research shows that the ways in which the individual responds to assessment will affect the outcomes of the developmental experience. Jones and Whitmore (1995) found that even though participation in an assessment center did not predict promotion (in comparison with a control group), those individuals who followed developmental recommendations had more career motivation, worked well with others, and were more likely to be promoted. T. Byham and Wilkerson (2003) found that relatively few managers engaged in follow-up development activities after an assessment center. These studies and others suggest there may be a number of personal characteristics that differentiate among people who do and do not benefit from the experience of participating in an assessment center.

What are the qualities of a person who is likely to benefit from a diagnostic or development assessment center? These qualities may include: readiness to develop, motivation to engage in training, a learning goal orientation, and involvement in developmental activities. Walter (2004) found that a measure of readiness to develop containing questions about awareness of one's developmental needs, activities to search for developmental opportunities, and taking actions to develop predicted students' developmental activities during the semester and their final course grade. In a meta-analysis of 20 years of training research, Colquitt, LePine, and Noe (2000) found that motivation to learn (defined simply as the desire to learn the training material) predicted a variety of learning outcomes (including knowledge, skill acquisition, and transfer) beyond the effects of cognitive ability. A variety of research studies suggest that a learning goal orientation involving a desire to improve one's competence (as opposed to a performance goal orientation involving demonstrating one's competence to others) (Dweck & Leggett, 1988; Nicholls, 1984) is related to feedback seeking behavior (Tuckey, Brewer, & Williamson, 2002), solicitation of help (Middleton & Midgely, 1997) and transfer of training (Ford, Smith, Weissbein, Gully, & Salas, 1998). Involvement in work-related learning and development activities has been shown to relate to intentions to participate in development and ultimately to participate in developmental activities (Maurer, Weiss, & Barbeite, 2003).

Needed Research

There have been few studies of the effects of feedback on assessment center participants beyond the Fleenor and Jones and Whitmore studies and the polling of participants at the end of various assessment centers. It would be interesting to know what types of feedback lead to greater acceptance of the findings in promotion programs, and whether good feedback leads to more favorable impressions of the organization in selection programs. In diagnostic programs, it would be helpful to understand what types of feedback lead participants to engage in more conscientious developmental planning, and more importantly, what leads participants to engage in further developmental activities, and ultimately to perform better on the job. Based on research in other fields, we might expect that specific and descriptive (rather than general and evaluative) feedback would be more helpful in developmental programs, but the research by Goodman et al. (2004) cited earlier warns that specific feedback may, in fact, lead to fewer exploration behaviors so essential to true learning. There has been no research on these issues in the assessment center context.

SUMMARY AND CONCLUSIONS

We can look on the feedback session as both the "end" and the "beginning." It is the end in the sense that feedback is the culmination of all the work that has been done to develop, implement, and execute an assessment center. As we have seen, feedback is effective only if the dimensions have been chosen correctly, the exercises have been designed properly, and the assessors observe, classify, and judge behavior accurately. "Correctly," "properly," and "accurately" must be interpreted in light of the purpose of the assessment center. There is no one best way to carry out each of these steps. In this chapter we have seen how feedback must be tailored to provide the kinds of information needed by decision makers and participants alike.

Verbal feedback should be given in all types of assessment programs; written feedback should usually be given to employees but need not be given to external applicants. Written feedback is briefer and more general in promotion programs, and longer and more detailed in diagnostic programs. The content of feedback in diagnostic and training programs should be much more detailed so that participants can learn from the experience. In contrast, for reasons of security, exercise materials should usually not be reviewed in detail in feedback after a selection or promotion program.

Feedback is most commonly given by human resource management staff members, but management assessors can be effective in giving feedback to the participants' immediate supervisors in a diagnostic program, as the first step in developmental planning. Managers, human resource staff, and outside consultants can be helpful facilitators in a developmental program.

Aside from the participant, who should be given the results of an assessment center? There are very good reasons for giving feedback to the participant's immediate supervisor in a diagnostic program, and for not giving the immediate supervisor feedback in promotion programs. In a training program, the participant is often the only one who gets feedback.

The feedback session is also a beginning, in the sense that the assessment information must now be put to good use in the organization. In selection and promotion programs, the assessment center results provide input, along with other types of information, to these important personnel decisions. The assessment center ratings should be used in conjunction with other sources of information about the candidate's background, education, work performance, and potential. In diagnostic programs, the assessment center diagnosis of strengths and weaknesses is only the first step in planning follow-up developmental activities for each individual. The individual and his or her supervisor must sit down and combine the assessment results with information about the individual's performance on the job. Together they should lay out specific action steps. As in the medical field, a diagnosis is not very helpful if no treatment is forthcoming. In development programs, the feedback is an indication of what the person is doing well and what needs to be improved, but for the training to have any effect, there must be opportunities to try out new behaviors and get further feedback.

The assessment center process is particularly good at providing feedback that is helpful for all these purposes. Most organizations find that feedback on assessment center results is well received—compared with feedback on other evaluative information such as performance appraisals—because the assessments are based on specific behavioral observations rather than general impressions. It is informative to compare the behavioral feedback from an assessment center to the feedback that might be given if an intelligence test were used to make selection/promotion decisions, to diagnose development needs, or to foster learning. Although IQ tests may have high predictive validity, it is unlikely that feedback to assessees would be very helpful or received very favorably if the feedback read anything like this: "You were not recommended for promotion because of low IQ" or "You are low on intelligence, get smarter" or "Undertake some activities to get more intelligent." Finally, the intense involvement of multiple assessors gives the feedback credibility. Armed with assessment center results, human resource managers find that they are in a good position to help employees make important decisions and launch productive development plans.

Questions remain about what assessment centers really measure and whether they are worth the cost. In the next chapter, we examine in some detail further issues about the accuracy and interpretation of overall assessment center ratings and compare their effectiveness and cost with some alternative assessment methods.

Participant's Name: Bob Leonard

Reviewed with Department Head
Program Staff: Chuck Stuart, Bill Blake, Randy Golden

The purpose of this report is to summarize the program staff's observations of the participant, to assist individuals and their supervisors in identifying strengths and development needs, and to help in planning developmental activities.

Overall Summary
Bob appeared to be very sincere and active in this program. He thought the session was slightly more intense than he expected, although he was not noticeably affected by this. He felt that many of the exercises were realistic and job related. We observed distinct strengths and developmental needs in some dimensions, although we observed that degrees of performance in one dimension area were reflected in other dimensions.

Summary of Demonstrated Strengths
Bob demonstrated strengths in *Problem Analysis, Judgment, Oral Communication and Sensitivity*. He demonstrated an appreciation of delegation, control, planning and organizing, and leadership. These however were observed to offer room for good improvement.

Summary of Developmental Needs
Developmental needs were observed in *Planning and Organizing, Delegation, Control, Leadership and Development of People*. We will illustrate within each dimension how we feel these areas can be enhanced.

Comments
This report is segmented by dimensions. A dimension will include a definition and a narrative description of the participant's behavior in the program.

Management Skills

Planning and Organizing
The ability to anticipate as well as to lay out one's work and subordinae's work effectively. To be able to summarize divergent information and effectively coordinate tasks, materials, and manpower.

Observations recorded in this dimension indicate a developmental need exists. Although Bob has a good theoretical approach to Planning and Organizing, some difficulties were encountered in the application of it. We observed examples of Planning and Organizing primarily in the Compensation Committee and the In-Basket. In the Compensation Committee Bob planned the presentation of his candidate very well, and followed through with an effective presentation of the candidate. Bob indicated during his In-Basket interview that his approach was to sort items into: 1. personnel problems, 2. production problems, 3. schedule problems. He stated that on his return, his priorities would be: 1. sit down with Bill, 2. get with O'Brian, 3. have introductory meeting with 'his people.

FIG. 9.3.   (*Continued*)

215

Examples indicating less planning and organizing occurred in the Background Interview, L.K. Fawcett, and the Interview Simulation.

- Background Interview: When asked what plans and goals he had, he responded, "I don't know." He indicated that he personally doesn't get involved in planning his section's work (unless his help is solicited).

- L.K. Fawcett: Bob didn't schedule the last hour of the day for two plumbers. He put 2 men on a 1-man job because "I didn't know what to do with the other man except have his idle." He interrupted jobs for lunch rather than have plumbers work straight through and take lunch after the job.

- Interview Simulation: Although Bob planned his interview to cover past and current job performance, no planning for future goals of improved performance were indicated. As a result, the objective of a commitment to better performance was not obtained. Bob indicated during the feedback interview that he felt this goal and objective was achieved. We discussed this point; I explained that we looked at this rather narrowly. The goal was improved performance and acceptance of the fact that performance had fallen.

We also observed that Bob has a tendency to "live with things" rather than chart out a method of change. When reviewing the work load problem his section had, he indicated that a "system study" was made of the operation. Although he recognized the problem, he himself did not initiate this. In the Management Problems exercise, many opportunities were passed up by Bob. For example, Bob got the group's attention by saying "I'm sure there are lots of things you could do . . ." but then dropped it with no specific plans being made. This feeling will be discussed further in other dimensions.

We encourage Bob to consider priorities of his daily assignments, attack the most important issues first and stick with them. We encourage development of the "execution" phase of this planning. Personal assessment of his success in completing these plans will help monitor his growth.

Delegation

Turning over a specific job or responsibility to the appropriate person(s) with some reporting control and accountability: giving adequate, but not overly detailed instructions; ability to use subordinates effectively and to understand when a decision could best be made.

This dimension was observed to be a developmental need. Bob indicated a willingness to delegate, e.g., "try to let them be on their own" (Background Interview). In the In-Basket, of the 14 items, 9 were sent to Bill, 2 to Suzy, and 2 to Tom O'Brien. Bob's delegation was generally clear and understandable. We did observe two aspects of delegation, which offer room for development.

1. He frequently gives instruction to his subordinates, i.e., delegates activities, fact finding, etc. but he was not observed transferring responsibility and/or decision making to subordinates, e.g., "Let's order enough to get some feedback from the trade, but still order from our regular suppliers." "You decide" delegation was not observed.

2. Bob did not use any control mechanisms to check if work was accomplished. He did not give due dates and he did not ask for specific answers to his memos. He did not make a list to follow up on his requests.

We feel that, as the definition indicates, delegation should include some aspects of responsibility, decision making, and accountability to most effectively utilize subordinates (and to stimulate their own personal development).

FIG. 9.3. Diagnostic report of supervisory skills workshop.

Chapter 10

Varieties of Validity Evidence
for Assessment Centers

The last five chapters have given a detailed view of each of the key elements of the assessment center method. We now step back from our detailed analysis of the elements to take a broader look at the effectiveness of the method as a whole: We analyze the extent to which the assessment center has validity. Validity is a general concept covering evidence that an assessment or development procedure is capable of achieving its stated purposes. Because any assessment technique can be used for a variety of purposes, many different types of evidence must be considered. For our purposes here, we consider whether the accumulated evidence supports the three main applications of the assessment center method covered in this book: prediction for selection/ promotion, diagnosis, and development. As we do this, our evaluation of validity covers all the steps taken to develop and implement an assessment center, because the results of all these steps provide relevant evidence. Specifically, we see that in the better assessment centers:

- Dimensions are chosen on the basis of careful job analysis or competency modeling. Different dimensions are chosen for different purposes, and different definitions for dimensions are written for different levels of jobs, different organizations, and different cultures.
- Simulation exercises are designed to elicit behavior relevant to dimensions. Different types of exercises and different content in the same type of exercise are prepared for different applications.
- Assessors are trained to observe, record, classify, and scale behaviors. The competence of assessors to fulfill their roles is established.

- Information is integrated either in a discussion to achieve consensus among assessors, or in a statistical formula. Steps are taken to design the consensus discussion to minimize the potential biases that can interfere with, and to maximize the benefits of, the quality of group decision making. Statistical formulae for integration are cross validated.
- A method is designed to provide feedback to participants, and possibly their managers, to serve the objectives of the assessment center.

Documentation of each of these steps provides an essential basis for establishing the validity of an assessment center.

Several questions must still be addressed in our consideration of whether assessment centers are a valid human resource management technique. For example:

- Is there evidence to support the contention that assessment centers fulfill the functions organizations use them for?
- Do assessment centers actually measure the dimensions they are designed to measure?
- Do assessment centers make accurate predictions about the individual's potential, development needs, or future success?
- What alternative explanations can be given for why assessment centers work?
- How does the assessment center method compare with other evaluation methods?
- Do assessment centers have utility, that is, do the benefits outweigh the costs?
- What do participants and assessors think about in assessment and how do they feel about assessment center procedures?

We have already laid the groundwork for the answers to these questions in our review of assessment center research. For example, we have seen in chapter 5 that dimensions are selected to represent critical aspects of performance required for the job of interest. In chapter 6 we showed how exercises are built to simulate important challenges in relevant work settings. In chapter 7, we described the training that assessors are provided to ensure they carry out the processes of observing, recording, classifying, and scaling behaviors. That chapter also reviewed evidence that assessors can observe and evaluate behavior with considerable reliability. In chapter 8, we described the processes followed in assessment centers to increase the potential advantages and overcome the potential disadvantages of group decision making. That chapter also reviewed evidence that assessors show considerable interrater reliability and agreement in ratings of performance dimensions and overall performance after they have shared observations. We now address more complex questions about the ability of assessment centers to achieve organizational aims.

THE VARIETY OF VALIDITY EVIDENCE RELATED TO ASSESSMENT CENTERS

The question "What do assessment centers really measure?" must ultimately be answered by empirical research evidence. However, the conclusion—whether or not the assessment center process is of value—cannot be determined by one correlation statistic or one research study. The many studies that provide evidence about content of the exercises, evidence of the internal structure of the assessments, relationships among different measures of the same attributes, relationships between assessment data and many types of criteria (including performance on the job), changes in assessment center scores over time, differences in assessments of different subgroups (e.g., men and women, different racial groups, different age groups), and the contributions to an organization's overall human resource objectives—all must be examined. All of this evidence must then be interpreted to provide support for or refutation of the claims being made about the validity of the assessment center method (Aguinis, Henle, & Ostroff, 2001; Landy, 1986; Schmitt, Cortina, Ingerick, & Wiechmann, 2003).

In decades past, validity evidence was classified into three separate categories, and researchers and practitioners frequently referred to "content validity," "criterion validity" (which included "concurrent validity" and "predictive validity"), and "construct validity" as separate and distinct "validities." Authors sometimes wrote that "Test X has content validity" or "Test Y does not have construct validity." Such statements are no longer considered appropriate, and probably never were. Experts in the field have since recognized that all evidence related to a test must be interpreted to provide evidence for the validity of results stemming from a particular assessment (Landy, 1986; Schmitt et al., 2003). Binning and Barrett (1989) emphasized that even though there are many different types of evidence we can examine, validity boils down to an interpretation of all the accumulated evidence.

This modern approach to test validation has been codified in *Standards for Educational and Psychological Testing* (AERA et al., 1999): "A sound validity argument integrates various strands of evidence into a coherent account of the degree to which existing evidence and theory support the intended interpretation of test scores for specific uses. . . . Ultimately, the validity of an intended interpretation of test scores relies on all the available evidence relevant to the technical quality of a testing system" (p. 17). The *Standards* describes several strands of evidence that must be intertwined to form conclusions about test validity:

- Test content: analyses of the relationship of test content and the construct to be measured, and the extent to which the content domain represents the performance domain. Evidence can come from expert judgments about the relative importance of the assessment content and its comparability to the actual job.
- Evidence of internal structure: investigations of the relationship among test items and test components. Scores on similar items/dimensions should be logically related.
- Response processes: studies of the processes test takers engage in while taking the test. This can be done by asking participants about their strategies for responding and how they reacted to the testing situation.
- Convergent and discriminant relationships: studies of the relationship of the measure with other measures of the same and different constructs. Similar constructs should be related; dissimilar constructs should be unrelated.
- Test-criterion relationships: studies of the relationships of the measure with measures of performance deemed important by individuals in the organization. Test scores should predict performance or performance changes due to assessment center feedback or developmental coaching.
- Validity generalization: meta-analyses of test-criterion relationships obtained from many validity studies. The relationship should not be a function of statistical and measurement artifacts.
- Consequences of testing: investigations of whether the testing process results in positive and negative consequences that are intended and unintended. Particular attention should be focused on the intended positive consequences and the unintended negative consequences. This sort of evidence has also been termed "consequential validity" (Messick, 1998).

THE RELATIONSHIP BETWEEN THE TYPE OF EVIDENCE AND THE PURPOSE OF THE ASSESSMENT CENTER

As we have described throughout this book, assessment centers are used primarily for three purposes: prediction for selection/promotion, diagnosis, and development. Thus, we have emphasized that when used for different purposes, assessment centers must be designed and implemented in different ways. Assessment centers for different purposes will vary in terms of their dimensions, instructions in exercises, methods of observation and rating, procedures for integrating information from observers, and feedback to participants and others in the organization.

We now undertake a discussion of the different kinds of evidence that are available to understand the validity of assessment centers used for different purposes. When assessment centers are used for selection and promotion we are making an inference that assessment center ratings of overall performance will predict future job performance. When they are used for diagnostic purposes, we infer that the strengths and weaknesses identified are accurate, and that participants will engage in some follow-up action to remediate weaknesses. When assessment centers are used for development, we are assuming that participants will learn/develop in some way as a result of the assessment center experience itself or will engage in additional development following the assessment and feedback. Specifying the type of validity evidence relevant to these different purposes provides a framework for interpreting the research findings to date, and understanding the overall effectiveness of the assessment center method. Table 10.1 provides an outline of the types of evidence that have been gathered and that are relevant to three applications of the assessment center method. We discuss each of the "cells" of the table in the sections that follow.

VALIDITY EVIDENCE RELATED
TO SELECTION/PROMOTION PROGRAMS

When assessment centers are used to select external applicants into an organization or to promote internal employees from one position into one or more higher level positions, the inference being made is that the assessment procedure measures a general attribute of potential to be successful in a new job. This general attribute is often a global ability such as "general managerial ability" or "general sales ability." Each of these general abilities is a composite set of more specific abilities. In much the same way that an intelligence test is often a measure of "general mental ability," defined as a complex set of specific abilities (e.g., verbal reasoning, quantitative analysis, spatial visualization), an assessment center may be designed to measure "general managerial ability," defined as a complex set of specific task and interpersonal abilities relevant to managing an organization. For selection/promotion assessment centers, a wide variety of evidence has been accumulated. This evidence suggests that well-built assessment centers demonstrate validity.

TEST CONTENT

The content of assessment centers designed for selection and promotion is typically built to simulate the "target job" (i.e., the job or set of jobs for which the person is being considered). Some assessment centers are built

TABLE 10.1
Varieties of Validity Evidence

Evidence based on:	Application of Assessment Center		
	Selection/promotion	Diagnosis	Development
Test content	Job analysis and competency modeling Simulations SMEs' and assessors' judgments	Multiple measures of distinct performance dimensions	Selection of developable dimensions
Internal structure	Agreement on observations Convergence across exercises Interrater agreement Correlations among dimensions	Mixed evidence regarding structure of within-exercise dimension ratings	Multiple opportunities to learn and get feedback
Response processes	Positive responses of participants and assessors	Positive responses of participants and assessors	Changes in attitudes, understanding, and performance
Convergent and discriminant evidence	Correlation of OAR with other assessment method (e.g., cognitive and personality measures)	Correlations of final dimension ratings with other assessments of dimensions	Dimension differentiation, internal & external construct validation, analysis of DAC & multisource agreement on dimension ratings
Test-criterion relations	Correlations of OAR with performance, progress, salary Incremental validity	Correlation of dimension scores and future performance on dimensions	Pre-post change in dimension effectiveness
Validity generalization	Schmidt & Hunter (1998); Gaugler et al. (1987); Hardison & Sackett (2004)	Arthur, Day, et al. (2003); Woehr & Arthur (2003)	NA
Consequences of testing	No or smaller subgroup differences Less adverse impact Positive reactions	Awareness of strengths and weaknesses Readiness to engage in development	Participants learn about themselves and improve professionally

to screen candidates for a specific job. Applicants may be assessed for "external sales person." Inside an organization, police patrol officers may be assessed for promotion to "lieutenant." In each of these applications, the content of the exercises is often built to closely represent the activities of the target job in a specific organization. Alternatively, some assessment centers are built to assess potential for a wider range of jobs. For example, college recruits may be assessed for selection into "management trainee" positions in a variety of departments, divisions, and functional assignments; or first-level supervisors throughout the organization may be assessed to identify long-range potential to move into mid and higher level management throughout the organization. In these latter applications, the content of the exercises is often built to resemble a wide range of applicable situations. In all of these applications, the exercises are built to assess a complex set of behaviors that constitute potential for effective performance in the target job or jobs.

Referring to Table 10.1, we begin by examining evidence of whether content of an assessment center is appropriate. The validity inference is supported if the assessment center begins with a careful identification of job tasks and the attributes underlying effectiveness on the tasks through systematic job analysis and/or competency modeling. As described in chapter 5, assessment center developers typically compile lists of job tasks on the basis of reading source documents, observing and interviewing job incumbents or their supervisors, and then use questionnaires to obtain judgments from other subject matter experts to confirm the importance or criticality of job tasks. Subject matter experts also provide ratings of importance of lists of knowledge, skills, abilities, and other characteristics (KSAOs) related to performance effectiveness. Finally, judgments of the linkage of KSAOs to job tasks provide a final piece of evidence that is typically collected before construction of the assessment exercises.

Additional bits of validity evidence come from the process of developing organizational simulations to simulate important job situations and to contain the types of problems, challenges, and opportunities the incumbents in the target job(s) face. Details on how organizations build and validate organizational simulations can be found in Thornton and Mueller-Hanson (2004).

After the initial construction of the exercises, subject matter experts are routinely asked to judge the relationship of the materials in the simulation exercise to the job situation. Information about content representativeness consists of evidence concerning testing activities. Two requirements must be considered here: Do the test materials present a representative sample of situations employees face on the job and, are the required responses to the test materials a representative sample of the performance requirements on the job. Content validity evidence typically consists of judgments by experts that both these requirements have been met. The testing procedure need not cover the *entire* job, but it must cover important and critical job duties (Society for Industrial and Organizational Psychology, 2003).

Judgments about the similarity of exercises to job situations are the most common type of evidence used to demonstrate the validity of assessment centers in individual organizations (Spychalski et al., 1997). Organizations typically defend an assessment center by pointing out that (a) the dimensions are chosen on the basis of job analysis, (b) the exercises include important and frequently encountered job activities, (c) behavior in the exercises can be classified into the critical performance dimensions, and (d) trained assessors can make consistent and accurate observations of participant behavior. Gathering meaningful content validity evidence is not an easy process. Sackett (1987) pointed out that when using content validity evidence to validate an assessment center, we must look at several features of the assessment situation in addition to the points just listed, such as the instructions given to participants, scoring systems used by the assessors, and methods of interpretation of the assessment results. These features are important because they can affect assessment center ratings.

Although there has been some opposition to the process of content validation of assessment centers when they are used to assess management potential (Sackett, 1987), counterarguments have been offered (e.g., Norton, 1981). In our opinion, evidence of content representativeness is quite relevant to understanding the assessment center process. Such evidence is consistent with the pattern of evidence required by researchers to show the overall validity of any test (Binning & Barrett, 1989; Landy, 1986). Indeed, it is complementary to the results of statistical studies showing that assessment centers provide accurate predictions of managerial performance.

Other critical bits of evidence are gathered during and after assessor training. Assessors are asked to judge if the exercises provide opportunities to observe behaviors relevant to the dimensions identified to be important in the job analysis. Thornton and Mueller-Hanson (2004) provide examples of how such information can be gathered.

INTERNAL STRUCTURE

Evidence of logical patterns of assessment at the level of individual assessors was presented in chapter 8. Research described in that chapter leads to several conclusions: Assessors demonstrate interrater agreement in the observation and rating of behaviors related to specified dimensions. In addition, correlations of ratings of the same dimension observed in different exercises provide evidence of convergence of measurement at the exercise level. After hearing reports of behavioral evidence from several exercises, assessors rate overall dimension performance with high levels of agreement and reliability. Correlations among final dimension ratings show meaningful clusters of dimensions such as decision-making abilities and administrative skills (Thornton & Byham, 1982).

RESPONSE PROCESSES

Participants report that they take the process seriously, they find it challenging, and that it assesses important dimensions of job performance. Assessors carry out several complex cognitive processes (Zedeck, 1986), but reviews of research in this area (Lievens & Klimoski, 2001) have shown that these processes are not completely understood. Lievens and Klimoski provide an analysis of the assessor as a social information processor. They analyze the roles of expectancies, cognitive structures, controlled vs. automatic processes, motivations, social interactions, and accountability on observation and judgment. They conclude that the "quality" of assessment center ratings varies considerably: "some centers have it, others do not" (p. 269). As described in chapter 8, high-quality assessment centers manage the procedures that influence social information processing and lead to more accurate ratings.

CONVERGENT AND DISCRIMINANT EVIDENCE

Convergent and discriminant validation strategies look for evidence that the overall assessment center method correlates with other overall assessment methods such as cognitive ability tests and personality questionnaires. It is important to note that we are not referring here to the evidence presented in studies that examined the convergent and discriminant validity of within-exercise dimension ratings. We do not consider that evidence related to the convergence and discriminance of the assessment center method as a whole. That evidence is reviewed in the section on evidence related to diagnostic assessment centers.

Assessment center ratings have been found to be related to other measures of conceptually related constructs. For example, meta-analytic evidence has shown overall assessment ratings to correlate .67 with cognitive ability, .50 with openness, .50 with extraversion, .35 with emotional stability, .25 with openness, and .17 with agreeableness (Collins, Schmidt, Sanchez-Ku, Thomas, McDaniel, & Le, 2003). These studies show that the overall assessment rating, reflecting assessors' judgments of management potential converges on measures of other characteristics known to be related to managerial effectiveness. Lest one conclude that the assessment center is measuring only these other characteristics, we next present evidence of the validity and incremental validity of assessment centers over other methods when predicting criterion performance.

TEST-CRITERION RELATIONS

The inference that is being made is that the overall assessment scores on the assessment center are related to some measure of success. For assessments of this type, the assessment technique is assumed to measure the candidate's potential to meet some standard of performance in the future. The standard may be expressed in some measure of effectiveness, referred to as a criterion. The criterion may be preliminary success measures such as completion of a required training program, a subsequent direct measure of effectiveness such as sales or profit, some indirect measure such a progress in management rank or salary, or some index of employment stability such as tenure, absenteeism, or accident rate.

Numerous individual studies have demonstrated that assessment centers predict a variety of criterion measures of managerial performance, including salary progress, attainment of predicted levels of mid-management, success in training, and ratings of managerial effectiveness. There is little question, even among the most severe critics of assessment center methods, that the overall assessment rating consistently predicts a wide variety of criteria of managerial success. Table 10.2 summarizes several reviews of the research findings with regard to the predictive validity of overall assessment

TABLE 10.2
Reviews of the Predictive Validity of the
Overall Assessment Rating (OAR)

Author	Summary
Byham (1970)	OAR identifies managers who make progress in rank; success rate of assessed managers is greater than nonassessed managers; correlation of OAR and performance ranges from .27 to .64
Cohen et al. (1974)	Median correlation with performance is .33, with potential is .63, with promotion is .40
Thornton & Byham (1982)	OAR predicts a variety of criteria (e.g., promotions, performance ratings)
Hunter & Hunter (1984)	Estimated correlation of OAR and job performance .43
Schmitt et al. (1984)	Estimate correlation with a variety of criteria .40
Gaugler et al. (1987)	Meta-analysis found estimated true validity was .37 in relation to progress, performance, ratings
Hardison & Sackett (2004)	Meta-analysis found estimated true validity was .31

ratings, starting with Byham's (1970) seminal article in the *Harvard Business Review* and ending with the most recent statistical analysis of prior studies.

In summary, the best estimates of the relationship between overall assessment center ratings and measures of success in management range from about .31 to .43. This means that people who get higher scores on the overall assessment rating will probably be more successful on the job than people who score lower. It should be clear from these results that, at the very least, the criterion-related validity evidence is positive, that is, the overall assessment rating is related to career success. It should be noted that the studies included in these reviews were both published and unpublished; that some of the research was carried out for purely academic purposes and some for practical use in the organization; and that some studies involved various criteria ranging from progress in management ranks, ratings of training or on-the-job performance, and observation by independent researchers of job effectiveness. These studies, therefore, represent a broad sampling of various viewpoints of success.

Correlation coefficients are sometimes difficult to interpret, and thus other methods of presenting the results may be helpful. Data from the Management Progress Study summarized in Table 10.3 clearly illustrate the predictive accuracy of the assessment center. It can be seen that 48% of the college graduates who were predicted by the assessment center to reach middle management had actually attained this level in 1965 (i.e., up to 8 years after assessment), whereas only 11% of those who were not predicted to reach middle management had done so. The figures are even more dramatic for non-college people: 32% of those predicted to reach middle management had done so, whereas only 5% of those receiving low ratings had done so. The predictions after 8 years and 16 years show even more accuracy, that is, more and more people who had been assessed highly were actually promoted to middle management. (It can also be seen that many of the low-rated participants with college degrees got promoted by the 16th

TABLE 10.3
Evidence of Predictive Accuracy in the Management Progress Study

Predicted to reach middle management	Percentage Attaining Middle Management		
	(8 years or less)	*Year 8*	*Year 16*
College sample			
Yes	48	64	89
No or Question	11	32	66
Noncollege sample			
Yes	32	40	63
No or Question	5	9	18

Source. Bray and Grant (1966); Bray et al. (1974); Howard (1997).

year of the study.) In this study the assessment center results were never revealed to anyone in the organization and never used for promotion decisions. Therefore, the results are a pure measure of predictive accuracy.

Variations in Predictive Validity Evidence

What does the accuracy of the assessment center depend on? The answer to that question was explored in depth by Gaugler et al. (1987) who studied the variables that correlated with the criterion-related validity coefficient. The idea of some variable correlating with validity coefficients may be somewhat difficult to grasp. Figure 10.1 illustrates this idea by showing that the criterion validity coefficient increases with the number of different types of exercises. This relationship is not perfect; it can be seen that an assessment center with many different types of exercises can still have lower validity. But the trend is clear.

A variable that correlates with the validity coefficients is called a "moderator variable" (Zedeck, 1986). The Gaugler et al. (1987) analysis looked for many different types of moderator variables, including characteristics of participants and assessors, features of the assessment center procedures, and types of assessment devices used.

Several features of the assessment center were found to be correlated with the validity coefficients across the large group of the studies reviewed. Assessment centers were more effective when a wide variety of types of assessment techniques was used, when psychologists were added as assessors (along with managers), and when peer evaluations were gathered. These findings give us some clues about the variables that contribute to the higher validities of assessment centers and tell us why assessment centers work.

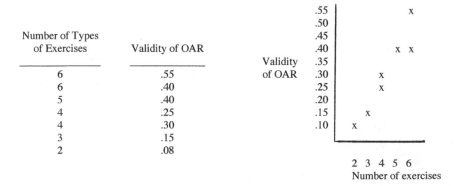

FIG. 10.1. Illustration of a variable correlating with the validity of assessment centers.

Further evidence that situational variables affect validities comes from a study of a regionally administered assessment center used to select secondary school principals (Schmitt et al., 1990). It was found that the assessment center was more accurate in predicting a criterion of effectiveness as perceived by teachers when a larger percent of the assessors were principals (as opposed to university professors), when the assessment was conducted in several districts (as opposed to one district), and when the assessors had not previously worked closely with the participants. The authors concluded that the quality of implementation of the assessment center is an important determinant of assessment effectiveness.

Detailed references and summaries of recent criterion-related validity studies can be found in numerous sources (e.g., Lievens & Thornton, in press; Thornton & Rupp, 2003). These studies provide additional evidence supporting the predictive validity of overall ratings, and extend the evidence to other jobs, longer time periods, and other settings. Validity evidence has been provided for airline pilots (Damitz et al., 2003), police officers (Dayan, Kasten, & Fox, 2002; Krause et al., 2004), students (Bartels, Boomer, & Rubin, 2000; Riggio, Mayes, & Schleicher, 2003; Waldman & Korbar, 2004), and retail sales (O'Connell, Hattrup, Doverspike, & Cober, 2002). The predictive accuracy for salary progress over a 7-year period was demonstrated by Jansen and Stoop (2001). Lievens, Harris, Van Keer, and Bisqueret (2003) validated an assessment center for selecting European managers for a cross-cultural training program in Japan.

STATISTICAL VERSUS JUDGMENTAL COMBINATION OF DIMENSION RATINGS TO PREDICT CRITERIA

A variety of methods have been used to combine dimension ratings to predict external criteria. A frequent question concerns the best way to combine the dimension ratings: some statistical combination or a judgmental combination. Research evidence is decidedly mixed. Some studies show the superiority of the statistical/actuarial approach (Borman, 1982; Herriot et al., 1985; Tziner & Dolan, 1982; Wingrove et al., 1985; Wollowick & McNamara, 1969), others support the clinical/judgmental/consensual discussion approaches (Lebreton, Binning, & Hesson-McInnis, 1998; Tziner et al., 1994), and still others show no difference in predictive accuracy (Chan, 1996; Feltham, 1988b; Huck, 1974; Jansen & Stoop, 2001; Moses, 1973; Pynes & Bernardin, 1992). The major conclusion from reviewing these findings is that the studies cannot be compared because different exercises and dimensions are used, data are integrated in different ways at different points in the aggregation process, different types of criteria are measured after different time periods, and so forth. Thus, no conclusions can be made about which integration method is best at this stage of the assessment center process.

INCREMENTAL VALIDITY

Assessment centers show incremental validity over other predictors of effectiveness. When combined with cognitive ability tests, Schmidt and Hunter (1998) found that assessment centers showed only small incremental validity (2%). In contrast, other studies have found significant incremental validity over cognitive ability tests (Dayan, Kasten, & Fox, 2002; Krause et al., 2004), as well as supervisory ratings (Chan, 1996), personality tests (Goffin, Rothstein, & Johnston, 1996), biodata (O'Connell et al., 2002), and a behavioral description interview (Lievens et al., 2003). These studies clearly demonstrate that assessment centers are measuring some unique attributes in comparison with the attributes measured by other methods.

VALIDITY GENERALIZATION

Meta-analyses, using validity generalization techniques to control for statistical and measurement artifacts, have provided estimates that the "true" validity of assessment centers is quite substantial. These analyses demonstrate that assessment centers predict a variety of criterion measures of managerial performance, including salary progress, attainment of predicted levels of mid-management, success in training, ratings of managerial effectiveness. The level of average validity has varied from a high of .43 (Hunter & Hunter, 1984), to .37 (Gaugler et al., 1987), to .31 (Hardison & Sackett, 2004). The difference in validity estimates has not been explained but may be due to different samples of individual studies that were aggregated or the difference in quality of assessment center operations over time. The lower validity for studies of more recent assessment centers may be due to one or more of the following factors: shorter length of recent assessment centers; the use of assessors other than midlevel managers, which was more common in the 1980 and 1990s; inconsistencies in administration. Another factor that affects the final estimate of true validity is the level of criterion reliability used when correcting for attenuation. Lievens and Thornton (in press) pointed out that the validity estimate of .37 found by Gaugler et al. (1987) may be an *under*estimate because that study used a relatively conservative (i.e., high) value of reliability of .77. In comparison, if the criterion reliability value of .52 (i.e., the value that Viswesvaran, Ones, & Schmidt, 1996, found for the interrater agreement of job performance ratings) is used for correction in the Gaugler et al. meta-analysis, the estimated validity goes up from .37 to .45.

CONSEQUENCES OF TESTING

Returning to the last row of Table 10.1, we are reminded of the importance of considering the consequences of testing. A potential, negative consequence of using an assessment technique to assess potential and predict performance is the presence of subgroup differences among racial, ethnic, gender, and age groups). Differences in average scores among subgroups will lead to adverse impact against members of the subgroups if top-down selection is used (Gatewood & Feild, 2001). Although adverse impact is not the same as differential validity or differential prediction, differences in selection rates among protected subgroups may hinder an organization from obtaining the level of diversity it is seeking in its workforce, may expose the organization to scrutiny of compliance agencies, and subject it to legal challenges. Therefore, organizations have been seeking valid assessment methods that eliminate or minimize subgroup differences. Some evidence suggests that assessment centers (in comparison with written cognitive ability tests) tend to show lesser levels of subgroup differences.

Studies have shown little difference between the overall assessment ratings among groups of Whites and Blacks (Goldstein, Yusko, & Nicolopoulos, 2001; Huck & Bray, 1976) and Men and Women (Alexander, Buck, & McCarthy, 1975; Anderson & Thacker, 1985; Huck & Bray, 1976; Moses, 1973; Moses & Boehm, 1975; Ritchie & Moses, 1983; Schmitt & Hill, 1975; Shore et al., 1997). By contrast, one study (Schmitt & Mills, 2001) found a majority sample scored higher than the minority sample in a telephone simulation, but this difference on the simulation was one half the size of the difference on traditional paper-and-pencil tests. Other studies of gender differences found that women (compared to men) showed slightly higher assessment ratings (Bobrow & Leonards, 1997; Shore, 1992; Schmitt, 1993; Walsh, Weinberg, & Fairfield, 1987).

Another line of evidence related to the consequences of testing is the literature on test takers' reactions to various assessment techniques. Numerous studies have shown that participants in assessment centers have a variety of positive reactions (Thornton & Byham, 1982). In addition, test takers have more favorable impressions of assessment centers than cognitive ability tests and personality tests (Chan, 1996). Applicant reactions to various selection practices are important because favorable reactions are related to positive attitudes toward the organization (Bauer et al., 1998; Howard, 1997). With the workforce becoming more diverse (Triandis et al., 1993) and women and minorities entering positions they have not traditionally

held, it is increasingly important to use fair selection procedures and to ensure that applicants are aware of the aspect of the program that ensures this
fairness.

SUMMARY

Taken together, these lines of evidence show that assessment centers have
considerable validity when used to make inferences about potential to succeed among external applicants for selection and internal candidates for
promotion. Evidence of job-relevant content, meaningful internal relationships among dimension ratings, and convergent and discriminant relationships with other measurement methods provide a firm basis for validity inferences. In addition, substantial levels of correlations of assessment center
ratings with criteria of job performance have been found to generalize to a
wide variety of indicators of success. Overall assessment ratings show relatively little adverse impact on minority groups and little differential validity.
Assessment center ratings show incremental validity over other predictor
measures. More research studies, for example using qualitative analyses,
are needed to better understand the thought processes of assessors during
the observation, classification, and evaluation of behaviors.

EVIDENCE OF VALIDITY FOR DIAGNOSTIC
ASSESSMENT CENTERS

When assessment centers are used to diagnose strengths and weaknesses of
individuals, the inference that is being made is that the assessment ratings
provide an accurate evaluation of separate, identifiable dimensions of effective performance. It is assumed that each individual is strong in some performance attributes and weak in others. The information from this assessment can be used in two different ways: capitalizing on strengths, or
remediating weaknesses. The approach of capitalizing on strengths places
the focus on each individual's special capabilities to contribute to organizational effectiveness (Buckingham & Clifton, 2001). The assessment information can help the individual find his or her niche and help the organization place the individual in a position for optimal contribution. The
approach of remediating weaknesses places the focus on helping each individual identify his or her developmental needs. It assumes that each person
has a set of limiting factors, and improvement will come from engaging in
some activities to overcome these weaknesses. In this book, we emphasize
the second approach. We demonstrate how assessment centers have been

used to identify developmental needs, guide persons into appropriate developmental actions, and engage in learning experiences.

For assessment centers used for diagnosis, a wide variety of evidence has been accumulated. This evidence suggests that well-built assessment centers demonstrate validity for this purpose.

TEST CONTENT

The content of assessment centers for diagnosis often includes exercises and dimensions that are somewhat different from these features in selection/promotion centers. The exercises for diagnostic centers often closely resemble the job currently held by the incumbents. For example, one large manufacturing organization constructed three somewhat different diagnostic programs for administrative assistants, first-level supervisors, and second-level managers. Each program had exercises that simulated job activities relevant to the respective positions: coordinating projects, organizing day-to-day operations, or overseeing multiple departments. The dimensions were chosen to reflect the attributes needed for effective performance in the separate, current jobs. Although the title of some dimensions remained the same, the complexity of the dimension often changed to capture the unique application of the dimension. For example, "planning and organizing" was assessed in each program but the required and desirable behaviors differed: For administrative assistants, planning and organizing meant scheduling diverse project members; for supervisors, it meant anticipating how to handle last minute absenteeism; for managers, it meant anticipating seasonal fluctuations in demand for the product.

The content of diagnostic exercises and dimensions are validated in much the same way as selection/promotion exercises and dimensions: careful job analysis, construction of exercises by experienced test developers, confirmation by organizational experts, and judgments of comparability of materials and job requirements by knowledgeable subject matter experts and assessors. In addition, studies of content representativeness of diagnostic assessment centers should also show the independence of dimensions. The conceptual distinction of dimensions can be tested by asking subject matter experts if it is feasible for a person to show combinations of strengths and weaknesses on two dimensions. For example, if the complex area of decision making is important in the job, the program may wish to diagnose managers' strengths and weaknesses in the various elements of decision making, for example, problem identification, generating alternative solutions, evaluating costs and benefits of alternatives, and making the choice. If it is conceivable that a person can be, say, effective at "generating alternatives" yet ineffective at "evaluating alternatives" (or vice versa), then the dimensions are conceptually distinct. If effective generating and evaluating always go together, then the dimensions are probably not candidates for differential assessment. Instructions for exercises can then state that assessees are to carry out the decision-making processes, and assessors can observe behaviors revealing performance levels.

INTERNAL STRUCTURE

Here is where the major controversy has arisen in evaluating the validity of assessment centers. One line of evidence has been generated over the past 20 years which some people have interpreted to mean that assessment centers do not have "construct validity" and are not up to the task of diagnosing developmental needs among performance attributes. In this section we describe this evidence to date, present alternative arguments that have received support, and point out why this line of reasoning has limited relevance for evaluating assessment center validity.

Before presenting our review of the internal studies, we summarize the following points:

- A series of well-done internal validity studies have concluded that evidence does not support the construct validity of assessment centers
- Other internal studies using the same method of construct validation have produced evidence that assessment centers do have construct validity to measure intended constructs
- All of the internal validity have limited relevance to understanding the validity of assessment centers to measure intended constructs.

Recent analyses of what some authors call "construct validity" involve studies of the relationships of dimension ratings after several individual exercises. As described in chapters 7 and 8, these ratings are called "within-exercise dimension ratings." Sometimes they are referred to as "post exercise dimension ratings." For example, after the group discussion, one assessor may rate the participant on Leadership, Problem Solving, and Oral Communication; after the interaction simulation with a problem employee, a second assessor may rate the participant on the same three dimensions; and after a case analysis and presentation, a third assessor may rate the participant on the same three dimensions. The following relationships have been studied:

- Correlations between ratings of the same dimension across different exercises. For example, these include the correlations of Leadership demonstrated in the group discussion, interaction simulation, and case presentation. In the terminology of the multitrait–multimethod matrix (Campbell & Fiske, 1959), these correlations are called "mono-trait–heteromethod" correlations. They are traditionally interpreted to be an indication of convergent validity.

- Correlations between ratings of different dimensions within each separate exercise. For example, these include the correlations of Leadership, Problem Solving, and Oral Communication within the group discussion (and within the interview simulation, within the case presentation, etc.). There correlations are called "heterotrait–monomethod" correlations, and have been interpreted to indicate method bias. When they are high, and accompanied by high correlations in the next category, they have been interpreted to mean that discriminant validity is lacking.
- Correlations between ratings of different dimensions across different exercises. For example, these include the correlation of Leadership in the group discussion with Problem Solving in the interaction simulation. These are called "heterotrait–heteromethod" correlations. When they are high, and accompanied by method bias, this pattern has been interpreted to mean that discriminant validity is lacking.

Within-exercise dimension ratings have been investigated in several ways: examination of correlations, factor analysis, and analysis of variance.

Examination of the Multitrait–Multimethod Matrix

A long line of research evidence has demonstrated that within-exercise dimension ratings tend to show adequate convergent correlations but low discriminant correlations. That is, the convergent correlations of the same dimension rated in different exercises are relatively large (i.e., approximately in the range of .40 to .50). But, there tends to also be a relatively large amount of method bias, that is, large correlations of different dimensions within each exercise, with correlations in the range of .50 to .70. In addition, even the heterotrait–heteromethod correlations often are higher than might be expected. Summarizing this body of literature, some researchers (Sackett & Tuzinski, 2001) concluded that assessment center ratings do not demonstrate the expected patterns of convergent and discriminant validity, that is, the correlations do not support the pattern one might expect of high correlations of the same dimension rated in different exercises, along with lack of correlations among ratings of supposedly distinct dimensions, either within exercises or across exercises.

Other studies show more promise of improving this form of construct validity by altering the processes of the assessment center. Kolk (2001) reviewed 37 studies and found that the convergent validity improved from .35 to .67 and the discriminant validity improved (i.e., declined) from .68 to .60 when assessors rated the performance on the dimensions across exercises (in comparison with rating dimensions within the exercise). In addition, Kolk found that if the common-rater effect was eliminated by having each assessor rate only one dimension, then there was some improvement in discriminant validity. Lievens (1998) reviewed 21 studies that examined the effects of several variables on this form of construct validity, and made several practical recommendations that will increase this form of construct validity:

- Use a small number of conceptually distinct dimensions which are concretely defined.
- Train assessors, including psychologists, with frame-of-reference training procedures.
- Develop exercises that generate a large amount of behavior clearly related to a few dimensions; train role players to elicit relevant behaviors.
- Provide assessors with observation and rating aides (e.g., checklists, lists of key behaviors).

Factor Analysis

Factor analysis is a systematic method of identifying clusters of variables that tend to correlate highly with each other. "Factors" are identified that represent the commonalities among the variables. In the present example, there would be nine correlations resulting from the combination of three dimensions being assessed in three exercises. If the correlations of the same dimensions across exercises tend to be *high*, and the correlations of different dimensions in the same exercise tend to be *low*, then "dimension factors" emerge and we can conclude that dimensions (i.e., the constructs being measured) are being measured. On the other hand, if the correlations of the same dimensions across exercises tend to be *low* and the correlations of the different dimensions in the same exercise tend to be *high*, then "exercise factors" emerge and we conclude that exercises are driving the ratings. Factor analyses have shown mixed findings, with the majority of studies showing that exercise factors dominate (for summaries of these studies, see Lance, Foster et al., 2004; Lievens & Conway, 2001; Sackett & Tuzinski, 2001), but other studies showing both exercise and dimension factors emerging (Donahue et al., 1997; Lievens & Conway, 2001; Kudisch et al., 1997; Louiselle, 1980).

Analysis of Variance

Another statistical method of investigating the within-exercise dimension ratings involves analysis of variance. Exercises and dimensions are viewed as factors in an experiment. The ratings are analyzed to determine if there is primarily a "dimension effect" or an "exercise effect." According to this argument, if dimensions such as Leadership, Problem Solving, or Oral Communication are really what the assessors are evaluating, then the dimension effect should be large. That is, the ratings of dimensions across exercises should explain variance in the ratings. On the other hand, if the exercise effect is large, then what the assessors are focusing on is really candidates' overall performance in one exercise versus another exercise.

The analysis of variance techniques used to investigate these data vary considerably, and controversy exists regarding the assumptions underlying these analyses. These assumptions are referred to as "models" underlying the data. The technical details of the various hypothetical models are beyond the scope of this chapter. The interested reader is referred to the following sources to learn about the rationale for various models. Lievens and Conway (2001) used a correlated dimension-correlated uniqueness model and found that the within-exercise dimension ratings showed equal proportions of exercise and dimension variation. Lance, Lambert, et al. (2004) contend that the analytic method used by Lievens and Conway (2001) actually overestimated dimension effects. Using a method Lance, Lambert et al. prefer (i.e., a 1-dimension-correlated exercise and 1-dimension-correlated uniqueness model), the results reveal that exercise variance predominates over dimension variance.

Summary

In summary, the major conclusion that many researchers have derived from these findings has been either "assessment centers do not display construct validity" or "assessment centers do have construct validity, but the constructs measured are not the intended dimensions." These researchers conclude that assessment center ratings do not reflect ratings of performance dimensions but rather reflect generalized performance in separate exercises.

CRITIQUE OF THIS LINE OF EVIDENCE

What are we to make of these analyses of within-exercise dimension ratings? On the one hand, we could say that this sort of internal analysis of within-exercise dimension ratings is one valuable source of evidence for understanding the construct validity of assessment centers. Sackett and Tuzinski (2001) provide a strong rationale to support this position.

We offer a markedly different point of view. We assert that all of the various and often sophisticated analytical techniques of within-exercise dimension ratings are theoretically and methodologically misplaced. At best, these analyses are of limited value and must be interpreted in conjunction with many other types of evidence before one can conclude that assessment centers do not have construct validity to measure dimensions.

First, we emphasize that the assessment center method was founded on the basic principle that evaluations of performance must be based on aggregations of observations by multiple assessors of multiple behaviors relevant to multiple dimensions in multiple exercises. No one can be identified in the assessment center literature for asserting that the judgment by *one* assessor of behavior relevant to *one* dimension in *one* exercise has meaning by itself. The entire rationale for the assessment center method has been that meaningful assessment comes only after aggregating across *multiple* sources of information.

Second, to view the within-exercise dimension rating on one dimension by one assessor as a meaningful entity is analogous to asserting that a single item in a test is meaningful. Test developers certainly expect that single items have limited reliability and would not be correlated very highly with other single items (Nunnally & Bernstein, 1994). In the same way, we would not expect a high level of agreement between one rating of a single assessor after observing a single exercise with another single rating of the dimension in another single exercise. All psychometric theory is based on the notion that individual items have limited accuracy and accurate measurement is attained by summing across sets of items. Analogously, in an assessment center, the accurate evaluation of a person's performance on a dimension is accomplished by aggregating across observations of multiple behaviors in multiple exercises by multiple assessors.

Third, within-exercise dimension ratings are confounded with assessor effects. That is, in analysis of variance terms, assessors are typically nested in exercises. This means that these ratings include the effect of the exercise itself and the effect of the assessor. Attempts to disentangle these effects have not been completely successful (Kolk, Born, & Van der Flier, 2002).

Fourth, we do not believe the multitrait–multimethod comparison is appropriate because *exercises* are not different *methods*. Exercises are somewhat different forms of behavioral simulations, but they are not distinctly different methods to the same extent as a behavioral simulation is different from a background interview or a test (in paper-and-pencil or computer-administered format). In other sections of this review, we discuss what we see as the more appropriate comparison of truly different methods, for example, overall dimension ratings from an assessment center in comparison with measures of similar and different constructs measured with different methods (e.g., tests, questionnaires, ratings by others).

Fifth, most of the data for these studies have come from assessment centers using a specific method of obtaining and aggregating the ratings, namely, the method calling for assessors to provide within-exercise dimension ratings. This method is quite different from the original behavior reporting method (Bray & Grant, 1966). In chapter 7, the distinction is made between methods that call for assessors to rate dimensions after viewing each exercise. This method is useful in clarifying the evaluative component of the assessors' role, and may facilitate communication of information in the assessor discussion. But, this very method of calling for ratings on the dimensions (in comparison with the method of simply recording and sharing only behavioral observations) may instill an artificial method bias and heighten the correlations among within-exercise dimension ratings. Harris, Becker, and Smith (1993) reported a study which allegedly addressed this issue. They claimed the study compared the behavior reporting method to the within-exercise rating method. The results showed the typical lack of discriminant validity (i.e., dimension ratings within an exercise correlated higher than ratings of the same dimension across exercises). Closer reading of the study reveals that this study was not a true representation of the behavior reporting method because assessors made dimension ratings for each exercise, then made overall dimension ratings. The behavior reporting method does *not* call for dimension ratings for each exercise. Research on data emanating from an assessment center using the behavioral observation method has shown correlations with external measures of constructs similar to the assessment center dimensions (Thornton, Tziner, Dahan, Clevenger, & Meir, 1997). The reader will quickly note that when the behavioral reporting method is used, the types of internal analyses reviewed in this section are not possible. Why, because within-exercise dimension ratings are not made!

To conclude this section, we acknowledge that a responsible interpretation of this body of evidence regarding internal relationships of within-exercise dimension ratings can be interpreted in different ways. Fortunately, we do not have to rely on this limited body of evidence alone when forming conclusions about the validity of assessment center dimensions. Many other bodies of evidence are available. We now review other sets of research evidence that allow much clearer support for the validity of diagnostic assessment centers.

Correlations Among Final Dimension Ratings

Correlations among the final dimension ratings provide insight into the structure of assessments after information is aggregated across assessors and exercises. Thornton (1992) reviewed early studies and found that, whereas some showed a high level of correlation and thus indicated that assessors' ratings may be influenced by some general impression of the candidates, other studies generally yielded two to four factors. Schmitt (1977) found three factors; Shore et al. (1990) found two a priori factors of performance and style dimensions; Thornton et al. (1997) found four factors. In a more recent study, Kolk (2001) found three factors that conformed to a theoretical framework of Feeling, Thinking, and Power.

Thus, factor analysis studies of final dimension ratings indicate that the dimensions are not representative of completely separate concepts, because only a few factors are needed to explain the variation in assessors' ratings. On the other hand, more than one general "halo" impression is needed to explain the assessors' final dimension ratings.

Convergent and Discriminant Evidence

In this section we review evidence regarding the correlation of final dimension ratings from assessment centers with assessments of the same or similar constructs measured by different methods. These sorts of evidence involve comparisons of measurement of the dimensions in assessment center ratings with scores or ratings from truly different methods such as tests, questionnaires, or judgments by others. We hasten to emphasize the distinction we are making between this body of evidence and the body of evidence reviewed in the section on internal structure. In that earlier section, convergence referred to correlations across different exercises. We do not consider exercises to be different methods. We believe that it is far more informative to compare final dimension ratings with truly different methods.

Assessment center ratings on performance-related dimensions were found to correlate with cognitive ability tests whereas interpersonally related dimensions related personality inventories measuring conceptually similar traits (Shore, Thornton, & Shore, 1990). The results of all such studies are not totally supportive. For example, Chan (1996) was unable to replicate the same pattern.

Correlations With Criterion Measures

Arthur, Day et al. (2003) conducted a meta-analysis of 34 studies that investigated the correlation of dimension ratings with job-related measures of performance (e.g., job performance, salary, promotion). They aggregated diverse dimension labels into six broad dimensions (consideration of others, communication, drive, influencing others, organizing and planning, and problem solving). The results of combining 258 correlations yielded estimated true criterion correlations ranging from .25 to .39 for the six dimensions. A combination of four of the six dimensions using multiple regression showed a correlation of .45 with the criterion measures. Arthur et al. compared this figure with the estimated true validity of overall assessment ratings (namely, .37) found by Gaugler et al. (1987). The percent of variance in performance explained by the predictor can be estimated by computing the square of the correlation coefficient. Thus, using information at the dimension level explains 43% more variance in performance than using the overall assessment rating (.45 squared = 20% compared to .37 squared = 14%).

This analysis shows the importance of distinguishing between the *method* of assessment and the *constructs* that are being assessed. The analysis demonstrates that assessment center ratings of dimensions are meaningful assessments of performance constructs. Arthur, Day et al. (2003) pointed out that their analysis showed a relatively high correlation among dimensions (i.e., .56) and that figure highlights the limitation of demonstrating other forms of construct validity involving discriminant patterns of correlations.

The value of studying the relationship of dimension ratings was demonstrated in the 7-year longitudinal study by Jansen and Stoop (2001). In addition to the validity of the overall assessment rating, these researchers found that dimension "firmness" was predictive over the entire period, but the "interpersonal" dimension became valid only in later years. The increasing validity of this noncognitive dimension over time supports the findings from other research (Goldstein, Zedeck, & Goldstein, 2002).

Consequences of Diagnosis

Diagnostic assessment centers can result in many positive consequences for the participants and the organization. As described in the case study on a diagnostic assessment center in chapter 2 and the section on diagnostic feedback in chapter 9, the result of this assessment is feedback about behavior and the initiation of plans for development. Our experience with diagnostic assessment centers, as well as surveys in other centers, shows that when participants receive thorough feedback from credible assessors, participants demonstrate strong readiness to engage in subsequent training programs. When the supervisor of the participant is involved, and when the organization has support programs in place, participants follow up with developmental activities. Although a portion of assessees do not follow up (T. Byham & Wilkerson, 2003; Jones & Whitmore, 1995), those who do engage in developmental actions experience career success. As explained in chapter 9, as the workforce becomes more diverse, demographic characteristics of feedback providers and recipients must be taken into consideration when designing feedback to gain maximal effectiveness.

SUMMARY

The evidence regarding the validity of diagnostic assessment centers is supportive of inference that the method measures distinct constructs, with one
exception. If one focuses only on the discriminant validity of within-
exercise dimension ratings, the evidence may suggest that assessors' ratings
do not measure intended constructs. By contrast, much of the other extensive rich evidence supports the inference that diagnosis has been accomplished. Subject matter experts confirm that exercises elicit behavior relevant to dimensions. Final dimension ratings aggregated across assessors
and exercises correlate with other methods of measurement of related constructs and with criteria of job performance on these dimensions. Diagnostic assessment centers have positive consequences for participants and organizations. Participants demonstrate readiness to learn and if they engage in
follow up action, they experience career growth.

VALIDITY EVIDENCE RELATED TO
DEVELOPMENTAL ASSESSMENT CENTERS

When assessment centers are used for developmental purposes, the inference is made that participants grow professionally as a result of the experience. The expected outcome may be that participants:

- develop a better understanding of job-related performance dimensions;
- learn some new skills;
- are motivated to engage in developmental activities.

We now turn to the evidence that supports the validity of assessment centers
for developmental purposes.

TEST CONTENT

The "content" of DACs includes the aspects of the simulation exercises, the
dimensions assessed, and the feedback provided. The exercises in a DAC
are realistic simulations of tasks that participants are likely to encounter in
their current jobs or tasks they are likely to encounter in the near future.
The content of these exercises is more geared toward current situations
than the content of exercises in selection and promotion assessment centers which is cast in the future.

When assessment centers are used for development, the dimensions are chosen to be ones that are "developable." This means that the dimensions are knowledge, skills, abilities, or other characteristics that can be developed as a result of the assessment center experience or as a result of some type of training or experience in a reasonable amount of time after the DAC (Rupp et al., 2003). Examples of "developable" dimensions are certain aspects of oral communication, interpersonal communication, and problem analysis. By contrast, some dimensions would probably not be appropriate for a developmental assessment center because more extensive, in-depth training is needed for their development, or development of these dimensions may be an unreasonable or inappropriate goal for the organization to take on. Such dimensions might include basic intelligence, emotional stability, or organizational commitment.

The distinction of "developable" dimensions implies a continuum from highly stable traits to easily modifiable human characteristics. Such a continuum was presented by Rupp et al. (2003), and is presented in Fig. 10.2. For some dimensions, improvement may come with little more than the opportunity to participate in some activity that gives the participant self-insight, which can then result in behavioral change. By contrast, change on other dimensions may require extensive, formal education or in-depth, lengthy, and individualized training. Furthermore, the dimensions identified here refer to complex sets of behaviors. It is quite possible that various aspects of a dimension may develop at different rates, or in response to different interventions. For example, both nonverbal communication and audience-appropriateness are classified as elements of oral communication. It may be quite easy to develop nonverbal communication techniques such as eye contact and effective gestures, yet be quite difficult to learn how to gauge the appropriateness of one's communication for one's audience. Future research at this level is needed, exploring the developability of not only the broad dimension classes but also the individual behaviors of which they are composed. The top half of Fig. 10.2 presents a preliminary scaling of a few dimensions along such a continuum. The location of these initial dimensions is suggested by the results of the study presented here, as well as by previous research and experience. Systematic study over time is needed to confirm or refine the proposed placement.

Additionally, one must consider the element of time that is implied by the notion of developability. Some dimensions may be changed relatively quickly with little effort, whereas others may require considerably more effort over an extended period of time. A recent meta-analysis (Arthur, Bennett, Edens, & Bell, 2003) found that training methods may be differentially effective for different kinds of skill, but the authors note that the reason for this is not yet clear. Systematic research is needed to identify the factors that influence the rate and degree of development for various dimensions.

Nearly impossible to develop	Very difficult to develop	Difficult to develop	Reasonable possibility to develop	Somewhat easy to develop
Motivation	Adaptability	Interpersonal Skills	Listening	Non-verbal communication
	Conscientiousness	Leadership	Problem solving techniques	
			Planning and organizing techniques	
				"One trial learning"
	Long-term practice with coaching	Counseling	Feedback alone	Participation in simulation alone
		Education programs	Lecture	Self insight
	Extensive counseling	Long training programs	Readings	
		Courses	On-the-job experience with coaching	
		Mentoring		
		Skill practice		

FIG. 10.2. A scale of developability of dimensions/competencies with associated development/training methods. From Rupp et al. (2003).

The lower half of Fig. 10.2 presents a preliminary scaling of intervention methods. At the far right are those interventions that are relatively easy to implement. For example, simply by participating in a short presentation, a person might gain the self-insight that he or she fidgets too much and could easily learn to stand still and not make distracting hand gestures. Research findings suggest that assessment center participants can, in fact, gain such self-awareness, even before feedback is given (Schmitt et al. 1986). At the other extreme are more extensive and elaborate methods designed to foster complex, long-term behavioral change, such as coaching, formal education, or even psychotherapy. Development of complex leadership skills is likely to require multiple opportunities to practice and receive guidance. Therefore, it is plausible that a carefully structured developmental assessment center can lead to improvement in selected aspects of performance dimensions, but that additional development strategies may be necessary to fully develop other aspects of complex dimensions. Rupp et al. (2003) provided preliminary evidence that dimensions predicted to be developable were seen to be so by U.S. and Korean managers.

Finally, the extent to which individuals develop on the dimensions during and following DAC participation is dependent on the extent to which they come to understand their relative strengths and developmental needs. This relies heavily on the format and quality of the feedback provided. As discussed in chapter 4, DACs can include multiple opportunities for self-evaluation and detailed behavioral feedback, coaching, and goal setting focused on dimension improvement.

INTERNAL STRUCTURE

A basic assumption of a developmental assessment center is that assessors can observe behaviors and give meaningful feedback related to performance dimensions. Research has shown that there is reliability and validity in these behavioral observations. For example, Ladd et al. (2002) found that assessors show a high level of interrater agreement when observing behavior in exercises. Schleicher et al. (2002) found that the reliability of dimension ratings improved with frame-of-reference training (in comparison with a control condition) on the dimensions of Communication (.76 to .83), Decision Making (.69 to .89), and Leadership (.65 to .75). Validity evidence comes from studies of the accuracy of behavioral observation as well. Thornton and Zorich (1980) found that assessors trained in observation methods observe 48% of the behaviors displayed in a videotaped simulation exercise. Gaugler and Thornton (1989) established that trained assessors demonstrated two types of dimension-level observation accuracy. Assessors recorded approximately 50% to 60% of the observations "keyed" by expert raters, and approximately 70% to 80% of the assessors' observations were "good" observations (i.e., the observations were specific behavioral statements of what the assessee actually said or did).

As described in chapters 3 and 4, in a DAC, the participant is provided multiple opportunities to exhibit behavior, receive feedback, and practice the behavior again. Multiple opportunities for development are provided in several ways:

- Experientially: Due to the active and intensive nature of the exercises, participants "learn by doing." Behavioral role modeling might also take place in group exercises.
- Within a single exercise: The participant may be given feedback and a chance to adjust his or her performance. For example, during a case analysis/presentation, the participant gives a presentation, is provided immediate feedback (e.g., "Eliminate distracting, irrelevant phrases such as 'ya know' "), and asked to make a second presentation.
- Across exercises: The participant can practice the skill in a subsequent exercise (e.g., in an interaction simulation that follows a presentation).
- Across blocks of exercises: For example, the developmental assessment center may be designed to provide feedback in the late morning after one set of three exercises, and then the participant practices the skills in a second block of parallel exercises in the afternoon.
- Over time. The developmental assessment center may be part of a long-term development program where the assessee receives repeated feedback, coaching, and career tracking, and later returns for another development center.

Gibbons, Rupp, Baldwin, and Holub (2005) provided validity evidence related to the internal structure of DAC dimensions. The assessors in the DAC studied by these authors completed rating scales for three subdimensions per dimension, essentially creating a multiitem measure of each dimension. This technique allowed for an investigation of the internal structure at the dimension level. Within-exercise confirmatory factor analyses were conducted to explore whether assessors ratings within each exercise differentiated between dimensions or reflected general halo error. Results showed that a multifactor model reflecting the dimensions assessed in each exercise fit the data significantly better than a single factor model. This provides evidence for the internal structure of DACs, which is critical for this type of assessment center, where dimension differentiation is so crucial.

RESPONSE PROCESSES

Validity evidence related to response processes comes from studies of how participants change their attitudes, understanding, and performance as a result of the assessment experience. Survey responses show that participants report they gain insight into strengths and weaknesses as a result of participation and feedback.

Rogers (2005) showed that students and managers develop better understanding of the performance constructs, such as analysis and synthesis as a result of getting feedback about participation in developmental activities. Rogers applied an innovative set of analyses to detect whether individual participants experienced "alpha," "beta," or "gamma" change as a result of developmental experiences. Alpha change is actual change in the ability itself, beta change is recalibration of scale of measurement of the change, and gamma change is a re-conceptualization of the attribute being assessed. Evidence of gamma change is particularly relevant because it demonstrates that the participant has developed a deeper understanding of the dimensions. In Rogers' studies, different participants demonstrated different types of change.

Related to this, Woo and Sims (2005) found evidence that the extent to which assessees gain this deeper understanding of the dimensions (as indicated by their agreement with assessor's ratings) predicts both their engagement in the development program as well as their agreement with DAC feedback one month following the DAC.

CONVERGENT AND DISCRIMINANT EVIDENCE

The general nature of convergent and discriminant validity evidence relevant for developmental assessment centers is much the same as the convergent and discriminant validity evidence relevant for other types of assessment centers. However, given the nature and complexity of many DAC programs (see chap. 4), there are often many different types of data collected as part of the program that might provide a wide range of validity evidence of this sort. DACs function at the dimension level of analysis, and therefore convergent and discriminant validity evidence must show that the dimensions measured are properly placed in a larger nomological network. There are three major ways this might be approached: showing differentiation between the dimensions, showing that dimension ratings are related to what they logically should be related to (convergent validity), and showing that dimension ratings are not related to what they logically should not be related to (discriminant validity).

   Dimension differentiation was discussed earlier as this also relates to the internal structure of the DAC. As described, there is some evidence that DAC exercises allow for the assessment of distinct dimensions and not simply some general exercise performance factor (Gibbons, Rupp, Baldwin, & Holub, 2005).

   Convergent and discriminant validity evidence can be provided by taking either the internal or external approach (Shore et al., 1990; Shore et al., 1992; Thornton & Rupp, 2003). Internal evidence could be gleaned by looking at the intercorrelations between dimension ratings, both within and across exercises. The Shore et al. studies provide a useful framework for classifying dimensions into performance-style dimensions and interpersonal-style dimensions that aid in making such comparisons. Rupp et al. (2004) used a similar framework to compare the intercorrelations of DAC ratings. Classifying dimensions into interpersonal (conflict management, leadership, fairness) and performance (oral communication, problem solving, information seeking, planning and organizing) categories, they found higher intercorrelations within the interpersonal category than across categories, though within the performance category the correlations were no higher. Note that although we argued earlier against the use of within-exercise dimension ratings, this study obtained reliable, multi-item ratings of dimensions within exercises, and only used these results as one small piece of evidence in a much larger validity study. The external approach, which we argue is more appropriate (Thornton & Rupp, 2003), involves looking at how dimension ratings correlate with external variables.

   A third way of obtaining convergent and discriminant validity falls somewhere between an internal and external approach in that it considers the agreement between the dimension ratings obtained in the DAC (i.e., assessor ratings) and ratings on dimensions collected from other sources external to the program (i.e., self, supervisor, peer, subordinate ratings on the dimensions). As described in chapter 4, DACs might incorporate the collection of multisource ratings as an additional source of feedback and to monitor improvement on the dimensions. These data can also be used to assess convergent and discriminant validity. To do this, a correlation matrix can be formed which crosses DAC dimension scores with multisource dimension scores collected immediately prior to DAC participation. An example of such a matrix is provided in Table 10.4, showing the agreement of DAC and multisource ratings on three dimensions. Similar to the logic of the multitrait–multimethod matrix approach (Campbell & Fiske, 1959), validity evidence is provided when correlations between DAC and multisource ratings of the same dimension are higher than correlations between DAC and multisource ratings of different dimensions. Of course, it would not be advisable to use multisource ratings collected at times following DAC participation in that at that point dimension proficiency is expected to be

TABLE 10.4
Matrix of Agreement Between DAC and Multisource Ratings
on Dimensions to Show Convergent and Discriminant Validity

DAC ratings made by assessors	Multisource Ratings Collected Immediately Prior to DAC Participation		
	Dimension 1	*Dimension 2*	*Dimension 3*
Dimension 1	+	−	−
Dimension 2	−	+	−
Dimension 3	−	−	+

Note. + denotes correlation coefficients that should be larger than correlation coefficients marked as −.

changing and thus agreement is not expected. More research along these lines in DACs is needed.

TEST-CRITERION RELATIONS

Validity evidence related to test-criterion relations involves the demonstration that effectiveness on the assessed dimensions has improved over time. Relatively little such evidence exists in the assessment center literature exploring this type of evidence. To thoroughly analyze the effectiveness of assessment centers for this purpose, we would need to have enough research on programs that assessed dimensions of different levels of "developability." For example, if the program assesses relatively stable dimensions, such as those assessed in programs designed to assess long range potential (e.g., the Management Progress Study or the Management Continuity Study; Howard & Bray, 1988), we would not expect much change over time. This is what was found: The experience of being assessed and experiencing a variety of developmental experiences on the job did not lead to appreciable increases in proficiency on the basic managerial dimensions. By contrast, in programs targeted at specific behavioral skills, the experience of participation in simulation exercises and receiving feedback led to improvements on these skills in a study by Latham and Saari (1979).

A few studies exist which explicitly sought to evaluate the effectiveness of DACs as training interventions (i.e., capable of catalyzing improvement on dimensions). Engelbrecht and Fischer (1995) collected data on managers who participated in a DAC and compared their supervisor ratings of performance following DAC participation to supervisor ratings of an equivalent group of managers that did not participate in the DAC. These authors found that supervisor ratings (using well-constructed BARS) of managers' proficiency on the dimensions action orientation, probing, and development collected 3 months following DAC participation were significantly higher than ratings of managers that did not participate in the DAC. They did not see an effect of DAC participation for the dimensions synthesis or judgment. They explained this lack of effect by arguing that these two dimensions reflect cognitive skills which are less developable than the others (Spangenberg, 1990).

One potential confound of the Engelbrecht and Fischer study was that the supervisors who conducted the ratings of the managers were also provided these individuals' DAC results, potentially leading to criterion contamination. A study by Rupp et al. (2004) collected data from a "pure" DAC, where results were provided to the participants only and solely for the purpose of their professional development. This DAC followed the model presented in chapter 4, where assessees participate, are assessed, and receive feedback multiple times within the course of the DAC itself. They found a significant improvement in performance from the morning to the afternoon at the multivariate level, with the strongest univariate effect for the dimension oral communication. An analysis of self-ratings at multiple time points throughout the DAC showed the same pattern of results. The finding of oral communication being the most developable dimension in a short timeframe corresponds with the continuum of developability presented in Fig. 10.2.

Seemingly less promising results were provided by Jones and Whitmore (1995) who found no significant differences in career advancement between groups who did and did not participate in a DAC. However, results did show that the percentage of developmental recommendations provided in the DAC that were followed by assessees predicted their subsequent advancement. When broken down by dimensions, those who followed developmental recommendations related to career motivation and working with others were the most likely to be promoted. Although Jones and Whitmore conclude from their data that the effectiveness of DACs as training interventions is limited, we instead argue that this was an extremely conservative, and in some ways inappropriate, test of DAC effectiveness. As we described earlier, the effectiveness of DACs is not shown by predicting broad (and often heavily contaminated) criteria by a one-time measure of dimension proficiency, but rather by showing that participation in the DAC and subsequent developmental activities lead to improvement on the dimensions. Of course, while we would expect that over time, continued improvement on multiple relevant dimensions would positively predict career advancement, this type of longitudinal research on the effectiveness of the DAC method as it has been described here has yet to be conducted. Future research is certainly needed in this domain (Lievens & Klimoski, 2001; Thornton & Rupp, 2003) and the work at AT&T in decades past can serve as an excellent model. We continue to think that use of reliable multisource dimension ratings collected longitudinally before and following DAC participation could prove a useful method of collecting DAC validity evidence.

CONSEQUENCES OF TESTING

Participants in developmental assessment centers learn about themselves and improve professionally. They also develop a better appreciation of the organization's interest in the development of organizational members. For example, Rupp et al. (2004) analyzed the program evaluations collected from participants following a development assessment center. They found that DAC participants were impacted positively by their experience in the DAC program attitudinally, cognitively, and behaviorally. As we discuss in chapter 11, DACs can also be used to promote diversity and perceptions of fairness in organizations, among both assessors and assessees.

SUMMARY

The use of the assessment center method to foster development of performance skills is relatively new in comparison with traditional applications for selection and promotion. Thus, less research evidence has accumulated to establish their worth. The evidence that has been gathered is supportive: Developmental assessment centers provide the conditions to foster skill development, motivate employees to undertake planning for further development, and lead to follow-up developmental activities. The emphasis in these applications is on developable dimensions, multiple opportunities to practice in simulations, and the providing of systematic feedback and coaching. Evidence shows that a portion of the participants develop a better understanding of performance constructs, and subsequently demonstrate better skills on the job. Another positive consequence is that participants report a better appreciation of the organization's interest in their development.

WHY DO ASSESSMENT CENTERS WORK?

Klimoski and Brickner (1987) raised a fundamental question about assessment centers: "Why do assessment centers work?" From their point of view, there was general acknowledgment that assessment centers are effective at predicting progress in an organization, but there is still widespread opinion about why assessment centers work. Klimoski and Brickner summarized several criticisms of the measurement inherent in assessment centers and offered alternative explanations of why assessment centers work. In the years since this challenge, much evidence has accumulated to answer their question. We conclude that the traditional explanation is most defensible: Assessors observe behaviors, make judgments about dimensions relevant to job success, and then possibly derive an overall assessment rating. We now present evidence that refutes each of the following alternatives.

CRITERION CONTAMINATION

Klimoski and Brickner argued that because assessment centers are expensive, people in organizations want to make use of their findings. The overall assessment ratings cannot be kept secret, and they are used for operational decisions. Subsequent decisions, such as promotions, salary increases, and even performance ratings are influenced by the assessment ratings themselves. As a result, the relationship of assessments and criteria will be artificially high.

There is little question that in some assessment centers, criterion contamination has been present, that is, the decision to promote the individuals was based in part on the assessment ratings. At the practical level, that is what we hope happens! However, when evaluating the quality of assessment center research, the issue is whether predictive accuracy is found when actual criterion contamination is NOT present. The answer is very clear: High levels of criterion predictive accuracy are found in many centers where contamination is absent (Thornton & Byham, 1982). Gaugler et al. (1987) provided evidence, summarized in Table 10.5, that many types of research designs (e.g., pure research studies, studies with no feedback of the ratings, concurrent validation designs, and studies of operational programs where the assessment data are used for decision making) give about the same estimate of average predictive validity.

The analysis also showed the accuracy of predictions was not a function of the type of criterion used to measure managerial success. Assessment ratings predicted not only progress criteria, such as promotions and salary

TABLE 10.5
Predictive Validity of Assessment Centers Evaluated
by Different Research Designs

Research Design	Estimated Validity
Experiment	.36
Predictive study without feedback	.43
Predictive study with feedback	.39
Concurrent validity	.42

Source.   Gaugler et al. (1987).

progress (which may be contaminated, but are not necessarily so), but also criteria such as ratings of on-the-job performance, success in training, and ratings by independent evaluators. It is hard to imagine that all of these criteria could be severely contaminated.

In addition, Gaugler et al. (1987) made judgments about the quality of each individual research study with regard to whether criterion contamination was present and whether the study was technically sound in other ways (e.g., was the sample representative of employees, could other reasons explain the results, and so on). They then computed an index of "quality" of the study. The quality of the study was related to the level of accuracy, such that the higher quality studies showed more predictive accuracy than the lower quality studies.

Other examples of situations where actual criterion contamination (i.e., knowledge of assessment ratings on the part of people providing criterion ratings) was not present further illustrate this point. The results of the landmark study of the assessment center method at AT&T (Bray & Grant, 1966; Howard & Bray, 1988) cannot be explained by criterion contamination because no one in the organization, including participants themselves, ever saw the assessment ratings. The results were literally locked up at a remote location outside the company. In another study (Kraut & Scott, 1972), the criterion was promotion to the second level of management, which took place long after the assessment center had been conducted and after managers had time to demonstrate performance effectiveness at the first level. In this case it is safe to assume that the decision to promote to the second level was based more on job performance than assessment ratings made several years earlier. In both studies, the overall assessment rating was directly correlated with long-term managerial progress.

Another example of a long-range study with little chance of criterion contamination was carried out by Tziner, Ronen, and Hacohen (1990). The assessment center predicted two uncontaminated criteria (i.e., ratings by supervisors of performance and potential for further growth) gathered each year for 3 years after the assessment center was conducted. The results showed that the overall assessment rating and dimension ratings predicted both criteria. Other studies with uncontaminated criteria have also been reported (e.g., Gluski & Sherman, 2000; Rupp et al., 2004).

In summary, although criterion contamination may exist and, if present, will artificially raise the level of predictive accuracy, there is much evidence that assessment centers can predict a wide variety of criteria that are unlikely to be influenced by assessment center results. Furthermore, many other supportive studies have been conducted where assessment center results were not disseminated in the organization. Actual criterion contamination does not seem to be a plausible explanation of the only reason why assessment centers work.

SUBTLE CRITERION CONTAMINATION

Klimoski and Brickner speculated that because the assessors are often managers in the organization, they share the same biases about what constitutes good management with managers who will later provide performance appraisal ratings. Thus, any evidence of predictive accuracy will be "contaminated" and consequently spuriously high; both groups of evaluators may be wrong and may not be evaluating real job performance. The argument here is that assessment center research has used poor criteria, that is, ratings of performance and indices of progress are colored by biased perceptions of work effectiveness. Guion (1987) has used the example that police department administrators have an image of a good police supervisor that includes "being tall." Police department assessment center ratings given by management assessors, as well as ratings of job performance given by managers, were supposedly influenced by this image. According to this argument, the correlations between the assessment center ratings and the criterion ratings were largely due to these shared biases.

There are several weaknesses in this argument as it relates to much assessment center research. First, assessment center research has used a variety of different types of criteria, not just indices of promotion and judgmental ratings by upper level managers. Table 10.6 shows that predictive accuracy of the assessment ratings is present when different types of criteria are used (Gaugler et al., 1987). Criteria have included judgments by independent third-party observers (Bray & Campbell, 1968), ratings by subordinates (McEvoy & Beatty, 1989; Schmitt et al., 1990), turnover of subordinates in the manager's unit (K. C. Ague, personal communication, March 16, 1971), objective results in a management-by-objectives system for 600 middle and senior managers (Britz, cited in Spangenberg et al., 1989), and sales performance among telemarketing representatives (Squires, Torkel,

TABLE 10.6
Validity of Assessment Centers in Relation to Different Criteria

Type of Criterion	Estimated Validity
Performance	.36[a]
Potential rating	.53[a]
Dimension ratings	.33[a]
Training performance	.35[a]
Career progress	.36[a]
Multisource rating of dimension improvement	.39[b]/.21[c]

Sources. Gaugler et al. (1987); Rupp et al. (2004); Gibbons, Rupp, Baldwin, and Holub (2005).

[a]Correlation coefficient.

[b,c]Effect size (d) for the effect of a DAC intervention on change in dimension performance as rated by self (b) and subordinates (c).

Smither, & Ingate, 1988). Further, the developmental assessment center validity study by Rupp et al. (2004) showed change in dimension performance as rated by three different sources (i.e., self, subordinate, and external assessor).

It is hard to argue that all these criteria are influenced by some irrelevant image of a good employee. Assessment center researchers have faced all of the many criterion problems plaguing industrial and organizational psychologists (Aguinis et al., 2001; Schmitt et al., 2003) and have used the best methods available in the field to measure job performance. This counterargument does not mean that we should accept faulty criterion measures (and we do not have to do so because assessment center researchers have used good ones); it does mean that researchers in this area have dealt with the thorny issue of criterion measurement as effectively as other researchers in other areas of industrial psychology and human resource management.

In summary, subtle contaminations may be present in some criterion ratings, and when present, will probably inflate validity coefficients. At the same time, assessor judgments have predicted a variety of criteria, including ones that are not subject to subtle contaminations.

A second weakness of the subtle criterion contamination argument is that a variety of assessors have been used in assessment centers—not just higher level managers from within the organization. Assessment center staffs have included human resource managers, industrial and organizational psychologists, clinical and counseling psychologists, management consultants, and groups of managers from outside the organization. Even though there is not enough evidence to prove that all of these sources provide equally accurate predictions, some comparisons between types of assessors have been made. Studies have shown that assessment centers using psychologists are just as predictive as centers using managers; when both groups are used, the accuracy is even higher (Gaugler et al., 1987).

A third argument against the subtle criterion contamination hypothesis is that managers who supposedly hold the stereotype of what is a "good manager" cannot seem to make accurate predictions of managerial success without the aid of the assessment center process. There is virtually no evidence that performance appraisal ratings and predictions of success by managers who supervise the candidates can also predict success in higher levels of management (Bernardin & Beatty, 1984; McEvoy & Beatty, 1989; Murphy & Cleveland, 1991). Management's inability to identify personnel with potential for managerial success is what often leads organizations to turn to the assessment center method in the first place.

SELF-FULFILLING PROPHECY

The following logic has been put forth: As a result of being selected for and participating in an assessment center, employees are given the idea they are competent. Thus, they perform well in the assessment center and get good feedback. Later, they put forth the effort to develop managerial skills and thereby verify the assessors' judgments. There is evidence to support the idea that expectations held by supervisors about employees' performance can have powerful effects on the employees' self-confidence and subsequent job performance (Eden, 1990). The complex process whereby these expectations influence employee performance is less clear. According to one explanation, called the "Pygmalion effect" (Eden, 1984), if the supervisor is led to expect that a subordinate is highly qualified, then the supervisor treats that subordinate in special ways that lead to increased performance. In another process, when the individual himself or herself is told about perceived special talents, that person feels more competent and performs better. Eden (1988, 1990) has provided excellent summaries of studies that have demonstrated these effects in organizational settings and has speculated that similar processes may operate in assessment centers. Turnage and Muchinsky (1984) also speculated that the Pygmalion effect may be operating in assessment centers but provided no data. Although such a phenomenon is actually aligned with and fostered in a development assessment center, this issue is unlikely to be a problem for selection and diagnostic programs. That is, research evidence shows that predictive accuracy exists when no feedback is given to the participants themselves or to the immediate supervisor (Gaugler et al., 1987). Thus, while participants' expectations about their own competencies may influence performance, studies of assessment center predictions have been conducted when no feedback was provided to alter those expectations, and still the assessment center ratings predicted future success.

PERFORMANCE CONSISTENCY

Klimoski and Brickner (1987) also argued that performance consistency inflates correlations with criteria. Two arguments here are (a) background data about the participants give assessors information about their past performance, which is then used to predict future performance, and (b) assessors can predict future performance from present performance observed in the work-sample exercises; therefore we can avoid using abstract ideas like dimensions. The first contention here is that the assessors make predictions of future performance based on knowledge of past performance gleaned from the background interview or from the candidates' work record. Such information may enhance predictions, but many assessment centers are conducted in which the assessors do not know the names or backgrounds of the participants; in fact, in fire and police promotional assessment centers, participants often wear identification numbers so that their identities are kept secret. This practice perpetuates a long-standing procedure initiated in the studies by the Office of Strategic Services to select espionage agents (Office of Strategic Services, 1948).

The second contention in the performance consistency argument implies that behavior in simulation exercises predicts future behavior on the job, and therefore there is no need to make judgments about attributes or dimensions. Proponents of this view have given brief suggestions for how an alternative practice without attribute dimensions would actually be carried out (Lance, Foster, et al., 2004; Lance, Lambert et al., 2004; Thoreson, 2002), but no published evidence of effectiveness has been presented. We are left with speculation of how the assessment program would work, and no evidence of its effectiveness. Two possibilities seem logical. Assessors could be asked to rate overall performance in each exercise, or to sort behaviors into some other logical categories, such as tasks. The first technique has been used and some of the evidence of reliability of overall exercise ratings is shown in Table 10.7. The conclusion from these studies is that consistent and accurate ratings can be obtained, but overall exercise ratings are no more consistent and no more predictive of subsequent performance on the job than dimension ratings. This evidence by itself neither refutes nor supports the performance consistency argument, because all these assessment centers used human attributes as the guiding principle for job analysis, exercise design, assessor training, and categories for observation and judgment.

More importantly, there is no published research evidence from an assessment center conducted without the use of attribute dimensions as the framework for assessors' observations. Despite years of criticism of dimensions as the framework for building assessment centers and structuring assessors' observations and judgments, there has been no published research

TABLE 10.7
Studies of Assessor Agreement on Overall Exercise Evaluations

Exercise	Author	Average Level of Agreement
LGD	Bray & Grant (1966)	.75
	Gatewood et al. (1990)	.93
	Greenwood & McNamara (1967)	.64
	Tziner & Dolan (1982)	.83
Business game	Bray & Grant (1966)	.60
	Greenwood & McNamara (1967)	.74
	Tziner & Dolan (1982)	.92
In-basket	Bray & Grant (1966)	.92
	Tziner & Dolan (1982)	.84
Presentation	Tziner & Dolan (1982)	.69
Role-play	Tziner & Dolan (1982)	.82

into the effectiveness of an assessment center using some cognitive framework other than dimensions. Thus, we are left with only speculation that this alternative is an effective procedure.

There is evidence that the combination of exercise ratings and dimension ratings correlates more highly with managerial success than either set of ratings alone (Wollowick & McNamara, 1969). Thus, it seems inappropriate to recommend dropping dimension ratings and certainly premature to adopt some other procedure until research evidence is provided.

Although there is no evidence in an applied assessment setting that task categories provide a meaningful way to organize behavioral observations, an experimental test of the effectiveness of task ratings was conducted by Adams (1990). She found that there was no difference in the accuracy of ratings using task categories in comparison with attribute categories, although ratings of task categories increased the recall of specific behaviors. More research along these lines is clearly warranted.

MANAGERIAL INTELLIGENCE

A final argument made by Klimoski and Brickner is that assessment center ratings reflect the level of intellectual functioning of candidates, but are not evaluations of managerial performance dimensions. There is no doubt that managerial tasks require intellectual abilities. Aptitude or intelligence tests consistently predict success in managerial positions, and these tests correlate with performance in assessment centers (Klimoski & Brickner, 1987; Thornton & Byham, 1982). The real issue is whether situational exercises measure anything over and above what can be obtained with intelligence tests alone. Again, studies (Chan, 1996; Dayan et al., 2002; Goffin et al., 1996; Krause et al., 2004; Wollowick & McNamara, 1969) clearly show that the combination of test scores and ratings of dimensions predicted progress more accurately than either the tests or ratings alone. We can conclude that both intelligence test scores and dimension ratings from exercises are predictive of managerial success.

Summary

There is an element of truth in each of the alternative explanations of why assessment centers work, but no one of the explanations is totally adequate in explaining assessment center accuracy. At the same time, a review of assessment center research reveals considerable evidence to refute each of the alternative explanations. There is certainly not enough evidence to favor one of the alternative explanations over the traditional explanation. In fact, in our opinion, the preponderance of evidence supports the notion that assessment centers work because assessors can and do observe behaviors displayed in situational exercises, classify those behaviors into meaningful categories representing human attributes, make judgments of overall performance, and accurately predict meaningful measures of managerial performance.

THE UTILITY OF ASSESSMENT CENTERS: COMPARING BENEFITS AND COSTS

A human resource management procedure has utility if the benefits from the technique exceed the costs by some significant amount. Utility is a way of thinking (Cascio, 1982) about the various costs and benefits that result from the use of a selection or training procedure. Whereas validity evidence tells us the extent to which the test correlates with measures of job performance, utility tells whether job performance improvements in employees selected using the new assessment procedure are enough to justify the costs of administering the test. Utility analysis requires that we compare the new test with the organization's existing selection procedure to demonstrate that there is some improvement in the benefit–cost ratio.

The most valuable innovation of utility analysis is the ability to express the value of the selection procedure in economic terms. Techniques of utility analysis allow us to derive precise estimates of the benefit of the improved procedure in dollar amounts. There are many ways that utility analysis can be conducted (Boudreau, 1983; Cascio, 1998). We will use a formula given by Schmidt, Hunter, McKenzie, and Muldrow (1979) because it shows most clearly the essential ingredients of utility analysis. In addition, this method has been widely used to evaluate personnel selection procedures, including assessment centers. With this method, utility is measured with the following formula:

$$U = t\ N_s\ (r_1 - r_2)\ SD_y\ L\ /\ SR - N_s\ (c_1 - c_2)\ /SR$$

where t = average tenure of selected people, N_s = the number selected, r_1 = validity of the new procedure, r_2 = validity of the old procedure, SD_y = unrestricted standard deviation in performance in dollar terms, L = ordinate of the normal curve at the selection ratio (a technical term that need not be explained here), SR = selection ratio (i.e., the ratio of the number of people hired to the number of applicants), c_1 = cost of new method, and c_2 = cost of old method.

The key ingredients of the utility analyses (using slight variations of the utility formula above) from assessment center studies by Cascio and Ramos (1986) and Burke and Frederick (1986) are presented in Table 10.8. In

TABLE 10.8
Results of Two Utility Studies of Assessment Centers

Key Variables	Cascio & Ramos (1986)		Burke & Frederick (1986)	
	Interview	Assessment Center	Interview	Assessment Center
Validity	.13	.388	.16	.59
Cost per assessee	$300	$688	$383	$2000
Standard deviation of job per- formance (SD_y)		$10,081		$12,789 to 38,333
Utility (gain per selectee per year)		$2,676		$2,538 to 21,222

both cases, an assessment center was compared with an interviewing process for selecting managers, because that was the selection method used previously. A high level of utility is demonstrated: The economic gain from the use of the assessment center is at least $2,500 per selectee per year, and can be as high as $21,000 per selectee per year. What this means is that, even though the assessment center is more expensive than the interview, the benefits of better prediction far outweigh these higher costs. Investments in the more accurate procedure pay off in economic returns. Before we can accept these figures, we must evaluate the credibility of the numbers put into these utility formulae.

VALIDITY ESTIMATES

The validity figures of the assessment centers in these studies are very reasonable and may in fact be too low. In the Cascio and Ramos study, the validity was .39, a value corresponding very closely with the estimate of the average validity found in the analyses reviewed earlier in this chapter. The estimate of .59 in Burke and Frederick is higher, but within the range of validities reported in Thornton and Byham (1982), Gaugler et al. (1987), and Hardison and Sackett (2004). In other words, .59 is a high figure, but validities at this level were found in other research studies, and we have some evidence about what factors lead to higher validity.

Another reason to speculate that these validity estimates may be too low is the evidence that the predictive accuracy of assessment centers increases over time. The practical reality of conducting research in organizations dictates that criterion data are collected between a few months and a couple years after the assessments have been made; it is very difficult to wait much longer to gather the success measures. Thus, most of the studies of predictive accuracy cover a relatively short time span. A few organizations have checked the accuracy of predictions over longer periods and found that predictive accuracy improves with time. We saw one example of this pattern where the assessments at AT&T were more accurate after 8 years and 16 years than at earlier points in time. IBM has also found that its assessment centers are more accurate over time. Using level of management as the criterion, Wolfson (1988) reported that the predictive accuracy for people assessed in 1984 or earlier was .29, for people assessed in 1982 or earlier was .31, and for those assessed in 1980 or earlier was .37.

VALIDITY OF ALTERNATIVE PROCEDURES

Both the Cascio and Ramos and the Burke and Frederick utility studies involve a comparison of the assessment center with a background interview, the procedure that was used traditionally in these organizations. The assumed validities of the interview were .13 and .16, average validities found in reviews of the literature at the time of the studies. These estimates of the validity of the interview may be lower than the validity of the interview process when it is carried out in a structured, systematic, and standardized manner. Subsequent reviews (Buckley & Russell, 1999; Harris, 1989; Weisner & Cronshaw, 1988) suggest that the interview can be as accurate as an assessment center, but many organizations start up an assessment center because they find their interviewing process is not effective in identifying effective managers. If the interview process is more accurate than the ones studied in Table 10.8, the utility of the assessment centers will be lower than the estimates reported here.

Another comparison might be made between assessment centers and aptitude tests. Research findings are inconsistent: One review (Schmitt et al., 1984) suggested that assessment centers were more predictive of job performance than aptitude tests, whereas another review (Hunter & Hunter, 1984) concluded that aptitude tests had predictive accuracy greater than the estimates for assessment centers. Looking across these and other studies, it appears that aptitude tests have an average validity that is about the same as assessment centers. Because of this, and because they are less costly, they might appear to be preferable. The problem with this conclusion is that there is very little variability in the validities of aptitude tests (Murphy, 1988). By contrast, we have seen that the accuracy of a well-designed and well-executed assessment center can be much higher (Chan, 1996) and assessment centers are not plagued with the adverse impact typically found with aptitude tests.

There are several other arguments that can be given for using the assessment center method. First, paper-and-pencil tests are often not as acceptable as assessment centers to candidates or managers as the basis for making decisions about selection or promotion. Candidates often feel they do not have a chance to show relevant abilities on aptitude tests. In essence, the tests do not have the "face validity" of situational tests. Furthermore, some applicants believe they do not have control over the outcome of aptitude tests, whereas they believe they can do something to prepare for situational tests and improve the skills required to perform well on them.

Another reason for not using aptitude tests, even though they may be just as valid and less costly, is that many people believe such tests are unfair to minorities and women. Even though this perception may not be accurate—in fact, aptitude tests do not show differential validity or biased prediction of job success (Hartigan & Wigdor, 1989; Schmidt, 1988)—the perception of unfairness is very powerful. Organizations often want to avoid the difficulties of defending an unpopular human resource management procedure, if possible. Because the assessment center method is perceived as unbiased, it provides a desirable alternative. Equally important is the evidence that assessment centers have been shown to be fair to minorities and women (Huck & Bray, 1976; Thornton & Byham, 1982).

A final argument for using an assessment center over paper-and-pencil tests is that the results can be much more helpful in understanding the candidates' individual strengths and weaknesses related to placement and later supervision on the job. The rich behavioral information is helpful in understanding how the person will react on the job. By contrast, results of aptitude tests usually give only one or two scores that are not very helpful in this regard.

COSTS

An examination of costs in the utility analyses for assessment centers shows, at the low end, just "out-of-pocket" costs for materials, meals, etc. At the high end, the cost includes developing and running the program. The costs of participants' and assessors' time are often omitted because the assessment experience can be considered a training opportunity for all participants. Thus, the salary expenses are balanced by training benefits and need not be included in the utility formula, which deals only with payoffs from better selection. Although there may be some debate about the actual costs to include in the analysis, research by Cascio and Silby (1979) showed that utility results for assessment centers are not very sensitive to the cost figures. In other words, widely different cost figures do not have much influence on final utility figures. These results are not intuitively obvious, but they make sense when the relatively small costs of assessment are compared to the very great economic benefits of sound judgment coming from effective managers (e.g., cost savings of thousands of dollars).

VARIATION IN JOB PERFORMANCE

By contrast, utility analysis is highly sensitive to the value used for SD_y, the standard deviation of job performance expressed in dollar terms. SD_y is an estimate of the monetary differences in job performance between more effective and less effective managers in the target position. The rationale for this part of the utility analysis can be understood more clearly with an example. If every sales clerk sells about the same amount of merchandise, then the variation in job performance (SD_y) is small. By contrast, if some sales clerks sell thousands of dollars' worth of merchandise while others sell only hundreds of dollars worth, then the variation in job performance (SD_y) is large, and a new, more accurate selection procedure will probably have utility for the organization.

Objective measures of the economic effects of variation in job performance are difficult to obtain. Fortunately, the various methods of estimating SD_y give approximately the same results (Burke & Frederick, 1986; Reilly & Smither, 1985; Weekly, Frank, O'Conner, & Peters, 1985). Thus, we can have confidence in the overall results of these utility analyses. The Burke and Frederick study (1986) is helpful because a range of SD_y figures was included in the study, and we can see the effects on the utility results. Even if we use the lowest estimate of SD_y, we can see that the assessment center clearly is a good investment. The payoff is at least $2,500 dollars per year for each manager selected with the assessment center method and may be as great as $21,000 per year per manager.

Other utility studies have been carried out with very similar results. Hogan and Zenke (1986) found that the dollar-value gain for the assessment center for selecting school principals was $58,000. Huck (1987) found that the utility of an assessment center for selecting 29 managers out of 132 candidates was $554,000, translating into a return on investment of 210%. Feltham (1988a) found that the utility of an assessment center in England was £550,000 (approximately $1,000,000). Tziner et al. (1994) found the assessment center had utility in a study of high-level managers in an Israeli corporation. Finally, Goldsmith (1990) compared three procedures used to select first-line supervisors in the nuclear division of a public utility: (1) a paper-and-pencil test of judgment combined with autobiographical information (validity .30); (2) an assessment center (validity = .43); (3) an assessment center combined with two interviews, reference checks, and procedure number one (validity = .55). The utility of the assessment center as opposed to procedure number one was $1,744,445, and the utility of procedure number three as opposed to number one was $9,205,639. We can see the increased benefit from gathering additional valid information. The wide variation in utility figures is a result of studying different types of jobs and different criteria but the conclusion is clear: Assessment centers are sound economic investments.

OTHER BENEFITS OF ASSESSMENT CENTERS

The utility analyses discussed in the preceding section show that the economic payoff from selecting better employees far outweighs the additional costs incurred with the assessment center method. However, the utility of an assessment center is even greater because these analyses consider only the primary benefits of selecting, diagnosing, and developing better employees. There are many secondary benefits that come from implementing the assessment center method. Participants learn more from the assessment center experience than from cognitive tests, personality questionnaires, or background interviews. In an assessment center, participants gain insights into their own styles of behavior and can observe the ways in which other participants handle the same situations. These benefits come even in a selection or promotion program, where there are no formal training activities. Participants also benefit from the feedback they receive at the end of the program. Even with the often-limited feedback that accompanies a selection or promotion program, participants learn how the assessors evaluate their decision making and interaction styles. And although no formal follow-up activities may be planned to remediate deficiencies, individuals can use the results to launch their own self-improvement plans.

Assessors also benefit from their service on an assessment center staff. Through the assessor training and through their interactions with other assessors, individuals learn many valuable lessons about management, principles of behavioral observation, standards for evaluating subordinates, and successful decision-making techniques. Assessors themselves report that the experience is beneficial (Thornton & Byham, 1982), and, more importantly, research has shown that assessors learn new skills (Lorenzo, 1984). Lorenzo found that, compared to a control group of managers who had no assessor training or experience, the experimental group of managers who were given assessor training and served as assessors for 3 months showed better skills in interviewing to obtain information, in evaluating that information, and in verbally communicating and defending the information.

Curiously, other research has shown that service as an assessor in an assessment center program did not make managers more effective participants when they were assessed in a higher level assessment center program (Struth, Frank, & Amato, 1980). The authors offer several possible explanations for the lack of advantage in the higher level program: Different skills were being assessed in the higher level program; the managers did not assess highly because they were being compared with truly outstanding participants in the higher level program; or the managers learned valuable skills from their participation as assessors, but not the skills needed in the higher level assessment program.

Setting up an assessment center can have additional benefits to the organization far beyond those mentioned. Alon (1977) pointed out that there were many positive effects on his organization following the assessment center. Working together on the definitions of dimensions and the assessment of candidates led to a better "alignment of perspectives among all levels of management regarding a model of supermarket store manager" (p. 229). Managers learned from each other about the behavior that contributes to the effective operation of the entire organization, thereby furthering the development of the company itself.

Finally, when assessment centers are aligned with both the human resource strategy as well as the broader business strategy, as we discuss in the next chapter, the assessment center has direct and indirect effects on the accomplishment of the strategic mission of the organization. For example, the assessment center program may assist the organization in building a diverse workforce, and also contribute to the broader social milieu by promoting fairness and equal opportunities for all members of society.

SUMMARY AND CONCLUSIONS

For each of the three applications of the assessment center method featured in this chapter, considerable evidence of validity has been reviewed. In each section, evidence related to the content of exercises and behavioral responses, internal and external relationships of ratings to measures of comparable constructs, relationships of ratings to measures of effectiveness on the job, and various intended and unintended consequences of this method was explored. The preponderance of evidence supports the validity of the assessment center method for predicting job performance, diagnosing strengths and weaknesses, and developing performance dimensions. Although all studies do not provide supportive evidence for each of the assessment center operations examined, the reasons why assessment centers do not work in some organizations is not clear.

One set of factors that affects the effectiveness of assessment centers, as well as most human resource management interventions, is the internal and external environment of the organization. In the next chapter we explore the organizational context in which assessment centers operate. In the final chapter we summarize our conclusions, make predictions about the future of assessment centers, and propose some areas where research is sorely needed, including a program to investigate why some assessment centers do not work.

Chapter 11

Assessment Centers, Human Resource Management, and Organizational Strategies

Up to this point, we have described the theory, research, and practice of the assessment center method. In this chapter, we describe the context in which assessment centers are conducted. When discussing the assessment center method we have demonstrated that assessment programs come in all shapes and sizes. Even though they all conform to the basic requirements specified in the *Guidelines* (i.e., simulations, multiple assessment methods, multiple assessors, etc.; International Task Force, 2000), assessment centers are "plastic" (Howard, 1997). As we have shown, there are wide differences in each of the elements of the assessment center method. What explains these differences? Aside from the differences that result when assessment centers are designed for different purposes, differences result from factors in an organization's internal and external environment. In this chapter we examine:

- how assessment center practices are integrated with the organization's business strategy;
- how assessment centers serve an organization's human resource management strategy;
- how assessment dimensions can integrate a number of human resource management practices;
- how assessment center practices are influenced by the external environment of the organization, specifically the legal system.

INTEGRATING ASSESSMENT WITH THE BUSINESS STRATEGY

At a very broad level, assessment centers are designed to serve the organization's business strategy. The business strategy guides many activities in an organization, including human resource management practices. Likewise, the business strategy influences assessment center practices. The business strategy of an organization may be explicit or implicit; it may be highly articulated and publicized or it may be rather vague and not highly visible. If the strategy is in fact vague, and/or if the AC developer has not been involved in the formulation of the business strategy, he or she may need to seek help from an insider to decipher the strategy and incorporate it into the AC program. Next, we describe several different organizational strategies (as presented by Gomez-Mejia, Balkin, & Cardy, 2004) and discuss how they might manifest themselves in an organization's AC program.

Evolutional Strategy

An organization that has an evolutionary strategy changes rapidly, often through the acquisition of new businesses. Reorganizations occur repeatedly and, as a result, the organization may hire and fire employees rapidly as well. In this type of setting, assessment centers are often used to identify high potential employees for new and changing roles, or to aid in the acculturation process when companies merge. Dimensions often assessed in these sorts of programs include flexibility, entrepreneurship, and risk taking.

In addition, the assessment center can simulate the dynamic cultural elements of an organization with an evolutionary strategy. For example, the exercises may simulate companies merging, dealing with a recent reduction in force, or conflicts between employees from different organizational (or national) cultures who have recently been assigned to work together.

Steady-State Strategy

Organizations with a steady-state strategy have an inward focus. These types of organization grow by developing new products in their area of expertise. They tend to foster employee loyalty and provide long-term employment stability. Assessment centers might serve this context in a number of ways. First, since retention and loyalty are paramount in these types of settings, investing in a developmental assessment center program might be a good investment, in that it conveys the company's commitment to the employees and allows for a intensive focus on a specific set of dimensions determined to be imperative to the organization's core mission (e.g., skills needed for detailed work planning and tight supervision). These types of programs demonstrate to employees that the organization is interested in their long-term development.

Overall Cost Leadership Strategy

Organizations that seek primarily to gain competitive advantage through lowering costs are said to have an overall cost leadership strategy. In this context, tasks and responsibilities are typically highly structured. As such, selection, promotion, and diagnostic centers can be easily developed using explicit job descriptions and job requirements. Assessment can involve the assessment of relatively technical skills and provide detailed descriptions of job-specific training needs. The company may also want to use simulation exercises strategically to tap into the intellectual capital of its employees. That is, leaderless group discussions might be focused on making a particular product more efficiently or lowering labor costs.

Differentiation Business Strategy

Organizations holding a differentiation business strategy excel by developing unique products and services. The firm may differentiate itself on the basis of technology, customer service, or product quality. In this setting, assessment centers can be used to foster individual or group creativity. Furthermore, the assessment center may be used to foster broader organizational development goals, such as creating a "learning culture" where formality is discouraged and innovation rewarded. Consequently, assessment centers in this context may cover a broader range of job categories, dimensions may be more "competency"–like, and participation in the center may be less targeted at a particular "level" in the organizational hierarchy.

Focus Strategy

Firms stressing low cost and differentiation from competitors in serving a narrow segment of a market are said to have a focus strategy. These types of organizations may benefit from assessment programs of all kinds. Whereas they might implement developmental centers to nourish their need for differentiation, they might also use more traditional centers to select individuals for well-defined jobs, or to diagnose the skill deficiencies present in their workforce. The dimensions assessed, diagnosed, or developed would differ depending on the purpose of the assessment, and in this case an integrated assessment program where these various components complement one another might prove quite effective.

Summary

There is no such thing as "the assessment center." As assessment center developers make choices about the many features of a specific program, they need to consider the organization strategy that is guiding decisions about many business practices. The dimensions and their definitions, the types of exercises and their content, the types of feedback and who delivers it, and how the assessment center information is disseminated throughout the organization will all be designed to serve the organization's business strategy.

RECOMMENDATIONS FOR LINKING ASSESSMENT CENTERS WITH THE BUSINESS STRATEGY

A challenge for human resource staff and assessment center developers is to learn how to tie human resource management interventions to the organization's strategy. Cascio (1998) provided a set of guidelines for making any human resource management intervention more intimately tied to the organization's strategy. Our adaptation of these suggestions in the practice of assessment centers is provided here.

1. A member of the assessment center design team should be someone who has participated in the development of the corporate business strategy. The designer needs to understand factors internal and external to the organization that influence the organization and its human resource management practices.

2. The assessment center designer should work with managers from diverse functions in the organization, such as production, quality, and finance in setting up the assessment center. Collaboration across subdepartments in the human resource management department is also important. For example, for a developmental assessment center to be most effective, units involved in assessment should coordinate with units conducting training and education.

3. The assessment center designer should clarify to upper management how the assessment center helps achieve business objectives. Many organizations develop a list of "core competencies." These competencies should form the foundation for the dimensions to be assessed, or at the very least, the dimensions should be able to be classified into the core competency system.

4. The purpose of the assessment center should be defined in light of business objectives (e.g., select new staff with more entrepreneurial skills to

advance the organization in a new area of business objectives; train current staff in proficiencies needed to handle increased responsibilities).

5. Assessment center elements should be designed to match the purpose of the assessment center, and the purpose of the assessment center should align with the HR strategy, which should align with the overall business strategy.

6. The assessment center should be executed in a timely and efficient manner. Assessment center designers should avoid designing a burdensome process that will overly tax those who implement it, because this may keep the individuals involved (e.g., subject matter experts, assessors, etc.) from meeting the organization's strategic goals by keeping them from their other responsibilities

7. The assessment center should be evaluated periodically to establish and repeatedly demonstrate its ability to contribute to business objectives.

Following these guidelines will ensure that the assessment center is maximally effective and intimately integrated with organizational strategy. To be effective and survive, private organizations must be productive and earn a profit and public organizations must provide high-quality, cost-effective services. Thus, the goal of an effective assessment center is to maximize these outcomes: select, promote, develop, and retain highly "productive" employees. The processes of assessment will ultimately be tested against these results.

ASSESSMENT CENTERS IN THE CONTEXT OF HUMAN RESOURCE MANAGEMENT

The objectives of human resource management are to attract, retain, and motivate employees (Schuler & Huber, 1990). Assessment centers contribute to these objectives. Applicants tend to respond favorably to assessment centers, in comparison with other assessment techniques such as cognitive ability tests and personality questionnaires. When assessment centers are used for making promotional decisions, candidates see them as fair. When they are used for diagnosis and development, they show employees that the organization is interested in individuals' development. The achievement of these HRM goals is contingent on making specific HRM interventions compatible with the organization's environment.

As a framework of this discussion, we can build on a model of human resource management set forth by Ivancevich (2004). Figure 11.1 provides a diagnostic model of human resource management processes. Ivancevich pointed out that any human resource management program is influenced

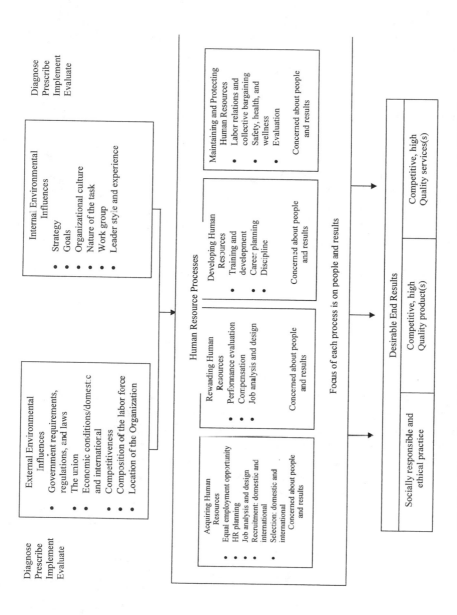

FIG. 11.1. Diagnostic model for human resource management. From Ivancevich (2004). *Human resource management*. Reproduced with permission of the McGraw-Hill Companies.

271

by (and has influences on) the external and internal environments of the organization. The figure depicts many of the external environmental influences (including governmental regulations and laws, economic conditions, and the labor force availability) and internal environmental influences (including the organization's tasks, strategies, goals, and culture) that impact human resource processes. These factors have an impact on many of the practices for acquiring, rewarding, developing, and maintaining human resources. Examples abound for how assessment center programs are influenced by these factors:

- Concerns about vulnerability to legal challenges that exercises may not be standardized have led some police and fire jurisdictions to eliminate group discussions and interview simulations from their arsenal of simulation exercises.
- Economic conditions have led some organizations to outsource their assessment program to reduce the cost of using middle management as assessors.
- Organizations with a trusting growth culture have matched participants with their on-the-job managers in a diagnostic assessment program.
- One organization's revised competency model includes a renewed emphasis on entrepreneurialship and thus a new set of dimensions clarifying higher expectations in this realm.

Internal and external influences have had effects on assessment centers applied to each of the four human resource processes in Fig. 11.1. One aspect of *acquiring* human resources is the need to recruit and select new staff with "the right stuff." When establishing an assessment center, the dimensions the organization wishes new recruits to bring to the organization are articulated through the processes of job analysis to understand job requirements and competency modeling to clarify new expectations imposed by strategic objectives. When done thoroughly, the process of building a selection center contributes greatly to organizational effectiveness. This process includes defining what is *the right stuff* the organization is seeking in specific and behavioral terms and building behaviorally anchored rating scales to evaluate performance in simulation exercises.

With reference to *rewarding* human resources, assessment centers have typically not been used for performance appraisal or compensation purposes for work on the current job. On the other hand, assessment centers have been used to certify competencies that qualify a person for increases in pay in skill-based pay systems bonuses. Also called competency-based or knowledge-based pay systems, these systems pay employees not for jobs they hold, but for the skills they possess and thus the number of jobs they can do (Cascio, 1998; Schuler & Huber, 1990). These systems encourage employees to learn new skills. Whereas tests provide a measure of knowledge, assessment centers provide one mechanism for certifying that employees can demonstrate complex skills. In addition, an IT organization used an assessment center along with knowledge tests and a portfolio to certify their consultants to offer support services to clients. Being certified allowed the consultant to work on advanced projects and earn more money. The dimensions uncovered in the job analysis and assessed in the assessment center can also be used as performance appraisal criteria. This is an example of an integrated human resource system.

As we have demonstrated throughout this book, assessment centers are being increasingly used for *developing* human resources, the processes depicted in the third box from the left in Fig. 11.1. When used for this purpose, the organization's strategies, goals, and culture have a profound influence on the definition of the dimensions being assessed. The general requirement of "leadership skill" and the wish for managers to be "good leaders," must be refined in light of what leadership means in each specific organization. Whereas relatively directive leadership is what may be sought in the operational ranks of a fire rescue organization, highly participative leadership may be what the organization is seeking for supervisors of research scientists or software designers in a computer organization.

Maintaining human resources (i.e., the processes depicted in the box to the far right of the figure) must also take into account the internal and external environment. When designing an assessment center, the architect will want to consider not only formal collective bargaining requirements, but also less formal but still highly important expectations which may be present when there are strong membership associations in the work groups affected (e.g., associations of minority fire fighters, fraternal order of police officers, and so on). Assessment center practices may also be affected by city regulations, legal precedence, and traditional past practices that require objective measures of merit and fitness.

USING ASSESSMENT CENTER OPERATIONS
TO PROMOTE WORKPLACE DIVERSITY

The demographic landscape is yet another situational variable that plays a role in shaping the social context of the organization (Cleveland & Shore, 1992). Given that the workplace is becoming increasingly diverse (Triandis et al., 1993) and diversity at most organizational levels is largely welcomed in many of today's organizations (Raggins, Townsend, & Mattis, 1998), assessment center architects should look for ways in which AC programs can assist organizations in meeting their strategic diversity goals.

Arthur and Doverspike (2005) offered many suggestions for achieving diversity and reducing discrimination through HR practices, many of which could be incorporated in an assessment center program. The first involves incorporating diversity values into the set of criteria from which employees are selected. Identifying a prodiversity or antidiscrimination attitude that can be reliably measured and on which individuals differ would allow for the selection of individuals who may be more passionate about assisting the organization meet its diversity goals. Of course adding such a "predictor" into the selection system would require an expansion of the criterion space to include the facilitation of such goals. Potential attributes suggested by Arthur and Doverspike include racism, modern racism, modern sexism, openness, cosmopolitanism, and implicit cognitions.

Assessment centers may be especially useful in defining and assessing prodiversity attitudes and behaviors in that a "diversity" dimension could be defined behaviorally according to the values and context of the organization. Simulation exercises could be designed to challenge these values, and the diversity dimension assessed through the explicit behaviors displayed by assessees. Proficiency on this dimension could then be combined with ratings on other job-relevant dimensions to determine an applicant's overall assessment rating in hopes of selecting/promoting employees that not only have the skills to carry out the job effectively, but also will strive to meet the organization's diversity goals. Arthur and Doverspike remind HR practitioners, however, that fakability on this sort of dimensions should be taken into consideration, due to the social desirability now associated with diversity initiatives.

Diversity initiatives might also be imbedded into developmental assessment center programs. Take for example the challenges often faced by older workers in training contexts (see Sterns & Doverspike, 1989). Arthur and Doverspike argue that these obstacles might be overcome by both training managers to be aware and sensitive to these issues, and to provide special incentives and rewards to older workers participating in training programs. We know of one study that has systematically explored the impact of DACs on older workers. Gibbons and Rupp (2004) found no systematic age bias in a DAC program and found older workers to respond quite favorably to the training experience. Furthermore, this lack of age bias was shown despite bias shown in subjective multisource ratings collected on the same group of mangers. Baldwin, Rupp, and Bashshur (2005) discussed how DACs might be used to promote fairness among managers. Organizations with a substantial proportion of older employees within its workforce might consider adding additional components to such a program to build awareness among management of the unique challenges faced by this and other often marginalized subgroups (e.g., women, minorities, and so forth). Designers of such programs might consider looking to the literature on diversity training (see Bendick, Egan, & Lofhjelm, 2001) for guidance in the area. Arthur and Doverspike (2005), in reviewing this literature, suggest that such programs:

- avoid ironic reversals
- incorporate action steps
- provide adequate time for the training
- ensure training isn't simply an expression of the trainer's values
- avoid coming across as simply being politically correct
- clearly define goals
- ensure buy-in from top management
- simultaneously integrate and differentiate the training with affirmative action efforts.

Pettigrew (1998), based on a similar review, suggested that such programs focus on:

- learning about the other groups
- behavioral change
- creating positive emotions associated with the outgroup
- create insight about individuals' own ingroups
- implement social sanctions for participating in diversity initiatives and assisting with the facilitation of diversity goals.

In summary, there are many ways in which assessment center programs might incorporate process and content elements that will assist the organization in meeting its strategic goals for promoting a diverse and effective workforce. As the workforce continues to become more diverse on a multitude of variables, such goals will become more and more important for modern organization to remain successful and competitive.

DIMENSIONS AS AN INTEGRATING MECHANISM FOR HUMAN RESOURCE MANAGEMENT FUNCTIONS

Assessment centers can serve to integrate many human resource management practices. The dimensions assessed in an assessment center provide one integrative mechanism. Ideally, one human resource management unit would be responsible for organizational analysis, job analysis, and competency modeling, and would coordinate the identification of core competencies and operationalizing these into behavioral dimensions, but these diagnostic processes may be conducted by disparate and disconnected organizational units. The behavioral dimensions then provide the basis for many human resource practices, such as selection, training, performance appraisal, and performance management.

Some examples of how dimensions have been used are listed below:

- Assessment center dimensions can be derived from the organization's overall competency model. For example, an organization may be placing renewed emphasis on customer service. This competency has been operationalized in dimensions such as listening skill and problem analysis.
- The dimensions can be used as the framework for performance appraisal and performance management systems. Behavioral dimensions often help explain the reasons why employees do not meet performance goals in a management-by-objectives or performance management system.
- The content of training programs can be structured around the skills embodied by assessment center dimensions. Training and development can be targeted at "developable" dimensions (i.e., knowledge, skills, and abilities that can be developed in a reasonable period of time with the training techniques available to organizations).
- Management succession plans can include information coming from assessment outcomes. Succession plans are often based on the matching of individual strengths with job and organizational requirements. Assessment center diagnoses of managerial strengths provide a road map of the placement process.

Assessment centers provide many mechanisms for integrating human resource functions. Entrance into training and development programs can be guided by assessment center findings. In one organization two human resource management policies were established: (a) The diagnosis of a development need in their assessment center must be followed with a planned developmental activity, and (b) Attendance at a training program or involvement in a developmental assignment must be justified with documentation of real need (e.g., an assessment center diagnosis). Integration also occurs because the diagnosis of training needs with an assessment center often makes people ready for active involvement in a training program. The same cannot be said for the assessment provided by most intelligence tests.

The integration discussion can be the place where diagnosis of information from multiple sources can be combined. Some consulting firms use results of ability tests and personality questionnaires to explain reasons why assessment center participants demonstrate the behavior they show in performance exercises. Howard (1997) discussed the ways in which information from multisource feedback ratings can be combined with assessment information. These two methods are complementary in the sense that multisource feedback shows how persons are perceived on the job, whereas the assessment performance shows their abilities. Succession planning in organizations can be guided by accurate information about each manager's inventory of skills and abilities.

ASSESSMENT CENTERS AND THE EXTERNAL ENVIRONMENT: LEGAL CONSIDERATIONS

Organizations that operate in highly contentious and litigious environments (e.g., those confronting some police and fire jurisdictions) often wish to design and implement an assessment center in ways that minimize vulnerability to complaints and lawsuits. The influence of the legal environment has led to a number of practices in assessment centers in these organizations.

- avoiding exercises that call for interaction among candidates, for example, not using a leaderless group discussion because the group dynamics may differ from group to group;
- avoiding exercises that involve role players, for example, not using interaction simulations such as an performance review meeting with a problem employee because different role players may interact differently with different candidates;
- designing exercises to minimize interactions between assessors and candidates, for example, not allowing assessors to ask follow-up questions about in-basket responses;
- adhering to strict time for preparation for and execution of exercises;
- taking steps to ensure that assessors and candidates have the chance to review who will be matched in exercises to avoid pairs that have any familial or business relationship;
- randomly assigning assessors to candidates.

All of these steps lead to a high level of standardization, and help protect the organization against any liability for treating candidates unfairly. In the following section we explore how assessment centers have fared when challenged in lawsuits.

Results of Legal Decisions Involving Assessment Centers

Thornton and Byham (1982) reviewed the first 10 cases arising in the 1970s and Thornton (1992) summarized a few subsequent cases that involved challenges to human resource systems that involved assessment centers.

There was no instance where the court ruled against the assessment center method. Successful defenses were due in large part to the extensive research behind the assessment center method, evidence that the method was developed following state-of-the-art procedures and then implemented in a consistent way, and evidence was fair to minorities and women. In the past several years, many other legal challenges have arisen, and assessment centers have been discussed in the rulings by judges on many employment discrimination litigation cases. The rulings in these cases give some indication of the courts' view of the status of the assessment center method. The litigated situations have involved selection, promotion, and layoffs where the plaintiff alleges discrimination in some employment practice on the basis of race, gender, or age. In most of these situations, some form of the assessment center method (or one or more simulation exercises) is used in combination with other assessment techniques. This makes it difficult to form definitive conclusions about the judiciary's opinion about assessment centers per se. Nevertheless, a review of a sample of cases provides insights into what assessment center practices are most defensible in bench trials before a judge. It is important to note, however, that these insights may not generalize to jury trials.

Judicial rulings mentioning "assessment centers" can be classified into several categories, ranging from cases where the ruling dealt directly with the administration, validity, or fairness of the assessment center method to cases where the assessment center was mentioned only as a tangential matter. In the following sections, citations of legal cases state only the names of the plaintiff and defendant; full legal citations are presented in Appendix B.

Substantive Rulings on Assessment Centers

A first set of cases involve "substantive rulings," or cases where the judge stated a conclusion about the validity and fairness of the assessment center method.

- In the classic case of *Firefighters Institute for Racial Equality et al. v City of St. Louis*, the ruling specifically stated that even though the promotional examination using a written test and an assessment center resulted in disparate impact on Black applicants, it was sufficiently valid. Prominent industrial psychologists served as expert witnesses for both plaintiffs and defendant. Pieces of evidence included the fact that the written test had a disparate impact on Blacks whereas the means for the assessment center scores for Blacks and Whites were virtually identical (2.864 vs. 2.865 respectively).

- In *Garza v City of Inglewood*, the judge ruled in favor of the City using an assessment center to select candidates for captain in the police department.

- In *Rudder et al. v District of Columbia* the judge entered a ruling in favor of the District in using an assessment center for promotion to positions of captain, lieutenant, and sergeant in the fire department even though adverse impact was shown. This was because the District provided evidence of validity and the plaintiff could not show illegal discrimination.

- In *NAACP-Metro Branch et al. v City of Montgomery* the court accepted two affidavits attesting to the validity of the assessment center for promotion in the fire department.

- In *Sapp v City of Warner Robins*, a gender discrimination case, the judge ruled that the assessment center was a legitimate screening procedure for police sergeants.

- *Wilson v Michigan Bell Telephone* involved a complaint that the assessment center discriminated against a Black male applying to a management position. The judge ruled in favor of the defendant and looked favorably on validity evidence presented, which was based on published research.

- *Cousin v Board of Trustees of the Houston Municipal School District* supported the use of an assessment center for selection of school principal.

Summary Judgment for Assessment Center User

Another category of cases involved those where one party requested summary judgment before a trial. A summary judgment refers to prompt disposition of a suit without trial when there is no dispute over the facts and the judge can make a decision based only on the law. These judgments are typically requested by the defendant (the organization) in order to dismiss the case brought by the plaintiff. Summary judgment is granted by the judge in such a situation only if the plaintiff has not provided enough evidence, even when interpreted in the most favorable light, to potentially win the case.

- In *Cunningham et al. v Village of Mount Prospect et al.*, summary judgment was awarded in favor of the City in using an assessment center as a second part of a promotional exam for police and fire officers.

- In *Hunter v City of Warner Robins, Georgia*, the assessment center was endorsed and the City was permitted to reduce the exam score for a tardy candidate.

- In *Long v City of Kansas City*, the judge dismissed a claim of age discrimination in promotion to fire chief after a promotional exam involving an assessment center.
- In *Palmer et al. v Kroger*, the judge dismissed a case in favor of a company that was using an assessment center to select store managers.
- In *Housley v Boeing*, the plaintiff challenged the assessment center as a part of a promotional examination for first-level supervisor, but the judge ruled in the company's favor.
- In *Felton et al. v City of Auburn*, a promotional exam in the fire department was upheld.
- In *Pyles v Boeing*, an assessment center for selecting first level supervisors was upheld.
- *Belfield v Cheasapeake & Potomac Telephone* found an assessment center could be used for selection to engineering assistant.

Settlement Agreement or Consent Decree to Use Assessment Centers

Parties in a legal case often come to some agreement on how to settle their differences before the trial occurs. The settlement agreements must then be reviewed and approved by the judge. Judges do not always approve agreements. Settlement agreements involving the implementation of an assessment center are often arranged when prior selection or promotional procedures are challenged by candidates as unfair or invalid. Examples of settlement agreements involving assessment centers in both public and private organizations are summarized next.

- In *Stewart et al. v US Department of the Treasury*, the parties agreed and the judge approved the agreement that an assessment center would be installed as part of a promotional system.
- In *Reynolds v Alabama Department of Transportation*, a consent decree said that DOT administrators could be used for the administration of assessment centers or other structured exams but not service ratings.
- In *United States v City of Milwaukee*, the court approved a consent order to use an assessment center for promotion to police sergeant.
- In *Williams v Weirton Steel*, the consent decree included a provision that the organization use an assessment center to evaluate candidates for first-level plant manager.
- *Stearns v Ponderosa* found that an assessment center could be used to facilitate the identification and development of women for management positions.

Injunction Against Assessment Center Denied

One party can file a motion to enjoin the other party from taking some action. Relevant to the present discussion, the plaintiff may file a motion to prevent an organization from using an assessment center as part of a promotional process. In the following cases, the judge refused to enjoin the organization from using an assessment center.

- In *Adams et al. v City of Chicago*, the judge denied a motion to stop the City from using an exam process that involved an assessment center to promote police sergeants.
- In *Sharr et al. v Department of Transportation*, the judge denied the plaintiffs' motion to enjoin when an assessment center that was normally run in one day was actually conducted over two days.

COURT DECISIONS NOT SUPPORTIVE OF ASSESSMENT CENTERS

Not all court decisions involving assessment centers have been supportive of the method. Although assessment centers may be valid and less discriminatory than alternatives such as cognitive ability tests, they are not always endorsed by the courts. The potential for plausible alternative assessment procedures or irregularities in administration of the assessment center may lead judges to rule against the use of assessment centers. The rulings in these cases can be quite informative for assessment center operations.

Cases Involving Claims of Plausible Alternatives

In an adverse impact case, three steps are followed: First, the plaintiff must show that the assessment procedure has a disparate negative effect on a legally protected group; second, the defendant can show that the procedure was valid and job-related; third, the plaintiff can show that an alternative procedure would serve the organization's interest and not have as much adverse impact. In some cases that proceeded to Step three, plaintiffs have suggested that an assessment center is an alternative to some other procedure shown to have adverse impact. However, in a number of cases, the mere mention of an assessment center as a possible alternative for promotion has not been enough to convince the judge that the challenged procedure should be ruled invalid.

- In *Simmons et al. v City of Kansas City*, the judge refused to overturn a three-part exam including a written test, oral interview, and supervisory evaluation (and substitute an assessment center) because of alleged racial discrimination in promotion of police officers.

- In *Allen et al. v District of Columbia*, the judge refused to overturn a promotional exam that involved an assessment center just because there was an assertion of an alternative.
- In *Cotter et al. v City of Boston*, the judge expressed skepticism that an assessment center (or an oral interview) was a feasible alternative to a written examination in a police promotional system.

Limitations on Assessment Center Operations

The courts have not given unfettered endorsement of assessment center practices. In the following cases, judges have recognized the need to consider important factors in assessment center applications.

- In *Meisser et al. v Federal Deposit Insurance Corporation* the judge ruled that the FDIC failed to make reasonable accommodation for a deaf person in the administration of an assessment center (and other examination procedures).
- In *Sanchez et al. v City of Santa Anna*, it was determined that because of the costs of administering an assessment center, the City did not have to implement an assessment center as an alternative to a written test for promotion to sergeant in the police department.
- In *San Antonio Hispanic Police Officers' Organization et al. v City of San Antonio*, the judge granted an injunction against the City from using the results from an assessment center because of problems in administration, and approved a settlement agreement that eliminated the assessment center.
- In *Perez v Federal Bureau of Investigation*, the court criticized several aspects of the assessment center method: failure to revise dimensions in light of changes in the organization; a dearth of Hispanic assessors; inconsistent use of the findings across different assessment center programs in the organization.

Conclusions

Because of the inherent complexity of most employment litigation, it is often difficult to ascertain the actual role played by any one element of a case. This ambiguity is further complicated by the fact that judges do not always directly address the operation of the assessment center. However, despite these complexities, several lessons can be gleaned from this review. It appears that an assessment center will have a better chance of being viewed favorably by the courts if the following practices are followed.

- Evidence is presented to support the validity of the assessment center. Evidence may be in form of a demonstration of the representativeness of content of the exercises in relation to job duties (i.e., what is sometimes labeled "content" validity), or evidence that the assessment scores are related to measures of job effectiveness.
- Evidence is provided that the assessment does not have adverse impact on protected groups. If adverse impact is present, more convincing validity evidence will need to be provided.
- It is demonstrated that the assessment center has been conducted in a uniform manner with all candidates. Minor variations in administrative conditions may not disqualify an assessment center but major deviations may.
- The corps of assessors is representative of diversity in the candidate group.
- Evidence is presented that assessors are trained thoroughly and monitored carefully.

PRINCIPLES THAT EXPLAIN SUSTAINABILITY OF ASSESSMENT CENTERS

Experience with assessment centers over the past several decades has led to some general principles explaining why some assessment centers die off in some organizations and why others survive over time in other organizations.

Reasons for failure are relatively easy to discern. Since the 1970s, we have been involved with numerous assessment centers. We have planned, initiated, implemented, conducted, observed, consulted on, evaluated, and listened to stories about many assessment centers. Here are a few reasons why assessment centers fail:

- Poor planning: appropriate people not involved; failure to get support from top-level executives.
- Burdensome preliminary work: excessive time on job analysis and development of exercises.
- Troubles in assessor training: assessors felt the process was too difficult; a practice participant caused disruptions.
- Misuse of findings: use of information from a program advertised to be diagnostic was actually used for promotion.

- No demonstration of validity.
- Dwindling support from top executives for the time and money to run the program.
- Leakage of confidential information from early to later programs.
- Failure to provide useful feedback.

Looking at successful assessment centers, we can see that sustainable programs are, at a minimum, technically sound and carefully implemented. Beyond those basic requirements, assessment center programs survive if they become institutionalized as a regular part of an organization's broader human resource management functions and strategic plan. Sustainable programs have support from many levels in the organization. Support from executive levels is critical in providing the resources of time and money. Regular presentations to an executive management committee lead to continued support. In addition, successful assessment center programs have support from key line managers in functional areas. For example, a marketing vice president may support a program that has provided useful information in the promotion of sales staff into sales management positions.

Assessment center programs are sustainable if the designers take active steps to recognize and satisfy the needs of several different constituencies. Caldwell et al. (2003) described seven ethical duties that assessment center administrators in public safety organizations owe to seven stakeholders. This analysis addressed a change in the conceptualization of assessment centers noted by Lievens and Klimoski (2001), namely "that nowadays multiple stakeholders are involved in assessment centers . . . including assessees, assessors, assessment center users, and the organization" (p. 246). Lievens and Klimoski did not elaborate on this new scrutiny of assessment centers, but we can see the need for assessment center designers and implementers to be more cognizant of the many responsibilities of running an effective and efficient assessment center. Table 11.1 presents a matrix of assessment center duties. The ever enlarging circle of persons to whom assessment center administrators have responsibility include the candidate (i.e., assessees), assessors, managers in operational departments, human resource representatives in the organization, city administrators, and the public. In addition, assessment center staff has duties to their families. The duties owed to these constituencies include the need to practice competent assessment and evaluate the quality of the assessment program and treat everyone with procedural fairness and courtesy, comply with all laws and regulations, and display financial prudence.

Each of the seven duties related to each of the seven recipients is manifested in different ways. A few examples will illustrate the complex pattern of actions that foster a sustainable assessment center. City administration or

TABLE 11.1
Assessment Center Duties Matrix

	City Admin	Department	Candidates	Assessors	The Public	HR Professionals	Self & Family
Competence	"Best Practice"	Objective fit	Clear and fair	Proper training	Match needs	Error-free process	Model excellence
Legal Compliance	Minimize liability	Follow guidelines	Job-related & unbiased	Clarify issues	Avoid blunders	Anticipate risks	Access legal experts
Need to Inform	Cost/benefit counsel	Keep involved	Prepare & explain	Explain demands	Inform & involve	Share results	Recognize demands
Procedural Fairness	Publicize & follow plan	Avoid any hint of bias	Adequate preparation	Note conflicts of interest	Avoid those with bias	Research pitfalls	Create "squeaky clean" reputation
Interactional Courtesy	Prevent "surprises"	Protect interests & involve	Orient, debrief, & protect	Respect & reciprocate	Educate and report	Share info & participate	Recognize conflicts and prepare
Quality Assurance	Conduct validation studies	Coordinate to check results	Provide appropriate feedback	Document their ability	Involve qualified experts	Network and use experts	Constantly improve skills
Financial Balance	Keep costs reasonable	Achieve real needs	Ensure quality of process	Reimburse fairly	Achieve "best result"	Compare costs with others	Pursue quality and economy

Source. Caldwell et al., 2003 (Table 1).

top-level executives in a private corporation want the assessment center to be "state-of-art," that is, demonstrate best practices. The assessment center must not incur unreasonable expenses and must withstand legal scrutiny.

The assessment center will be sustainable if it serves the real needs of managers in operational departments. This service involves selecting, promoting, and developing employees who are a good fit with the job and departmental requirements. The assessment center must involve the department in the program and avoid any hint of bias. In addition, assessment centers in public organizations must be operated with an eye to the general public who want public agencies to be run efficiently, to select appropriate personnel, and to be open to public scrutiny. Finally, an assessment center will be sustainable if assessment staff members consider their own needs in the process of developing and administering the programs. At the least, they must avoid "burnout" that can come from overly burdensome processes. At best, they can use legal and professional advisors to improve their own skills and to create a valid and defensible program.

By satisfying these duties to multiple stakeholders, developers of assessment centers can build programs that provide valuable services to an organization over many years.

CONCLUSION

Assessment centers do not exist in a vacuum. They contribute to organizational effectiveness and thrive only if they fit with the internal environment of the organization and with the organization's external environment. We have observed two extreme situations: premature demise and long life. On the one end, we have seen an assessment center emerge stillborn even after developers conducted all the technically sound work in development. Why? Because the program did not have the backing of key executives who were initiating strategic objectives which they believed would not be served by the nascent assessment center program. Could this have been avoided? Maybe not. But, if the development team had included someone knowledgeable about the emerging organizational objectives and if a thorough organizational analysis had been done, then a better fit of the assessment center and the organization may have been accomplished.

Two long lived assessment center programs illustrate the other extreme (i.e., organizations with programs that thrived for years). AT&T and several Bell System companies maintained assessment centers for more than 50 years, starting in the mid-1950s. These programs were based on solid research and they provided accurate assessments that helped the organization identify manage potential in a time of organizational stability and expanding opportunities for promotion among talented managers. The second example is Suisse Credit Bank. For more than 25 years and continuing to the present day, the organization has used the assessment center method to identify and develop talent in locations throughout Europe. The method has top-level support throughout the organization, largely because it provides an integrated mechanism for several human relations management programs including selection, performance management, career planning, and development.

Chapter 12

Assessment Centers:
A Look Back and a Look Forward

In this chapter we summarize our views on the current level of knowledge regarding the assessment center method, speculate about what the future holds for assessment center practice, and propose a research agenda to explore the many unanswered questions that remain in our field.

WHAT HAVE WE LEARNED?

There is certainly no dearth of published information about the assessment center method and its effectiveness. In fact, popular articles, papers from presentations at conferences, and scientific research reports abound. In fact, there is probably no other human resource management intervention that has been subjected to more empirical research than assessment centers! Several conclusions can be gleaned from this research, and we summarize them here.

Assessment Centers Are Widespread

Assessment centers are used extensively throughout the United States, the United Kingdom, Germany, South Africa, and many other countries throughout the world. They are used in private organizations representing widely diverse industries, and in public agencies at the city, state, and federal levels, and in the military in several counties. Many consulting organizations around the world offer services in developing and implementing the assessment center method. Indeed, certain forms of the assessment center method have been refined to a point where appropriately trained human resource managers can successfully implement simple, standardized assessment centers.

Assessment Centers Are Used for a Variety of Purposes and Jobs

Assessment centers are used for a variety of human resource management purposes. Originally, assessment centers were developed to identify managerial potential and to aid in making promotion decisions into management. Now, assessment centers are used for many additional purposes including external selection, diagnosis of training needs, certification of competency, individual development, team building, and organizational development. The dimensions and exercises have been adapted for use with numerous jobs ranging from manufacturing workers and customer service representatives to scientists and chief executive officers.

Assessment Center Procedures Vary Widely

There are a variety of different ways in which assessment centers are designed and implemented. There is no single "assessment center method." As a reflection of this diversity, the name of the conference devoted almost exclusively to this method was changed in 1997 from the "International Congress on the Assessment Center Method" to "International Congress on Assessment Center Methods." Note the plural *methods*. Every element of the method is carried out in different ways in different programs: Dimensions can be various combinations of skills, abilities, and other characteristics; simulations are various combinations of individual, group, written, and verbal exercises; assessors include operational and human resource managers and internal and external consultants with backgrounds in various disciplines; observations and judgments of individual assessors are recorded on different forms; judgments across assessors are integrated via discussion and consensus or mechanically; feedback is given in different forms by different individuals to various persons. There is a very large number of combinations of these variables instituted in any given assessment center. Thus, when speaking about "an assessment center," one must be very careful to qualify the meaning of that generic term.

Assessment Centers Are Valid

Assessment centers are valid. This bold statement is made in light of the extensive evidence that has accumulated over the past 50 years, and in full recognition of the controversy about some of the data showing that within-exercise dimension ratings do not show the pattern of relationships that some researchers expect. Well developed assessment centers are valid for making inferences about current levels of a wide range of abilities, predicting future performance in a wide variety of jobs, assessing strengths and weaknesses on performance dimensions in a variety of jobs. In addition, assessment centers are effective for developing individuals' skills and team members' working relationships. Validity evidence comes in the variety of forms called for in modern professional standards:

- Representative content is built into exercises that simulate job activities and performance demands.
- Assessors are trained to observe and evaluate behavior related to specified dimensions, and have been shown to be able to reliably and validly do so.
- Relationships of dimension ratings with other measures of the same, related, and different performance dimensions follow expected patterns.
- Overall assessment center scores are related to scores on other methods measuring performance.
- Overall assessment center scores are related to a wide variety of criterion measures of job performance.
- Participants in assessment centers express positive reactions to assessment centers and experience growth and development.
- The use of the assessment center has many *expected* positive benefits and does not have negative unexpected consequences.

These various pieces of validity evidence fall into the outdated, but sometimes still-used categories of content validity, criterion validity (including concurrent validity and predictive validity), and construct validity, and support the modern, unified view that highlights various forms of accumulated validity evidence.

Not All Validity Evidence Is Supportive

A number of studies have revealed assessment centers that do not demonstrate the level of validity that supports the intended use of the method. Despite the preponderance of evidence demonstrating support for the three major inferences from assessment center ratings described in this book (namely prediction of success, diagnosis of strengths and weaknesses, and development of performance skills), some studies show some assessment center operations do not work as intended. In some assessment centers, some dimensions do not depict important aspects of job effectiveness, some exercises are not realistic simulations, some assessors are not trained adequately or motivated sufficiently, and some assessment centers are not run in a standardized manner. In addition, the pattern and correlates of ratings from some assessment centers do not demonstrate expected relationships. The reasons why some assessment centers work and others do not work are not clear.

Assessment Centers Can Assist Organizations in Promoting Diversity

Throughout the book, we have highlighted the fact that demographic diversity is on the rise at all levels of the modern organization (Triandis et al., 1993). We have also highlighted the special challenges this presents, such as women and minorities risking bias in performance evaluations due to their taking on jobs and roles that are stereotypically associated with demographic characteristics different from their own (Cheng, 1997; Heilman et al., 2004; Tomkiewicz et al., 1998), group decision making being impacted by dissimilarity among group members (Chattopadhyay, 1999; Riordan & Shore, 1997), and fairness perceptions impacting feedback acceptance when feedback providers and recipients differ from one another (Leung et al., 2001).

The good news is that we see many organizations embracing diversity as a strategic goal (Raggins et al., 1998). We have pointed out many ways in which assessment center operations might assist organization in facilitating such goals. Such practices include selecting a diverse assessor panel, considering group composition effects among both assessors in integration discussion, and assessees participating in group exercises. We also discussed the incorporation of a prodiversity dimension to be assessed and developed in the AC program, and using diversity strategically to maximize feedback acceptance following the AC.

THE FUTURE OF ASSESSMENT CENTERS

Next, we look into the future to try to anticipate what direction the practice of assessment centers will take. Some of the current trends will likely continue and those directions are clear. Other future developments are harder to predict. The full story of assessment centers is still unfolding. The past few years have seen many new applications of the traditional methods, as well as many innovations in assessment center development, validation, and implementation. These extensions will surely continue. To build on Howard's (1997) characterization of the future of assessment centers, we predict a number of future advances.

First, we predict that the "plastic" structure of assessment centers will be reshaped. We envision continued "tweaking" of all elements:

- different definitions of basic dimensions (e.g., leadership to include elements of charisma);
- slight variations of the format and content of the standard arsenal of simulation exercises (e.g., interview simulation over the telephone for customer service reps);
- refinements of methods for recording, classifying, and integrating behavioral observations (e.g., use of PCs to record observations and prepare reports);
- computer assisted methods of sharing observations and ratings across assessors.

Second, we foresee a continued rise in high-tech assessment simulations. This includes higher fidelity simulations of office settings (e.g., those that incorporate computers, telephones, emails, etc.). We fully realize a similar prediction was made some time ago, but Kudisch et al. (1999) did not detect much of this sort of assessment technology in use in actual organizations. We again predict an increase in high-tech assessment for a number of reasons:

- the rapid development of electronic media;
- the need to lessen the involvement of highly paid assessors;
- the pressure for "objectivity" that ostensibly comes from automated systems of presenting simulation stimuli and recording and scoring responses.

Computerizing the assessment center may not be feasible for some organizations. That is, if assessees must respond to simulation exercises on a computer, it may be difficult for assessment center programs that must process large numbers of candidates to set up enough work stations to conduct secure assessments in the window of time available. However, computerization may save time, money, and resources in other aspects of the assessment center program, such as by computerizing/automating assessor functions and the integration of assessment center information. For technology to markedly affect the evolution of assessment centers, practical innovations will need to be made that don't simply computerize everything, but rather change the fundamental ways that behavior is elicited and evaluated.

Another future direction in assessment in general is the increased use of computerized techniques that eliminate the need for participants to demonstrate overt, complex behaviors. One form of this assessment is the computerized in-basket in which participants choose among a set of preselected alternatives. Another is the computerized situational judgment test, which requires a choice of preferred actions to video-presented comments by a subordinate in a low-fidelity interaction simulation.

Although these methods have their place as other forms of assessment, we want to be clear that we do not see such methods as replacements or substitutes for assessment center simulation exercises. To be clear about our objection, we emphasize that it is not the automated presentation of the stimuli (i.e., the electronic memos in the in-basket or the comments of the subordinate), but rather the presentation of preselected options for behavior that make these techniques very different from behavioral assessment. The behavior of choosing among alternatives is not the same as constructing and actually demonstrating the behavior one wishes to make in response to complex interactions with other humans. Future research is needed which compares these behavioral and nonbehavioral forms of assessment.

With the expansion of the global economy, we predict an ever-widening expansion of assessment centers into cross-cultural and multicultural settings. Many newly industrialized countries are seeing the adoption of assessment center methods. We envision two patterns of implementation of assessment centers: an importation of standard methods from one country to another (most notably from highly industrialized countries such as the United States and the United Kingdom to lesser industrialized countries); and the development of indigenous assessment centers, that is, the construction of assessment centers based on local job analyses, using definitions of dimensions that fit with local customs, and employing integration and feedback methods relevant to that country. What is less discernable is whether the choice of these routes will be determined on the basis of conscious decision making or expediency. Both routes of cross-cultural adoption are appropriate, in certain circumstances.

Finally, we see increased implementation of developmental assessment centers (i.e., programs devoted to improving skills within and after the program itself). Two converging forces will propel this movement. First, the diagnosis that comes from a diagnostic assessment center may not be enough payoff for organizations, and thus may opt for programs that are both diagnostic and developmental. Second, the changing nature of work and the dynamic nature of organizations mean employees must adapt more frequently. Developmental assessment centers provide one mechanism for fostering the necessary learning.

RESEARCH NEEDS

In light of what we do not presently know about the assessment center method, outstanding questions about the method, as well as anticipated future directions, more research is needed. In this last section, we identify several research needs and opportunities.

Alterations in the Assessment Center Method

Despite the extensive research that has been conducted and reviewed in this book (and elsewhere), the assessment center method continues to be applied in many different ways in many different countries. What must be asked is "To what degree do the current research findings generalize to assessment centers which vary from the standard practice?" The need to conduct research to answer this question depends on just how much assessment centers of today and the future do and will deviate from this standard. At one extreme are assessment centers that make only minimal modifications to the standard assessment center design. In this case, no new research studies are needed; we can probably generalize from past research to the new situation. The following situations might fall in this category: A new type of business game is used for managers; assessors are provided computers to take notes on behavioral observations; assessors watch an exercise via video conferencing technology. At another extreme are assessment centers that vary substantially from the standard method. Research is almost certainly required to substantiate the validity of these more progressive practices. Examples in this category might include: a never-before-used dimension; students used as assessors; new methods for assessors to share observations and integrate evaluations.

Assessors

More research is needed to understand what types of assessors are capable of carrying out what functions in assessment centers. Early assessment centers were staffed by assessors who had extensive training in industrial, clinical, counseling, and educational psychology. The next generation of assessors was middle-level managers who were familiar with the organization and target jobs being assessed. Another wave of assessors included human resource specialists, many of whom had training in behavioral sciences. Today, assessment centers are being staffed by persons with less formal training in psychology, behavioral science, or human resource management. These assessors may very well be capable of carrying out all functions with equal reliability and validity, but research is needed to establish which assessors can carry out which functions.

In addition, whereas the role of assessor has traditionally been one involving the observing, recording, reporting, and scaling of behaviors, with the rise of developmental assessment centers, the role has been expanded to one of "development facilitator." That is, assessors may be required to provide feedback, do career coaching, recommend training, set goals, track development, and so on. Whereas the skills required to carry out the traditional assessor roles were more analytical in nature, these new roles require much more interpersonal skill. Research is needed to sort out if these roles should be carried out by the same or different people, or what types of people can effectively carry out both roles.

Dimension-less Assessment Centers

We also need empirical research into the alternative constructs that have been mentioned by those who have criticized the traditional dimensions as constructs as the foundation of assessment centers. Potential alternatives include tasks, roles, and exercises. We have described the so-called construct validity controversy over whether assessors' ratings reflect dimensions or some other concepts. What has not been forthcoming is any description of how to design and implement an assessment center without dimensions. Despite the past 25 years of claims that dimensions do not work and vague assertions that other "constructs" are more appropriate, there has been no published research demonstrating the reliability or validity of other structures of assessment centers. In the process of preparing this book, we have searched extensively for published accounts of alternative constructs and inquired with relevant scholars to solicit evidence of the validity of alternative constructs. None have turned up as of this writing.

Cross-Cultural Applications

Among the many areas where research is needed is the cross-cultural application of assessment centers in countries that differ in customs from the major industrialized countries. A first step is to compile a detailed account of how assessment centers are designed, implemented, and evaluated around the world. Anecdotal information suggests that some practices common in the United States and the United Kingdom are adopted without change, whereas other methods and techniques are altered to meet local customs and values. Two surveys (Krause & Gebert, 2003; Kudisch et al., 1999) provide some insights into cross-cultural similarities and differences in practices, but much more evidence awaits discovery. Based on cultural differences in human resource management techniques in general, it is reasonable to speculate that differences in national cultural values are related to assessment center practices. Research to empirically investigate these speculations is underway (Krause & Thornton, 2004).

Effects of Diagnostic Assessment Centers

Another area begging for research involves the consequences of diagnostic assessment centers. Aside from the evidence that participants tend to react positively to the assessment center method, what other changes take place in assessees as a result of assessment? Research is needed that investigates how to match developmental interventions with assessment diagnoses and what interventions are effective for developing specific developmental needs in different types of people. Knowledge of these sorts of aptitude/treatment interactions is sorely needed.

Follow-up After Diagnostic and Developmental Assessment Centers

We also need more thorough studies of what factors in individuals and organizations lead to meaningful follow-up after diagnosis and feedback. The track record here is mixed: Some assessment and development programs show systematic follow-up, whereas other evidence shows disappointing amounts of follow-up activity after diagnosis. But this again is a question of both aptitude and treatment. The wide variance in the extent to which follow-up is encouraged following diagnostic centers makes it difficult to sort out these issues at present.

Still another area of much needed research is that of developmental assessment centers. DACs have been built on well-developed theories of learning and development, and upon well established practices in the fields of human resource training and development. But these theories have not been thoroughly tested in the context of developmental assessment centers. Preliminary research findings are supportive, but we need studies of a wider array of dependent variables. Do assesses develop a better understanding of management concepts as a result of being assessed and receiving feedback? What types of organizational support for such programs are needed? What factors in individuals and organizations lead to skill development, applications of these skills on the job, and ultimately better work performance and organizational effectiveness? We know this sort of research is not easy: Longitudinal designs are needed; experimentation in real organizations is difficult to justify; the time of managers is precious. Still, innovative research programs may be able to yield valuable information.

Social Information Processing

Finally, we reiterate Lievens and Klimoski's (2001) call for research into the assessor as a social information processor. Summarizing research in this area up to 2000, they conclude that the quality of assessment center ratings are a function of conceptually distinct dimensions, exercises that provide opportunities to observe behavior relevant to the dimensions, and assessors who are motivated and capable of providing quality judgments. They suggest that we need additional research to discover how to improve social judgment accuracy in assessment center ratings, including the role of expectations and cognitive structures in assessors, the contributions of both controlled and automatic processing of information, and how the social context affects assessment center judgments.

We support these recommendations, but also argue for the importance of considering both the specific procedure used to observe, classify, and integrate observations, as well as the purpose of the assessment center. As we have described in some detail in chapters 7 and 8, there are a wide variety of procedures that are followed by individual assessors and groups of assessors in gathering information and forming conclusions about dimension performance. These procedures include various combinations of judgmental and statistical procedures, all of which probably have an impact on how assessors process social information. Research will need to sort out what procedures have what impact on what judgment processes.

The second factor that will need to be considered in understanding social information processing is the purpose of the assessment center. As we have repeatedly emphasized, assessment centers are used for different purposes, namely selection/placement, diagnosis, and development. The purpose of the assessment center is very likely to have a profound effect on how assessors perceive, integrate, and judge behavior. Future research will contribute substantially if it examines the effect of assessment center purpose on the content and processes of social perception.

Why Don't Some Assessment Centers Work?

A comprehensive research agenda is needed to explain why some assessment centers do not work. The most cursory review of the assessment center literature reveals an array of evidence—some supportive, but some not supportive of the inferences made from assessment center results. Our detailed analysis of the extensive research over nearly 40 years shows a mixture of evidence on each element of the assessment center method. What explains the discrepancies in these findings? Even though we have attempted to identify the most valid practices, and we have put forth our conclusions based on extant literature, it is clear that more research is needed.

Our suggested approach for this research program is to focus on the factors that explain why a given assessment center does *not* work. Recall that Klimoski and Brickner (1987) proposed several alternate explanations of why assessment centers work. Those notions focused much research and discussion in subsequent years. We turn their challenge on its head and propose a research agenda to explore reasons why some assessment centers do not work. By "work," we mean demonstrate reliability and validity for intended inferences.

A working list of explanations of why an assessment center does not work includes the following: An assessment center will not work if:

- adequate job, organization, and situation analyses are not conducted;
- dimensions are ill-defined, conceptually indistinct, and exceed 7 or 8 in number;
- assessors are incompetent, poorly trained, and ill-motivated;
- the assessment procedures are unstandardized and inconsistent across time or participants;
- the design of the program elements does not match the purpose of the assessment center.

No single study will be able to investigate all these possible explanations at once. Conclusions will need to be drawn by examining a number of related studies, possibly using quantitative methods (e.g., meta-analysis), where the assessment practices vary in some systematic way.

SUMMARY

For nearly 50 years the assessment center method has been a valuable human resource management intervention. In that period we see examples of continuity and change in the method. Starting the mid-1950s, a select few large organizations conducted assessment centers in much the same way to identify management potential. Based on systematic and extensive research into the reliability and validity of assessment center ratings, the reputation of the method rose steadily. Numerous organizations adopted and then adapted the method to assess personnel in a wide range of jobs. New applications for diagnostic and developmental purposes emerged. What remained constant were the essential features of the assessment center method: observation of overt behavior on multiple dimensions in simulation exercises by multiple assessors and then integrated in some systematic judgmental or statistical manner. What changed were the dimensions being assessed, the methods of recording and integrating observations, the level of technology built into the process, the types of assessors, and the methods of feedback.

Waves of additional research studies investigated innovations on virtually all elements of the method. Moving from relatively straightforward studies of the relationship of assessment ratings with external criteria to quite sophisticated studies of judgment processes, the preponderance of findings support the new applications. Controversy arose and still persists over the cognitive frameworks that assessors use when observing and evaluating the complex social behavior displayed in simulation exercises. Additional research is needed to fully understand how the purpose of the assessment center, the various elements of the method, and the organizational and cultural context interact to affect the outcome of assessment center ratings. We envision lively debates surrounding the currently unsolved issues. In the meantime, practitioners will continue to use the assessment center method as a human resource management intervention to help select, promote, diagnose, and develop organizational personnel.

CONCLUSIONS

So, after all this, we present our final conclusions. Are assessment center methods always perfectly reliable, valid, and nondiscriminatory? Certainly not. But, they do have a solid track record of prediction, diagnosis, and development.

Do assessors' ratings from all assessment center methods conform to the expectations we have about internal and external relationships? Certainly not. But, many assessment centers provide valuable assessments of many dimensions related to performance effectiveness in many jobs.

Are assessment center methods the only, or the best, method of predicting employee success? Certainly not. But, assessments from the method predict success in a variety of criteria in a variety of jobs over various time periods, and they add incremental predictive power in combination with other methods.

Are assessment center methods a panacea for all human resource management problems? Certainly not. But, the various instantiations of assessment centers are valuable interventions for a variety of human resource management needs. Assessment centers are effective in predicting, diagnosing, and developing performance effectiveness in organizations.

In the end, we are reminded of the prologue to an old television show in the United States staring Hal Holbrook that went something like this: The government of the United States is a poor form of government, and yet it is the best form of government devised by men. Analogously, we close with this: Some say the assessment center is a poor human resource management intervention, yet we say it is the best of human resource management intervention devised by men and women.

Epilogue

To twist Voltaire's philosophical debate in Candide about whether
this is the best world or the best of all possible worlds,
we assert that the assessment center method may not be
the best human resource management intervention
but it is the best of all possible human resource management interventions.

Guidelines and Ethical Considerations for Assessment Center Operations

Source: International Task Force on Assessment Center Guidelines. (2000). Guidelines and ethical considerations for assessment center operations. *Public Personnel Management, 29*, 315–331.

PURPOSE

This document is intended to establish professional guidelines and ethical considerations for users of the assessment center method. These guidelines are designed to cover both existing and future applications. The title "assessment center" is restricted to those methods that follow these guidelines.

These guidelines will provide: (1) guidance to industrial/organizational psychologists, organizational consultants, human resource management specialists and generalists, and others designing and conducting assessment centers; (2) information to managers deciding whether or not to institute assessment center methods; (3) instruction to assessors serving on the staff of an assessment center; and (4) guidance on the use of technology in assessments.

HISTORY OF GUIDELINES

The rapid growth in the use of the assessment center method in recent years has resulted in a proliferation of applications in a variety of organizations. Assessment centers currently are being used in industrial, educational, military, government, law enforcement, and other organizational settings. Practitioners have raised serious concerns that reflect a need for standards or guidelines for users of the method. The 3rd International Congress on the Assessment Center Method, which met in Quebec (May 1975), endorsed the first set of guidelines. These were based on the observations and experience of a group of professionals representing many of the largest users of the method.

Developments in the period 1975–79 concerning federal guidelines related to testing, as well as professional experience with the original guidelines, suggested that the guidelines should be evaluated and revised. Therefore, the 1979 guidelines included essential items from the original guidelines but also addressed the recognized need for: (1) further definitions, (2) clarification of impact on organizations and participants, (3) expanded guidelines on training, and (4) additional information on validation.

Since 1979 the use of assessment centers has spread to many different organizations that are assessing individuals representing diverse types of jobs. During this period pressures to modify the assessment center method came from three different sources. First, there had been attempts to streamline the procedures to make them less time-consuming and expensive. Second, new theoretical arguments and evidence from empirical research had been interpreted to mean that the assessment center method does not work exactly as its proponents originally had believed, suggesting that the method should be modified. Third, many procedures purporting to be assessment centers had not complied with previous guidelines because the guidelines may have been too ambiguous. Revisions in the 1989 third edition were designed to incorporate needed changes and to respond to some of the concerns raised from 1979–89.

The 1989 revision of these guidelines was begun at the 15th International Congress on the Assessment Center Method in Boston (April 1987) when Dr. Douglas Bray held discussions with many attendees.

Subsequently, Dr. Bray and Dr. George Thornton solicited additional comments from a group of assessment center practitioners. The 1989 Task Force provided comments on drafts of a revision prepared by Bray and Thornton. A later draft was circulated and discussed at the 16th International Congress held in May 1988 in Tampa.

The 1989 guidelines were written in response to comments obtained at the 1988 Congress and from members of the Task Force. The 1989 guidelines were endorsed by a majority of the Task Force and by participants at the 17th International Congress held in May 1989 in Pittsburgh.

Changes in the 1989 guidelines from prior editions included: (1) specification of the role of the job analysis; (2) clarification of the types of attributes/dimensions to be assessed and whether or not attributes/dimensions must be used; (3) delineation of the processes of observing, recording, evaluating, and aggregating information; and (4) further specification of assessor training. The current revision of these guidelines was initiated at the 27th International Congress on Assessment Center Methods in Orlando (June 1999) when Dr. David R. MacDonald conducted discussions with a number of assessment center experts in attendance, and also solicited input at a general session regarding aspects of the guidelines needing to be (re-)addressed. A primary factor driving the revision was the passage of a full decade since the 1989 edition. Other factors included an interest in the integration of technology into assessment center methods and recognition of the need for more specific definitions of several concepts and terms.

Input from members of the Task Force for the 2000 Edition was synthesized into a final draft that was presented and endorsed at the 28th International Congress held in May 2000 in San Francisco, attended by 150 participants representing Australia, Belgium, Brazil, Canada, Columbia, Germany, India, Indonesia, Italy, Japan, Mexico, Netherlands, Philippines, Singapore, Sweden, Switzerland, Taiwan, United Arab Emirates, United Kingdom, and the United States of America.

ASSESSMENT CENTER DEFINED

An assessment center consists of a standardized evaluation of behavior based on multiple inputs. Several trained observers and techniques are used. Judgments about behavior are made, in major part, from specifically developed assessment simulations. These judgments are pooled in a meeting among the assessors or by a statistical integration process. In an integration discussion, comprehensive accounts of behavior, and often ratings of it, are pooled. The discussion results in evaluations of the performance of the assessees on the dimensions/competencies or other variables that the assessment center is designed to measure. Statistical combination methods should be validated in accordance with professionally accepted standards.

There is a difference between an assessment center and assessment center methodology. Various features of the assessment center methodology are used in procedures that do not meet all of the guidelines set forth here, such as when a psychologist or human resource professional, acting alone, uses a simulation as a part of the evaluation of an individual. Such personnel assessment procedures are not covered by these guidelines; each should be judged on its own merits. Procedures that do not conform to all the guidelines here should not be represented as assessment centers or imply that they are assessment centers by using the term "assessment center" as part of the title.

The following are the essential elements for a process to be considered an assessment center:

1. **Job Analysis**—A job analysis of relevant behaviors must be conducted to determine the dimensions, competencies, attributes, and job performance indices important to job success in order to identify what should be evaluated by the assessment center.

The type and extent of the job analysis depend on the purpose of assessment, the complexity of the job, the adequacy and appropriateness of prior information about the job, and the similarity of the new job to jobs that have been studied previously.

If past job analyses and research are used to select dimensions and exercises for a new job, evidence of the comparability or generalizability of the jobs must be provided.

When the job does not currently exist, analyses can be done of actual or projected tasks or roles that will comprise the new job, position, job level, or job family.

Target dimensions can also be identified from an analysis of the vision, values, strategies, or key objectives of the organization.

Competency-modeling procedures may be used to determine the dimensions/competencies to be assessed by the assessment center, if such procedures are conducted with the same rigor as traditional job analysis methods. Rigor in this regard is defined as the involvement of subject matter experts who are knowledgeable about job requirements, the collection and quantitative evaluation of essential job elements, and the production of evidence of reliable results. Any job analysis or competency modeling must result in clearly specified categories of behavior that can be observed in assessment procedures.

A "competency" may or may not be amenable to behavioral assessment as defined herein. A competency, as used in various contemporary sources, refers to an organizational strength, an organizational goal, a valued objective, a construct, or a grouping of related behaviors or attributes. A competency may be considered a behavioral dimension for the purposes of assessment in an assessment center if it can be defined precisely and expressed in terms of behaviors observable on the job or in a job family and in simulation exercises. A competency also must be shown to be related to success in the target job or position or job family.

2. **Behavioral Classification**—Behaviors displayed by participants must be classified into meaningful and relevant categories such as dimensions, attributes, characteristics, aptitudes, qualities, skills, abilities, competencies, and knowledge.

3. **Assessment Techniques**—The techniques used in the assessment center must be designed to provide information for evaluating the dimensions previously determined by the job analysis.

Assessment center developers should establish a link from behaviors to competencies to exercises/assessment techniques. This linkage should be documented in a competency-by-exercise/assessment technique matrix.

4. **Multiple Assessments**—Multiple assessment techniques must be used. These can include tests, interviews, questionnaires, sociometric devices, and simulations. The assessment techniques are developed or chosen to elicit a variety of behaviors and information relevant to the selected competencies/dimensions. Self-assessment and 360° assessment data may be gathered as assessment information. The assessment techniques will be pretested to ensure that the techniques provide reliable, objective and relevant behavioral information for the organization in question. Pre-testing might entail trial administration with participants similar to assessment center candidates, thorough review by subject matter experts as to the accuracy and representativeness of behavioral sampling and/or evidence from the use of these techniques for similar jobs in similar organizations.

5. **Simulations**—The assessment techniques must include a sufficient number of job-related simulations to allow opportunities to observe the candidate's behavior related to each competency/dimension being assessed. At least one—and usually several—job-related simulations must be included in each assessment center.

A simulation is an exercise or technique designed to elicit behaviors related to dimensions of performance on the job requiring the participants to respond behaviorally to situational stimuli. Examples of simulations include, but are not limited to, group exercises, in-basket exercises, interaction (interview) simulations, presentations, and fact-finding exercises.

Stimuli may also be presented through video-based or virtual simulations delivered via computer, video, the Internet, or an intranet.

For simple jobs one or two job-related simulations may be used if the job analysis clearly indicates that only one or two simulations sufficiently simulate a substantial portion of the job being evaluated. If a single comprehensive assessment technique is used, then it must include distinct job-related segments.

Assessment center designers also should be careful to design exercises that reliably elicit a large number of competency-related behaviors. In turn, this should provide assessors with sufficient opportunities to observe competency-related behavior. The stimuli contained in a simulation parallel or resemble stimuli in the work situation, although they may be in different settings. The desirable degree of fidelity is a function of the purpose of the assessment center. Fidelity may be relatively low for early identification and selection programs for non-managerial personnel and may be relatively high for programs designed to diagnose the training needs of experienced managers. Assessment center designers should be careful that the content of the exercises does not favor certain assessees (e.g., assessees in certain racial, ethnic, age, or sex groups) for irrelevant reasons.

To qualify as a behavioral simulation for an assessment center as herein defined, the assessment method must require the assessee to overtly display certain behaviors. The assessee must be required to demonstrate a constructed response. Assessment procedures that require the assessee to select *only* among provided alternative responses, such as seen only in multiple-choice tests or computerized in-baskets, do not conform to this requirement. Likewise, a situational interview that calls for only an expression of behavioral intentions does not conform. Neither do "low fidelity" simulations and situational interviews. Though they may yield highly reliable and valid assessment ratings, they do not constitute behavioral assessment required in assessment centers.

Assessment center materials often are intellectual property protected by international copyright laws. Respect for copyrights and the intellectual property of others must be maintained under all circumstances.

6. **Assessors**—Multiple assessors must be used to observe and evaluate each assessee.

When selecting a group of assessors, consider characteristics such as diversity of race, ethnicity, age, sex, organizational level, and functional work area.

Computer technology may be used to assess in those situations in which it can be shown that a computer program evaluates behaviors at least as well as a human assessor.

The maximum ratio of assessees to assessors is a function of several variables, including the type of exercises used, the dimensions to be evaluated, the roles of the assessors, the type of integration carried out, the amount of assessor training, the experience of the assessors, and the purpose of the assessment center. A typical ratio of assessees to assessors is two to one.

A participant's current supervisor should not be involved in the assessment of a direct subordinate when the resulting data will be used for selection or promotional purposes.

7. **Assessor Training**—Assessors must receive thorough training and demonstrate performance that meets the guidelines in the section, "Assessor Training," *prior to* participating in an assessment center.

8. **Recording Behavior**—A systematic procedure must be used by assessors to record specific behavioral observations accurately at the time of observation. This procedure might include techniques such as handwritten

notes, behavioral observation scales, or behavioral checklists. Audio and video recordings of behavior may be made and analyzed at a later date.

9. **Reports**—Assessors must prepare a report of the observations made during each exercise before the integration discussion or statistical integration.

10. **Data Integration**—The integration of behaviors must be based on a pooling of information from assessors or through a statistical integration process validated in accordance with professionally accepted standards.

During the integration discussion of each dimension, assessors should report information derived from the assessment techniques but should not report information irrelevant to the purpose of the assessment process.

The integration of information may be accomplished by consensus or by some other method of arriving at a joint decision. Methods of combining assessors' evaluations of information discussed in the assessors' integration sessions must be supported by the reliability of the assessors' discussions.

Computer technology also may be used to support the data integration process provided the conditions of this section are met.

NON-ASSESSMENT CENTER ACTIVITIES

The following kinds of activities *do not* constitute an assessment center:

1. Assessment procedures that do not require the assessee to demonstrate overt behavioral responses are not behavioral simulations, and thus any assessment program that consists solely of such procedures is not an assessment center as defined herein. Examples of these are computerized in-baskets calling only for multiple-choice responses, situation interviews calling only for behavioral intentions, and written competency tests.

Procedures not requiring an assessee to demonstrate overt behavioral responses may be used within an assessment center but must be coupled with at least one simulation requiring the overt display of behaviors.

2. Panel interviews or a series of sequential interviews as the sole technique.

3. Reliance on a single technique (regardless of whether it is a simulation) as the sole basis for evaluation. However, a single comprehensive assessment technique that includes distinct job-related segments (e.g., large, complex simulations or virtual assessment centers with several definable components and with multiple opportunities for observations in different situations) is not precluded by this restriction.

4. Using only a test battery composed of a number of paper-and-pencil measures, regardless of whether the judgments are made by a statistical or judgmental pooling of scores.

5. Single-assessor evaluation (i.e., measurement by one individual using a variety of techniques such as paper-and-pencil tests, interviews, personality measures, or simulations).

6. The use of several simulations with more than one assessor but with no pooling of data (i.e., each assessor prepares a report on performance in an exercise, and the individual, unintegrated reports are used as the final product of the center).

7. A physical location labeled as an "assessment center" that does not conform to the methodological requirements noted above.

ORGANIZATIONAL POLICY STATEMENT

Assessment centers operate more effectively as part of a human resource system. Prior to the introduction of a center into an organization, a policy statement should be prepared and approved by the organization. This policy statement should address the following areas:

1. **Objective**—This may be selection, diagnosis for development, early identification, evaluation of potential, evaluation of competency, succession planning, or any combination of these.

An assessment center participant should be told, prior to assessment, what decision(s) will or might be made with assessment data. If the organization desires to make decisions with the data other than those communicated to the participant prior to assessment, the decision(s) should be clearly described to the participant and consent obtained.

2. **Assessees**—The population to be assessed, the method for selecting assessees from this population, procedure for notification, and policy related to assessing should be specified.

3. **Assessors**—The assessor population (including sex, age, race, and ethnic mix), limitations on use of assessors, assessor experience, and evaluation of assessor performance and certification requirements, where applicable, should be specified.

4. **Use of Data**—The process flow of assessment records within the organization, individuals to receive reports, restrictions on access to information, procedures and controls for research and program evaluation purposes, feedback procedures to management and employees, and the length of time data will be maintained in files should be specified. Particularly for a selection application, it is recommended that the data be used within two

years of the date of administration because of the likelihood of change in the participant or the organization.

5. **Qualifications of Consultant(s) or Assessment Center Developer(s)**—The internal or external consultant(s) responsible for the development of the center or of the exercises/simulations for the center should be identified and his or her professional qualifications and related training specified.

6. **Validation**—The statement should specify the validation model being used. If a content-oriented validation strategy is used, documentation of the relationship of the job/job family content to the dimensions and exercises should be presented along with evidence of the reliability of the observations and rating of behavior. If evidence is being taken from prior validation research, which may have been summarized in meta-analyses, the organization must document that the current job/job family and assessment center are comparable and generalized to the jobs and assessment centers studied elsewhere. If local, criterion-related validation has been carried out, full documentation of the study should be provided. If validation studies are under way, there should be a schedule indicating when a validation report will be available.

ASSESSOR TRAINING

Assessor training is an integral part of the assessment center program. Assessor training should have clearly stated training objectives and performance guidelines.

The following issues related to training must be considered:

1. **Training Content**—Whatever the approach to assessor training, the objective is to obtain reliable and accurate assessor judgments. A variety of training approaches may be used, as long as it can be demonstrated that reliable and accurate assessor judgments are obtained. The following minimum training goals are required:

  a. Thorough knowledge of the organization and job/job family or normative group being assessed to provide an effective context for assessor judgments.

  b. Thorough knowledge and understanding of the assessment dimensions, definitions of dimensions, relationship to job performance, and examples of effective and ineffective performance.

  c. Thorough knowledge and understanding of the assessment techniques, relevant dimensions to be observed in each portion of the assessment center, expected or typical behavior, examples or samples of actual behaviors, etc.

d. Demonstrated ability to observe, record, and classify behavior in dimensions, including knowledge of forms used by the center.

e. Thorough knowledge and understanding of evaluation and rating procedures, including how data are integrated.

f. Thorough knowledge and understanding of assessment policies and practices of the organization, including restrictions on how assessment data are to be used, when this is a requirement of assessors.

g. Thorough knowledge and understanding of feedback procedures, where appropriate.

h. Demonstrated ability to give accurate oral and written feedback, when feedback is given by the assessors.

i. Demonstrated knowledge and ability to play objectively and consistently the role called for in interactive exercises (e.g., one-on-one simulations or fact-finding exercises) when role-playing is required of assessors. Non-assessor roleplayers also may be used if their training results in their ability to play the role objectively and consistently.

2. **Training Length**—The length of assessor training may vary due to a variety of considerations that can be categorized into three major areas:

a. Instructional Design Considerations
   • The instructional mode(s) utilized
   • The qualifications and expertise of training of assessors who have no expertise of the trainer
   • The training and instructional sequence

b. Assessor Considerations
   • Previous knowledge and experience may require less training assessment techniques
   • The use of professional psychologists training; simple assessment centers may require less
   • Experience and familiarity with the organization and the target position(s)/job(s)/job families or target level
   • The frequency of assessor participation
   • Other related qualifications and expertise

c. Assessment Program Considerations
   • The target position's level of difficulty
   • The number of dimensions/competencies to be rated

- The anticipated use of the assessment information (e.g., immediate selection, broad placement considerations, development)
- The number and complexity of the exercises
- The division of roles and responsibilities between assessors and others on the assessment staff (e.g., administrator and other support staff)
- The degree of support provided to assessors in the form of observation and evaluation guides

It should be noted that length and quality of training are not synonymous. Precise guidelines for the minimum number of hours or days required for assessor training are difficult to specify. However, extensive experience has shown that, for the initial training of assessors who have no experience in an assessment center that conforms to the guidelines in this document, a typical assessment center may require two days of assessor training for each day of the administration of assessment center exercises. Assessors who have experience with similar assessment techniques in other programs may require less training. More complex assessment centers with varied formats of simulation exercises may require additional training; simple assessment centers may require less.

In any event, assessor training is an essential aspect of an assessment program. The true test of training quality should be assessor competence as described by the performance guidelines and certification that follow.

3. **Performance Guidelines and Certification**—Each assessment center should have clearly stated performance guidelines for assessors. These performance guidelines should include, at a minimum, the following areas:

a. The ability to rate behavior in a standardized fashion
b. The ability to recognize, observe, and report the behaviors into the appropriate dimensions, etc.
c. The ability to administer an exercise, if the assessor serves as exercise administrator

Some measurement is needed to indicate that the individual being trained is capable of functioning as an assessor. The measurement of assessor performance may vary and could include data in terms of (1) accuracy of rating performance, (2) critiques of assessor reports, and (3) observation as an evaluator. It is important that, prior to their actual duties, assessors' performance is evaluated to ensure that individuals are sufficiently trained to function as assessors and that such performance is periodically monitored to ensure that skills learned in training are applied.

Each organization must be able to demonstrate that its assessors can meet minimum performance standards. This may require the development of additional training or other prescribed actions for assessors not meeting these performance guidelines.

The trainer of assessors should be competent to enable individuals to develop the assessor skills stated above and to evaluate the acquisition of these skills.

4. **Currency of Training and Experience**—The time between assessor training and initial service as an assessor must not exceed six months. If a longer period has elapsed, prospective assessors should attend a refresher course or receive special coaching from a trained assessment center administrator.

Assessors who do not have recent experience as an assessor (i.e., fewer than two assessment centers over two consecutive years) should attend a refresher course before they serve again or be given special coaching by a trained assessment center administrator.

INFORMED PARTICIPATION

The organization is obligated to make an announcement prior to assessment so that participants will be fully informed about the program. Ideally, this information should be made available in writing before the center. A second option is to use the material in the opening statement of the center. While the information provided will vary across organizations, the following basic information should be given to all prospective participants.

1. **Objective(s)**—The objective(s) of the program and the purpose of the assessment center. The organization may choose to disclose the dimensions measured and the general nature of the exercises prior to the assessment.
2. **Selection**—How individuals are selected to participate in the center.
3. **Choice(s)**—Any options the individual has regarding the choice of participating in the assessment center as a condition of employment, advancement, development, etc.
4. **Staff**—General information on the assessor staff, including composition and assessor training.
5. **Materials**—What assessment center materials completed by the individual are collected and maintained by the organization.
6. **Results**—How the assessment center results will be used and how long the assessment results will be maintained on file.

7. **Feedback**—When and what kind of feedback will be given to the participants.

8. **Reassessment**—The procedure for reassessment (if any).

9. **Access**—Who will have access to the assessment center reports and under what conditions.

10. **Contact**—Who will be the contact person responsible for the records and where the results will be stored or archived.

VALIDATION ISSUES

A major factor in the widespread acceptance and use of assessment centers is related directly to an emphasis on sound validation research. Numerous studies demonstrating the predictive validity of individual assessment center programs have been conducted in a variety of organizational settings and reported in the professional literature. However, the historical record of the validity of this process cannot be taken as a guarantee that a given assessment program will or will not be valid or generalized to a new application.

Ascertaining the validity of an assessment center program is a complicated technical process, and it is important that validation research meet both professional and legal standards. Research should be conducted by individuals knowledgeable in the technical and legal issues pertinent to validation procedures. In evaluating the validity of assessment center programs, it is particularly important to document the selection of the dimensions, etc., assessed in the center. In addition, the relationship of assessment exercises to the dimensions, attributes, or competencies assessed should be documented as well.

Validity generalization studies of assessment center research suggest that overall assessment ratings derived in a manner conforming to these guidelines show considerable predictive validity. Such findings support the use of a new assessment center in a different setting if the job, exercises, assessors, and assessees in the new situation are similar to those studied in the validation research and if similar procedures are used to observe, report, and integrate the information. The validity generalization studies of the predictive validity of the overall assessment rating do not necessarily establish the validity of the procedure for other purposes such as diagnosis of training needs, accurate assessment of skill level in separate dimensions, or the developmental influence of participation in an assessment center.

The technical standards and principles for validation appear in *Principles for the Validation and Use of Personnel Selection Procedures* (Society for Industrial and Organizational Psychology, Inc., 1987) and *Standards for Educational and Psychological Testing* (American Psychological Association [APA], 1999).

RIGHTS OF THE PARTICIPANT

In the United States the federal government enacted the Freedom of Information Act and the Privacy Act of 1974 to ensure that certain safeguards are provided for an individual against an invasion of personal privacy. Some broad interpretations of these acts are applicable to the general use of assessment center data.

Assessment center activities typically generate a large volume of data on an individual who has gone through an assessment center. These assessment data come in many forms and may include observer notes, reports on performance in the exercises, assessor ratings, peer ratings, paper-and-pencil or computerized tests, and final assessment center reports. This list, while not exhaustive, does indicate the extent of information about an individual that may be collected.

The following guidelines for use of these data are suggested:

1. Assessees should receive feedback on their assessment center performance and should be informed of any recommendations made.

2. Assessees who are members of the organization have a right to read any formal summary written reports concerning their own performance and recommendations that are prepared and made available to management. Applicants to an organization should be provided with, at a minimum, what the final recommendation is and, if possible and if requested by the applicant, the reason for the recommendation.

3. For reason for test security, assessment center exercises and assessor reports on performance in particular exercises are exempted from disclosure, but the rationale and validity data concerning ratings of dimensions and the resulting recommendations should be made available upon request of the individual.

4. The organization should inform the assessee what records and data are being collected, maintained, used, and disseminated.

5. If the organization decides to use assessment results for purposes other than those originally announced and that can impact the assessee, the assessee must be informed and consent obtained.

REFERENCES

The guidelines have been developed to be compatible with the following documents:

American Educational Research Association, American Psychological Association, and National Council on Measurements in Education. (1999). *Standards for educational and psychological testing.* Washington, DC: American Psychological Association.

Society for Industrial and Organizational Psychology Inc., American Psychological Association. (1987). *Principles for the validation and use of personnel selection procedures* (3rd ed.). College Park, MD.

GLOSSARY

Assessee: An individual whose competencies are measured by an assessment center.

Assessment Center: A process employing multiple techniques and multiple
assessors to produce judgments regarding the extent to which a participant
displays selected competencies.

Assessor: An individual trained to observe, record, classify, and make reliable judgments about the behaviors of assessees.

Competency: Also called *dimension*. The constellation or group of behaviors
that are specific, observable, and verifiable and that can be reliably and logically classified together and that are related to job success.

Dimension: See *Competency*.

Feedback: Information comparing actual performance to a standard or desired level of performance.

High (or Low) Fidelity: The extent to which an assessment center simulation requires the assessee to actually display behaviors related to one or
more selected competencies. Fidelity is related to the realism of the simulation as compared to an actual job situation, task, etc.

Job Analysis: The process (typically a combination of techniques such as interviews with and observations of incumbents; job checklists; interviews with
upper-level managers/executives) used to determine the competencies
linked to success or failure in a job, job role, or job grouping.

Reliability: The extent to which a measurement process yields the same results (given identical conditions) across repeated measurements.

Simulation: An exercise or technique designed to elicit behaviors related to
dimensions of performance on the job requiring the participants to respond behaviorally to situational stimuli.

Validity: The extent to which a measurement tool or process, such as an assessment center, yields useful results. Multiple validities might be measured
(e.g., "construct," "content," "face," "predictive," "social") depending upon
the questions being explored and the tool or process being investigated.

References to Employment Discrimination Cases Involving Assessment Centers

Adams et al. v City of Chicago. No. 94-5727, 1996 U.S. Dist. Lexis 3567.

Allen et al. v District of Columbia. Civil Action No. 92-555 (CRR), 812 F. Supp. 1239; 1993 U.S. Dist. Lexis 1908.

Belfield v Cheaseapeake & Potomac Telephone. Civil Action No. 78-1373, 1980 U.S. Dist. Lexis 10405, 22 Empl. Prac. Dec. (CCH) P30,641.

Cotter et al. v City of Boston. Civil Action No. 99-11101-Wgy, 193 F. Supp. 2d 323; 20002 U.S. Dist. Lexis 4922.

Cousin v Board of Trustees of the Houston Municipal Separate School District. No. EC 77-92, 488 F Supp. 75, 1980 U.S. Dist. Lexis 10727, 28 Fair Empl. Prac. Cas. (BNA) 166.

Cunningham v Village of Mount Pleasant et al. No. 02 C 4196, 2004 U.S. Dist. Lexis 3153.

Felton, W.C. et al. v City of Auburn. CA No. 96-D-0385-E, 968 F. Supp. 1476; 1997 U.S. Dist. Lexis 9592.

Firefighters Institute for Racial Equality et al. v City of St. Louis. Civil Action No 74-30C(2), 74 C 200(2), U.S. Dist. Lexis 12512, 23 Empl. Prac. Dec. (CCH) P31,040.

Firefighters Institute for Racial Equality et al. v City of St. Louis. Nos 74-30C(3), 74-200C(3), 470 F. Supp. 1281, 1979 U.S. Dist. Lexis 11968, 19 Fair Empl. Prac. Cas. (BNA) 1643, 20 Empl. Prac. Dec. (CCH) P30,202.

Garza v City of Inglewood. Case No. CV 87-7251-AAH Consolidated with No. CV 89-5582-AAH, 761 F. Supp. 1475; 1991 U.S. Dist. Lexis 5461; 60 Empl. Prac. Dec. (CCH) P41,977; 91 Daily Journal DAR 4836.

Housley v Boeing Company. Case No. 00-2429-JWL, 177 F. Supp.2d 1209, 2001 U.S. Dist. Lexis 21004

Hunter v City of Warner Robins, Georgia et al. C.A. 93-86-2-MAC (WDO), 842 F. Supp. 1460; 1994 U.S. Dist. Lexis 1298.

League of Martin et al. v City of Milwaukee. Civil Action No. 81-C-1465, 588 F. Supp. 1004, 1984 U.S. Dist. Lexis 16062, 42 Fair Empl. Prac. Cas. (BNA) 562; 35 Emply Prac. Dec. (CCH) P34, 894.

Long v City of Kansas City. Civil Action No. 93-2073-EEO; 1994 U.S. Dist. Lexis 9142.

Meisser et al. v Federal Deposit Insurance Corporation. No. 91 C 3242, 1994 U.S. Dist. Lexis 16525.

NAACP-Montgomery Metro Branch et al. v City of Montgomery. Civil Action No. 95-D-1590-N. 188 F.R.D. 408; 1999 U.S. Dist. Lexis 14615.

Palmer et al. v Kroger Company. Case No. 92-77235; 1994 U.S. Dist. Lexis 8283.

Perez v Bureau of Investigation et al. No. EP-87-CA-10, 714 F. Supp. 1414, 1989 U.S. Dist. Lexis 8426; 49 Fair Empl. Pracc. Cas. (BNA) 1349; 52 Empl. Prac. Dec. (CCH) P39, 518.

Pyles v Boeing Company. Civil Action No. 00-2394-KHV; 2002 U.S. Dist. Lexis 24787.

Reynolds et al. v Alabama Department of Transportation et al. Civil Action No. 85-T-665-N, 1994 U.S. Dist. Lexis 20921.

Rudder et al. v District of Columbia. Civil No. 92-2881 (CRR), 890 F. Supp. 23, 1995 U.S. Dist. Lexis 8948.

San Antonio Hispanic Police Officers' Organization et al. v City of San Antonio, et al. Civil Action No. SA-94-CA-242. FB, 188 F.R.D. 433; 1999 U.S. Dist. Lexis 13005.

Sanchez et al. v City of Santa Anna. CV 79-1818 KN, 928 F. Supp. 1494; 1995 U.S. Dist. Lexis 21224.

Sapp v City of Warner Robins. Civil Action No. 82-218-2-Mac (WDO), 655 F. Supp. 1043, 1987 U.S. Dist. Lexis 1930, 43 Fair Empl. Prac. Cas. (BNA) 486.

Scott v City of Overland Park. Civil Action No. 83-2219, 595 F. Supp. 520; 1984 U.S. Dist. Lexis 23698; 41 Fair Empl. Prac. Cas. (BNA) 1211.

Sharr et al. v Department of Transportation. Civil No. 02-1513-JO, 247 F Supp. 2d 1208; 2003 U.S. Dist. Lexis 3192.

Simmons et al. v City of Kansas City. Civil Action No. 88-2603-0, 1992 U.S. Dist. Lexis 20231.

Stearns v Ponderosa. Civil Action No. C81-0524-L (G), 1982 U.S. Dist. Lexis 14486; 29 Empl. Prac. Dec. (CCH) P32,979.

Stewart et al. v U.S. Department of the Treasury. Civil Action No. 90-2841, 948 F. Supp. 1077; U.S. Dist. Lexis 18470; and 225 F. Supp. 2d 6, 2002 U.S. Dist. Lexis 16328.

United States of America v City of Milwaukee. Civil Action No. 74-C-480; 102 F.R.D. 218, 1984 U.S. Dist. Lexis 16061.

United States of America v City of Montgomery. Civil Action No. 3739-N, Civil Action No. 75-19-N, 788 F. Supp. 1563; 1992 U.S. Dist. Lexis 4893; 65 Fair Empl. Prac. Cas. (BNA) 447.

Williams v Weirton Steel. Nos. 69-30-W, 72-50-W, 80-75-W, 1983 U.S. Dist Lexis 18961; 31 Fair Empl. Prac. Cas. (BNA) 1415.

Wilson v Michigan Bell Telephone. Civil Action No. 80-71849, 550 F. Supp. 1296, 1982 U.S. Dist. Lexis 15812; 30 Fair Empl. Prac. Cas. (BNA) 427, 31 Empl. Prac. Dec. (CCH) P33,356.

References

Abelson, R. P. (1981). Psychological status of the script concept. *American Psychologist, 36,* 715–729.

Adams, S. R. (1990). *Impact of assessment center method and categorization scheme on schema choice and observational, classification, and memory accuracy.* Unpublished doctoral dissertation, Colorado State University, Ft. Collins, CO.

Aguinis, H., Henle, C. A., & Ostroff, C. (2001). Measurement in work and organizational psychology. In N. Anderson, D. S. Ones, H. K. Sinangil, & C. Viswesvaran (Eds.), *Handbook of industrial, work, and organizational psychology* (Vol. 1, pp. 27–50). Thousand Oaks, CA: Sage.

Alba, J. W., & Hasher, L. (1983). Is memory schematic? *Psychological Bulletin, 93,* 203–231.

Aldag, R. J., & Fuller, S. R. (1993). Beyond fiasco: A reappraisal of the groupthink phenomenon and a new model of group decision processes. *Psychological Bulletin, 113,* 533–552.

Alexander, H. S., Buck, J. A., & McCarthy, R. J. (1975). Usefulness of the assessment center method for selection to upward mobility programs. *Human Resource Management, 14,* 10–13.

Alon, A. (1977). Assessment and organizational development. In J. L. Moses & W. C. Byham (Eds.), *Applying the assessment center method* (pp. 225–240). New York: Pergamon Press.

American Board of Professional Psychology. (1988). *The assessment center procedure for the diplomate examination in clinical psychology.* Columbia, MO: Author.

American Educational Research Association, American Psychological Association, & American Council on Measurement in Education. (1999). *Standards for Educational and Psychological Tests.* Washington, DC: American Psychological Association.

American Psychological Association. (1992). Ethical principles of psychologists and code of conduct. *American Psychologist, 47,* 1597–1611.

Anastasi, A., & Urbina, S. (1997). *Psychological testing.* Upper Saddle River, NJ: Prentice-Hall.

Anderson, L. R., & Thacker, J. (1985). Self-monitoring and sex as related to assessment center ratings and job performance. *Basic and Applied Social Psychology, 6,* 345–361.

Anderson, N. H. (1974). Cognitive algebra: Integration theory applied to social attribution. In L. Berkowitz (Ed.), *Advances in experimental social psychology* (Vol. 7, pp. 1–101). New York: Academic Press.

Anderson, N. H. (1981). *Foundations of information integration theory.* New York: Academic Press.

Argyris, C. F., & Schon, D. (1974). *Theory in practice.* San Francisco, CA: Jossey-Bass.

Arnold, G. T. (1987). Feedback and career development. In H. W. More & R. C. Unsinger (Eds.), *The police assessment center* (pp. 167–201). Springfield, IL: Charles C. Thomas.

Arnold, J. (2001). Careers and career management. In N. Anderson, D. S. Ones, H. K. Sinangil, & C. Viswesvaran, *Handbook of industrial, work, and organizational psychology, Vol. 2. Organizational psychology* (pp. 115–132). London: Sage.

Aronson, E., Wilson, T. D., & Akert, R. M. (2002). *Social psychology* (4th ed.). Upper Saddle River, NJ: Prentice-Hall.

Arthur, W., Jr., Bennett, W., Jr., Edens, P. S., & Bell, S. T. (2003). Effectiveness of training in organizations: A meta-analysis of design and evaluation features. *Journal of Applied Psychology, 88*, 234–245.

Arthur, W., Jr., Day, E. A., McNelly, T. L., & Edens, P. S. (2003). A meta-analysis of the criterion-related validity of assessment center dimensions. *Personnel Psychology, 56*, 125–154.

Arthur, W., & Doverspike, D. (2005). Achieving diversity and reducing discrimination in the workplace through human resource management practices: Implications of research and theory for staffing, training, and rewarding performance. In R. L. Dipboye & A. Colella (Eds.), *Discrimination at work: The psychological and organizational bases* (pp. 305–327). Mahwah, NJ: Lawrence Erlbaum Associates.

Arvey, R. D., & Murphy, K. R. (1998). Performance evaluation in work settings. *Annual Review of Psychology, 49*, 141–168.

Asher, J. J., & Sciarrino, J. A. (1974). Realistic work sample tests: A review. *Personnel Psychology, 27*, 519–533.

Atchley, E. K., Smith, E. M., & Hoffman, B. J. (2003, September). *Examining the relationship between performance, individual differences, and developmental activities. Getting more bang for the buck from DPACs.* Paper presented at the 31st International Congress on Assessment Center Methods. Atlanta, Georgia.

Baker, T. A. (1986). *Multitrait-multimethod analysis of performance ratings using behaviorally anchored and behavioral checklist formats.* Unpublished master's thesis, Old Dominion University, Norfolk, VA.

Baldwin, A., Rupp, D. E., & Bashshur, M. (2005). *Managerial justice training: An application of developmental assessment centers.* Theory Advancement. Presented at the 20th annual conference of the Society for Industrial and Organizational Psychology, Los Angeles, California.

Baldwin, T. T., & Ford, J. K. (1988). Transfer in training: A review and directions for future research. *Personnel Psychology, 41*, 63–105.

Bandura, A. (1977). *Social learning theory.* Englewood Cliffs, NJ: Prentice-Hall.

Bandura, A. (1986). *Social foundations of thought and action.* Englewood Cliffs, NJ: Prentice-Hall.

Bandura, A. (1997). *Self-efficacy.* New York: Freeman.

Banks, M. H. (1988). Job components inventory. In S. Gael (Ed.), *The job analysis handbook for business, industry, and government.* New York: Wiley.

Barker, L. I., Wahlers, K. J., Cegala, D. J., & Kibler, R. J. (1983). *Groups in process.* Englewood Cliffs, NJ: Prentice-Hall.

Bartels, L. K., Boomer, W. H., & Rubin, R. S. (2000). Student performance: Assessment centers versus traditional classroom evaluation techniques. *Journal of Education for Business, 75*, 198–201.

Bass, B. M. (1950). The leaderless group discussion. *Personnel Psychology, 3*, 17–32.

Bass, B. M. (1954). The leaderless group discussion. *Psychological Bulletin, 51*, 465–492.

Bauer, T. N., Maertz, C. P., Dolen, M. R., & Campion, M. A. (1998). Longitudinal assessment of applicant reactions to employment testing and test outcome feedback. *Journal of Applied Psychology, 83*, 892–903.

Bendick, M., Egan, M. L., & Lofhjelm, S. M. (2001). Workforce diversity training: From anti-discrimination compliance to organizational development. *Human Resource Planning, 24*, 10–25.

Bennett-Alexander, D. D., & Pincus, L. B. (1998). *Employment law for business.* Boston, MA: Irwin/McGraw-Hill.

Bentz, V. J. (1967). The Sears experience in the investigation, description, and prediction of executive behavior. In R. R. Wickert & D. E. McFarland (Eds.), *Measuring executive effectiveness* (pp. 147–205). New York: Appleton-Century-Crofts.

Bernardin, H. J., & Beatty, R. W. (1984). *Assessing human behavior at work.* Boston, MA: Kent.

Bernardin, H. J., & Buckley, M. R. (1981). Strategies in rater training. *Academy of Management Review, 6,* 205–212.

Bernardin, H. J., & Walter, C. W. (1977). Effects of rater training and diary keeping on psychometric error in ratings. *Journal of Applied Psychology, 62,* 64–69.

Binning, J. F., Adorno, A. J., & Kroeck, K. G. (1997, April). *Validity of behavior checklist and assessor judgmental ratings in an operational assessment center.* Paper presented at the annual conference of the Society for Industrial and Organizational Psychology, St. Louis, MO.

Binning, J. F., & Barrett, G. V. (1989). Validity of personnel decisions: An examination of the inferential and evidential bases. *Journal of Applied Psychology, 74,* 478–494.

Bobrow, W., & Leonards, J. S. (1997). Development and validation of an assessment center during organizational change. *Journal of Social Behavior & Personality, 12,* 217–236.

Bobrow, W., & Schultz, M. (2002, October). *Applying technical advances in assessment centers.* Paper presented at the 30th International Congress on Assessment Center Methods, Pittsburgh, PA.

Boehm, V. R. (1985). Using assessment centers for management development—Five applications. *Journal of Management Development, 4*(4), 40–51.

Bohlander, G., & Snell, S. (2004). *Managing human resources* (13th ed.). Mason, OH: Thomson/South-Western.

Borman, W. C. (1977). Consistency of rating accuracy and rating errors in the judgment of human performance. *Organizational Behavior and Human Performance, 20,* 238–252.

Borman, W. C. (1978). Exploring the upper limits of reliability and validity in job performance ratings. *Journal of Applied Psychology, 63,* 135–144.

Borman, W. C. (1982). Validity of behavioral assessment for predicting recruiter performance. *Journal of Applied Psychology, 67,* 3–9.

Borman, W. C., & Brush, D. H. (1993). More progress toward a taxonomy of managerial performance requirements. *Human Performance, 6,* 1–21.

Boudreau, J. W. (1983). Economic considerations in estimating the utility of human resource productivity improvement programs. *Personnel Psychology, 36,* 551–576.

Boyle, S., Fullerton, J., & Wood, R. (1995). Do assessment/development centres use optimum evaluation procedures? A survey of practice in UK organizations. *International Journal of Selection and Assessment, 3,* 132–140.

Braaten, L. (1990). Can assessment add value to the selection and development of sales managers? In C. W. Stucker (Ed.), *Proceedings of the 1989 National Assessment Conference* (pp. 18–21). Minneapolis, MN: Personnel Decisions, Inc.

Bracken, D. W., Timmreck, C. W., & Church, A. H. (2001). Introduction: A multisource feedback process model. In D. W. Bracken, C. W. Timmreck, & A. H. Church (Eds.), *The handbook of multisource feedback: The comprehensive resource for designing and implementing MSF Processes.* San Francisco, CA: Jossey-Bass.

Brannick, M. R., & Levine, E. L. (2002). *Job analysis.* Thousand Oaks, CA: Sage.

Brannick, M. T., Michaels, C. E., & Baker, D. P. (1989). Construct validity of in-basket scores. *Journal of Applied Psychology, 74,* 957–963.

Bray, D. W. (1964). The management progress study. *American Psychologist, 19,* 419–429.

Bray, D. W., & Campbell, R. J. (1968). Selection of salesmen by means of an assessment center. *Journal of Applied Psychology, 52,* 36–41.

Bray, D. W., Campbell, R. J., & Grant, D. L. (1974). *Formative years in business: A long-term AT&T study of managerial lives.* New York: Wiley.

Bray, D. W., & Grant, D. L. (1966). The assessment center in the measurement of potential for business management. *Psychological Monographs, 80* (17, Whole No. 625), 1–27.

Brockner, J., & Wiesenfeld, B. M. (1996). An integrative framework for explaining reactions to decisions: Interactive effects of outcomes and procedures. *Psychological Bulletin, 20,* 189–208.

Brummel, B., & Rupp, D. E. (2004). *Creating parallel simulation exercises.* Unpublished manuscript. University of Illinois.

Buckingham M., & Clifton, D. O. (2001). *Now, discover your strengths.* New York: The Free Press.

Buckley, M. R., & Russell, C. J. (1999). Validity evidence. In R. W. Eder & M. M. Harris (Eds.), *The employment interview handbook* (pp. 35–48). Thousand Oaks, CA: Sage.

Burke, M. J., & Frederick, J. T. (1986). A comparison of economic utility estimates for alternative SDy estimation procedures. *Journal of Applied Psychology, 71,* 334–339.

Burke, R. J., & McKeen, C. A. (1996). Do women at the top make a difference? Gender proportions and experiences of managerial and professional women. *Human Relations, 49,* 1093–1104.

Burrus, J. (2004). *Simulations in assessment centers and the anchoring and adjustment heuristic.* Unpublished manuscript, University of Illinois.

Bycio, P., & Zoogah, B. (2002). Exercise order and assessment center performance. *Journal of Occupational and Organizational Psychology, 75,* 109–114.

Byham, T. M., & Wilkerson, B. A. (2003, April). *Factors affecting the acceptance and application of developmental feedback from an executive development program.* Paper presented at the 18th annual conference of the Society for Industrial and Organizational Psychology, Orlando, Florida.

Byham, W. C. (1970). Assessment center for spotting future managers. *Harvard Business Review, 48,* 150–160, plus appendix.

Byham, W. C. (1977). Assessor selection and training. In J. L. Moses & W. C. Byham (Eds.), *Applying the assessment center method* (pp. 89–126). New York: Pergamon Press.

Byham, W. C. (1990). *Dimensions of effective performance for the 1990s.* Pittsburgh, PA: Development Dimensions International.

Byham, W. C., & Temlock, S. (1972). Operational validity—A new concept in personnel testing. *Personnel Journal, 51,* 639–647, 654.

Byham, W. C., Smith, A. B., & Paese, M. J. (2000). *Grow your own leaders. Acceleration pools: A new method of succession management.* Pittsburgh, PA: DDI Press.

Caldwell, C., Gruys, M. L., & Thornton, G. C., III (2003). Public service assessment centers: A steward's perspective. *Public Personnel Management, 32,* 229–249.

Campbell, D. T., & Fiske, D. W. (1959). Convergent and discriminant validation by the multitrait-multimethod matrix. *Psychological Bulletin, 56,* 81–105.

Campbell, W. J. (1986). *Construct validation of role-playing exercises in an assessment center using BARS and behavioral checklist formats.* Unpublished master's thesis, Old Dominion University, Norfolk, VA.

Campion, M. A. (1994). Job analysis for the future. In M. G. Rumsey, C. B. Walker, & J. H. Harris (Eds.), *Personnel selection and classification* (pp. 1–12). Hillsdale, NJ: Lawrence Erlbaum Associates.

Carpenter, M. (2002). The implications of strategy and social context for the relationship between top management team heterogeneity and firm performance. *Strategic Management Journal, 23,* 275–284.

Carrick, P., & Williams, R. (1999). Development centres: A review of assumptions. *Human Resource Management Review, 9,* 77–91.

Cascio, W. F. (1982). *Costing human resources: The financial impact of behavior in organizations.* Boston, MA: Kent.

Cascio, W. F. (1989, October). *Assessment data and personnel decisions.* Paper presented at the 1989 National Assessment Conference, Minneapolis, MN.

Cascio, W. F. (1998). *Managing human resources* (5th ed.), Boston, MA: McGraw-Hill/Irwin.

Cascio, W. F. (2002). Changes in workers, work, and organizations. In W. C. Borman, D. R. Ilgen, & R. J. Klimoski (Eds.), *Comprehensive handbook of psychology, Vol. 12: Industrial and organizational psychology* (pp. 107–130). New York: Wiley.

Cascio, W. F., & Ramos, R. A. (1986). Development and application of new method for assessing job performance in behavioral/economic terms. *Journal of Applied Psychology, 71*, 20–28.

Cascio, W. F., & Silbey, V. (1979). Utility of the assessment center as a selection device. *Journal of Applied Psychology, 64*, 107–118.

Chaiken, S., & Stangor, C. (1987). Attitudes and attitude change. In M. R. Rosenzweig & L. W. Porter (Eds.), *Annual review of psychology* (Vol. 38, pp. 575–630). Palo Alto, CA: Annual Reviews.

Chan, D. (1996). Criterion and construct validation of an assessment centre. *Journal of Occupational and Organizational Psychology, 69*, 167–181.

Chan, D., Schmitt, N., Sacco, J. M., & DeShon, R. P. (1998). Understanding pretest and posttest reactions to cognitive ability and personality tests. *Journal of Applied Psychology, 83*, 471–485.

Chatman, J. A., & Flynn, F. J. (2001). The influence of demographic heterogeneity on the emergence and consequences of cooperative norms in work teams. *Academy of Management Journal, 44*, 956–974.

Chattopadhyay, P. (1999). Beyond direct and symmetrical effects: The influence of demographic dissimilarity on organizational citizenship behavior. *Academy of Management Journal, 42*, 273–287.

Chen, P. Y., Carsten, J., & Krauss, A. D. (2003). Job analysis: The basis for developing criteria for all human recourse programs. In J. E. Edwards, J. C. Scott, & N. Raju (Eds.), *Human resources program-evaluation handbook* (pp. 27–48). Thousand Oaks, CA: Sage.

Cheng, C. (1997). Are Asian American employees a model minority or just a minority? *Journal of Applied Behavioral Science, 33*, 277–290.

Clause, C. S., Mullins, M. E., Nee, M. T., Pulakos, E., & Schmitt, N. (1998). Parallel test form development: A procedure for alternative predictors and an example. *Personnel Psychology, 51*, 193–208.

Cleveland, J. N., & Shore, L. M. (1992). Self- and supervisory perspectives on age and work attitudes and performance. *Journal of Applied Psychology, 77*, 469–484.

Cochran, D. S., Hinckle, T. W., & Dusenberry, D. (1987). Designing a developmental assessment center in a government agency: A case study. *Public Personnel Management, 16*(2), 145–152.

Cohen, B. M., Moses, J. L., & Byham, W. C. (1974). *The validity of assessment centers: A literature review.* Monograph II. Pittsburgh, PA: Development Dimensions Press.

Cohen-Charash, Y., & Spector, P. E. (2001). The role of justice in organizations: A meta-analysis. *Organizational Behavior and Human Decision Processes, 86*, 278–321.

Collins, J. M., Schmidt, F. L., Sanchez-Ku, M., Thomas, L., McDaniel, M. A., & Le, H. (2003). Can basic individual differences shed lights on the construct meaning of assessment center evaluations? *International Journal of Selection and Assessment, 11*, 17–29.

Colquitt, J. A. (2001). On the dimensionality of organizational justice: A construct validation of a measure. *Journal of Applied Psychology, 86*, 356–400.

Colquitt, J. A., Conlon, D. E., Wesson, M. J., Porter, C. O. L. H., & Ng, K. Y. (2001). Justice at the millennium: A meta-analytic review of 25 years of organizational justice research. *Journal of Applied Psychology, 86*, 425–445.

Colquitt, J. A., LePine, J. A., & Noe, R. A. (2000). Toward an integrative theory of training motivation: A meta-analytic path analysis of 20 years of research. *Journal of Applied Psychology, 85*, 678–707.

Constable, A. (1999). *Development centres.* Paper presented at the Human Resource Development Conference, London, Roffey Park Management Institute.

Cooper, W. W. (1981). Ubiquitous halo. *Psychological Bulletin, 90,* 218–244.

Costa, P. T., Jr., & McRae, R. R. (1992). *Revised NEO Personality Inventory (NEO-PI-R) and NEO Five-factor Inventory (NEO-FFI) professional manual.* Odessa, FL: Psychological Assessment Resources.

Coulton, G. F., & Feild, H. S. (1995). Using assessment centers in selecting entry-level police officers: Extravagance or justified expense? *Public Personnel Management, 24,* 223–254.

Cronbach, L. J. (1970). *Essentials of psychological testing.* New York: Harper & Row.

Cropanzano, R., Prehar, C. A., & Chen, P. Y. (2002). Using social exchange theory to distinguish procedural from interactional justice. *Group and Organizational Management, 27,* 324–351.

Cropanzano, R., & Randall, M. L. (1993). Injustice and work behavior: A historical review. In R. Cropanzano (Ed.), *Justice in the workplace: Approaching fairness in human resource management.* (pp. 1–20). Hillsdale, NJ: Lawrence Erlbaum Associates.

Cropanzano, R., & Schminke, M. (2001). Using social justice to build effective work groups. In M. Turner (Ed.), *Groups at work: Advances in theory and research* (pp. 143–171). Hillsdale, NJ: Lawrence Erlbaum Associates.

Crudup, B. (2004). *Innovation: Life, inspired.* New York: Thirteen/WNET New York.

Damitz, M., Manzey, D., Kleinmann, M., & Severin, K. (2003). Assessment center for pilot selection: Construct and criterion validity and the impact of assessor type. *Applied Psychology: An International Review, 52,* 193–212.

Dawes, R. (1979). The robust beauty of improper linear models in decision making. *American Psychologist, 34,* 571–582.

Dayan, K., Kasten, R., & Fox, S. (2002). Entry-level police candidate assessment center: An efficient tool or a hammer to kill a fly? *Personnel Psychology, 55,* 827–849.

Dipboye, R. L. (1985). Some neglected variables in research on discrimination in appraisals. *Academy of Management Review, 10,* 116–127.

Dodd, W. E. (1977). Attitudes toward assessment center programs. In J. I. Moses & W. C. Byham (Eds.), *Applying the assessment center method* (pp. 161–183). New York: Pergamon Press.

Donahue, L. M., Truxillo, D. M., Cornwell, J. M., & Gerrity, M. J. (1997). Assessment center construct validity and behavioral checklists: Some additional findings. *Journal of Social Behavior and Personality, 12,* 85–108.

Dugan, B. (1988). Effects of assessor training on information use. *Journal of Applied Psychology, 73,* 743–748.

Dulewitz, V. (1991). Improving assessment centers. *Personnel Management, 23*(6), 50–55.

Dunning, D. (1995). Trait importance and modifiability as factors influencing self-assessment and self-enhancement motives. *Personality and Social Psychology Bulletin, 21,* 1297–1306.

Dweck, C. S., & Leggett, E. L. (1988). A social-cognitive approach to motivation and personality. *Psychological Review, 95,* 256–273.

Eagly, A. H., Makhijani, M. G., & Klonsky, B. G. (1992). Gender and the evaluation of leaders: A meta-analysis. *Psychological Bulletin, 111,* 3–22.

Earley, P. C., & Mosakowski, E. M. (2000). Creating hybrid team cultures: An empirical test of international team functioning. *Academy of Management Journal, 43,* 26–49.

Ebbesen, E. B. (1981). Cognitive processes in inferences about a person's personality. In E. Higgins, C. Herman, & M. Zanna (Eds.), *Social cognition: The Ontario symposium* (Vol. 1, pp. 247–276). Hillsdale, NJ: Lawrence Erlbaum Associates.

Eden, D. (1984). Self-fulfilling prophecy as a management tool: Harnessing Pygmalion. *Academy of Management Review, 9,* 64–73.

Eden, D. (1988). Creating expectation effects in OD: Applying self-fulfilling prophecy. In R. W. Woodman & W. A. Rassman (Eds.), *Research in organizational change and development* (Vol. 2, pp. 235–267). Greenwich, CT: JAI Press.

Eden, D. (1990). *Pygmalion in management: Productivity as a self-fulfilling prophecy.* Lexington, MA: Lexington Books.

Edison, C. E. (2003, September). *From assessment center feedback to human performance improvement.* Paper presented at the 31st International Congress on Assessment Center Methods. Atlanta, Georgia.

Einhorn, H. J., Hogarth, R. M., & Klempner, E. (1977). Quality of group judgment. *Psychological Bulletin, 84,* 158–172.

Engelbrecht, A. S., & Fischer, A. H. (1995). The managerial performance implications of a developmental assessment center process. *Human Relations, 48,* 387–404.

Equal Employment Opportunity Commission, Civil Rights Commission, Department of Labor, & Department of Justice. (1978). Uniform Guidelines on Employee Selection Procedures. *Federal Register, 43*(166), 38290–38309.

Feldman, J. (1981). Beyond attribution theory: Cognitive processes in performance appraisal. *Journal of Applied Psychology, 66,* 127–148.

Feltham, R. (1988a). Validity of a police assessment centre: A 1–19-year follow-up. *Journal of Occupational Psychology, 61,* 129–144.

Feltham, R. (1988b). Assessment centre decision making: Judgmental vs. mechanical. *Journal of Occupational Psychology, 61,* 237–241.

Fenwick, G. D., & Neal, D. J. (2001). Effect of gender composition on group performance. *Gender, Work, and Organization, 8,* 205–225.

Fine, S. A., & Cronshaw, S. F. (1999). *Functional job analysis: A foundation for human resources management.* Mahwah, NJ: Lawrence Erlbaum Associates.

Finkin, M. W. (2004). *Privacy in employment law* (2nd ed.). Washington, DC: BNA Books.

Finkle, R. B. (1976). Managerial assessment centers. In M. D. Dunnette (Ed.), *Handbook of industrial and organizational psychology* (pp. 861–888). Chicago, IL: Rand McNally.

Finkle, R. B., & Jones, W. S. (1970). *Assessing corporate talent: A key to managerial manpower planning.* New York: Wiley Interscience.

Fishbein, M., & Azjen, I. (1975). *Belief, attitude, intention, and behavior. An introduction to theory and research.* Reading, MA: Addison-Wesley.

Fiske, S. T. (1993). Social cognition and social perception. *Annual Review of Psychology, 44,* 155–194.

Fiske, S. T., & Taylor, S. E. (1984). *Social cognition.* Reading, MA: Addison-Wesley.

Flanagan, J. C. (1954). The critical incident technique. *Psychological Bulletin, 51,* 327–349.

Fleenor, J. W. (1988). *The utility of assessment centers for career development.* Unpublished doctoral dissertation, North Carolina State University.

Fleenor, J. W., & Brutus, S. (2001). Multisource feedback for personnel decisions. In D. W. Bracken, C. W. Timmreck, & A. H. Church (Eds.), *The handbook of multisource feedback: The comprehensive resource for designing and implementing MSF processes.* San Francisco, CA: Jossey-Bass.

Fleishman, E. A., & Quaintance, M. K. (1984). *Taxonomies of human performance: The description of human tasks.* Orlando, FL: Academic Press.

Fleishman, E. A., & Reilly, M. E. (1992). *Administrator guide F-JAS: Fleishman job survey.* Palo Alto, CA: Consulting Psychologists Press.

Fletcher, C. (1991). Candidates' reactions to assessment centres and their outcomes: A longitudinal study. *Journal of Occupational Psychology, 64,* 117–127.

Fogli, L. (1985). *Coremart.* Pheasant Hill, CA. Author.

Folger, R., & Cropanzano, R. (1998). *Organizational justice and human resource management.* Thousand Oaks, CA: Sage.

Ford, J. (2001, September). *Automating the collection and scoring of written (non multiple choice) assessment center data.* Paper presented at the 29th International Congress on Assessment Center Methods, Frankfurt, Germany.

Ford, J. K., Smith, E. M., Weissbein, D. A., Gully, S. M., & Salas, E. (1998). Relationships of goal orientation, metacognitive activity, and practice strategies with learning outcomes and transfer. *Journal of Applied Psychology, 83*, 218–233.

Foster, S. L., & Cone, J. D. (1986). Design and use of direct observation. In A. R. Cimincro, M. S. Calhoun, & H. E. Adams (Eds.), *Handbook of behavioral assessment* (2nd ed., pp. 253–322). New York: Wiley.

Fraley, R. C., & Roberts, B. W. (2005). Patterns of continuity: A dynamic model for conceptualizing the stability of individual differences in psychological constructs across the life course. *Psychological Review, 112*, 60–74.

Francis-Smythe, J., & Smith, P. M. (1997). The psychological impact of assessment in a development center. *Human Relations, 50*(2), 149–167.

Frank, F. D. (1990, May). *Video testing: An alternative to assessment centers.* Paper presented at the 18th International Congress on the Assessment Center Method.

Franks, D., Ferguson, E., Rolls, S., & Henderson, F. (1999). Self-assessments in HRM: An example from an assessment centre. *Personnel Review, 28*, 124–133.

Frederiksen, N., Saunders, D. R., & Wand, B. (1957). The in-basket test. *Psychological Monographs, 71*(9, Whole No. 438).

Fritzsche, B. A., Brannick, M. T., & Fisher-Hazucha, J. F. (1994, April). *The effects of using behavioral checklists on the predictive and construct validity of assessment center ratings.* Paper presented at the annual conference of the Society for Industrial and Organizational Psychology, Nashville, TN.

Garcia, L. T., Erskine, N., Hawn, K., & Casmay, S. R. (1981). The effect of affirmative action on attributions about minority group members. *Journal of Personality, 49*, 427–437.

Gatewood, R. D., & Feild, H. S. (2001). *Human resource selection* (5th ed.). Mason, OH: South-Western.

Gaugler, B. B., Rosenthal, D. B., Thornton, G. C., III, & Bentson, C. (1987). Meta-analysis of assessment center validity. *Journal of Applied Psychology, 72*, 493–511.

Gaugler, B. B., & Thornton, G. C., III. (1989). Number of assessment center dimensions as a determinant of assessor accuracy. *Journal of Applied Psychology, 74*, 611–618.

Geddes, D., & Konrad, A. M. (2003). Demographic differences and reactions to performance feedback. *Human Relations, 56*, 1485–1513.

Ghiselli, E. E., Campbell, J. P., & Zedeck, S. (1981). *Measurement theory for the behavioral sciences.* San Francisco, CA: Freeman.

Gibbons, A. M., & Rupp, D. E. (2004, April). *Developmental assessment centers as training tools for the aging workforce.* Paper presented at the 19th annual meeting of the Society for Industrial and Organizational Psychology, Chicago, Illinois.

Gibbons, A. M., Rupp, D. E., Baldwin, A., & Holub, S. A. (2005, April). *Developmental assessment center validation: Evidence for DACs as effective training interventions.* Paper presented at the 20th annual meeting of the Society for Industrial and Organizational Psychology, Los Angeles, CA.

Gibbons, A. M., Rupp, D. E., Kim, M. J., & Woo, S. E. (2005, April). *Developable assessment center dimensions: A Korean investigation.* Paper presented at the 20th annual meeting of the Society for Industrial and Organizational Psychology, Los Angeles, CA.

Gluski, B. J., & Sherman, A. M. (2000, May). *Results of concurrent and content validation studies for supervisory assessment center transported from manufacturing to insurance services.* Paper presented at the International Congress on the Assessment Center Method, Pittsburgh, PA.

Goffin, R. D., Rothstein, M. G., & Johnston, N. G. (1996). Personality testing and the assessment center: Incremental validity for managerial selection. *Journal of Applied Psychology, 81*, 746–756.

Goldsmith, R. F. (1990). Utility analysis and its application to the study of the cost effectiveness of the assessment center method. In K. R. Murphy & F. E. Saal (Eds.), *Psychology in organiza-*

tions. Integrating science and practice (pp. 95–110). Hillsdale, NJ: Lawrence Erlbaum Associates.

Goldstein, A. P., & Sorcher, M. (1974). *Changing managerial behavior.* New York: Pergamon Press.

Goldstein, H. W., Yusko, K. P., & Nicolopoulos, V. (2001). Exploring Black-White subgroup differences of managerial competencies. *Personnel Psychology, 54,* 783–807.

Goldstein, H. W., Zedeck, S., & Goldstein, I. L. (2002). G: Is this your final answer? *Human Performance, 15,* 123–142.

Goldstein, I. L. (1986). *Training in organizations. Needs assessment, development, and evaluation* (2nd ed.). Monterey, CA: Brooks/Cole.

Goldstein, I., Schneider, B., & Zedeck, S. (1993). An exploration of the job analysis-content validity process. In N. Schmitt & W. C. Borman (Eds.), *Personnel selection in organizations* (pp. 3–34). San Francisco, CA: Jossey-Bass.

Gomez-Mejia, L. R., Balkin, D. B., & Cardy, R. L. (2004). *Managing human resources* (4th ed.). Upper Saddle River, NJ: Pearson Prentice-Hall.

Goodge, P. (1991). Development centres: Guidelines for decision makers. *Journal of Management Development, 10*(3), 4–12.

Goodge, P. (1997). Assessment and development centres: Practical design principles. *Selection and Development Review, 13,* 11–14.

Goodie, A. S., & Crooks, C. L. (2004). Time-pressure effects on performance in a base-rate tasks. *Journal of General Psychology, 131,* 18–28.

Goodman, J. S., Wood, R. E., & Hendrickx, M. (2004). Feedback specificity, exploration, and learning. *Journal of Applied Psychology, 89,* 248–262.

Goodstone, M. S., & Lopez, F. E. (2001). The frame of reference approach as a solution to an assessment center dilemma. *Consulting Psychology Journal: Practice & Research, 53,* 96–107.

Greenberg, J. (1986). Determinants of perceived fairness of performance evaluations. *Journal of Applied Psychology, 71,* 340–342.

Greenwood, J. M., & McNamara, W. J. (1967). Interrater reliability in situational tests. *Journal of Applied Psychology, 51,* 101–106.

Griffiths, P., & Allen, B. (1987). Assessment centres: Breaking with tradition. *Journal of Management Development, 6*(1), 18–29.

Griffiths, P., & Goodge, P. (1994). Development centres: The third generation. *Personnel Management, 26,* 40–44.

Guion, R. M. (1987). Changing views for personnel selection research. *Personnel Psychology, 40,* 199–213.

Guion, R. M. (1998). *Assessment, measurement, and prediction for personnel decisions.* Mahwah, NJ: Lawrence Erlbaum Associates.

Haaland, S., & Christiansen, N. D. (2002). Implications of trait-activation theory for evaluating the construct validity of assessment center ratings. *Personnel Psychology, 55,* 137–163.

Hackman, J. R., & Morris, C. G. (1978a). Group process and group effectiveness: A reappraisal. In L. Berkowitz (Ed.), *Group processes* (pp. 57–66). New York: Academic Press.

Hackman, J. R., & Morris, C. G. (1978b). Group tasks, group interaction process, and group performance effectiveness: A review and proposed integration. In L. Berkowitz (Ed.), *Group processes* (pp. 1–55). New York: Academic Press.

Hammond, K. R., McClelland, G. H., & Mumpower, J. (1980). *Human judgment and decision making. Theories, methods, and procedures.* New York: Praeger.

Hampson, S. E., John, O. P., & Goldberg, L. R. (1986). Category breadth and hierarchical structure in personality: Studies of asymmetries in judgments of trait implications. *Journal of Personality and Social Psychology, 51,* 37–54.

Hardison, C. M., & Sackett, P. R. (2004, April). *Assessment center criterion-related validity: A meta-analytic update.* Paper presented at the 19th annual conference of the Society for Industrial and Organizational Psychology, Chicago, Ill.

Harris, H. (1949). *The group approach to leadership testing.* London: Routledge and Paul.

Harris, M. H., Becker, A. S., & Smith, D. E. (1993). Does the assessment center scoring method affect the cross-situational consistency of ratings? *Journal of Applied Psychology, 78,* 675–678.

Harris, M. M. (1989). Reconsidering the employment interview: A review of recent literature and suggestions for future research. *Personnel Psychology, 42,* 691–726.

Hartigan, J. A., & Wigdor, A. K. (1989). *Employment testing.* Washington, DC: National Academy Press.

Hastie, R. (1986). Experimental evidence of group accuracy. In B. Grofman & G. Owen (Eds.), *Decision research.* Greenwich, CT: JAI Press.

Hastie, R., & Dawes, R. M. (2001). *Rational choice in an uncertain world: The psychology of judgment and decision making.* Thousand Oaks, CA: Sage.

Hastie, R., & Kumar, P. (1979). Person memory: Personality traits as organizing principles in memory for behavior. *Journal of Personality and Social Psychology, 37,* 25–38.

Hauenstein, P. C. (1994). *A key behavior approach for improving the utility of developmental assessment centers.* Paper presented at the Annual Conference of the Society for Industrial and Organizational Psychology, Nashville, TN.

Heilman, M. E. (1995). Sex stereotypes and their effects in the workplace: What we know and what we don't know. *Journal of Social Behavior and Personality, 10,* 3–26.

Heilman, M. E., Block, C. J., & Stathatos, P. (1997). The affirmative action stigma of incompetence: Effects of performance information ambiguity. *Academy of Management Journal, 40,* 603–625.

Heilman, M. E., Wallen, A. S., Fuchs, D., & Tamkins, M. M. (2004). Penalties for success: Reactions to women who succeed at male gender-typed tasks. *Journal of Applied Psychology, 89,* 416–427.

Heine, D. M., & Struth, M. R. (1989, May). *Computerized assessment centers.* Paper presented at the 17th International Congress on the Assessment Center Method, Pittsburgh, PA.

Heneman, H. G., & Judge, T. A. (2003). *Staffing organizations.* Middleton, WI: McGraw-Hill/Irwin.

Hennessy, J., Mabey, B., & Warr, P. (1998). Assessment centre observation procedures: An experimental comparison of traditional, checklist and coding methods, *International Journal of Selection and Assessment, 6,* 222–231.

Henry, S. E. (1988, August). *Nontraditional applications of assessment centers. Assessment in staffing plant start-ups.* Paper presented at the meeting of the American Psychological Association, Atlanta, GA.

Herriot, P., Chalmers, C., & Wingrove, J. (1985). Group decision making in an assessment centre. *Journal of Occupational Psychology, 58,* 309–312.

Hezlett, S. A., Ones, D. S., & Kuncel, N. R. (2000, May). Participation in development activities and its correlates: An investigation of gender differences. In C. D. McCauley (Chair), *Developments on Development: The Process and Consequences of Continuous Learning.* Symposium conducted at the 15th annual conference of the Society for Industrial and Organizational Psychology. New Orleans, LA.

Higgins, E. T., & Bargh, J. A. (1987). Social cognition and social perception. In M. R. Rosenzweig & L. W. Porter (Eds.), *Annual review of psychology* (Vol. 38). Palo Alto, CA: Annual Reviews.

Highhouse, S. (2002). Assessing the candidate as a whole: A historical and critical analysis of individual psychological assessment for personnel decision making. *Personnel Psychology, 55,* 363–396.

Hill, G. W. (1982). Groups vs. individual performance: Are N + 1 heads better than one? *Psychological Bulletin, 91,* 517–539.

Hinrichs, J. R. (1978). An eight-year follow-up of a management assessment center. *Journal of Applied Psychology, 63,* 596–601.

Hinrichs, J. R., & Haanpera, S. (1976). Reliability of measurement in situational exercises: An assessment of the assessment center method. *Personnel Psychology, 29,* 31–40.

Hinsz, V. B., Tindale, R. S., & Vollrath, D. A. (1997). The emerging conceptualization of groups as information processors. *Psychological Bulletin, 121,* 43–64.

Hintzman, D. L. (1986). "Schema abstraction" in a multiple-trace memory model. *Psychological Review, 93,* 411–428.

Hintzman, D. L. (1988). Judgment of frequency and recognition memory in a multiple-trace memory model. *Psychological Review, 95,* 528–551.

Hoffman, L. R. (1978a). The group problem-solving process. In L. Berkowitz (Ed.), *Group processes* (pp. 57–66). New York: Academic Press.

Hoffman, L. R. (1978b). Group problem solving. In L. Berkowitz (Ed.), *Group processes* (pp. 67–113). New York: Academic Press.

Hogan, J., & Zenke, L. L. (1986). Dollar-value utility of alternative procedures for selecting school principals. *Educational and Psychological Measurement, 46,* 935–945.

Hollenbeck, G. P. (1990). The past, present, and future of assessment centers. *The Industrial/ Organizational Psychologist, 28*(2), 13–17.

Howard, A. (1995). *The changing nature of work.* San Francisco, CA: Jossey-Bass.

Howard, A. (1997). A reassessment of assessment centers: Challenges for the 21st century. *Journal of Social Behavior and Personality, 12,* 13–52.

Howard, A., & Bray, D. W. (1988). *Managerial lives in transition: Advancing age and changing times.* New York: Guilford Press.

Huck, J. R. (1974). *Determinants of assessment center ratings for white and black females and relationship of these dimensions to subsequent performance effectiveness.* Unpublished doctoral dissertation, Wayne State University, Detroit, Michigan.

Huck, J. R. (1987). Costing the value of human resources. *A look at the economic utility of an assessment center selection process.* Paper presented at the Institute for Personnel Management, Stellenbosch, South Africa.

Huck, J. R., & Bray, D. W. (1976). Management assessment center evaluations and subsequent job performance of Black and White females. *Personnel Psychology, 29,* 13–30.

Hunt, D. M., & Michael, C. (1983). Mentorship: A career training and development tool. *Academy of Management Review, 8,* 475–485.

Hunter, J. E., & Hunter, R. F. (1984). Validity and utility of alternative predictors of job performance. *Psychological Bulletin, 96,* 72–98.

Hunter, J. E., & Schmidt, F. L. (1990). *Methods of meta-analysis: Correcting error and bias in research findings.* Newbury Park, CA: Sage.

Hunter, J. E., Schmidt, F. L., & Jackson, G. B. (1982). *Meta-analysis. Cumulating research findings across studies.* Beverly Hills, CA: Sage.

Iles, P., & Forster, A. (1994). Developing organizations through collaborative development centers. *Organization Development Journal, 12,* 45–51.

Ilgen, D. R., Fisher, C. D., & Taylor, M. S. (1979). Consequences of individual feedback on behavior in organizations. *Journal of Applied Psychology, 64,* 340–371.

International Task Force on Assessment Center Guidelines (2000). Guidelines and ethical considerations for assessment center operations. *Public Personnel Management, 29,* 315–331.

Ivancevich, J. M. (2004). *Human resource management* (9th ed.). Boston, MA: McGraw-Hill/ Irwin.

Jackson, S. E., Joshi, A., & Erhardt, N. L. (2003). Recent research on team and organizational diversity: SWOT analysis and implications. *Journal of Management, 29,* 801–830.

Jackson, S. E., Schuler, R. S., & Rivero, J. C. (1989). Organizational characteristics as predictors of personnel practices. *Personnel Psychology, 42,* 727–786.

Jacobsen, L., & Sinclair, N. (1990, March). *Assessing the writing of teacher candidates: Connecticut's method of holistic assessments.* Paper presented at the 18th International Congress on the Assessment Center Method, Anaheim, CA.

Jacobson, M. B., & Koch, W. (1977). Women as leaders: Performance evaluation as a function of method of leader selection. *Organizational Behavior and Human Performance, 20,* 149–157.

Janis, I. L. (1982). *Groupthink* (2nd ed.). Boston, MA: Houghton Mifflin.

Jansen, P. G. W., & Stoop, B. A. M. (2001). The dynamics of assessment center validity: Results of a 7-year study. *Journal of Applied Psychology, 86,* 741–753.

Johnson, M. K., & Raye, C. L. (1981). Reality monitoring. *Psychological Review, 88,* 67–85.

Joiner, D. A. (2002). Assessment centers: What's new? *Public Personnel Management, 31,* 179–185.

Jones, E. E., & Davis, K. E. (1965). A theory of correspondent inferences: From acts to dispositions. In L. Berkowitz (Ed.), *Advances in experimental and social psychology* (Vol. 2, pp. 220–266). New York: Academic Press.

Jones, G. T. (1972). *Simulations and business decisions.* Middlesex, England: Penguin.

Jones, R. G., & Whitmore, M. D. (1995). Evaluating developmental assessment centers as interventions. *Personnel Psychology, 48,* 377–388.

Jones, R. G., & Whitmore, M. D. (1995). Evaluating developmental assessment centers as interventions: Errata. *Personnel Psychology, 48,* 562.

Joyce, L. W., Thayer, P. W., & Pond, S. B. (1994). Managerial functions: An alternative to traditional assessment center dimensions? *Personnel Psychology, 47,* 109–121.

Kameda, T., Tindale, R. S., & Davis, J. H. (2003). Cognitions, preferences, and social sharedness. In S. J. Schneider & J. Santeau (Eds.), *Emerging perspectives on judgment and decision research* (pp. 458–485). Cambridge, UK: Cambridge University Press.

Kazdin, A. E. (1984). *Behavior modification in applied settings* (2nd ed.). Homewood, IL: Dorsey.

Kehoe, J. F., Weinberg, K., & Lawrence, I. M. (1985, August). *Dimension and exercise effects on work simulation ratings.* Paper presented at the meeting of the American Psychological Association, Los Angeles, CA.

Kintsch, W., & van Dijk, T. A. (1978). Toward a model of text comprehension and production. *Psychological Review, 85,* 363–394.

Kleinmann, M., & Strauss, B. (1998). Validity and application of computer simulated scenarios in personnel assessment. *International Journal of Selection and Assessment, 6,* 97–106.

Klimoski, R., & Brickner, M. (1987). Why do assessment centers work? The puzzle of assessment center validity. *Personnel Psychology, 40,* 243–260.

Kluger, A. N., & DeNisi, A. (1996). The effects of feedback interventions on performance: a historical review, a meta-analysis, and a preliminary feedback intervention theory. *Psychological Bulletin, 119*(2), 254–284.

Knowles, M. S. (1970). *The modern practice of adult education: Andragogy versus pedagogy.* New York: Association Press.

Knowles, M. S. (1973). *The adult learner: A neglected species.* Houston, TX: Gulf Publishing Co.

Kogan, N., & Wallach, M. A. (1967). Risk-taking as a function of the situation, the person, and the group. In G. Mandler, P. Mussen, & N. Kogan (Eds.), *New directions in psychology* (Vol. 3, pp. 111–266). New York: Holt.

Kolk, N. J. (2001). *Assessment centers: Understanding and improving construct-related validity.* Enschede, Netherlands: Printpartners Ipshamp.

Kolk, N. J., Born, M. P., & Van der Flier, H. (2002). Impact of common rater variance on construct validity of assessment center dimension judgments. *Human Performance, 15,* 325–338.

Kolk, N. J., Born, M. P., Van der Flier, H., & Olman, J. M. (2002). Assessment center procedures, Cognitive load during the observation phase. *International Journal of Selection and Assessment, 10,* 271–278.

Konz, A. M. (1988). *A comparison of dimension ratings and exercise ratings in assessment centers.* Unpublished doctoral dissertation, University of Maryland.

Krause, D. E., & Gebert, D. (2003). A comparison of assessment center practices inn organizations in German-speaking regions and the United States. *International Journal of Selection and Assessment, 11,* 297–312.

Krause, D. E., Kersting, M., Heggestad, E., & Thornton, G. C., III (2004). *Criterion validity of cognitive ability tests and assessment centers.* Unpublished paper, Colorado State University.

Krause, D. E., & Thornton, G. C., III. (2004, October). *Cultural values and assessment center practices in the Americas, Europe, and Asian countries.* Presentation at the 23rd International Congress on Assessment Center Methods, Las Vegas, NV.

Kraut, A. I., & Scott, G. J. (1972). Validity of an operational management assessment program. *Journal of Applied Psychology, 56,* 124–129.

Kruger, J. (1999). Lake Wobegon be gone! The "below-average effect" and the egocentric nature of comparative ability judgments. *Journal of Personality & Social Psychology, 77,* 221–232.

Kudisch, J. D., Avis, J. M., Fallon, J. D., Thibodeaux, H. F., III, Roberts, F. E., Rollier, T. J., & Rotolo, C. T. (1999, June). *Benchmarking for success: A look at today's assessment center practices worldwide.* Paper presented at the 27th annual meeting of the International Congress on Assessment Center Methods, Orlando, FL.

Kudisch, J. D., Avis, J. M., Fallon, J. D., Thibodeaux, H. F., Roberts, F. E., Rollier, T. J., & Rotolo, C. T. (2001, September). *A survey of assessment center practices in organizations worldwide: Maximizing innovation or business as usual?* Paper presented at the 16th annual conference of the Society for Industrial and Organizational Psychology, San Diego, CA.

Kudisch, J. D., Ladd, R. T., & Dobbins, G. H. (1997). New evidence on the construct validity of diagnostic assessment centers: The findings may not be so troubling after all. *Journal of Social Behavior and Personality, 12,* 129–144.

Kudisch, J., Lundquist, C., & Smith, A. F. R. (2002, October). *Reactions to dual-purpose assessment center feedback: What does it take to get participants to buy into and actually do something with their feedback?* Presentation at the 30th International Congress on Assessment Center Methods, Pittsburgh, PA.

Kunda, Z., & Sinclair, L. (1999). Motivated reasoning with stereotypes: Activation, application, and inhibition. *Psychological Inquiry, 10,* 12–22.

Ladd, R. T., Atchley, E. K. P., Gniatczyk, L. A., & Baumann, L. B. (2002, April). *An examination of the construct validity of an assessment center using multiple regression importance analysis.* Paper presented at the 17th Annual Conference of the Society for Industrial and Organizational Psychology, Toronto, Ontario, Canada.

Lamm, H., & Myers, D. G. (1978). Group-induced polarization of attitudes and behavior. In L. Berkowitz (Ed.), *Advances in experimental social psychology* (Vol. 11). New York: Academic Press.

Lance, C. E., Foster, M. R., Thoresen, J. D., & Gentry, W. A. (2004). Assessor cognitive processes in an operational assessment center. *Journal of Applied Psychology, 89,* 22–35.

Lance, C. E., Lambert, T. A., Gewin, A. G., Lievens, F., & Conway, J. M. (2004). Revised estimates of dimension and exercise variance components in assessment center post exercise dimension ratings. *Journal of Applied Psychology, 89,* 377–385.

Landy, F. J. (1986). Stamp collecting versus science: Validation as hypothesis testing. *American Psychologist, 41,* 1183–1192.

Landy, F. J. (2005). *Employment discrimination litigation: Behavioral, quantitative, and legal perspectives.* San Francisco, CA: Jossey-Bass.

Latane, B., & Darley, J. M. (1970). *The unresponsive bystander. Why doesn't he help?* New York: Appleton-Century-Crofts.

Latham, G. P., & Saari, L. M. (1979). Application of social-learning theory to training supervisors through behavior modeling. *Journal of Applied Psychology, 64,* 239–246.

Laughlin, P. R. (1980). Social combination processes of cooperative problem-solving groups on verbal intellective tasks. In M. Fishbein (Ed.), *Progress in social psychology.* Hillsdale, NJ: Lawrence Erlbaum Associates.

Laughlin, P. R. (1999). Collective induction: Twelve postulates. *Organizational Behavior and Human Decision Processes, 80,* 50–69.

Laughlin, P. R., Bonner, B. L., & Milner, A. G. (2002). Groups perform better that the best individuals on Letters-to-Numbers problems. *Organizational Behavior and Human Decision Processes, 88,* 605–620.

Laughlin, P. R., & Ellis, A. L. (1986). Demonstrability and social combination processes on mathematical intellective tasks. *Journal of Experimental Social Psychology, 22,* 177–189.

Laughlin, P. R., & McGlynn, R. P. (1986). Collective induction: Mutual group and individual influence by exchange of hypotheses & evidence. *Journal of Experimental Social Psychology, 22,* 567–589.

Lawler, E. (1994). From job-based to competency-based organizations. *Journal of Organizational Behavior, 15,* 3–15.

Lebreton, J. M., Binning, J. F., & Hesson-McInnis, M. S. (1998, August). *The effects of measurement structure on the validity of assessment center dimensions.* Paper presented at the Annual Meeting of the Academy of Management, San Diego, CA.

Lebreton, J. M., Gniatczyk, L. A., & Migetz, D. Z. (1999, April). *The relationship between behavior checklist ratings and judgmental ratings in an operational assessment center: An application of structural equation modeling.* Paper presented at the Annual Conference of the Society for Industrial and Organizational Psychology, Atlanta, GA.

Lee, G. (2000). The state of the art in development centres. *Selection and Development Review, 16,* 10–14.

Lee, G. (2003). Same old development centers? *Selection and Development Review, 19,* 3–6.

Lee, G., & Beard, D. (1994). *Development centres: Realizing the potential of your employees through assessment and development.* London: McGraw-Hill.

Leitenberg, H. (1976). *Handbook of behavior modification and behavior therapy.* Englewood Cliffs, NJ. Prentice-Hall.

Lerner, J. S., & Tetlock, P. E. (1999). Accounting for the effects of accountability. *Psychological Bulletin, 125,* 255–275.

Leung, W., Su, S., & Morris, M. W. (2001). When is criticism not constructive? The roles of fairness perceptions and dispositional attributions in employee acceptance of critical supervisory feedback. *Human Relations, 54,* 1155–1187.

Levine, J. M., & Moreland, R. L. (1998). Small groups. In D. T. Gilbert, S. T. Fiske, & G. Lindzey (Eds.), *The handbook of social psychology* (4th ed., Vol. II, pp. 415–469). Boston, MA: McGraw-Hill.

Lewin, K. (1951). *Field theory in social science.* New York: Harper.

Libby, R., Trotman, K. T., & Zimmer, I. (1987). Member variation, recognition of expertise and group performance. *Journal of Applied Psychology, 72,* 81–87.

Lievens, F. (1998). Factors which improve the construct validity of assessment centers: A review. *International Journal of Selection and Assessment, 6,* 141–152.

Lievens, F. (1999). *The effects of type of assessor training on the construct validity and accuracy of assessment center ratings.* Paper presented at the European Congress of Work and Organizational Psychology, Espoo-Helsinki, Finland.

Lievens, F. (2001). Assessor training strategies and their effects on accuracy, interrater reliability, and discriminant validity. *Journal of Applied Psychology, 86,* 255–264.

Lievens, F., Chasteen, C. S., Day, E., & Christiansen, N. D. (2004, April). *A large-scale investigation of the role of trait activation theory.* Paper presented at the 19th annual conference of the Society for Industrial and Organizational Psychology, Chicago, IL.

Lievens, F., & Conway, J. M. (2001). Dimension and exercise variance in assessment center scores: A large-scale evaluation of multitrait-multimethod studies. *Journal of Applied Psychology, 86,* 1202–1222.

Lievens, F., Harris, M. M., Van Keer, E., & Bisqueret, C. (2003). Predicting cross-cultural training performance: The validity of personality, cognitive ability, and dimensions measured by an assessment center and a behavioral description interview. *Journal of Applied Psychology, 88,* 476–489.

Lievens, F., & Klimoski, R. J. (2001). Understanding the assessment centre process: Where are we now? *International Review of Industrial and Organizational Psychology, 16,* 246–286.

Lievens, F., & Thornton, G. C., III. (in press). Assessment centers: Recent developments in practice and research. In A. Evers, O. Voskuijl, & N. Anderson (Eds.), *Handbook of selection.* London: Blackwell.

Linville, P. W., Fischer, G. W., & Salovey, P. (1989). Perceived distributions of the characteristics of in-group and out-group members: Empirical evidence and a computer simulation. *Journal of Personality and Social Psychology, 57,* 165–188.

Locke, E. A., & Latham, G. P. (1990). *A theory of goal setting and task performance.* Englewood Cliffs, NJ: Prentice-Hall.

Locksley, A., Borgida, E., Brekke, N., & Hepburn, C. (1980). Sex stereotypes and social judgment. *Journal of Personality & Social Psychology, 39,* 821–831.

London, M. (1997). *Job feedback: Giving, seeking, and using feedback for performance improvement.* Mahwah, NJ: Lawrence Erlbaum Associates.

Lopez, F. M., Jr. (1966). *Evaluating executive decision making: The in-basket technique* (AMA Research Study No. 75). New York: American Management Association.

Lorenzo, R. V. (1984). Effects of assessorship on managers' proficiency in acquiring, evaluating, and communicating information about people. *Personnel Psychology, 37,* 617–634.

Louiselle, K. G. (1980). *Confirmatory factor analysis of two assessment center rating procedures.* Paper presented at the 17th Annual IO/OB Graduate Student Conference, Minneapolis, MN.

Lovler, R., & Goldsmith, R. F. (2002, October). *Cutting edge developments in assessment center technology.* Paper presented at the 30th International Congress on Assessment Center Methods. Pittsburgh, PA.

Lowery, P. E. (1997). The assessment center process: New directions. *Journal of Social Behavior and Personality, 12,* 53–62.

Lyness, K. S., & Judiesch, M. K. (1999). Are women more likely to be hired or promoted into management positions? *Journal of Vocational Behavior, 54,* 158–173.

MacKinnon, D. W. (1977). From selecting spies to selecting managers—the OSS assessment program. In J. J. Moses & W. C. Byham (Eds.), *Applying the assessment center method* (pp. 13–30). New York: Pergamon Press.

Major, B. (1980). Information acquisition and attribution processes. *Journal of Personality and Social Psychology, 39,* 1010–1023.

Manz, C. C., & Sims, H. P. (1981). Vicarious learning: The influence of modeling on organizational behavior. *Academy of Management Review, 6,* 105–113.

Masterson, S. S., Lewis, K., Goldman, B. M., & Taylor, M. S. (2000). Integrating justice and social exchange: The differing effects of fair procedures and treatment on work relationships. *Academy of Management Journal, 43,* 738–748.

Maurer, S. D., Sue-Chan, C., & Latham, G. P. (1999). The situational interview. In R. W. Edder & M. M. Harris (Eds.), *The employment interview handbook* (pp. 159–179). Thousand Oaks, CA: Sage.

Maurer, T. J., Weiss, E. M., & Barbeite, F. G. (2003). A model of involvement in work-related learning and development activity: The effects of individual, situational, motivational, and age variables. *Journal of Applied Psychology, 88,* 707–724.

McCauley, C. D., & Hezlett, S. A. (2001). Individual development in the workplace. In N. Anderson, D. S. Ones, H. Sinangil, & C. Viswesveran (Eds.), *Handbook of industrial, work, and organizational psychology. Vol. 1: Personnel psychology* (pp. 313–335). London, UK: Sage.

McClelland, D. C. (1987, May). *Competency assessment: Future prospects and developments.* Paper presented at the International Congress on the Assessment Center, Boston, MA.

McConnell, J. J., & Parker, T. (1972). An assessment center program for multiorganizational use. *Training and Development Journal, 26*(3), 6–14.

McCormick, E. J., Jeanneret, P. R., & Mecham, R. C. (1989). *Position Analysis Questionnaire.* Logan, UT: PAQ Services.

McEvoy, G. M., & Beatty, R. W. (1989). Assessment centers and subordinate appraisals of managers: A seven-year examination of predictive validity. *Personnel Psychology, 42*, 37–52.

McGrath, J. E., & Kravitz, D. A. (1982). Group research. *Annual Review of Psychology, 33*, 195–230.

McIntyre, R. M., & Vanetti, E. (1988, August). *The effects of priming in a simulated assessment center environment.* Paper presented at the meeting of the American Psychological Association, Atlanta, GA.

Meehl, P. E. (1954). *Clinical versus statistical prediction: A theoretical analysis and a review of the evidence.* Minneapolis, MN: University of Minnesota.

Mehta, P. (1978). Dynamics of adult learning and development. *Convergence, 11*, 36–43.

Mero, N. P., & Motowidlo, S. J. (1995). Effects of rater accountability on the accuracy and the favorability of performance ratings. *Journal of Applied Psychology, 80*, 517–524.

Messick, S. (1998). Test validity: A matter of consequence. *Social Indicators Research, 45*, 35–44.

Middleton, M. J., & Midgely, C. (1997). Avoiding the demonstration of lack of ability: An underexplored aspect of goal theory. *Journal of Educational Psychology, 89*, 710–718.

Miner, F. C. (1984). Group versus individual decision making: An investigation of performance measures, decision strategies, and process losses/gains. *Organizational Behavior & Human Performance, 33*, 112–114.

Mintzberg, H. (1975). The manager's job: Folklore and fact. *Harvard Business Review, 53*, 49–61.

Mischel, W., Jeffry, K. M., & Patterson, C. J. (1974). The layman's use of trait and behavioral information to predict behavior. *Journal of Research in Personality, 8*, 231–242.

Mitchel, J. O. (1975). Assessment center validity: A longitudinal study. *Journal of Applied Psychology, 60*, 573–579.

Moscovici, S. (1985). Social influence and conformity. In G. Lindzey & E. Aronson (Eds.), *Handbook of social psychology* (pp. 347–412). New York: Random House.

Moses, J. L. (1973). The development of an assessment center for the early identification of supervisory potential. *Personnel Psychology, 26*, 569–580.

Moses, J. L., & Boehm, V. R. (1975). Relationship of assessment center performance to management progress of women. *Journal of Applied Psychology, 60*, 527–529.

Murphy, K. R. (1988). Psychological measurement: Abilities and skills. In C. L. Cooper & L. Robertson (Eds.), *International review of industrial and organizational psychology.* New York: Wiley.

Murphy, K. R., & Cleveland, J. N. (1991). *Performance appraisal: An organizational perspective.* Boston, MA: Allyn & Bacon.

Murphy, K. R., Jako, R. A., & Anhalt, R. L. (1993). Nature and consequences of halo error: A critical analysis. *Journal of Applied Psychology, 78*, 218–225.

Murphy, K. R., & Kroeker, L. P. (1988). *Dimensions of job performance.* San Diego, CA. Navy Personnel Research and Development Center, NPRDC-TN88-39.

Myers, D. G., & Lamm, H. (1976). The group polarization phenomenon. *Psychological Bulletin, 83*, 602–627.

Nathan, B. R., & Lord, R. G. (1983). Cognitive categorization and dimensional schemata: A process approach to the study of halo in performance ratings. *Journal of Applied Psychology, 68*, 102–114.

Neidig, R. D., & Martin, J. C. (1979). *The FBI's Management Aptitude Program Assessment Center (report no. 2): An analysis of assessors' ratings* (TM79-2). Washington, DC: Applied Psychology Section. Personnel Research and Development Center, U.S. Civil Service Commission.

Neidig, R. D., Martin, J. C., & Yates, R. E. (1978). *The FBI's Management Aptitude Program Assessment Center. Research report no. 1* (TM783). Washington, DC: Applied Psychology Section. Personnel Research and Development Center, U.S. Civil Service Commission.

Nevo, B. (1989). *The practical and theoretical value of examinee feedback questionnaires (EFeQ).* Paper presented at the conference, "The individual and organizational side of selection and performance evaluation and appraisal." Universitat Hohenheim, Stuttgart, Germany.

Nevo, B., & Jager, R. (1986). *Psychological testing. The examinee perspective.* Gottingen, Germany: Hogrefe.

Nicholls, J. G. (1984). Achievement motivation: Conceptions of ability, subjective experience, task choice, and performance. *Psychological Review, 91,* 328–346.

Nisbett, R., & Ross, L. (1980). *Human inference strategies and shortcomings of social judgment.* Englewood Cliffs, NJ: Prentice-Hall.

Northcraft, G. B., & Martin, J. (1982). Double jeopardy: Resistance to affirmative action from potential beneficiaries. In B. Gutek (Ed.), *Sex roles stereotyping and affirmative action policy.* Los Angeles: Institute of Industrial Relations, University of California.

Norton, S. D. (1981). The assessment center process and content validity: A reply to Dreher and Sackett. *Academy of Management Review, 6,* 561–566.

Nunnally, J. C., & Bernstein, I. H. (1994). *Psychometric theory* (3rd ed.). New York: McGraw-Hill.

O'Connell, M. S., Hattrup, K., Doverspike, D., & Cober, A. (2002). The validity of "mini" simulations for Mexican retail salespeople. *Journal of Business and Psychology, 16,* 593–599.

Office of Strategic Services Assessment Staff (1948). *Assessment of men: Selection of personnel for the Office of Strategic Services.* New York: Rinehart.

Pelled, L. H., Eisenhardt, K. M., & Xin, K. R. (1999). Exploring the black box: An analysis of work group diversity, conflict, and performance. *Administrative Science Quarterly, 44,* 1–28.

Pendit, V., & Thornton, G. C., III. (2001, September). *Development of a code of conduct for personnel assessment in Indonesia.* Paper presented at the 29th International Congress on Assessment Center Methods, Frankfurt, Germany.

Perry, E. (1997). A cognitive approach to understanding discrimination: A closer look at applicant gender and age. *Research in Personnel and Human Resources Management, 15,* 175–240.

Peterson, D. X., & Pitz, G. F. (1986). Effect of input from a mechanical model on clinical judgment. *Journal of Applied Psychology, 71,* 163–167.

Peterson, N. G., Mumford, M. D., Borman, W. C., Jeanneret, P. R., Fleishman, E. A., Levin, K. Y., Campion, M. A., Mayfield, M. S., Morgeson, F. P., Pearlman, K., Gowing, M. K., Lancaster, A. R., Silver, M. B., & Dye, D. M. (2001). Understanding work using the Occupational Information Network (O*NET): Implications for practice and research. *Personnel Psychology, 54,* 451–492.

Pettigrew, T. F. (1998). Intergroup contact theory. *Annual Review of Psychology, 49,* 65–85.

Petty, R. E., & Caccioppo, J. T. (1986). The elaboration likelihood model of persuasion. *Advances in Experimental Social Psychology, 19,* 123–205.

Pigors, P. (1976). Case method. In R. L. Craig (Ed.), *Training and development handbook* (2nd ed., pp. 35: 1–12). New York: McGraw-Hill.

Pigors, P., & Pigors, F. (1961). *Case method in human relations. The incident process.* New York: McGraw-Hill.

Pinolli, P. L., & Anderson, J. R. (1985). The role of learning from examples in the acquisition of recursive programming skills. *Canadian Journal of Psychology, 39,* 240–272.

Ployhart, R. E., & Ehrhart, M. G. (2002). Modeling the practical effects of applicant reactions: Subgroup differences in test-taking motivation, test performance, and selection rates. *International Journal of Selection & Assessment, 10,* 258–270.

Ployhart, R. E., & Ryan, A. M. (1997). Toward and explanation of applicant reactions: An examination of organizational justice and attribution frameworks. *Organizational Behavior & Human Decision Processes, 72,* 308–335.

Poteet, M. L., & Kudisch, J. D. (2003, September). *Straight from the horses mouth: Strategies for increasing feedback acceptance.* Paper presented at the 31st International Congress on Assessment Center Methods, Atlanta, Georgia.

Potemra, M. J. (2005). *Skill development in a university setting: An investigation of students' improvability beliefs, locus of control, academic self-efficacy, and learning oriented attitudes.* Unpublished master's thesis, Colorado State University.

Povah, N. (1986). Using assessment centers as a means for self-development. *Industrial and Commercial Training, 18*, 22–25.

Povah, N., & Ballantyne, I. (2004). *Assessment & development centres* (2nd ed.). Gower: UK.

Prahalad, C., & Hamel, G. (1990, May–June). The core competence of the corporation. *Harvard Business Review*, 79–91.

Prien, E. P., Schippmann, J. S., & Prien, K. O. (2003). *Individual assessment: As practiced in industry and consulting.* Mahwah, NJ: Lawrence Erlbaum Associates.

Primoff, E. S. (1975). *How to prepare and conduct job element examinations.* Washington, DC: Personnel Research and Development Center, U.S. Civil Service Commission (TS-75-1).

Pynes, J., & Bernardin, H. J. (1992). Mechanical vs consensus-derived assessment center ratings. *Public Personnel Management, 21*, 17–28.

Raggins, B. R., Townsend, B., & Mattis, M. (1998). Gender gap in the executive suite: CEOs and female executives report on breaking the glass ceiling. *Academy of Management Executive, 12*, 28–42.

Reilly, R. R., Henry, S., & Smither, J. W. (1990). An examination of the effects of using behavior checklists on the construct validity of assessment center dimensions. *Personnel Psychology, 43*, 71–84.

Reilly, R. R., & Smither, J. W. (1985). An examination of two alternative techniques to estimate the standard deviation of job performance in dollars. *Journal of Applied Psychology, 70*, 651–661.

Reynolds, D. (2003, September). *Assessing executive and leaders through a technology-based assessment center.* Paper presented at the 31st International Congress on Assessment Center Methods, Atlanta, GA.

Richards, W. (2002, October). *A digital portfolio to support learning and development.* Paper presented at the 30th International Congress on Assessment Center Methods, Pittsburgh, PA.

Riggio, R. E., Mayes, B. T., & Schleicher, D. J. (2003). Using assessment center methods for measuring undergraduate business student outcomes. *Journal of Management Inquiry, 12*, 68–78.

Riordan, C. M. (2000). Relational demography within groups: Past developments, contradictions, and new directions. *Research in Personnel and Human Resource Management, 19*, 131–173.

Riordan, C. M., & Shore, L. M. (1997). Demographic diversity and employee attitudes: An empirical examination of relational demography within work units. *Journal of Applied Psychology, 82*, 342–358.

Ritchie, R. J. (1994). Using the assessment center method to predict senior management potential. *Consulting Psychology Journal: Practice & Research, 46*, 16–23.

Ritchie, R. R., & Moses, J. L. (1983). Assessment center correlates of women's advancement into middle management: A 7-year longitudinal analysis. *Journal of Applied Psychology, 68*, 227–231.

Roberson, L., & Block, C. J. (2001). Racioethnicity and job performance: A review and critique of theoretical perspectives on the causes of group differences. *Research in Organizational Behavior, 23*, 247–325.

Robins, R. W., Noftle, E. E., Trzesniewski, K. H., & Roberts, B. W. (2005). Do people know how their personality has changed? Correlates of perceived and actual personality change in young adulthood. *Journal of Personality, 73*, 489–521.

Rogers, D. A. (2003). *The evaluation of gamma, beta, and alpha change in individuals following participation in a developmental assessment process.* Unpublished paper, Colorado State University.

Rogers, D. A. (2005, April). *Alpha, beta, and gamma change on assessees' understanding of DAC dimensions.* Paper presented at the 20th annual meeting of the Society for Industrial and Organizational Psychology, Los Angeles, CA.

Rohmert, W. (1988). AET. In S. Gael (Ed.), *The job analysis handbook for business, industry, and government* (pp. 843–859). New York: Wiley.

Rohrbaugh, J. (1979). Improving the quality of group judgment: Social judgment analysis and the Delphi technique. *Organizational Behavior and Human Performance, 24,* 73–92.

Rokeach, M. (1973). *The nature of human values.* New York: The Free Press.

Rosch, E., Mervis, C. G., Gray, W. D., Johnson, D. M., & Boyes-Braem, P. (1976). Basic objects in natural categories. *Cognitive Psychology, 8,* 382–439.

Rupp, D. E., Baldwin, A., & Bashshur, M. (2004, April). *Supervisory justice training: An application of developmental assessment centers.* Paper presented at the 20th annual meeting of the Society for Industrial and Organizational Psychology, Los Angeles, CA.

Rupp, D. E., & Cropanzano, R. (2002). Multifoci justice and social exchange relationships. *Organizational Behavior and Human Decision Processes, 89,* 925–946.

Rupp, D. E., Gibbons, A. M., Runnels, T., Anderson, L., & Thornton, G. C., III. (2003, August). *What should developmental assessment centers be assessing?* Paper presented at the 63rd annual meeting of the Academy of Management, Seattle, Washington.

Rupp, D. E., & Thornton, G. C., III. (2003, September). *Consortium to study developmental assessment centers.* The 31st International Congress on Assessment Center Methods, Atlanta, Georgia.

Russell, C. J. (1987). Person characteristic versus role congruency explanations for assessment center ratings. *Academy of Management Journal, 30,* 817–826.

Ryan, A. M., Daum, D., Bauman, T., Grisez, M., Mattimore, K., Nadloka, T., & McCormick, S. (1995). Direct, indirect, and controlled observation and rating accuracy. *Journal of Applied Psychology, 80,* 664–670.

Ryan, A. M., & Sackett, P. R. (1998). Individual assessment: The research base. In R. Jeanneret & R. Silzer (Eds.), *Individual psychological assessment: Predicting behavior in organizational settings.* San Francisco, CA: Jossey-Bass.

Rynes, S. L. (1991). Recruitment, job choice, and post-hire consequences: A call for new research directions. In M. D. Dunnette & L. M. Hough (Eds.), *Handbook of industrial and organizational psychology* (Vol. 2, pp. 399–444). Palo Alto, CA: Consulting Press.

Rynes, S. L., & Cable, D. M. (2003). Recruitment research in the twenty-first century. In W. C. Borman, D. R. Ilgen, & R. J. Klimoski (Eds.), *Handbook of psychology: Industrial and organizational psychology, Vol. 12* (pp. 55–76). New York: Wiley.

Sackett, P. R. (1982). A critical look at some common beliefs about assessment centers. *Public Personnel Management Journal, 2,* 140–147.

Sackett, P. R. (1987). Assessment centers and content validity: Some neglected issues. *Personnel Psychology, 40,* 13–25.

Sackett, P. R., & Hakel, M. D. (1979). Temporal stability and individual differences in using assessment information to form overall ratings. *Organizational Behavior and Human Performance, 23,* 120–137.

Sackett, P. R., & Tuzinski, K. (2001). The role of dimensions and exercises in assessment center judgments. In M. London (Ed.), *How people evaluate others in organizations* (pp. 111–129). Mahwah, NJ: Lawrence Erlbaum Associates.

Sackett, P. R., & Wilson, M. A. (1982). Factors affecting the consensus judgment process in management assessment centers. *Journal of Applied Psychology, 67,* 10–17.

Sagie, A., & Magnezy, R. (1997). Assessor type, number of distinguishable dimension categories' and assessment centre construct validity. *Journal of Occupational and Organizational Psychology, 70,* 103–108.

Salas, E., & Cannon-Bowers, J. A. (2001). The science of training: A decade of progress. *Annual Review of Psychology, 52,* 471–499.

Sanchez, J. I., & Levine, E. L. (2001). The analysis of work in the 20th and 21st centuries. In R. W. Woodman & W. A. Pasmore (Eds.), *Research in organizational change and development* (Vol. 7, pp. 71–89). Greenwich, CT: JAI Press.

Sawyer, I. (1966). Measurement and prediction, clinical and statistical. *Psychological Bulletin, 66*, 178–200.

Schalk, R., & Rousseau, D. M. (2002). Psychological contracts in employment. In N. Anderson, D. S. Ones, H. K. Sinangil, & C. Viswesvaran (Eds.), *Handbook of industrial, work, and organizational psychology* (Vol. 2, pp. 133–142). Thousand Oaks, CA: Sage.

Schein, E. H. (1970). *Organizational psychology.* Englewood Cliffs, NJ: Prentice-Hall.

Schippmann, J. S. (1999). *Strategic job modeling: Working at the core of integrated human resources.* Mahwah, NJ: Lawrence Erlbaum Associates.

Schippmann, J. S., Ash, R. A., Battista, M., Carr, L., Eyde, L. D., Hesketh, B., Kehoe, J., Pearlman, K., Prien, E. P., & Sanchez, J. I. (2000). The practice of competency modeling. *Personnel Psychology, 53*, 703–740.

Schippmann, J. S., Prien, E. P., & Katz, J. A. (1990). Reliability and validity of in-basket performance measure. *Personnel Psychology, 43*, 837–859.

Schleicher, D. J., & Day, D. V. (1998). A cognitive evaluation of frame-of-reference rater training: Content and process issues. *Organizational Behavior & Human Decision Processes, 73*, 76–101.

Schleicher, D. J., Day, D. V., Mayes, B. T., & Riggio, R. E. (2002). A new frame for frame-of-reference training: Enhancing the construct validity of assessment centers. *Journal of Applied Psychology, 87*, 735–746.

Schmidt, F. L. (1988). The problem of group differences in ability test scores in employment selection. *Journal of Vocational Behavior, 33*, 279–292.

Schmidt, F. L., & Hunter, J. E. (1998). The validity and utility of selection methods in personnel psychology: Practical and theoretical implications of 85 years of research findings. *Psychological Bulletin, 124*, 262–274.

Schmidt, F. L., Hunter, J. E., McKenzie, R., & Muldrow, T. (1979). The impact of valid selection procedures on workforce productivity. *Journal of Applied Psychology, 64*, 609–626.

Schmitt, N. (1977). Interrater agreement in dimensionality and combination of assessment center judgments. *Journal of Applied Psychology, 62*, 171–176.

Schmitt, N. (1993). Group composition, gender, and race effects on assessment center ratings. In H. Schuler, J. L. Farr, & M. Smith (Eds.), *Personnel selection and assessment: Individual and organizational perspectives* (pp. 315–332). Hillsdale, NJ: Lawrence Erlbaum Associates.

Schmitt, N., Cortina, J. M., Ingerick, M. J., & Wiechmann, D. (2003). Personnel selection and employee performance. In W. C. Borman, D. R. Ilgen, & R. J. Klimoski (Eds.), *Comprehensive handbook of psychology, Vol. 12: Industrial and organizational psychology* (pp. 77–105). New York: Wiley.

Schmitt, N., Ford, J. K., & Stults, D. M. (1986). Changes in self-perceived ability as a function of performance in an assessment centre. *Journal of Occupational Psychology, 59*, 327–335.

Schmitt, N., Gooding, R. Z., Noe, R. A., & Kirsch, M. (1984). Meta-analyses of validity studies published between 1964 and 1982 and the investigation of study characteristics. *Personnel Psychology, 37*, 407–422.

Schmitt, N., & Hill, T. E. (1975). Sex and race composition of assessment center groups as a determinant of peer and assessor ratings. *Journal of Applied Psychology, 62*, 261–264.

Schmitt, N., & Mills, A. E. (2001). Traditional tests and job simulations: Minority and majority performance and test validities. *Journal of Applied Psychology, 86*, 451–458.

Schmitt, N., Schneider, J. P., & Cohen, S. A. (1990). Factors affecting validity of a regionally administered assessment center. *Personnel Psychology, 43*, 1–12.

Schneider, B., & Konz, A. M. (1989). Strategic job analysis. *Human Resource Management, 28*(1), 51–63.

Schuler, H. (1993), Social validity of selection situations: A concept and some empirical results. In H. Schuler, J. L. Farr, & M. Smith (Eds.), *Personnel selection and assessment: Individual and organizational perspectives.* Hillsdale, NJ: Lawrence Erlbaum Associates.

Schuler, R. S., & Huber, V. L. (1990). *Personnel and human resource management* (4th ed.). St. Paul, MN: West.

Schweiger, D. M., Sandberg, W. R., & Rediner, P. L. (1989). Experiential effects of dialectical inquiry, devil's advocacy, and consensus approaches to strategic decision making. *Academy of Management Journal, 32,* 745–772.

Sherman, S. J., Judd, C. M., & Park, B. (1989). Social cognition. *Annual Review of Psychology, 3,* 281–326.

Shore, T. H. (1992). Subtle gender bias in the assessment of managerial potential. *Sex Roles, 27,* 499–515.

Shore, T. H., Shore, L. M., & Thornton, G. C., III. (1992). Construct validity of self- and peer-evaluations of performance dimensions in an assessment center. *Journal of Applied Psychology, 77,* 42–54.

Shore, T. H., Tashchian, A., & Adams, J. S. (1997). The role of gender in a developmental assessment center. *Journal of Social Behavior & Personality, 12,* 191–203.

Shore, T. H., Thornton, G. C., III, & Shore, L. M. (1990). Construct validity of two categories of assessment center dimension ratings. *Personnel Psychology, 43,* 101–115.

Silzer, R. F., & Louiselle, K. (1990, March). *Statistical versus assessor data: Application and recent research.* Paper presented at the 18th International Congress on the Assessment Center Method, Anaheim, CA.

Skarlicki, D. P., & Folger, R. (1997). Retaliation in the workplace: The role of distributive, procedural, and interactional justice. *Journal of Applied Psychology, 82,* 434–443.

Slivinski, L. W., Grant, K. W., Bourgeois, R. P., & Pederson, L. D. (1977). *Development and validation of a first-level management assessment centre.* Ottawa, Canada: Public Service Commission of Canada.

Smith, A. B. (1989). *A comparison of two assessment center integration methods.* Unpublished doctoral dissertation, Colorado State University.

Smith, A., & Reynolds, D. (2002, October). *Automating the assessment experience: The latest chapter.* Paper presented at the 30th International Congress on Assessment Center Methods, Pittsburgh, PA.

Smith, F. F., & Medin, D. L. (1981). *Categories and concepts.* Cambridge, MA: Harvard University Press.

Smith, P. C., & Kendall, L. M. (1963). Retranslation of expectations: An approach to the construction of unambiguous anchors for rating scales. *Journal of Applied Psychology, 47,* 149–155.

Smith-Jentsch, K. A., Salas, E., & Baker, D. P. (1996). Training team performance-related assertiveness. *Personnel Psychology, 49,* 110–116.

Sniezek, J. A., & Henry, R. A. (1989). Accuracy and confidence in group judgment. *Organizational Behavior and Human Decision Processes, 43,* 1–28.

Sniezek, J. A., & Henry, R. A. (1990). Revision, weighting, and commitment in consensus group judgment. *Organizational Behavior and Human Decision Processes, 45,* 66–84.

Snyder, L. A., Gibbons, A. M., Woo, S. E., & Kim, M. J. (2005, April). *An examination of the developability of dimensions in DACs.* Paper presented at the 20th annual meeting of the Society for Industrial and Organizational Psychology, Los Angeles, CA.

Society for Industrial and Organizational Psychology. (2003). *Principles for the validation and use of personnel selection procedures* (4th ed.). Bowling Green, OH: Author.

Sovereign, M. L. (1984). *Personnel law.* Reston, VA: Reston.

Spangenberg, H. H. (1990). *Assessing managerial competence.* Cape Town, South Africa: Juta.

Spangenberg, H. H., Esterhuyse, J. J., Visser, J. H., Briedenbann, J. E., & Calitz, C. J. (1989). Validation of an assessment centre against BARS: An experience with performance-related criteria. *Journal of Industrial Psychology, 15*(2), 1–10.

Spychalski, A. C., Quinones, M. A., Gaugler, B. B., & Pohley, K. (1997). A survey of assessment center practices in organizations in the United States. *Personnel Psychology, 50,* 71–90.

Squires, P., Torkel, S. J., Smither, J. W., & Ingate, M. R. (1988). *Validity and generalizability of a role-play test to select telemarketing representatives.* Paper presented at the meeting of the American Psychological Association, Atlanta, GA.

Stasser, G. (1992). Information salience and the discovery of hidden profiles by decision-making groups: A "thought" experiment. *Organizational Behavior and Human Decision Processes, 52,* 156–181.

Stasser, G., & Stewart, D. (1992). The discovery of hidden profiles by decision making groups: Solving a problem versus making a judgment. *Journal of Personality and Social Psychology, 63,* 426–434.

Steiner, I. (1972). *Group process and productivity.* New York: Academic Press.

Sterns, H. L., & Doverspike, D. (1989). Aging and the training and learning process. In I. Goldstein (Ed.), *Training and development in organizations* (pp. 299–332). San Francisco: Jossey-Bass.

Stewart, D. D., Billings, R. S., & Stasser, G. (1998). Accountability and the discussion of unshared, critical information in decision-making groups. *Group dynamics: Theory, research, and practice, 2,* 18–23.

Struth, M. R., Frank, F. D., & Amato, A. (1980). Effects of assessor training on subsequent performance as an assessee. *Journal of Assessment Center Technology, 3*(2), 17–22.

Swann, W. B. (1984). Quest for accuracy in person perceptive: A matter of pragmatics. *Psychological Review, 91,* 457–477.

Swim, J. K., Borgida, E., Maruyama, G., & Myers, D. G. (1989). Joan McKay versus John McKay: Do gender stereotypes bias evaluation? *Psychological Bulletin, 105,* 409–429.

Taylor, C. R. (1990, May). *Strategic job analysis.* Paper presented at the 18th International Congress on the Assessment Center Method, Anaheim, CA.

Taylor, M. S., Fisher, C. D., & Ilgen, D. R. (1984). Individual reactions to performance feedback in organizations: A control theory perspective. In R. Rowland & G. Ferris (Eds.), *Research in personnel and human resources management* (Vol. 2, pp. 81–124). Greenwich, CT: JAI Press.

Tetlock, P. E. (1983). Accountability and the complexity of thought. *Journal of Personality and Social Psychology, 45,* 74–83.

Tetlock, P. E. (1985). Accountability: The neglected social context of judgment and choice. In L. L. Cummings & B. M. Staw (Eds.), *Research in organizational behavior* (Vol. 7, pp. 297–332). Greenwich, CT: JAI Press.

Tett, R. P., & Guterman, H. A. (2000). Situation trait relevance, trait expression, and cross-situational consistency: Testing a principle of trait activation. *Journal of Research in Personality, 34,* 397–423.

Thibodeaux, H. F., & Kudisch, J. D. (2003). The relationship between applicant reactions, the likelihood of complaints, and organization attractiveness. *Journal of Business & Psychology, 18,* 247–257.

Thomson, H. A. (1970). Comparison of predictor and criterion judgments of managerial performance using the multitrait-multimethod approach. *Journal of Applied Psychology, 54,* 496–502.

Thompson, D. E., & Thompson, T. A. (1982). Court standards for job analysis in test validation. *Personnel Psychology, 35,* 865–874.

Thoresen, J. D. (2002, October). *Do we need dimensions? Dimensions limited or unlimited.* Paper presented at the meeting of the International Congress of Assessment Center Methods, Pittsburgh, PA.

Thornton, G. C., III. (1976). *The effects of feedback in developmental planning.* Paper presented at the Fourth International Congress on the Assessment Center Method, Portsmouth, NH.

Thornton, G. C., III. (1992). *Assessment centers in human resource management.* Reading, MA: Addison-Wesley.

Thornton, G. C., III. (1993). The effect of selection practices on applicants' perceptions of organizational characteristics. In H. Schuler, J. L. Farr, & M. Smith (Eds.), *Personnel selection and assessment. Individual and organization perspectives* (pp. 57–69). Hillsdale, NJ: Lawrence Erlbaum Associates.

Thornton, G. C., III, & Byham, W. C. (1982). *Assessment centers and managerial performance.* New York: Academic Press.

Thornton, G. C., III, & Cleveland, J. N. (1990). Developing managerial talent through simulation. *American Psychologist, 45,* 190–199.

Thornton, G. C., III, & Mueller-Hanson, R. A. (2004). *Developing organizational simulations: A guide for practitioners and students.* Mahwah, NJ: Lawrence Erlbaum Associates.

Thornton, G. C., III, & Rogers, D. A. (2001, September). *Developmental assessment centers: Can we deliver the essential elements?* Paper presented at the 29th International Congress on Assessment Center Methods, Frankfurt, Germany.

Thornton, G. C., III, & Rupp, D. E. (2003). Simulations and assessment centers. In J. C. Thomas (Ed.), & M. Hersen (Series Ed.), *Comprehensive handbook of psychological assessment, Vol. 4: Industrial and organizational assessment* (pp. 318–344). New York: Wiley.

Thornton, G. C., III, Tziner, A., Dahan, M., Clevenger, J. P., & Meir, E. (1997). Construct validity of assessment center judgments. *Journal of Social Behavior and Personality, 12,* 109–128.

Thornton, G. C., III, & Zorich, S. (1980). Training to improve observer accuracy. *Journal of Applied Psychology, 64,* 351–354.

Tillema, H. H. (1998). Assessment of potential, from assessment centers to development centers. *International Journal of Selection & Assessment, 6,* 185–191.

Tomkiewicz, J., Brenner, O. C., & Adeyemi-Bello, T. (1998). The impact of perceptions and stereotypes on the managerial mobility of African Americans. *Journal of Social Psychology, 138,* 81–124.

Triandis, H. C., Kurowski, L. L., & Gelfand, M. J. (1993). Workplace diversity. In M. D. Dunnette & L. M. Hough (Eds.), *Handbook of industrial and organizational psychology* (Vol. 4, pp. 769–827). Palo Alto, CA: Consulting Psychologists Press.

Truxillo, D. M., Bauer, T. N., Campion, M. A., & Paronto, M. E. (2002). Selection fairness information and applicant reactions: A longitudinal field study. *Journal of Applied Psychology, 87,* 1020–1031.

Tuckey, M., Brewer, N., & Williamson, P. (2002). The influence of motives and goal orientation on feedback seeking. *Journal of Occupational and Organizational Psychology, 75,* 195–216.

Turnage, J. J., & Muchinsky, P. M. (1984). A comparison of the predictive validity of assessment center evaluations versus traditional measures of forecasting supervisory job performance: Interpretive implications of criterion distortion for the assessment paradigm. *Journal of Applied Psychology, 69,* 595–602.

Tversky, A., & Kahneman, D. (1974). Judgment under uncertainty: Heuristics and biases. *Science, 185,* 1124–1131.

Tziner, A., & Dolan, S. (1982). Validity of an assessment center for identifying future female officers in the military. *Journal of Applied Psychology, 67,* 728–736.

Tziner, A., Meir, E. I., Dahan, M., & Birati, A. (1994). An investigation of the predictive validity and economic utility of the assessment center for the high-management level. *Canadian Journal of Behavioural Science, 26,* 228–245.

Tziner, A., Ronen, S., & Hacohen, D. (1990). *The assessment center once more under the surgeon's knife: A long-term validation study in a nonNorth American organization setting.* Unpublished manuscript, Tel Aviv University.

UK Industrial Society. (1996). Assessment & development centres. *Managing Best Practice, 29.*

Umeshima, M. (1989, May). *Combining outside assessors with peer assessors.* Paper presented at the 17th International Congress on the Assessment Center Method, Pittsburgh, PA.

U.S. Bureau of Labor Statistics. (2001). Contingent and alternative employment arrangements, February 2001 (USDL 01-153) [On-line]. Available: http://www.stats.bls.gov/newsrels.htm. Date accessed: January 10, 2004.

U.S. Bureau of Labor Statistics. (2002). Workers on flexible and shift schedules in 2001 (USDL 02-225) [On-line]. Available: http://www.stats.bls.gov/newsrels.htm. Date accessed: January 10, 2004.

U.S. Department of Labor Bureau of Labor Statistics. (2003). *Occupational outlook handbook.* Washington, DC: U.S. Bureau of Labor Statistics Office of Occupational Statistics and Employment.

U.S. Department of Labor Employment and Training Administration. (2002). O*NET. Washington, DC: Government Printing Office. [On-line.] Available: http://www.doleta.gov/programs/onet/, accessed August 1, 2004.

Viswesvaran, C., Ones, D. S., & Schmidt, F. L. (1996). Comparative analysis of the reliability of job performance ratings. *Journal of Applied Psychology, 81,* 557–574.

Waldman, D. A., & Korbar, T. (2004). Student assessment center performance in the prediction of early career success. *Academy of Management Learning and Education, 3,* 151–167.

Walsh, J. P., Weinberg, R. M., & Fairfield, M. L. (1987). The effects of gender on assessment center evaluations. *Journal of Occupational Psychology, 60,* 305–309.

Walter, M. (2004). *Approach to Development Experiences Questionnaire: Reliability and validity evidence.* Unpublished paper, Colorado State University.

Wanous, J. P., & Youtz, M. A. (1986). Solution diversity and the quality of group decisions. *Academy of Management Journal, 29,* 149–159.

Weekly, J. A., Frank, B., O'Conner, E. J., & Peters, L. H. (1985). A comparison of three methods of estimating the standard deviation of performance in dollars. *Journal of Applied Psychology, 70,* 122–126.

Wegner, D. M., & Bargh, J. A. (1998). Control and automaticity in social life. In D. T. Gilbert, S. T., Fiske, & G. Lindzey (Eds.), *The handbook of social psychology* (4th ed., pp. 446–496). New York: McGraw-Hill.

Weisner, W. H., & Cronshaw, S. F. (1988). A meta-analytical investigation of the impact of interview format and degree of structure on the validity of the employment interview. *Journal of Occupational Psychology, 61,* 275–290.

Weldon, E., & Gargano, G. M. (1985). Cognitive effort in additive groups: The effects of shared responsibility on the quality of multiattribute judgments. *Organizational Behavior and Human Decision Processes, 36,* 348–361.

Weldon, E., & Mustari, E. L. (1988). Felt dispensability in groups of coactors: The effects of shared responsibility and explicit anonymity on cognitive effort. *Organizational Behavior and Human Decision Processes, 36,* 348–361.

Wernimont, P. F., & Campbell, J. P. (1968). Signs, samples, and criteria. *Journal of Applied Psychology, 52,* 372–376.

Wiggins, J. S. (1973). *Personality and prediction: Principles of personality assessment.* Reading, MA: Addison-Wesley.

Wilkinson, B., & Byham, T. M. (2003, September). *Factors affecting the acceptance and application of developmental feedback from an executive development center.* Paper presented at the 31st International Congress on Assessment Center Methods. Atlanta, Georgia.

Wingrove, J., Jones, A., & Herriot, P. (1985). The predictive validity of pre- and post-discussion assessment centre ratings. *Journal of Occupational Psychology, 58,* 189–192.

Woehr, D. J. (1994). Understanding frame-of-reference training: The impact of training on the recall of performance information. *Journal of Applied Psychology, 79,* 525–534.

Woehr, D. J., & Arthur, W. (2003). The construct-related validity of assessment center ratings: A review and meta-analysis of the role of methodological factors. *Journal of Management, 29,* 231–258.

Woehr, D. J., & Huffcutt, A. I. (1994). Rater training for performance appraisal: A quantitative review. *Journal of Occupational & Organizational Psychology, 67,* 189–205.

Wolfson, A. D. (1988, August). *Assessing general management skills in technical functions.* Paper presented at the annual meeting of the American Psychological Association, Atlanta, GA.

Wollowick, H. B., & McNamara, W. J. (1969). Relationship of the components of an assessment center to management success. *Journal of Applied Psychology, 53*, 348–352.

Wonderlic, F. (1992). Wonderlic *Personnel Test User's Manual*, Libertyville, IL: Wonderlic Personnel Test.

Woo, S. E., & Sims, C. (2005, April). *The impact of agreement between self- and assessor-ratings on DAC engagement*. Paper presented at the 20th annual meeting of the Society for Industrial and Organizational Psychology, Los Angeles, CA.

Wyer, R. S., Jr., & Srull, T. K. (1986). Human cognition in its social context. *Psychological Review, 93*, 322–359.

Zedeck, S. (1986). A process analysis of the assessment center method. In B. M. Staw & L. L. Cummings (Eds.), *Research in organizational behavior. Vol. 8* (pp. 259–296). Greenwich, CT: JAI Press.

Author Index

Subject Index